FOREWORD

by Lord Montagu of Beaulieu

Great Britain's tradition of making excellent sports cars stretches back to the very start of motoring. I have been lucky enough to drive most of the best models—some as long-established as the vintage Bentleys, and others as modern as the latest Aston Martins and Jaguars.

On open roads, I have always found a combination of speed, character, road holding, and open-top atmosphere to be irresistible—and a British sports car provides all that.

Even though today's roads are often overcrowded, and speed limits seem to tighten all the time, at the right time and place I can still enjoy driving a modern Jaguar, a Lotus, an MG, a Morgan, or a TVR. It isn't just the performance which is so rewarding, but the thrill of it all, and the sheer character of all these fine cars.

As long ago as the 1910s there was the Prince Henry Vauxhall, in the 1920s there were the "vintage" Bentleys, but these were cars for lucky motorists with money to spare. It was in the 1930s that Britain brought sports-car enjoyment to everyman, with truly affordable two-seaters from MG, Morgan, and Singer. And at the same time a range of mid-size machines from AC, Frazer Nash, and SS-Jaguar all added to Britain's reputation for making fine open-top machines.

In the second half of the twentieth century, of course, the reputation of British sports cars went from strength to strength. Our motor industry found the right combination of performance, style, and selling price—and convinced the world that our sports cars were by far the best. Not only Jaguar, MG, and Aston Martin prospered, but also Austin-Healey, Lotus, Sunbeam, and Triumph all found new markets all over the world.

So, how did it all happen? Why should the British, more than any other nation except perhaps Italy, have taken the development of sports cars to such heights? Probably because we have always been a fun-loving race, and certainly because our industry has always been peopled by inventive designers and characters who wanted to get the most out of their motoring.

There was every reason, for instance, why another nation could have matched W.O. Bentley's great exploits in the 1920s. Because cars like the MG Midgets and Jaguar XK120s were developed around components from family cars, other European companies, surely, could have done the same?

Yet it did not happen.

Sports Cars

BRITISH

BRITISH SPORTS CARS

RAINER W. SCHLEGELMILCH

HARTMUT LEHBRINK

BRITISH SPORTS CARS

KÖNEMANN

Lord Montagu in front of the museum he founded, now the National Motor Museum, and (overleaf) outside his country house.

In Britain, somehow our designers managed to capture the right combination of value-for-money performance which most of our rivals could not beat. At the time, I suggest, no other nation could possibly have matched the rock-solid engineering of a vintage Bentley, the simple charm of a 1930s' MG Midget—or developed the 150-mph Jaguar E-Type to sell at such an absurdly low price.

Do I have a favorite British sports car? It would depend on the period, the occasion, and take a good deal of thought. But today, given fine weather and an agreeable companion, I would say my 1914 "Prince Henry" Vauxhall.

Montagu of Beaulieu

AC ACE & ACECA

The racing car with which private driver Cliff Davis created a sensation in the 2-liter class on the 1953 English circuits is what is commonly termed a special, pieced together from parts of different origins. The chassis came from John Tojeiro, who at that time made racing and sports cars to order. It was astonishingly simple yet guaranteed excellent roadholding: a tubular frame with crossmembers, independent suspension on all wheels—with wishbones below and horizontal transverse leaf springs above—and a double-joint cardan shaft. The engine came from Bristol and its genealogy goes back to the power plant from the BMW 328, a straight-six with side-mounted camshaft. The alloy superstructure is an unvarnished copy of the touring-bodied Ferrari Barchetta, just as it won 1949 at Le Mans—timelessly smart and still a feast for the eyes.

As soon as the brothers William and Charles Hurlock, from 1930 the heads of the small sports car factory AC (Autocarriers) at Thames Ditton, Surrey, England, set their eyes on this snappy one-off, they immediately decided to produce it in a small run. For the first 100 copies Tojeiro apparently received a royalty of £5 a piece. The finished product was unveiled at the London Motor Show in 1953. A couple of minor modifications from AC director Allan Turner made a world of difference to its lines, and hungering for freedom and adventure under the front bonnet was a six-cylinder engine of their own production, with a capacity of 1991cc, an overhead camshaft, and 86 (from 1958, 102) bhp. Since this was based on a construction, dating from 1919, by company founder John Weller, it was covered in the patina of venerable old age. Nevertheless, between 1954 and 1959 it

took the car to numerous victories in its class, including in the US, where the AC Ace became a much-loved import for ambitious sports drivers.

In 1956 the Hurlocks started to offer the ubiquitous Bristol engine as an option, along with an overdrive from Laycock de Normanville. Contemporary testers vied with each other in their praises. In fourth gear it allowed the driver to dawdle along at 19 mph (30 kph) when turning over at 1000 rpm, but also to zoom up to peak revs of 6000 rpm without as much as a sputter, with the real energy being released at 2500 rpm and all conversation between the two occupants becoming a total impossibility at 4000 rpm.

With time the Moss transmission was replaced by one of their own making, using an AC housing and innards from the Triumph TR3. The car's tail was likely to slide out when

Mediterranean borrowings, a shape that forms a beautiful whole—with no flourishes or fancy trimmings, just smooth rounded curves and nicely sweeping hips. Not even the door handles jut out and spoil the picture. Aluminum ensures lightness. Many people say that none of its automotive contemporaries could outmatch its beauty, not least thanks to its standard series spoked wheels.

Two examples of the fastidious love of detail are the easy-to-grab emergency tool-set, neatly arranged on a cap on the spare wheel, and the proud way the pedals bear the company name.

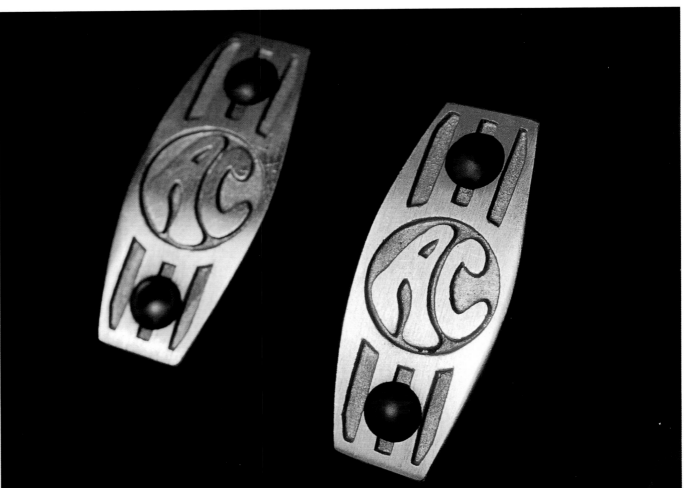

cornering at the limit, but kindly, not without first giving the pilot a friendly warning. One quirk was that in order to get into the car, it was necessary to pull out a section of the side window and operate a handle inside.

From October 1957 the car was presented with front disc brakes—first as an option, later as standard—and in 1962, the last year of production, the front section was given a final revamp. The windshield had always come in a pricey curved version and also in a cheaper one that was flat. At the Earls Court Motor Show of 1954 the roadster was flanked by the comfortable Aceca coupé, soon referred to appreciatively as the "businessman's express." Front-on it had the typical AC looks, but its fastback was evidently inspired by the Aston Martin DB2/4, which most likely didn't cost its creator Allan Turner too many sleepless nights. Roughly 110 lb (50 kg) heavier than its open-top brother, the Aceca responded somewhat more sluggishly, but thanks to its hardtop and better aerodynamics it managed a good 6 mph (10 kph) more.

Its evolution over the eight years of its life was a pretty cautious affair. Apart from the alterations that also affected the Ace, from 1958 the bottom corners of the windshield were changed from angular to round, and in 1960 the rain channels were built into the coachwork and not merely screwed on. *Autoparade* tester W.O. Probst emphasized the outstanding workmanship right to the last finicky detail, noting that the vehicle possessed a "horrendous amount of temperament" as a result of its excellent power-to-weight ratio of 16.3 lb (7.4 kg) per bhp, and stated that the limits when taking a brisk drive in the Aceca were not set by the car but by the driver's abilities.

In 1959 the Hurlocks received the short but gloomy tidings that their supplier, Bristol, was in dire straits; the brothers would have to make do without the universally loved engine. Luckily, help was at hand in the form of the six-cylinder motor of the Ford Zephyr, with 2.6 liters in five versions—from 85 through 120 to a wholesome 170 bhp. A company called Ruddspeed was responsible for the various tuning stages. Nor was AC lying on a bed of roses: Derek Hurlock, who succeeded Charles Hurlock at this time as the director, made no bones about the fact that the company's car venture had never seen any profit from either the 727 Aces or 329 Acecas. Fortunately Texan-born Carroll Shelby hit on the idea in the early 1960s of crossing a 4-liter Ford V8 with a chassis from AC. But that's another story in itself.

Designed by company founder John Weller during World War I, the AC six-cylinder in-line engine was still pretty well up with the times and gluttonously fed by three SU carburetors that gave it a new edge.

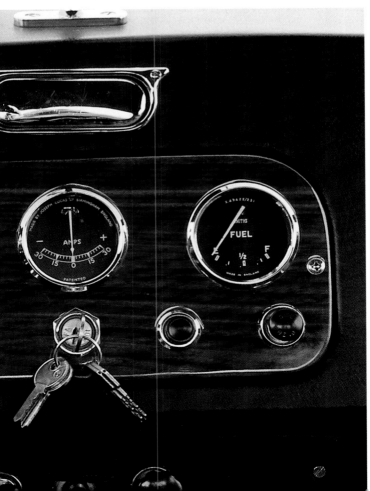

In fall 1954 the Hurlock brothers complemented the Ace roadster with the Aceca fastback, a vehicle for all-year traveling comfort. The dash has a tidy look about it, even if some of the information has slipped out of the driver's direct field of vision. Toward the end of the model's life, the six-cylinder engine from the Ford Zephyr was offered in five versions. The hottest of all, reworked by Tony Rudd, unleashed all of 170 bhp.

ALLARD J2X

There are, by and large, two ways of prospering in the comparatively small sports car segment. Either you take your cue from the competitors—or at least keep them in mind—or you occupy a relatively secure niche with a totally unmistakable product. Sydney Allard, born in 1920 and Chairman of the Allard Motor Co Ltd, based in Clapham, southwest London, belonged emphatically to the latter group. In modest circumstances, he linked up with a small team of engineers to hand-craft a combination of English grit and American power. It was a case of pairing a large-caliber V8 engine from the land of opportunity with a chassis boasting about as much comfort as a sparsely populated bed of nails. The chassis could be seen to an extent as somewhat underdressed. Indeed, there were no doors and aluminum was used only sparingly. Close-fitting, motorcycle-style front wings completed the look of a prehistoric and brutal precursor to the Lotus Seven. It was a recipe for veritable macho-mobiles, cars for men with hair on their chests—"daddies of the dragsters," as a tester later joked.

No two models were alike. In the uncertainty and confusion which followed World War II, American V8 power units were difficult to get hold of in the UK and a number of Allards were shipped over to the States without engine or transmission. There they were prepared for the road, often powered by engines tuned to deliver a full-throated roar. For the fearless amateur racing driver of the time, no other sporting machine could be maintained as efficiently or as quickly, and with as little hassle and expense.

The most famous of all Allards was the J2X. It was conceived in time for the start of the 1950 season and began life as the J2, a simple and low-slung two-seater with no trunk. It was built on a solid square-section tube frame, reinforced in strategically important areas. The rear wheels were located on a De Dion axle with coil springs, whilst the independent front suspension featured a swing-axle, with coil springs replacing the transverse leaf spring. This involved Sydney Allard sawing in half a rigid axle from Ford and bracketing the inner ends onto the chassis. The roadholding characteristics resulting from this method of construction took some getting used to. However, to the quietly fanatical Allard engineers, the real problem lay elsewhere: the Allard's drum brakes were sometimes overpowered by the car's effervescent energy.

Even the standard 4375cc Mercury V8 engine developed 110 bhp. A revised version with overhead valves and fitted

with light-alloy cylinder heads (supplied by future Corvette founder Zora Arkus-Duntov at his Ardun Engine Corporation on Broadway, New York) was capable of 140 bhp and gave the lightweight 2072-lb (940-kg) roadster a power/weight ratio of 15 lb (6.7 kg) per bhp. It was difficult to say exactly how low that figure could fall: a thundering Cadillac engine, for example, generated 180 bhp, making the power/weight ratio a mere 11.5 lb (5.2 kg) per bhp.

Sydney Allard was a capable driver behind the wheel of his outlandish creation, a fact borne out by the third place he gained in partnership with the American Tom Cole at Le Mans in 1950. In his youth, Allard had been hit in the left eye by a shot from an air rifle, which left him with seriously impaired vision—in the light of which his result at Le Mans becomes all the more impressive.

The last of the 99 J2 models produced was built in 1951, and the first of the 83 J2X cars was delivered not long after. The X indicated a modified chassis, the main changes being at the front which, in conjunction with repositioned forward-facing radius arms, enabled the engine to be mounted 7.5 inches (190 mm) further forward for better weight distribution and to give the occupants more legroom, even though the wheelbase remained the same. Delighted customers reported that the alterations had improved roadholding 100 percent. A wider range of power units had by then become available, with Allard paying precious little regard to the intense rivalries and competition that existed amongst the engine suppliers at the time. The power sources for the Allards came from Cadillac, Chevrolet, Lincoln, and Chrysler, as well as from the numerous tuning establishments which supplied the North American racing community.

Sydney Allard was briefly to taste glory once again, leading the race at the end of the first lap at Le Mans in 1953 in the J2R competition car, which had been developed from the J2X and had a full-width body, with the front wings absorbed into the main bodywork. Also during 1953, the last J2X to be produced in Clapham was delivered to its owner, the car having been completed the previous year. The Allard J-series cars had stumbled into the new era as dinosaurs of a bygone age. The Jaguar XK 120, the Triumph TR2, and the Austin-Healey 100 were setting new standards on the road, whilst the Jaguar C-Type and a spread of Ferrari models had taken control on the track.

However, hardened Allard enthusiasts, weather-beaten and conditioned by whatever nature brought to bear, could have only contempt for these upstarts.

For generations, the 24 Hours of Le Mans has been the ultimate test for British sports cars and, in 1950, Allard finished an impressive third. Two years on, motorcycle-style front wings were no longer permitted in the race, so the Clapham engineers adapted to the new situation and built 11 J2X cars with all-enveloping bodywork. Nine of these, however, were exported to the United States.

The smooth silhouette of the Allard J2X Le Mans puts the emphasis on horizontal lines and follows the trend established by the Ferrari Barchetta of 1948. The imposing air intake tunnel leads toward the air filter attached to the single Rochester downdraft carburetor, whose job is to feed the thirsty eight-cylinder Cadillac powerpack under the hood. As far as engine choice was concerned, the limits were set by the drivers themselves: they decided it had to be American and it had to pack a punch.

The TB 21 inherited the opulent curves that lap over its sparsely populated dashboard from its predecessor, the TB 14. As far as the statuette on the Alvis radiator is concerned, World War II marked the transition from hare to eagle—and from victim to aggressor, as it transpired: this ferocious-looking bird of prey poses a danger to pedestrians, making it advisable to remove the figure before any mandatory vehicle inspection. Built in-house, the six-cylinder engine was made to last, but is certainly not averse to burning fuel at the rate of 7.5 gallons per 60 miles (28 liters per 100 km) when pressed really hard.

ALVIS TB 21

The buildings of Alvis Ltd, on the Holyhead Road in Coventry, were among those reduced to rubble and ashes during a 12-hour bombing raid in November 1940. The destruction marked a second new beginning for a small firm that had made a name for itself as a maker of high-quality vehicles. The company lifted the curtain on its post-1945 era with a virtually unmodified reproduction of the pre-war range, in the form of the Fourteen. There was the TA 14 (a four-door sedan) and the two-door TB 14 drophead coupé, both powered by a 1892cc four-cylinder engine.

At the 1948 London Motor Show this small model range was complemented by the TB 14 Sports Tourer, adding a splash of exotic color in the process. Its strange front grill recalled Grand Prix cars of the time, such as the Alfetta 158, while its headlamps blinked out from behind the chromed grill bars in a style similar to that of the Peugeot 202 models of the same era. Built into one of the doors was a minibar, perhaps to give the

driver a self-service option on reasonably-priced refreshments at the opera festivals in Glyndebourne, for example. Indeed, the Sports Tourer also featured a complete beauty case where you would normally find the glove compartment, allowing the lady to powder her nose again before she arrived. Local body-work manufacturer AP Metalcraft was commissioned to build the car's body, which, with its strikingly curved doors, was not particularly attractive. The production run was 100 units. Further alterations were carried out to certain details—the headlamps, for example, were moved outwards on to the front of the wings. Meanwhile, the TA 14 was certainly quite quick off the blocks. Indeed, in 1953 the specialist publication *The Autocar* stopped the clock at 21.2 seconds for the sprint from 0–60 mph (up to 100 kph).

March 1950 saw the presentation of the TA 21 series, an indication that Alvis was back on track and in no way a closed shop to subtle innovations. The decision to unveil the car that spring at the Geneva Salon was a sign of Alvis's new horizons in the export market. At the heart of the sedan and drophead coupé was a short-stroke, 3-liter six-cylinder engine developing 86 bhp, which initially incorporated a Solex AAP twin-choke carburetor. The engine's robustness could be attributed in no small part to the seven bearings in which the crankshaft rotated. The chassis consisted of U-section longitudinal members braced by six crossmembers. The independent front suspension featured twin wishbones and coil springs, whilst the live axle and semi-elliptic springs of the rear suspension betrayed a construction principle the company was reluctant to give up. The front leading-shoe brakes had a tendency to shudder when applied at high speed.

The Sports Tourer, unveiled in the fall of 1950 as an offshoot of the TA 21, made no attempt to hide its similarity to the TA 14, although the body did have to be extended over a 3-inch (76-mm) longer wheelbase. In addition, the TB 14 nose section, which many had considered to be rather absurd, was replaced by the typical upright Alvis grill, which blended in surprisingly harmoniously with the smooth lines of the TB 21. Once again, 100 bodies were ordered from Metalcraft.

Meanwhile, two factors were having a somewhat negative effect on the fate of the open-top Alvis. Its predecessor had come up against superior opposition as early as 1948 in the shape of the Jaguar XK120, presented at the London Motor Show that October. Moreover, the Jaguar was £300 cheaper

and a good deal more attractive than its Coventry rival. Alvis's woes were then compounded in the spring of 1951, when English purchase tax doubled to 66.6 percent. Stunned, the company reduced the order placed with Metalcraft to 30 units. Sales had already proved sluggish compared to the sedan. The fact that the TB 21 with chassis number 25142 was finished in 1951 but not sold until a year later tells its own story. Production of the Alvis TB 21 was halted in 1953, spelling the end for a model that had not achieved the success the company hoped for, but nevertheless made a significant contribution to the rich tapestry of the British sports car industry.

The same could be said of Alvis as a whole. It was certainly true that the hard core of its well-heeled clientele, which included the Duke of Edinburgh, were extremely keen for the marque to survive. However, the company was dealt a series of crippling blows, including the defection of bodywork manufacturers Tickford (to Aston Martin) and Mulliners (to Standard-Triumph). For a while the Bern-based Swiss firm Graber filled the breach, its bodies later being produced under license by Park Ward of London. Eventually, though, Alvis reached a point where demand for its cars was going steadily downhill. In 1965, it conceded defeat and what remained of a once-proud maker of fine cars was taken over by Rover. The last model was delivered in fall 1967—a fourth-generation TF 21 sedan and every inch a character, just like the 6937 Alvis cars that went before it in the post-war era.

The radiator grill has reclaimed its defiant vertical position on the TB 21, a move that in fact represents a step backwards from the rounded but ungainly features of the previous two-seater model. Here is an example of how Alvis managed to blend a daringly modern design with tradition to give their devotees great pleasure, without necessarily appealing to everyone's tastes. However, its shape exudes a definite air of solidity.

ASTON MARTIN INTERNATIONAL

Fortunately, Thomas Mann used to say, few people know under what conditions and against what backgrounds art is sometimes created.

The same could be said of more than seven decades of Aston Martin history. An early example is the International model of 1929, a first-class product that was born out of regrettable circumstances. In 1926 two engine designers from Birmingham took over the seriously ailing firm. They were William Somerville Renwick and Augustus Cesare Bertelli, soon known familiarly as "Our Bert" for his jovial manner.

The two engineers acquired a new production plant on Victoria Road in Feltham in Middlesex, England, and in October that year they changed the name to Aston Martin Motors. But it was still not a bed of roses for the firm. In the first nine months of 1929 only seven vehicles were sold, and Our Bert could be seen knocking on doors everywhere as he tried to scrape together enough funds to carry on.

His persuasiveness certainly did not fall on deaf ears. The suppliers in particular gave him to understand that a jewel

like an Aston Martin simply could not be allowed to die. Finally he found a financially strong partner in Sidney C. Whitehead. A new name was needed; it was Aston Martin Ltd. In the course of the necessary management changes, Bertelli's brother Enrico, known as Harry, joined the undertaking, moving into a neighboring property with his coach-building plant, Enrico Bertelli Ltd. Until then Harry's skill at designing beautiful forms had mainly been expended on coach bodies. He had no time for paperwork and new ideas were sketched out in a scale of 1:1 in chalk on a huge slate.

The first fruit of the new team was the International, presented at the London Motor Show in 1929 and offered as a two-seater, or a four-seater on the same short chassis, with a wheelbase of 101.9 inches (2590 mm). The name was programmatic, for it contained the scarcely concealed message that the model met the requirements of the AIACR, Association Internationale des Automobile Clubs Reconnus. The International was designed to win the hearts of a

Much in the appearance of the Aston Martin bore witness to its nature as a sports car—the windshield that could be lowered, for instance, the Brooklands exhaust running round the outside, the dual access to the reserve tank in the pointed back. On the roughly 95 Internationals of the first series the oil tank of the dry-sump lubrication was visible in front between the ends of the chassis. The suspension of the front wheels was also clearly visible, with the friction shock absorber set lengthwise.

hand-picked, sporty clientele who had always been loyal to the firm's credo that racing was the origin of all things.

The appearance of the new model was certainly sporty, with its closely fitting motorcycle mudguards that turned with the steering wheel and kept the silhouette low in front. The lack of running boards made it easier to lubricate parts underneath and to adjust the brakes.

The 1.5-liter engine was also sporty, with a camshaft above, a gift from engineer Claude Hill who had moved to Aston Martin in the Renwick and Bertelli team. One striking feature was the dry-sump lubrication with a reservoir right at the front between the ends of the chassis, such as had proved its worth in Le Mans in 1928 in the two works cars, LM1 and LM2. For all those who like a little extra, a tuned-up Ulster version of the engine was available as an option from 1930 for £50 extra.

The International met with a good response, not least owing to delighted press reviews. The highly regarded magazine, *The Autocar*, for instance, was full of praise in its issue of September 18, 1931. The little Aston fully delivered the four things one expected of a genuine sports car. Its performance was unusually high; it held the road as if glued to it; it responded with precision; and it was a feast for the eyes. The reviewer was particularly impressed by the engine.

It purred softly in a cultured voice like a six-cylinder, and could accelerate in top gear from the lowest revs without demur. One could roll along smoothly but had lots of power in hand when needed, a very welcome quality on the over-crowded roads of today. One could easily run up to 5000 rpm—the engine always sprang to life and the plugs never oiled up.

The same praise was lavished on the body. It offered the comfort of a tourer and had none of the hardness one had come to expect of cars like the International. The positioning of the driver was excellent, between the easily and precisely adjustable bucket seat and the three-spoke steering wheel, which was set in exactly the right position. And it was a real pleasure to take the short, defiant little gearshift lever through the easily visible gates.

Our Bert and the men around him must have read the last sentence with particular pleasure. It was difficult to imagine, said the journalist, that the real enthusiast would not become addicted to the little Aston Martin straightaway.

This is a four-cylinder version by the engine specialist Claude Hill, in beautiful condition. A particular feature is the overhead camshaft and dry-sump lubrication. The engine is fed by two SU horizontal carburetors. The set of rods leading to the accelerator is clearly visible, as is their synchronizing link. A set of four reserve plugs on the wall is waiting to be used.

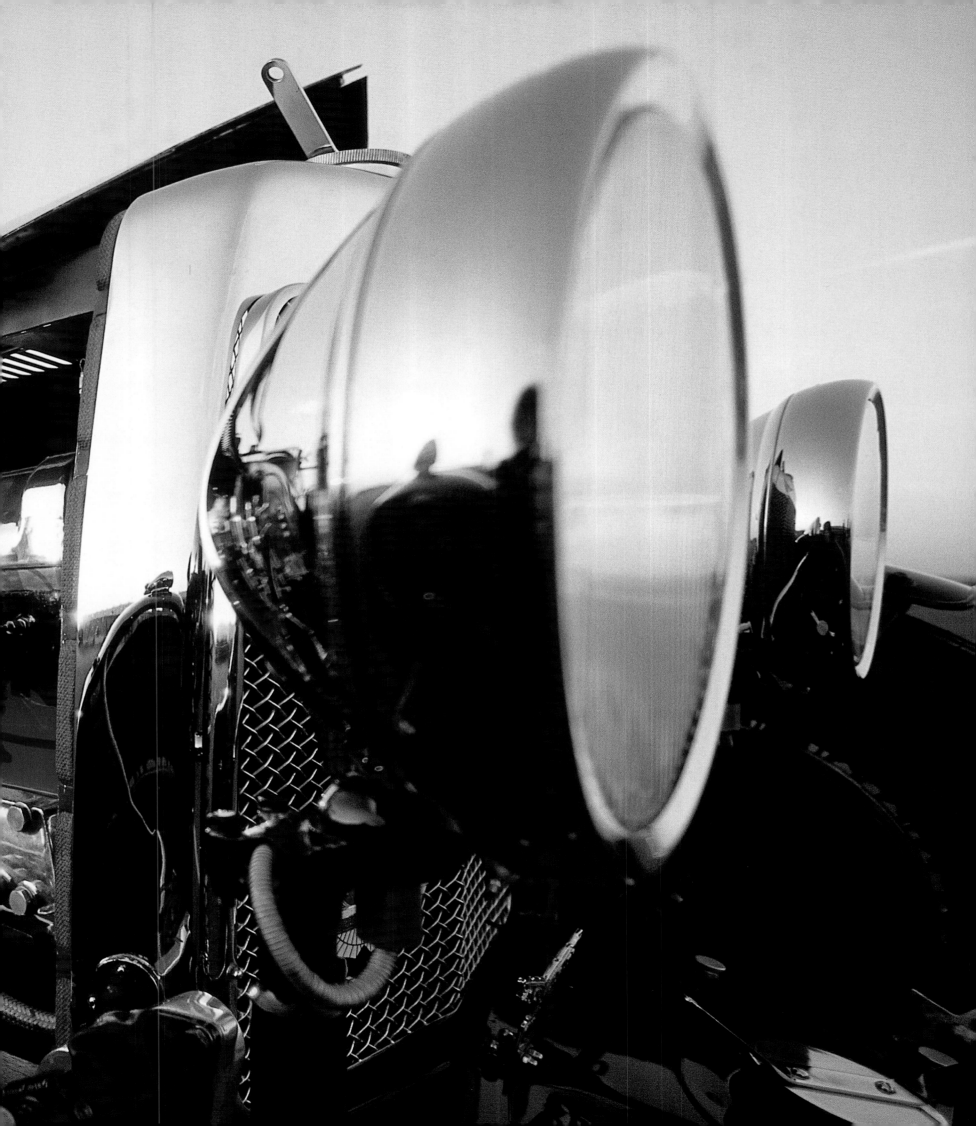

ASTON MARTIN DB1

Two things sustained Aston Martin through the darkness and privation of the war years—the principle of hope and its emblem, the Atom prototype of 1939, half conservative, half futuristic with a lattice tubular frame, an unusual suspension and electric Cotal transmission.

The unshakeable confidence that it would all turn out all right in the end found expression in a new beginning in February 1947. In late fall, 1946, David Brown, boss of a group of companies of the same name, found an inconspicuous little advert on the front page of *The Times*, which he was reading over his breakfast. His curiosity aroused, he answered it and found that Aston Martin chief Gordon Sutherland was offering his company for sale in this extremely unusual way. Brown took up his offer, and a price of £20,000 was agreed. The Atom, which had by now rather degenerated into yesterday's vision, also played a part in the deal. A trial run turned Brown's interest into a positive decision.

His first product was certainly inspired by what he had found, but it had to be much more sporty, the small but dynamic new owner told his engineers. Frank Feeley, who had styled the fine appearance of the mighty 12-cylinder Lagonda before the war, responded with a sensuously rounded aluminum body, although it did jut out rather too much in view of the relatively narrow track. The entire front section could be removed, giving totally unhindered access to the engine and the front-wheel suspension. At the same time, however, it made the car very vulnerable to impact. A narrow lid was provided for a quick look or slight adjustments. Two compartments in the fenders held the battery and the car's tools on the one side and the spare wheel, stood upright, on the other. A relatively modest trunk was concealed behind an external opening in the back. However, there was a bigger

luggage compartment behind the front bench seat for three that could also, if necessary, be used as less roomy accommodation for another passenger.

The triptych of grills in front primarily had a practical function. The central section carried air to the radiator, while those to left and right ventilated the drum brakes and wheel housings. Looking more closely the viewer would see the original version of what would be the future face of the Aston Martin. It would be mutated, varied, and styled right up to the present day.

Feeley's curving creation rested on a lattice of rectangular tubes. It was only cut out more deeply around the doors and was a rough outline of the silhouette of the first post-war Aston. The suspension was vaguely similar to Auto Union's Silver Arrow of the 1930s. It also had two longitudinal control arms with coil springs in front, a rigid axle with longitudinal control arms, coil springs, and a Panhard rod

behind. The engine, rather homely and hence actually a thorn in the flesh for David Brown, was a creation by veteran Claude Hill. It was a four-cylinder with a camshaft set high at the side, less costly and less complicated to make and maintain than the more sophisticated engines produced by Aston Martin before the war. The Cotal automatic transmission had been summarily jettisoned on the scrapheap of history and replaced by a robust four-gear transmission of David Brown's own manufacture.

In March 1948 the 2-liter sports car was announced—it was only later named DB1 by analogy—and the final form was shown at the Earl's Court Motor Show in October. In July, true to the firm's belief that fame, quality, and renown would come primarily from success in racing, a slimmed-down version was entered for the 24-hour rally in Spa. The mission was successful, with the two drivers, "Jock" Horsfall and Leslie Johnson, coming first. The motor magazines

outbid each other in their praise. A drophead coupé with the lines of a super sports car, enthused *Motor* on October 6, 1948, and *The Autocar* commented a year later that the 2-liter sports car was exactly what a contemporary fast car should look like.

Nevertheless, the model was a flop as far as sales were concerned, with a miserable 15 units sold. For there was the Jaguar XK120 with its timeless, racy silhouette, its silkily humming six cylinders, and with 160 bhp a good 70 bhp more powerful than the Aston Martin—and at £998 instead of £1333 it was also cheaper.

The entire superstructure of the Aston Martin 2-liter sports car, or DB1, could be lifted off, right up to the windshield. This had two advantages. Firstly, the mechanical parts were freely accessible. Secondly, there were virtually no joints, openings or any other potential sources of rattling, groaning, or hissing to break the smooth exterior of the three-seater. The battery (on the left) and the upright spare wheel (on the right) were, however, each located in their own casing. The voluptuous shape of the body was already indicated in the shape of the chassis beneath.

The interior architecture was equally liberal. The three-spoke steering wheel allowed the driver's glance to fall easily on the speedometer and rev counter, and the co-driver could also see how things were in the Aston Martin 2-liter sports car organism, as five other smaller dials were set near to him in a chronometer design. The radio was entirely his responsibility. If the four-cylinder engine needed modest attention, a narrow lid above it could be opened.

ASTON MARTIN DB2

The year 1947 was a key turning point in the life of the restless and energetic David Brown. Hardly had the turbulence raised by his acquisition of Aston Martin settled when he added another ailing car manufacturer to his empire, Lagonda. In an ideal exchange for the modest purchase price of £50,000 he got the good name, and as a real existing asset a sound six-cylinder engine of 2.6 liters, which Lagonda man Walter Owen Bentley contributed to the liaison.

True to its tradition, Aston Martin entered three works cars for the Le Mans 24 Hours race. They were based on the 2-liter sports model but built as coupés to minimize frictional loss from wind resistance. In two of them Claude Hill's reliable four-cylinder was at work, and in the third—registration number UMC 66—was Bentley's masterpiece. Admittedly UMC 66 did have to pull out before the end with a fault in its water pump, but it fathered the DB2 series, in which David Brown immortalized his initials for the first time.

The DB2 was presented at the New York Motor Show on April 12, 1950. It was very similar to the Le Mans prototype but 39 inches (1000 mm) higher. In its simple lines designer Frank Feeley had shown a lot of feeling for Italian flair but avoided any suggestion of plagiarism. The complete front section could now be tipped up forwards, while the spare wheel was stowed away in a little compartment accessible from outside and located above the tank in the back. The luggage space, or an oppressively narrow seat for an extra passenger, was behind the front bench seat, divided in two by the propshaft tunnel. The little gearshift was enthroned on this in front, if customers did not follow the current fashion and order a version with the gearshift beside the thin three-spoke steering wheel, which could be telescoped. As in the DB1, the beautiful body rested on a tubular skeletal frame that was extremely resistant to twist. The rear wheels were also hung on two transverse control arms, and this helped the DB2 to sit excellently on the road, skimming lithely over even really rough stretches. It was the smooth drive, with the gentle but energetic operation of the engine and the attractive appearance of the Aston Martin, that induced the ambitious Californian racing driver Phil Hill spontaneously to purchase one of the first DB2s that found its way onto the North American continent.

In its original form the DB2 had 108 bhp; the Vantage version, available toward the end of 1950, offered 125 bhp

While the radiator grill in earlier DB2s was a triptych, it is already one item here, a forerunner of future Aston Martin faces. The lid at the back conceals the spare wheel, which was laid flat.

and was immediately acknowledged as the one to buy for customers who wanted a little something extra. The radiator grill, initially in three sections, had now grown into a single unit. In a population of 411, of which about 100 were drophead coupés, the DB2 broke into the German and Italian domains and firmly installed the company on the sports car market.

For friends of the marque with children the DB2/4 came on sale in October 1953 and was available for the next two years. A total of 565 were sold. Two surgical operations permitted rudimentary seating above the rear axle. The DB2/4 was 69 inches (1780 mm) longer than its predecessor and slightly higher at the back. Two other measures certainly helped its line. The central bar on what was now a slightly curved front disk was dropped and the luggage compartment, under a large lid at the back, could be loaded from outside. From mid-1954 the model had a 3-liter engine of 140 bhp, offering more punch and more power.

In the Mark II evolution stage, of which 199 were sold by August 1957, the passengers had more headroom, while small fins at the back were a response to current fashion. The Mark II was also available with a hard top. The series was crowned from the 1957 Geneva Spring Show onwards with the DB Mark III, which achieved a record output of 550. The aggressively pointed radiator mouth of the racing DB3S suited it well, and the dials were now located under a curve directly in the driver's view, where in earlier models they were spread right across the dashboard.

In the skilful hands of exiled Pole Tadek Marek the engine had gained considerably in power. The driver of the DB Mk II had more than 162 bhp in his hands in its basic version, 178 bhp when a dual exhaust was doing its bit, and as much as 195 bhp with further boosting. From 1958 an overdrive was added to David Brown's transmission and a year later an automatic version was available. Girling brakes were first an option and later standard.

However, when the DB4 appeared the last descendant of the Atom tribe looked what it in fact was—pretty old.

Following pages: The charm of the Aston Martin DB2 was that designer Frank Feeley had taken up typical elements of contemporary Italian design, but incorporated them in his own very individual whole. The main instruments are big and easy to read, while less important sources of information are in the co-driver's field of vision.

ASTON MARTIN DB4

With the DB4 Aston Martin finally entered the top league of sports cars, where until then Ferrari, Maserati, and Mercedes had been able to play against each other almost undisturbed.

The DB4 was ceremoniously unveiled on October 10, 1958 at the Paris Salon. At the London Motor Show in Earl's Court a short time later it became a star, hailed with jubilation and national pride by a patriotic British press.

But it was not until 1959 that the first series models reached customers. The incubation period between decision and realization had been four years. Harold Beach of the Aston Martin staff had designed a box frame in the mid-1950s, over which a skeleton of large and smaller tubes was set and then clothed in a superstructure of great lightness and grace, particularly around the cabin area. The structure followed the *superleggera* principle of Carrozzeria Touring in Milan and was made under license from them. Nowhere was a break with tradition to be found. The Atom had had a similar spine, and the silhouette had echoes of the Mark III, for instance, which, 330 lb (150 kg) lighter and £600 cheaper, held its position as a substitute for the DB4 till 1959. For the DB4 was certainly expensive. In Germany, for instance, it

cost DM 46,000, while a Mercedes 300 SL Roadster could be purchased for as little as DM 33,000.

At the same time an entirely new six-cylinder engine had matured in Feltham since 1955. It was in aluminum, and so one third lighter than the previous engine. With 3.7 liters and the "square" cylinder measure of 36×36 inches (90×90 mm) it could be further developed. It was the masterpiece of the Polish engineer Tadek Marek, who had managed to reach England after a dangerous journey in the confusion of the war. The new engine was advertised as providing 243 bhp. The keen eye of the German industrial standard reduces it to about 210—still plenty.

The similarly rather blue-eyed promise that the DB4 could accelerate to 100 mph (160 kph) and be braked to a standstill again in half a minute was proved correct, to everyone's relief, by works test driver Roy Salvadori, who did it in 27.4 seconds, repeating the torture once more to provide undisputable proof.

Reg Parnell, head of racing and a former racing driver for Aston Martin, did it in just 20 seconds in the DB4GT, not least thanks to the huge Girling disc brakes. The DB4GT made its exit a year after the basic model. Intended as a

The fluid and racy lines of the Aston Martin DB4 were designed by Carrozzeria Touring in Milan. Following their *superleggera* principle the aluminum panels of its superstructure curve over a skeleton frame. The panorama window gives a good view, despite the relatively strongly canted A-pillar columns, and without hampering access to the interior. The space is generous in front, but it is much more cramped for passengers behind. Spoke wheels with central fastenings were included in the basic price.

weapon to fight the Ferrari 250 GT Short Wheel Base it was, admittedly, a loser in the war on the track, particularly when Ferrari's sheerly irresistible sublimation, the 250 GTO, appeared in 1962. But the DB4GT was still an extremely pleasing roadster. It could touch a top speed of 152 mph (245 kph), 12 mph (20 kph) faster than the normal DB4. 176 lb (80 kg) of weight had been jettisoned, largely by using plexiglass. The wheel base was shortened by 49 inches (1270 mm) to 92 inches (2362 mm) and the doors were much narrower. The tight rear seats had been dropped. For aerodynamic reasons the headlights now led a withdrawn existence behind plexiglass windows. Three dual carburetors by Weber, higher compression and sharper camshafts helped the engine to a realistic 267 bhp.

The DB4GT Zagato could do it all a little bit better, although after its presentation in Earl's Court in September 1960 it only achieved meager sales of 19 units, each one of which was in fact unique. Nine weeks would pass from the placing of the order with the small Carrozzeria in Terrazzano di Rho, where the rolling chassis supplied by Aston Martin would be covered with a thin skin of aluminum, to be exposed unprotected by bumpers to rough treatment on the

roads and tracks. But the use of even more aluminum and even more plexiglass reduced the weight by 275 lb (125 kg) compared with the DB4 Saloon. The Zagato's 285 greedy bhp were fed from a 30-gallon (135-liter) tank that, with the spare wheel that rode on top of it, almost filled the entire luggage space.

Chroniclers have identified five stages in the evolution of the DB4, in the course of which 170 improvements were made to the model. A total of 1103 Saloons and 75 GT (only the Zagato variants) were delivered to their delighted owners. Not until 1961 was the DB4 opened up in the form of a chic Convertible. At the same time the name Vantage was happily introduced, as usual to indicate more power. The DB4 Vantage could mobilize 240 bhp—exactly the strength that had been promised for the original exhibit at Earls Court in 1958.

No wonder that *Sporting Motorist* warned of "adultery" in June 1962—this car could come to mean more to you than your wife.

With the Zagato variant of the Aston Martin DB4GT in 1960 company chief David Brown culminated the series and set a brilliant seal on his creations to date. It was to become one of the most famous sports cars of all time. With its dual ignition and pampered by three dual carburetors by Weber the six-cylinder engine could produce 6000 rpm and 270 bhp, 27 more than the basic version. Without protective bumpers in front or behind the DB4GT Zagato was, however, dependent on careful handling by its driver and courtesy from other road users, a vulnerable aristocrat.

ASTON MARTIN DB6

The DB6 of 1965 was the third and final sublimation of the DB4, presented as usual at the patriotic forum of the London Motor Show. The tendency was clear. "In an Aston Martin," said company boss David Brown, "one should not only be able to move fast and safely, one should also feel comfortable and have a lot of room, even in the back."

The new model differed from its predecessor, the DB5, at first sight and on closer inspection. The side windows had quarter panes in front, which improved the ventilation, and bluntly rounded ends. The bumpers were not very robust and were in two separate entities. In front below the unprotected central section was an oil cooler, protected from flying grit by a wide mesh and horizontal bars. The model sloped down steeply at the back, with a pert spoiler lip above the edge. This strengthened the down-force at the back by 30 percent, as the company established in the wind tunnel.

Nevertheless, the DB6 was 19 inches (500 mm) longer, it offered 8 inches (200 mm) more headroom and had a more sloping windshield. The harmonious proportions of the series were thus basically untouched. Just in front of the rear wheel openings the engineer Albert Thickpenny had added 35 inches (900 mm) more wheelbase. In conjunction with flatter cushions, this provided much roomier accommodation for the passengers in the back. The same purpose was served by an unusual intervention under the skin. The two top longitudinal control arms were shortened, in order to make room for broader hips as well. Although the inscription "Superleggera" on the left and the right of the hood appeared to state the opposite, for a time the chassis was actually supplied by the works in Huddersfield without the typical tubular skeleton of the Milan Touring factory.

The DB6 was 19 inches (500 mm) longer than its predecessor the DB5. Nevertheless, its blunt back with the pert spoiler lip was an illustration of the theory and practice of Wunibald Kamm, Professor of Aerodynamics, and his belief in the efficiency of the smallest cross-section. The front bumper was divided and below the registration plate hung an air vent for the oil cooler. Other new features were the more strongly canted windshield and the quarter windows at the side, while the arrangement of the dials remained the same, although the size of some had changed.

From 1966 the DB6 was the first Aston Martin to be fitted with Servo steering, first as an option and then as standard. From 1963 the 4-liter tuned-up stages of Tadek Marek's light alloy engine were also standard, as were the headlights set behind plexiglass. The engine was available with three SU carburetors and 286 bhp, about 42 of which were thanks to the liberal SAE norm; a Vantage variant was also available with three Weber carburetors and 325 bhp, from which 53 can certainly be deducted. Whether the DB6 was delivered in one or the other version, with a five-speed transmission by ZF or a three-gear Borg-Warner automatic transmission, the price was always the same, £4998. The future looked rosy and soon the weekly output from Newport Pagnell was stepped up from 12 to 18 units.

But then dark clouds gathered on the horizon. In July 1966 the Labour Government under Harold Wilson devalued the pound and put purchase tax up by 10 percent. Demand began to ebb away. David Brown responded with a

dramatic measure, offering his beautiful products reduced by £1000, at a price that was below cost.

The DB6 came in two bursts, 1327 Saloons by July 1969 and 240 of a Mark II by November 1970. The new variant was already overshadowed by the new DBS model, from which, for rationalisation reasons, it took over the 6-inch (125-mm) rims with appropriate pneumatic tires that had to be set in wider wheel housings. The Cabriolet achieved a run of 215, initially still on the DB5 chassis.

As almost always the reception by the trade press was extremely positive. *Motor*, for instance, on January 8, 1966 said the Vantage now available was the fastest test car the magazine had ever known, making the 70 mph (113 kph) speed limit on British motorways look like a joke. But be careful—the brakes were so effective that many a driver behind would not be able to react quickly enough. In fact, the repairs department found itself dealing with a stream of vehicles with damage to the back. There was no fading at all, at most a slight smell of burning.

From 19 mph (30 kph), which was 800 rpm, the powerful six-cylinder engine would accelerate smoothly and without grumbling. The ZF transmission was a genial partner, although it was very irritable when cold, above all resisting attempts to move into second gear. Comfort was excellent for a car with a rigid rear axle, although it could certainly have been improved with independent suspension behind (prevented by the high cost of such a version).

The report concluded with fictitious dialog that was extremely flattering to the test model. The Aston Martin could say to 99 percent of all production cars: "anything you can do I can do better."

ASTON MARTIN
DBS V8/V8

Instead of the gentle curves of the DB6, a sharper profile. Careful research in the MIRA wind tunnel had made any distortion by a spoiler at the rear of the four-seater superfluous. Under the two little lids to left and right below the rear window stretched the filler tube for the tank. The engine was force-fed by mechanical injection into its intake ports. Nevertheless, the version shown here was a transitional model. Evidently, after the change of guard in Newport Pagnell, a few DBS labels were left, although all reference to the previous Aston Martin owner, David Brown, was actually to be removed.

For a quarter of a century David Brown had sustained the marque and the idea of Aston Martin. Later, while a progression of owners entered the noble little firm in Newport Pagnell, one model had provided continuity—the DBS V8, later known as just the V8.

The transitions were fluid. Tadek Marek and a project group had been working on the aluminum V8 since 1963. At 529 lb (240 kg) it was both light and a status symbol—it was to be the name of Aston Martin for the 1970s and 1980s. Conditions generally were difficult. The budget was tight and other commitments were taking up a lot of time. As many parts as possible were to come from current production, and to cap it all, the engine could only be given its certificate of maturity if it passed the crucial test on a racing track, in the Lola T70 of former Formula One champion John Surtees.

The new type DBS, for which Marek's V-weapon was actually intended, made its debut at the London Motor Show in 1967. Dudley Gershon was responsible for the chassis, which was based on the DB6 version but fitted with a De Dion axle for bigger tasks. In-house designer William Towns was entrusted with the appealingly proportioned but voluminous superstructure, although initially the well-known six-cylinder crouched, a little lost, in the spacious compartment for the engine.

It was not until September 1969 that the things that should have been together were united—the DBS and its 5340cc V8 with four overhead camshafts as well as a Bosch injection pump and 315 bhp fed to the rear axle by a five-speed ZF gearbox or, as an option, by the Chrysler Torqueflite

automatic transmission (although this lost a lot of power to transmission slip and heat). The top speed of 168 mph (270 kph) stated by the works proved a little generous. The publication *auto motor und sport* touched 150.1 mph (241.7 kph) but was still very impressed.

Some 405 DBS V8s had found their way to their owners when the company announced, in 1972, that the abbreviation DBS would be dropped. It was a sign of new owners. David Brown had finally tired of his finest but difficult subsidiary Aston Martin and sold it to Company Developments Ltd for the symbolic sum of £100. The new owners at first continued to feed the V8 into the market with almost no changes. It now had individual headlights instead of the former dual lights—but then bigger changes proved necessary.

The United States, an important export market, refused an entry certificate for this export from the Old World as its emissions were excessive, and so the injection system was ripped out and in 1973 a complicated bank of four Weber dual carburetors was installed in the hollow between the two banks of cylinders; the presence of these was indicated from outside by the big hump on the hood. But further problems loomed. Aston Martin was also suffering, in 1974, from the three-day week that did such damage to the British economy.

Finally, new Samaritans hastened to its aid in the persons of the American Peter Sprague and the Canadian George Minden, soon to be joined by two Britons, Denis Flather and Alan Curtis. Gradually the firm gathered momentum again, and in February 1977 it set a benchmark with the

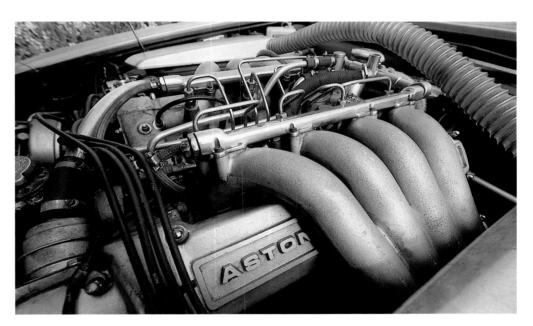

V8 Vantage, a 380 bhp version. At the rear it sprouted the obligatory spoiler and the swelling on the bonnet was now closed at its front, changes that were applied to all the Aston Martins from October 1978.

Three months earlier the cabriolet V8 Volante had seen the light of day, in response to growing demand on the North American market. It had an extremely solid electrically operated hydraulic hood designed by Harold Beach. Many critics saw it as shameless interference with a fine form when elements of the contemporary Vantage, such as the wider fenders, were added to it in 1986. Some customers, like Prince Charles, who had long been a loyal adherent of Aston Martin, preferred to do without these additions.

In the 11 years up to 1989 during which it was made, 849 Volantes were produced, and in the 20 years of the model's life up to the same year 2658 Saloons were made, 350 of which were Vantages. At the Geneva Motor Show in spring 1986 Victor Gauntlett and Peter Livanos, who had moved into the directors' suite in Newport Pagnell, revived an old business link. They signed an agreement with the brothers Gianni and Elio Zagato for a small, exclusive, and expensive run of 85 Zagato versions of the V8 Vantage, of which 35 would be Volantes.

But the coupé, with its 432 bhp, was denied entry to the club of 300 kph (186 mph) cars by a whisker. The French publication *Sport-Auto*, for example, could only register a top speed of 299 kph (186 mph).

ASTON MARTIN VIRAGE/V8

In the mid-1980s the Aston Martin V8 had finally become a monument to itself, a venerable motoring phenomenon, esteemed by all but elaborate and hence costly to make. When the company's teams rolled up their sleeves to create a new model, company chief Victor Gauntlett also threw out hierarchical principles.

To find an attractive new name, one that would maintain the tradition and also start with V, like Vantage and Volante, a competition was held among the staff and the members of the Aston Martin Owners Club. The winner was Virage, which was unusual and sounded dynamic. In 1994 it somehow got lost again.

Five teams were commissioned to put forward an appropriate design by the end of August 1986, the condition being that symbiosis with a shortened Lagonda chassis should be possible. The winners were the duo Ken Greenley and John Heffernan of the Royal College of Arts.

The existing engine was given a thorough update between April 1986 and December 1987 by Callaway in Connecticut, who were instructed that it was to feed off unleaded petrol and must meet the most stringent emission regulations conceivable. The lower half remained largely unchanged while in a much revamped head four valves per cylinder provided a greater liveliness. Fed by Weber-Marelli injection, the new engine achieved 330 bhp.

On its presentation at the Motor Show in Birmingham, England, in 1988 the Virage was acclaimed by all. The same applied to its open counterparts, a two-seater Volante at the same show two years later, a 2 + 2-seater version in spring 1992 and a four-seater in 1997. In August 1993 writer Mark Hughes of *Fast Lane* said of the two-seater that it was the most aristocratic Cabriolet ever, both British and brutal. Wherever one went it was the focus of interest, no doubt helped by the sonorous growl from the Volante's exhaust, which was much deeper than the sound from the familiar two-valve. The quality was outstanding, under the hood as well. It opened as if by magic when a button on the dashboard was pressed and sank down into its opening after the little rear side windows had dropped out of view. But all this was greatly at the expense of space in the trunk, which was small by any standards.

From 1993 a four-speed automatic transmission by Chrysler became available for the Virage, as an alternative to the ZF five-speed transmission. In the same year the name Lagonda was kissed awake from its long sleep with a four-

door long version. Automotive made-to-measure was now the slogan, and with it the company moved into a profitable market niche. The products included the ten Limited Edition coupés in British racing green of October 1994, and individual models made with the help of conversion kits, with up to 6.3 liters and 465 bhp, plus, of course, the appropriate surgical operations to body and mechanics.

The variety of powerful individual models was again crowned with a series car, the ultimate Vantage of October 1992, with two Eaton compressors blowing in 550 bhp. Primeval strength right from the depths took it up to 100 mph (160 kph) in ten seconds, making it the fastest Aston Martin of all times, although it just failed to reach the 186 mph (300 kph) mark, at 185 mph (298 kph). Externally, the Vantage was distinguished from the basic Saloon by a different front grill, flanked by three small lights on each side, where in the latter the lights of the VW Corrado looked innocently out into the world. The Vantage also had a differently shaped back with integrated spoiler lip. Many of its features were adapted to the Virage successor in a gently flowing evolution from March 1996. To the great confusion of chroniclers it was now called the V8 coupé, like earlier generations.

The swan song began for the V8 models in 1999 with a special run of 40 Vantage Le Mans. Like the latest evolution of the standard Vantage of 1998 they put forth 600 sturdy bhp, in memory of the historic Aston Martin victory on the Sarthe track 40 years before. The V8 era came gracefully to an end with a concluding mini-series of six Vantage Volantes in August 2000, each slightly different from the next. At the same time the extensive hand labor that had made the modest-looking works on both sides of Tickford Street in Newport Pagnell an enclave of tradition in a world full of brainless and soulless robots also came to a close. The Vanquish, the top Aston for the new millennium, did evolve in the old premises, but is being made in a comparatively modern way.

This is the Aston Martin Virage Volante in its original form, with 17-inch (4320-mm) rims, front lamps from the VW Corrado, rear lights from the VW Scirocco, and wing mirrors from the Citroën CX, borrowings that did no harm at all to its stately appearance. The solid textile hood of the Volante could be lowered or raised electrically with a touch of a button on the dashboard. The rear window was of heatable glass.

The Vantage, the top model of 1992, was a good deal more independent than the basic Virage, with 18-inch (4570-mm) rims, company-designed lights in front and behind, a new front spoiler and a different back end with integrated spoiler lip. The rear view is also aggressive.

Instruments and switches were well grouped and set in beautiful quality wood panels that were hand cut and fitted. The driver's seat could be adjusted to a large number of positions and gave excellent support. Passengers in the back, on the other hand, would feel rather let down although they too could enjoy the intoxicating scent of the Connolly leather, for which cows from the finest breeds had to sacrifice their hides.

Two compressors provided continuous power for the V8, and with 500 bhp the 5.3-liter engine of the Vantage was prominent among the most powerful production vehicles of all time; if only for that reason the pride of the men in Newport Pagnell in their marque was evident everywhere.

ASTON MARTIN DB7

At first sight the DB7, celebrated at its premiere in Geneva in 1994 as a new arrival in the domain of the Mercedes SL, the Porsche 928, and the Ferrari-Dreier, looked like a contemporary variation of typical Aston Martin styling. However, it proved to be a multicultural event, a successful combination of the traditional and the progressive, home and foreign products.

Since 1987 the noble firm in Newport Pagnell had been nestling under the wings of its mighty parent Ford, which first owned three-quarters of the shares and from 1994, all of them. Jaguar had also become a Ford subsidiary, and so there were family resemblances and admixtures—the dictate of the hour in the age of rationalization. From Jaguar came the chassis with its striking suspension elements such as dual track control arms in front and single track control arms behind, where the semi-axles were assigned a load-bearing function.

The 3.2-liter engine had also come out of the former competitor's drawer. It was a six-cylinder unit with two overhead camshafts, so it was actually as if made for the venerable Aston Martin tradition. However, the four-valve version had been given an energetic revamp, and it was attached to an Eaton compressor that blew in 317 bhp through a water-cooled intercooler that ensured maximum volumetric efficiency. It betrayed the hand of Walter Hayes, a former Ford manager, who had first worked for Aston Martin as consultant, and was chief executive from 1991 through 1994: it was he who had skilfully co-ordinated the entire project. This was the only possible form of boost, he insisted, the only way to make the engine respond to acceleration without shuddering. Finally, the production plant for the new model, Bloxham in Oxfordshire, also came from Jaguar, which had formerly used the works for its XJ220.

As far as the shape of the DB7 was concerned, Hayes literally pointed the young designer Ian Callum in the right direction by putting a DB4, a DB5, and a DB6 in his studio, encouraging him to be inspired to more of the same. Callum was not to be outdone and produced a design of flattering lines and proportions, in steel with composite parts. The elderly David Brown was so impressed that he spontaneously approved Callum's creation and assigned the right to use the letters DB that had lain around unused since 1972.

In its issue of October 19, 1994, however, the highly regarded trade journal *Autocar* saw the DB7 as similar to the E-Type Jaguar, the epitome of classical motor beauty. At a price of £78,500 it was the finest Gran Turismo one could buy for a five-figure sum. The DB7 did indeed rapidly become the company's best seller to date. In 1998, for example, 600 out of 700 vehicles sold by Aston Martin were DB7s.

With the Virage, the Volante was already being developed parallel to the saloon. This was also done with the DB7, whose open version was shown in January 1996 at the motor shows in Detroit and Los Angeles, awakening eager interest, particularly among North American buyers. But this was not enough. In March 1999 the DB7 Vantage made its debut in Geneva, a model with which the company succumbed to the discreet charm of the magic dozen. On June 30 that year *auto motor und sport* simply labeled it the best Aston Martin ever. The light and compact V12 under its bonnet was a joint production by Ford and Cosworth, providing a powerful 410 bhp. Following the instructions to the engineers the 410 bhp certainly did not wheeze, but responded instead with

a smooth but aggressive sound. A different radiator grill in polished metal with wider openings was part of a more efficient cooling system and announced the presence of the 12-cylinder engine. Account had also been taken of its primeval strength with new longitudinal transverse track arms in front and a horizontal rod behind. A sophisticated Visteon motor management system took care of the injection, sparking, anti-skid regulation, alarm, and exhaust and it could tell you the condition of the engine at any time. Huge discs with four-piston callipers by Brembo guaranteed literally breathtaking braking.

Inside the Vantage the driver and his passenger would find a number of buttons and switches from the Ford range,

and above all they would be met by the intoxicating scent of Connolly leather, for which cows of the noblest breed had sacrificed their hides. It covered the bucket seats, which could be adjusted to several positions, while a red ignition button on the central console recalled Pop Art. But with British discretion there was, of course, no indication of the 12 prestigious cylinders under the long hood.

The DB7, wrote a delighted reporter, was Aston Martin's seventh symphony. That applied to both the outside and the interior. Both were characterized by careful forethought and a conservative approach. The Beau from Bloxham contained a complex of references to its great forefathers without ever slipping into an anachronistic retro-look. The rims on the sporty, attractive five-spoke design of the coupé shown here are a special version.

Instead of the tuned six-cylinder engine an aesthetically appealing tuned V12 resided in the engine compartment of the DB7 Vantage—shown here in the Volante version. The 48 valves in its heads did their job under the thumb of four camshafts above. Despite diverse components from the familiar Ford repertoire the interior spoilt passengers with the ambience that was to be expected of a luxury liner of this price class. It all started with the scent of Connolly leather.

ASTON MARTIN VANQUISH

Originally it looked as if the engineers at Aston Martin, used to the ceaseless refinement of venerable concepts, had only been allowed out into the creative playground for a short while. "Series production was not planned," said Bob Dover, then head of the firm, when the Vantage project study was presented at the North American Auto Show in Detroit in January 1998.

It was as if master chef Paul Bocuse had shown a crowd of hungry and thirsty gourmets a spread of superb goodies from his kitchen and cellars and then cleared it away again. A sufficient number of automotive gourmets, particularly in the United States, could not contain their disappointment, and so after the show the company quickly jettisoned the idea of limiting the project to a unique prototype to bolster their ego and go in a museum. The vision from Buckinghamshire was simply too good to be true.

But a few things needed to be done before the new model officially made its bow at the Geneva Motor Show in the spring of 2001 under the un-British and rather aggressive name of Vanquish, and the first series units could roll out of the antique factory sheds in Tickford Street in Newport Pagnell on June 15. Certainly the form was close to perfection, a tightly fitting suit of breathtaking cut from which the power simply oozed. Nevertheless, Scot Ian Callum, creator of the DB7 and now by virtue of office entrusted with creating beauties for Jaguar under the joint roof of the Premier Automotive Group, revised his design slightly. The flanks were made slightly broader, the back slightly higher. For the rest, he said, the Vanquish remained a true Aston Martin—straight lines, very masculine, and a bit conservative.

Secondly, Dover's successor Ulrich Bez had a few criticisms to make of what he saw as weak points in the interior, like ventilation outlets from the sensible Ford Ka model. You didn't necessarily have to rub it in to the owner of a Vanquish that the noble product belonged to the huge Ford family. He also spontaneously ordered the huge aluminum-covered central console to be redesigned. Thirdly, 50 prototypes were tortured and battered over one million test miles. One trial model, for instance, with code number SCFAC13332, had to shiver for more than 5000 miles under arctic conditions before being allowed to warm up for a further 7500 in the glittering heat of the Nevada and Californian deserts.

But it was all set for top marks. It took eight weeks in Newport Pagnell to set a single Vanquish on its wheels, although the amount of hand labor had been greatly reduced. The main structure was formed from a tray of glued and riveted aluminum sheets with a central tunnel of carbon fiber attached. This precious material was also to be found in the A-pillars and in the front section, where it was combined with steel and aluminum elements to promote exemplary behavior in a crash. Most of the rear section was plastic reinforced with fiberglass.

The Vanquish was enveloped in sheet aluminum, no longer hammered by hand but pressed warm. It was supplied by the British firm Superform, which also dressed the Morgan Aero 8. Aston Martin covered the panels with eight coats of lacquer, allowing customers to exercise even the most exquisite taste in color, as in the Connolly leather inside, where 130 sq ft (12 sq m) of fine Wilton carpeting were also laid.

The same 6-liter V12 was installed as in the DB7 Vantage, although it was now assembled by expert hands in the Ford Cosworth plant. With careful changes it had been increased by 40 bhp to 457 and would bring the coupé, with its weight of 3968 lb (1800 kg), up to 60 mph (97 kph) in five seconds. It could also reach a top speed of 190 mph (306 kph). The brutal symphonic sound emitted by the two fat exhaust tubes left no-one in any doubt that there was enormous power there, although it was produced in the noblest way.

The automatic transmission was developed in co-operation with the Italian specialist Magneti Marelli. The six gears of this wolf in wolf's clothing could be changed manually as well in the twinkling of an eye, literally in 250 milliseconds, using paddles behind the steering wheel.

The chassis was co-ordinated with Lotus and guaranteed good roadholding. Voluminous 19-inch (482-mm) light alloy wheels with Yokohama tires of 255/40 ZR19 in front and 285/40 ZR19 behind were suspended on dual triangular transverse control arms in forged aluminum all round. They were tailor-made for the Vanquish and signed with the AML initials. Tire pressure and temperature were individually monitored, as part of the all-embracing electronic management of this top Aston Martin, while huge internally ventilated disc brakes by Brembo would put a complete curb on motion.

The Vanquish is available as a two-seater or as a 2+2. The 300 examples per year the company plans to make will presumably not even meet the most insistent demand. One thing is certain: as usual, an owner must state in his will who is to get the Aston Martin after his death.

The Aston Martin has something of the feral predator in its appearance, as if it were about to spring on its prey, bring it down and devour it. The huge mouth of the radiator, initially the last variation on a theme that started with the 2-liter sports car, is flanked by supplementary headlights and the indicator.

The silhouette of the new Aston Martin flagship unites a wide range of references to earlier models by the famous firm, combining traditional elements with the contemporary stylistic features of a supercar. The short overhang at the back is striking, as is the spoiler lip integrated in the lid of the trunk. White instruments watch over the health of the mighty V12, whose increase in power over the DB7 Vantage is partly due to new intakes and exhaust.

AUSTIN-HEALEY 100

Love at first sight sometimes brings about spontaneous reactions. Strolling through the London Motor Show in Earl's Court in October 1952, Leonard Lord, boss of the newly established British Motor Corporation, stood as if rooted to the spot, staring at an ice-blue open two-seater, the Healey 100.

Its beautiful form was from the pen of Gerry Coker, who had been with Donald Healey's sports car plant in Warwick for two years. The shape concealed relatively ordinary fare. A box frame taken under the axle with cross struts, designed by Healey engineer Barrie Bilby, independent suspension at the front with dual triangular transverse control arms and coil springs, a rigid axle at the rear suspended on semi-elliptical springs and located by Panhard rod. The 2660cc, 94 bhp four-cylinder engine came from the Austin A40, as did the transmission. The first gear was rarely ever used, and an overdrive unit could be switched on when in third or

The encounter between the two men was the start of a wonderful success story. A total of 25 pilot vehicles were made in Warwick, then the whole enterprise was moved to the Austin garrison in Longbridge.

Between March 1953 and August 1955, 10,688 examples of the 100/4 BN1 were made there and sold at the ridiculously low price of £750—£100 less than the price tag on the Healey stand in Earl's Court. During the next 12 months the slightly modified BN2 followed in a production series of 3924. This had a four-speed transmission plus overdrive, and was equipped with a more robust rear axle. At about the same time 1159 Austin-Healey 100Ms were made in response to the many requests. Its two-tone paintwork, a leather strap stretched across the bonnet and air slits cut into the engine cover indicated the presence of 112 bhp beneath. With 132 bhp, nurtured by the renowned tuner Harry Weslake from an alloy cylinder head, the 100S could do even better. Unlike the others it had a light metal body, an elliptical radiator grill and Dunlop disc brakes all round. It was only made in 1955, and in a strictly limited number as a special offer for a sporty clientele, although it did not acquire a great reputation.

The 100/6 BN4 arrived in August 1956. Its six-cylinder motor from the Austin Westminster had 2639cc but was more a status symbol than a spur to spectacular achievement, delivering only 102 bhp. The BN4—of which a volume of 10,289 had been made by 1959—weighed 418 lb (190 kg) more than the previous four-cylinder version. The striking features of the Six were its windshield, now rigidly upright, the oval air intake in front of it, with a grill of vertical rods, and the small air inlet on the edge of the bonnet. This model also had external door handles.

The chassis was extended roughly to their height, and the wheelbase was stretched by 1.8 inches (46 mm) to 92 inches (2336 mm), making room for an emergency seat at the back. Disc wheels were already available as an option in 1956. A chic hard top was available from 1957, and from the same year the big Healey was assembled in the MG factory in Abingdon, alongside the Sprite and MGA.

In November 1957 the company responded to a general call for more power by tuning the engine to 117 bhp. In the same configuration and with much the same performance, the six-cylinder motor was moved into the engine compartment of the 4150 BN6 from April 1958—a model that again only offered the joy of the road to strictly two persons. The final comment in the report in *Road & Track* applied to this model as to all the others. It said that this Austin-Healey was an extraordinary all-rounder, a lucky find for the many enthusiasts who wanted a sports car at a moderate price, with a good appearance, fine performance, and good reliability.

The Austin-Healey 100S was announced in fall 1954 and only 50 were made. Its sports background and intent were very evident in its striking appearance. It had no bumpers and the body ends had been given a pleasing new shape. The radiator grill was smaller and oval, the windshield was lower and could not be laid flat. The car had disc brakes all round and two-tone paintwork, often blue and white.

fourth gear. The windshield could be laid flat, further underlining the sportiness of the exhibit.

That evening Leonard Lord invited Healey to his hotel. Compliments flowed with the drinks, and Donald Healey told his host—among other things—that the blue car was certainly not a lame duck or an elegant plaything; the firm had just tested it in Belgium, where they had achieved 112 mph (180 kph) on the highway between Jabbeke and Aeltre.

The two men parted friends—and partners. From the very next day the Hundred was to be called the Austin-Healey, and what was particularly flattering for Donald Healey was the fact that no changes were to be made to it at all. No wonder: the Austin-Healey 100 was a perfect example of how entirely normal components could be put together in such a way as to achieve a literally breathtaking result, as the American magazine *Road & Track* said in July 1954.

The engine of the 100S also differed from the norm. The cylinder head was of aluminum alloy, and the induction and exhaust ports, carburetor and manifold had all been moved to the right. On the left were the ignition distributor and the dynamo. The opening to the tank, elsewhere concealed under the lid of the trunk, rose up from the bodywork behind the driver.

AUSTIN-HEALEY SPRITE

What they needed, remarked BMC boss Leonard Lord in the mid-1950s in a conversation with Donald Healey and his son Geoffrey, was an inexpensive little open two-seater based on the Austin 35, to set beside the Hundred.

So began the story of the frog-eye, a born favorite, the cheery little sports car of which 48,999 examples were sold, quite apart from the countless second- and third-hand sales by owners who—for whatever reason—chose to suffer the painful parting. The little car was quite simply youthful, and a godsend for boys—a priceless contribution to the love life of a whole generation, for with a Sprite outside the house it was much easier for you to get the nice girl from next door, and maybe a few from round the corner as well.

And because it was so greatly loved its weaknesses were willingly forgiven, weaknesses such as its phlegmatic behavior. The bright yellow model tested by *auto motor und sport* in 1958 was taken up to a top speed of 126 kph (80 mph) and took a full half-minute to reach 100 kph (60 mph). Owners seemingly weren't even put off by the fact that they were unpleasantly reminded of bad weather—even when the hood was up—albeit in a gently filtered form. Nor were they troubled that, in order to save costs, the company had done without such elementary ergonomic comforts as external door handles.

The frog-eyed Sprite's headlamps protruded rudely from the front of the car, earning the model its nickname; for some they were what gave the little Healey its real flair. The BMC engineers had made a virtue of necessity here: originally, shuttered headlights were envisaged, but the idea was dropped as being too expensive, and it was additionally feared that they would not meet with the approval of the American car import authorities. In the end there was no time to design a more sophisticated solution.

But one thing at a time. On January 31, 1957 Lord's successor, George Harriman, was presented with a prototype of the AN5 model, BMC internal Project 13 from the Austin Drawing Office, ADO. Exactly one year later the first Sprite Mk I was being given its last polish. The name Sprite was already well used—by a Riley and a Daimler. Drawn by Healey's in-house designer, Gerry Coker, and with a sure hand, the Mk I had little of a special nature to offer technically: a monocoque body entirely of steel, independent front suspension using dual transverse control arms, coil springs and lever dampers, and a rigid axle with piston dampers behind, suspended on quarter-elliptical leaf springs set lengthways below and longitudinal control arms above.

AHS 58

Some 42.5 bhp had been won from the 948cc BMC A-series engine, with slight modifications including special outlet valves, valve springs, and crankshaft bearings, and a compression ratio of 8.3:1.

The order for production went to the MG works in Abingdon with the express approval of the BMC governor there, John Thornley. There a truly remarkable collage was put together from widely disparate sources. The substructure came from John Thompson Motor Pressings in Wolverhampton, the rest of the body from the Pressed Steel Company in Swindon. The engine, transmission, and steering were from Morris Minor, in Coventry. In the Healey headquarters in Warwick trade was blooming in extras such as the Shorrocks compressor, which coaxed the Sprite up to 65 bhp, a top speed of 90 mph (145 kph) and generally very lively performance. But a price was paid in the life expectancy and vulnerability of the tiny four-cylinder engine. A special tuning manual was available for the eager home mechanic.

Apart from the few critical remarks that were necessary to maintain his reputation for thoroughness, Reinhard Seiffert,

the very severe reviewer and future chief editor of *auto motor und sport*, writing in the article cited above, allowed himself to be won over by the charm of the little test model he had driven, priced at DM 6990. Above all, he liked its exemplary handling: the steering required only two-and-a-third turns of the two-spoke steering wheel to get from lock to lock, and with its low center of gravity the Sprite lay on the road like a board, with a barely noticeable tendency to understeer.

Seiffert regarded the striking goitre look of the car as an amusing trademark of this nimble creature, and it was this that the London tuner, Sprinzel, removed from his considerably more elegant Sebring Sprite. The aim was to achieve less wind resistance, and in another special variant the frog eyes were lost in a form-has-to-follow-function manner. But in the process the little elf from Abingdon lost its flair.

Created as a half-hearted emergency solution, the protruding headlights on the Sprite became the trademark of this star of the 1-litre class. In the corners of its radiator mouth, here seen entirely without the protection of the usual slim bumper, there seemed to lurk a permanent little smile.

Under the huge and surprisingly heavy hood the 948cc four-cylinder BMC A-series engine crouched low, looking lost. There was no lid to the trunk, so the spare wheel was difficult to access and luggage could only be loaded and unloaded when the seats were folded down. And to be polite, the fixtures and fittings were "of spartan charm." But one would always forgive the Sprite anything.

AUSTIN-HEALEY 3000

With the production of the last Austin-Healey Sixes, types BN4 and BN6, and the first 3000 in March 1959, we reach the second part of the success story. A total of 42,922 3-liter models followed until the car bearing chassis number 43,026 marked the end on March 14, 1968. The time had come: as early as February 1965 *Road & Track* had remarked sourly that the car was due for honorable retirement, and that BMC should start again with a clean sheet.

Gentle evolution was characteristic of the model's progress. The transition from the 100/6 had gone smoothly with no breaks or jumps. The engine was opened up to 2912cc, the compression ratio increased from 8.5 to 9:1, and as a result of these cautious operations the car delivered 124 bhp. That disc brakes were only now installed at the front was remarkable, as the 100S of 1955 had four.

Despite downbeat comments from Pat Moss, an inspired driver with high-octane blood in her veins, just like her famous brother Stirling, the 3000 was regarded as a plaything for tough guys who were only afraid of death sometimes, and of the devil never. In 1962 one of these models advanced to eighth place in the general category at Le Mans before a piston fault intervened. And the model was able to chalk up 40 overall wins at major rallies under the direction of Competition Manager Marcus Chambers. They were linked to the names of the best of the sport—the twins Donald and Erle Morley, for example, Paddy Hopkirk, Rauno Aaltonen, Timo Makinen, Pat Moss, and Ann Wisdom. The Big Healey won the long-distance Liège-Rome-Liège twice, and was the only British sports car to do so, as the company proudly advertised.

In its issue of August 28, 1959 *The Autocar* noted the differences from the 100/6. At 32.8 seconds the 3000 took five seconds less to reach 100 mph (160 kph) and at 114 mph (183.5 kph) it was 5 mph (8 kph) faster. The engine coped well with the extra 110lb (50 kg), despite the longer rear axle ratio of 3.9:1 (in the 100/6 it was 4.1:1). The car had welcome accelerative punch, even from low engine speeds. In city traffic it proved willing and disciplined, although its driver always felt the urge to head for the open highway. The overdrive that could be switched on to the third and fourth gear had a noticeable effect on noise reduction and the fuel consumption.

The Mk I in its BT7 and BN7 versions was followed in 1961 by the Mk II, made for two years in the same variants, with three carburetors instead of the former two. In 1962 it was joined, again for two years, by the Mk II BJ7 with 131 bhp. The change back to twin SU carburetors cost only one unnoticeable horsepower. The BJ7 was replaced by the Mk III BJ8 until production ended. The BMC technicians were still able to coax a solid 148 bhp from its six cylinders. Servo brakes gave greater safety, while the walnut veneer on the dashboard was a visual delight and crank-operated windows provided greater comfort. From chassis number 26,705 in 1964 more space was freed-up for rear axle travel by curving the frame downwards and replacing the Panhard rod with dual overhanging arms. These all had tangibly positive effects on the driving experience offered by the Austin-Healey 3000. Incidentally, in BMC code, N stands for two-seater, T for 2+2 seater and J for Convertible.

In the *Road & Track* test report quoted above, the reviewer noted the slight understeer in the 3000 that made the car so easy for the normal consumer to control in extremis. On empty roads it was possible to slide the car's tail out on fast cornering—as rally drivers do—and control the car's line with the gas pedal alone, particularly on smooth-surfaced roads. On undulating roads the Healey was inclined to jump, as its predecessors had done. The steering required a little too much effort at low speed but sorted itself out nicely at normal driving speeds. The additional accommodation behind the front seats was essentially an annex to a trunk that was already fairly full of battery and spare wheel. The hand-cranked windows made the Convertible very much more winter-proof, although a lot of choke was always needed for starting-up in cold weather. In 1968 there was a brief epilog when Donald Healey produced three prototypes with 4-liter engines from the Vanden Plas. The idea did not catch on, so the Austin-Healey cult car and its various metamorphoses belong to the past.

At a fleeting glance the Austin-Healey 3000, unveiled in the hot summer of 1959, could not be distinguished from its predecessor, the 100/6. Only the oblique digits "3000" set into the radiator grill normally showed the presence of the 3-liter behind. Where the model was supplied with spoked wheels the front disc brakes could be seen behind them.

The arrangement of the instruments, in groups of two to the left and right of the steering column, and set into a narrow oval surrounded by a chrome rim, hadn't changed either. The trunk, in which the spare wheel and the battery were already taking up too much space, was reached by opening a big cover over a low loading edge.

3000

BENTLEY 4½-LITER SUPERCHARGED

For the avowed Bentley brotherhood there is no doubt: this noble marque reached its zenith in the years of independence between 1920 and 1931 in Cricklewood. In fact, they would go even further and state that in that long-gone decade the British sports car, in both spirit and letter, was born under the sign of the winged B.

The father of all this was Walter Owen Bentley, known simply to everybody by his initials W.O. He laid the foundation for a very British institution in 1919 when he bought a shop near Baker Street in London and set about building the first car to bear his name, together with his partners Frank T. Burgess and Harry Varley. Bentley's training as a railway engineer perhaps explains the robustness, the sheer solidity of his products.

The debutant with the EX.1 chassis, which was neither quite finished nor really roadworthy when it was launched at the first London Motor Show after the war, and which was still in a very crude state when it received its certificate of roadworthiness on December 11, 1919, was nonetheless a foretaste of what was to come in the future.

Its 3-liter, four-cylinder engine reflected the philosophy behind the 1914 racing engines. The block and head formed a single unit and the crankshaft and camshaft each rotated in five bearings—the latter driven by a bevel shaft mounted at the front in the crankcase. The pistons were made of light alloy, a separate pan collected the oil from the force-feed lubrication system, and each combustion chamber had two spark plugs, while the twin magnetos were synchronized by a transverse shaft. The cylinder dimensions of 3 × 6 inches (80 × 149 mm) matched the British rating formula, which set a ratio for the bore and number of cylinders.

The car's frame was formed by U-section side members with four transverse beams and two tubular supports. The rigid axles were suspended on semi-elliptical springs, while friction dampers controlled the spring movements. Initially the brakes acted only on the rear wheels, but on all four after 1923. A five-year warranty was granted on the chassis, although not without subjecting the car to a thorough works test once the body had been fitted. A total of 1622 chassis left the factory up to 1929, the bodies for many of them fitted by Vanden Plas or Gurney Nutting. The Bentley 3-liter took prestigious victories at Le Mans in 1924 and 1927.

By the late 1920s, however, the options for further development were as good as exhausted. Furthermore, the competition was becoming a threat—for example, the Vauxhall 30/98. Since the 6½-liter Bentleys voraciously devoured tires when racing, they were not really an alternative. Consequently, series production of the 4½-liter was launched in Cricklewood in 1927. This was the spitting image of its predecessor and was dismissed by many as a hangover from the Edwardian era. Of the 665 chassis up to 1931, 653 had a wheelbase of 130 inches (3302 mm), while only 12 opted for the shorter 118-inch (2984-mm) wheelbase.

Up to 1929 this model was fitted with a traditional cone clutch, and after this date with a plate clutch. Since the engine—fed by two SU carburetors—with its output ranging from 105 to 115 bhp, had only a low overall weight-to-load factor, its life expectancy was almost of Old Testament proportions. Sporting successes came thick and fast: for example victory at Le Mans in 1928 or second to fourth places in the 1930 race, where the car had to give way to another Bentley, a Speed Six.

The marathon French race was obviously also in mind in the design of the "Blower" Bentley, which was the top of the

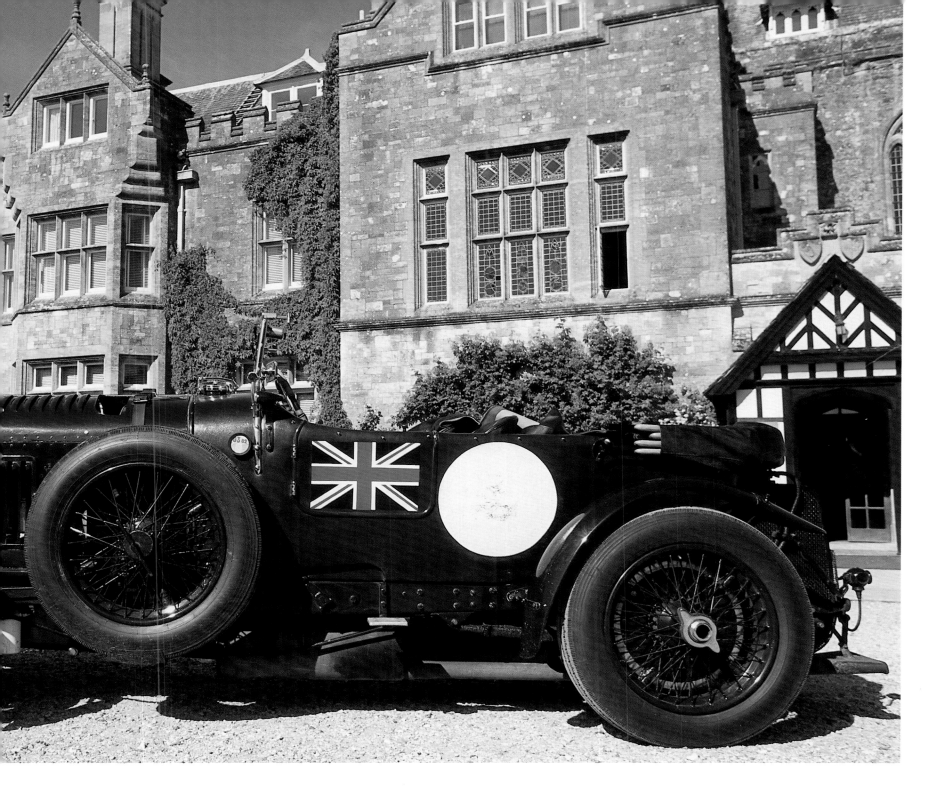

range from 1929 onwards. A minimum of 50 units were required to obtain type approval, and 55 supercharged 4½-liter cars were built up to 1931. The car was financed by Dorothy Paget and developed by Sir Henry Birkin and Amherst Villiers, who were also responsible for the twin-impeller blower that worked on the Roots principle. The standard chassis was reinforced with more robust front transverse beams, and the power plant was completely overhauled: the block, crankshaft, conrods, pistons, and the ribbed oil pan were new.

The blower and the two SU carburetors were stowed not far from the radiator under a metal grill between the chassis side bars. The road-going version delivered 182 bhp, while the hottest race-tuned car developed up to 250 bhp with a corresponding top speed of between 100 and 125 mph (160 and 200 kph). The Le Mans-tested racing car of the

Birkin-Paget Team reached no less than 62 mph (100 kph) in first gear. The closed-top variants of this majestic vehicle in particular made an extended journey a tortuous affair because of the infernal levels of noise.

Although the "Blower" Bentley gave the winged B in the company's badge a second meaning at a higher level, founding father W.O. was not at all happy with it. And rightly so: the 4½-liter's forced induction system raised its fuel consumption from an acceptable US 13.8 mpg (imperial 16.6 mpg) to a gluttonous US 8.4 mpg / imperial 10 mpg (respectively 17 and 28 liters per 100 km). Major shortcomings in the oil-feed system, plus cooling problems, put potential owners off. Above all, it lacked the accustomed success on the racetrack—in particular, it never won the race for which it should really have been tailor-made: Le Mans.

Undoubtedly a powerful personality, towering and threatening: in its day the Bentley "Blower" 4½-liter could show a clean pair of heels to almost everything on British and Continental roads. The car in the photo began its life as a Sportsman's coupé with a Vanden Plas body, was later converted to a Le Mans Replica and now forms part of the collection at the National Motor Museum at Beaulieu in Hampshire, England.

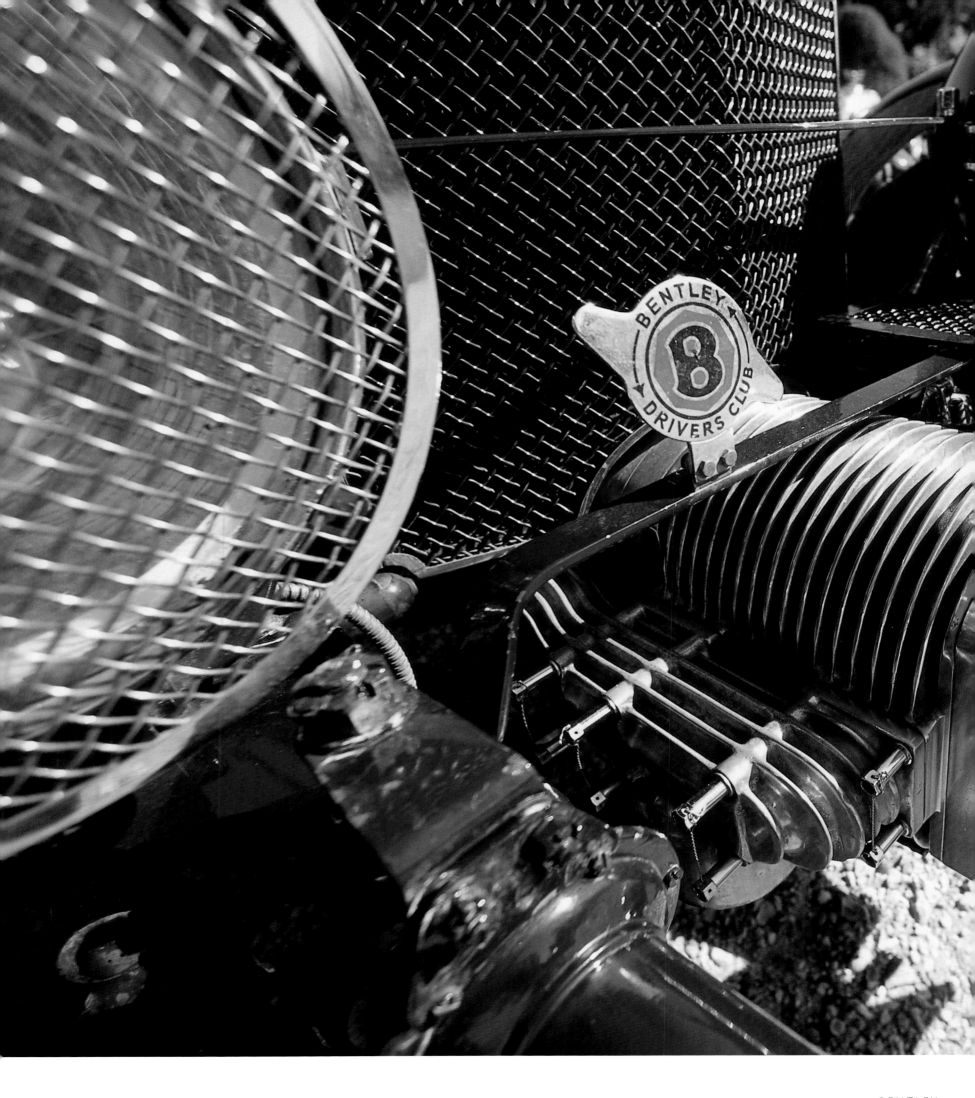

The supercharger in all its gleaming glory protrudes from below the radiator. It blows 182 bhp into the enormous four-cylinder engine, though it swallows 35 bhp of this for its own operation. The grill (left), typical of the Birkin competition cars, is intended to protect the carburetors against outside interference. Nowadays racing cars have smaller steering wheels than road-going cars, but in the past they were larger than average since considerable force had to be applied.

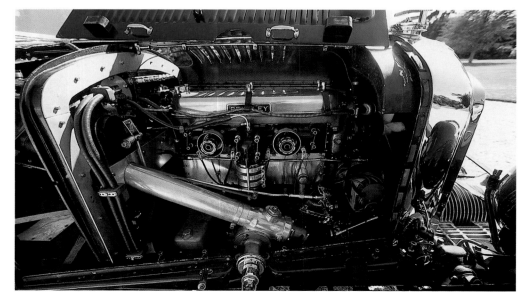

BRISTOL 404

As the world started to recover from the war in 1945 the Bristol Aeroplane Company set up a small car company to make use of spare capacity. The philosophy was to build a small number of cars by hand to the high standard of the aircraft industry and in accordance with some of its traditional principles. Furthermore, it wished to remain as self-sufficient as possible. This elitist approach attracted the critics: why should Bristol buy in a part for £5, some scorned, when they could make it themselves for £30?

The company's first opus, the 400, which was shown at the 1947 Geneva Motor Show, actually sported a first-class pre-war design from Bavaria. The chassis was derived from the BMW 326, a closed box-section frame with rear outriggers, a live rear axle and longitudinal torsion rods, independent front suspension with upper A-arms and transverse leaf springs, in modular form for ease of removability. The engine was based in principle on that of the BMW 328, an in-line six-cylinder unit with side-mounted camshaft and a displacement of 1971cc, delivering 90 bhp. The car was hardly discreet as it passed by: the forest of pushrods operating the valves "sounded like a thousand grandmothers knitting," wrote one perceptive listener. The body was clearly inspired by the BMW 327.

Yet it was by no means a pirate copy. The model's original, rather unwieldy name also explains why: Frazer-Nash-Bristol. Frazer-Nash boss H.J. Aldington had had friendly contacts with BMW even before the war, acquired the sales and manufacturing license for Britain, and had been awarded the design plans of types 327 and 328 as reparation payments. Bristol bought the rights, then Aldington re-acquired them—hence his company's name also appeared on the product.

This model was joined in October 1948 by the Bristol 401, a saloon freshly styled in *superleggera* fashion by Carrozzeria Touring of Milan, which revealed a great deal of attention to aerodynamic detail and was well protected

against front and rear-end collisions by unusually sturdy bumpers. At Geneva in 1949 Bristol whetted the appetites of wealthy would-be purchasers with its new offering, the drophead 402, whose beautiful lines betrayed the masterful hand of Pinin Farina. In early 1953 the 403 emerged as the contemporary evolution of the 401, with a stronger crankshaft and larger intake valves, meaning that the knitting grannies were now delivering 100 bhp. The brakes and suspension were also modified, though the family likeness to its German forebears was still unmistakable.

Only when the 404 was launched in the fall of that same year was this kinship largely gone. Its two-seater coupé body was a clear sign that the wind tunnel's opinion had been sought. The straight waistline ended in a gentle curve both at the front and at the rear where delicate fins were reminiscent of the huge tail fins of the type 450 racing coupé. The unadorned functionality of the engine air intake was also recycled from elsewhere in the Bristol group: the conglomerate's Brabazon aircraft sported something very similar. As in the Aston Martin DB1, the spare wheel was housed in a compartment on the left behind the front axle and thus did not disturb the car's clean lines at all. There was no external access to the trunk. The alloy body sat on a frame made of pitch pine with an aluminum substructure in the door areas. All the gauges and instruments providing the driver with information on the operating status, general wellbeing, and current performance of the Bristol 404 were grouped in a housing behind the steering wheel. Two engines were available, a lower-powered version delivering 107 bhp and a pokier 127 bhp, not dissimilar to the marque's Formula Two power plants.

Only 40 Bristol 404s were ever built, and there were two reasons for this. On the one hand, the Jaguar XK140 stole the show and the clientele, as it was superior in every regard and only half the price of the 404, which came in at an expensive £3542 15s 10d, including purchase tax. On the other hand, the extremely successful businessman and amateur racing driver Stanley Howard Arnolt offered the Arnolt-Bristol in the US, which featured a smart body by Bertone on a 404 chassis—and at half the price of the original. Quite a few people even claimed that the American version from Chicago was much more attractive than its English counterpart.

In the 404 the Bristol Aeroplane Company relishes the chance to remind us of its main work. The engine air intake, with its unadorned aggression, is borrowed from one of the company's aircraft. The razor-sharp sculpted fins at the rear hint at the gigantic vertical tail fins of the 450 Sport coupé that won its class in the 1953 Reims 12 Hours. Both are the product of the wind tunnel.

The 404's power plant is similar to the successful Bristol racing engine, with three Solex carburetors and its exhaust manifold with six outlets. Its spare wheel is housed vertically in a compartment in the left-hand fender, while the battery and other electrical systems are in the corresponding place on the other side.

The instruments are covered to prevent reflections on the windshield.

Caterham boss Graham Nearn had two main problems in the second half of the 1980s. Firstly, the rapid increase in demand for the nippy Caterham (né Lotus) Super Seven cult car was outgrowing its modest birthplace at Caterham Hill, Surrey, originally a smoke-blackened forge in the middle of an orchard. Nearn quickly located more spacious premises in Kennet Road, Dartford. In October 1987 the company was just in the process of moving everything to the new site when the infamous Hurricane Gilbert wreaked havoc at the old premises, the somber symbolism of which was not lost on the Caterham crew.

However, their energy was impaired neither by the move nor by the worst that the weather could throw at them. On the contrary: innovation was the order of the hour—insofar as it is required at all for such a coveted antique. A De Dion axle with brake discs of 9 inches (228 mm) diameter was offered as an alternative to the standard live axle with drum brakes at the rear. In 1988 the Seven's bad-weather equipment was improved and its radiator was enlarged. Countless extras, such as quality leather upholstery supplied by Oxted,

CATERHAM

meant that even the most unusual tastes among the marque's fans were catered for.

Nearn's liking for limited editions served the same purpose, for example the Prisoner model in British racing green with a yellow nose and bright red interior displayed at the 1990 London Motor Show, which recalled the eponymous popular TV series from the 1960s. Actor Patrick McGoohan, who drove a Lotus Seven as his runaround in the series, happily gave the project his blessing and even undertook the journey from Hollywood to London for the event. From the same year onwards a honeycomb structure offered greater protection against side impacts.

On the other hand, the era of the Ford Kent pushrod engine and the twin camshaft Cosworth BDR engine, both available since 1968, was coming to an end. Here, too, there was no shortage of quick solutions. The Ford engine was replaced by a Rover K-series four-cylinder unit of 1.4 liters with double overhead camshafts. As it was made entirely from alloy, it was 66 lb (30 kg) lighter than its predecessor. The sumptuously staged launch in London's Docklands in July 1991 was accompanied by a great many kind words on the Rover deal.

About a year earlier the HPC variant had been launched at the new production plant in Dartford, the result of a promising commercial tie-up with Vauxhall and—as everyone soon agreed—the best Seven of all time. Under the

slim hood sat the 16-valve 2-liter engine, a Cosworth creation weighing in at a mere 278 lb (126 kg) and developing 150 bhp in its standard version, which had powered the Vauxhall Astra GTE since May 1988. In the Seven HPC it was fed by two Weber 45 DCOE double-barrel carburetors which, in conjunction with a modified exhaust manifold, ensured an extra 25 bhp and which, like its dry-sump lubrication, was a concession to the Japanese market where such details were prized as technical delicacies.

The De Dion axle was a standard feature, as were the limited-slip differential and the set of alloy wheels weighing only 15 lb (6.7 kg). This sporty number tipped the scales at only 1300 lb (590 kg) at the curb, so every bhp had to move a mere 7.5 lb (3.4 kg).

This resulted in staggering performance figures: the factory quoted 4.9 seconds for the 0–60 mph (up to 100 kph) from a standing start and a top speed of 130 mph (209 kph), and also revealed a touching sense of responsibility for its customers. The High Performance Course (HPC—hence the name) was compulsory for owners up to the age of 25 years,

SEVEN

and recommended as a voluntary option for those who were older. For all those who like it even hotter, Swindon Racing Engines offered three tuning stages of 218, 225, and 235 bhp, while the 1992 JPE version (standing for Jonathan Palmer Evolution) went even further. Palmer had just finished his grand prix career, and his version had 250 bhp under the bonnet.

However, more stringent emissions regulations put a stop to this proliferation. As early as 1993, when the HPC could be bought not only as a kit but also fully factory-assembled and was sporting a new grill with a Seven logo, the carburetors had to be stripped out and replaced by the originally designed injection system, resulting in a 10 bhp reduction in performance. Despite this step, it was excessive exhaust emissions which caused production of the model to be halted in 1996 after a total of 387 had been built (238 with carburetors, 149 with fuel injection).

That's the bad news. The good news is that the Caterham Seven is, in principle, immortal and just about indestructible.

Launched in August 1990 in Dartford, the Seven HPC with its 2-liter Vauxhall engine is the fastest Caterham to date.

The Caterham Seven HPC's aesthetic appeal and driver enjoyment are due precisely to its bare minimalism. Its pleasing simplicity once again makes it a work of art with lovingly functional design details. It's not often that you see the window from which the spur ends of the twin Weber carburetors peek out, or the bizarrely efficient routing of the exhaust gases, for example. The upside-down tachometer shown below underlines how individual owners liked to add a personal touch to their car.

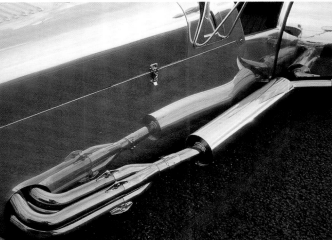

CATERHAM 21

After 21 years of a strict Seven monoculture Caterham boss Graham Nearn rang the changes for himself and his team, albeit after a few heated exchanges with his staff members Jez Coates and Reg Price: a new Caterham-specific model was required to augment the persistently popular evergreen, a little breath of fresh air after so much continuity. The project name was derived from its trigger: C21, later shortened to 21.

The initial move, of course, was to consult the Lotus history books. Something along the lines of the Eleven, once a fully enclosed racing variant of the original Seven, was out of the question because it would never have been wholly approved of by the European licensing authorities. They had enough trouble with them already. This was because it was proving increasingly difficult to obtain continued approval for the Caterham Seven in the light of the ever more

the Seven the driver searched in vain for somewhere to rest his clutch foot. The frame was suitably stiffened, the same power plant was used, and the suspension configuration was retained with a modified sway bar at the front.

The prototype of a chassis, commissioned from Arch Motors, was completed in March 1994. A few days before Christmas, Jez Coates engaged former Caterham employee Iain Robertson as the designer, agreed a modest fee and gave a broad outline of the remit: a traditional British sports car, lightweight, with clean and uncomplicated lines, as if an outer skin had been stretched over a skeleton. At the same time the 21 had to appear subtly sexy to the eye of the beholder. Four proposals were submitted, and the first proved the popular favorite.

Jez Coates took delivery of the chassis in April 1994, and both he and Iain Robertson then got to work in a shed on Coates' estate. He felt, he declared later, like a modern-day Michelangelo. Using the comparatively rough-and-ready tool of a power saw, they sculpted the left half of the car from polystyrene blocks and then simply filled in the missing half with a mirror.

To give the prototype a high-quality finish from the outset, they had it clad in aluminum by Roach Manufacturing Ltd in Ower, Hampshire, England. Like its colleague, the Seven, the rest of it was a collage of components of mixed origin: the JPE power plant for example (Rover engines were later supplied for the most part), together with the inside door handles from Vauxhall or the indicators from Suzuki, while the instruments were borrowed from the Seven and simply rearranged.

The Caterham 21 had a promising launch. At the Birmingham Motor Show in October 1994 its highly polished bodywork made a literally gleaming impression. It helped also that it was featured on the BBC's motoring program *Top Gear* as the finished article with former racing driver Tiff Needell at the wheel.

Shortly after the show the prototype was dispatched to Rawlsons in Dover, a plastics specialist, where composite bodies were to be manufactured as an option. A slight asymmetry in the area of the taillights was discovered and rectified here. The alloy skin, which required 1000 hours of work, was the responsibility of Caterham importer Tanaka in Tokyo. *Autocar* magazine tester Andrew Frankel reported that the test-model had the typical Caterham feel when driving, which could only be intended as a compliment. The gorgeous model also cut a good figure at the traditional fall show for special cars in Essen, Germany.

One stumbling block for the Caterham 21, however, was its high price—originally no less than £18,750 in kit form. Furthermore, competitors such as the Mazda MX-5 and the BMW Z3 appeared and overwhelmed it. Thus it was that up to and including November 2000 only 68 models were built, though its creators could bask in the joy of having made a beautiful dream come true.

stringent standards that were calling the acceptability of its emissions and its crash performance into question. Two other possible parameters were also rejected: a frameless, lightweight composite monocoque à la Lotus Elite, and the mid-engine principle. A small company with a workforce of only 60 would not have been up to such extravagant challenges.

What was feasible, however, was what Chris Rees in his Caterham monograph calls "a slippery son of the Seven"—a streamlined derivative of the marque's standard model. The fact that the company's philosophy—that the engineering under the Seven's skin could change, but that its look was absolutely inviolable—was turned on its head in the process, seems to have caused no one to lose any sleep. Nonetheless, enlarging the front track width by 3 inches (76 mm) to the same size as the rear, while retaining the wheelbase, meant that there was even room for a support on the left where in

RIGHT: A Ford crossflow engine with five-speed transmission being attached to the chassis of a limited-edition Seven for export to Japan. The model is recognizable by the aluminum motorcycle fenders at the rear.

The Supersport version of the Rover K-series engine gets a sharper camshaft to boost performance from 120 bhp to 135 bhp.

CATERHAM CARS LIMITED

BIRTH OF THE GLORIOUS SEVEN

Derek Gilbert of Caterham installing the inlet duct on the Ford engine.

As the carburetors needed more room a hole had to be made in the hood.

Derek Gilbert attaching the four-point harness, available as an option. The inner panels of the model for export to Japan were coated in red.

DAIMLER SP250

For the very proper Daimler family, which produced high-quality limousines in the 1950s such as the Regency Empress and the Majestic, the SP250, first unveiled on April 4, 1959 at the International Automobile Exhibition in New York, was something of a wayward son. It quickly divested itself of its original name, "Dart," since Chrysler already had a Dodge model of this name to which it held the rights.

In January 1964—by which time 1200 left-hand-drive and 1445 right-hand-drive models of this bizarre roadster were running, mainly on British and US roads—the curtain came down on its production. The end was ushered in by the opposition of Sir William Lyons, the head of Jaguar, who had taken control of the oldest British car marque in 1960 and

Turner's masterpiece was implanted in a chassis that was almost a clone of the Triumph TR3A: a box-section frame with crossbracing, independent front suspension with A-arms of unequal length configured above each other and coil springs with telescopic shock absorbers mounted inside them. There was a live rear axle above the chassis members suspended with semi-elliptic leaf springs, and efficient Girling disk brakes all round which, like the clutch, only bit at the end of lengthy pedal travel.

As for the material for the two-seater bodywork with a padded emergency seat space behind the front bucket seats, the decision was taken to use fiberglass, in order to avoid high investment costs because of the tight budget. The result was as striking as it was ugly. In their attempts to create something entirely unmistakable, the Daimler designers obviously lost all feel for proportion and cobbled together a heterogeneous synthesis of incompatible features such as the absolutely horizontal tail fins, the forward-bulging engine air intake and headlights emerging from the fenders. Worse still: in the first generation at least, cracks formed around the hinges, headlights, and door handles, and also in the region of the fenders and the hood, which were reminiscent of those that appear in a desert drying out again after a downpour.

In this period the SP250 flexed so much that the doors sometimes suddenly sprang open on poor road surfaces, leaving the occupants in a state of constant uncertainty. A hardtop, available from October 1960, had a stabilizing effect, while the B specification introduced in April 1961 featured reinforcements to the frame and body. Previous optional extras, such as full-width bumpers instead of the then standard overriders at front and rear, and an adjustable steering wheel, became part of the standard specification at the same time. From February of the same year a Borg Warner automatic transmission was available as an alternative to the manual transmission, whose first gear could still only be engaged after double-declutching. Additional, even if somewhat basic, comfort was provided in a C version available from March 1963: a cigarette lighter, for example, and a demister.

Contemporary reviewers were pleasantly surprised by details such as the cavernous trunk, a spacious lockable glove compartment, and the leather lining of the dashboard on which unusually large and well positioned instruments provided the necessary information. Weighing-in at 2090 lb (948 kg) at the curb, the Daimler SP250 was an uncommonly lively runabout. Its top speed of about 120 mph (193 kph) and its 0–60 mph (up to 100 kph) performance of 8.8 seconds meant that it could hold its own amongst its illustrious competitors. Understeer was a defining feature, with the car tending to drift a little on uneven surfaces as a friendly warning to the driver to beware of losing his rear end.

There were, therefore, also a large number of positive features—but they did not help the Daimler Dart, a.k.a. the SP250, to survive.

In contrast to the generally moderate rise behind the lavishly chromed, oval front grill, the SP250's headlights are strikingly sculpted and dominate their surroundings with a decidedly bulging look. Fender fins also sprout in similarly capricious style at the front and rear of the fiberglass body. The desire for a distinctive design was obviously achieved at the expense of balanced proportions.

had been an outspoken critic of the project from the start. Initially, however, the car owed its genesis to someone else, the newly appointed Daimler manager Edward Turner, who had made his name developing motorcycle engines.

He was responsible for the SP250's compact, lightweight V8, an over-square engine with a high, side-mounted camshaft, whose cylinder banks were angled at 90° to each other. The valve gear revealed its creator's pedigree in motorcycle design. The engine was extremely responsive and delivered a silky-smooth 140 bhp at 5800 rpm, and even then it was not under undue strain. Handled cautiously and maintained with loving care, the SP250 had a long life expectancy. An initial prototype demonstrated its qualities as early as the summer of 1958.

The impression that some things were only half thought-through in the Daimler's design is also confirmed at the rear end where the angular tail fins are not in harmony with their basically rounded surroundings. Nonetheless, the Daimler SP250 offers a surprisingly large amount of trunk space, and even quite large items can be stowed in its lockable glove compartment. Its powerful, lightweight, and compact V8 engine, which is never put under excessive strain, is a creation of engine specialist Edward Turner.

SP250

ELVA COURIER

The windshield is generously sized, so even tall passengers do not have to duck beneath the soft top which can be removed without a trace, and the dashboard is well supplied with instruments. The Elva Courier made concessions to the fashion of the time with its tail fins. Under the hood the very familiar BMC B-series engine, also in service in the MGA, waits for the call to action.

Like his celebrated colleague Colin Chapman, racing car manufacturer Frank Nichols, who was based in Hastings, Sussex, England, took the decision at some stage in the 1950s to bolster his income by producing road-going sports cars. People seek inspiration for a name in different ways: Lotus has a hint of poetry, a whispered secret known only to Chapman and his wife Hazel. The story behind the Elva name, on the other hand, is rather more prosaic: when a prototype suddenly moved, someone called out in French "elle va!"—it really works. Voilà!

The fact that a great dynamic nature was included in the purchase price is also evidenced by the model name, Courier, for the first road-going Elva sports car in 1958. The ideal owner had to have two qualities, Nichols announced, not without self-irony: a waterproof head and a pneumatic butt. The Elva Courier really was a car for pipe smokers who were prepared to risk having their pipe extinguished by the rain coming in through the crude soft top. The renowned specialist magazine *The Autocar* described this phenomenon the same year with typically British understatement: "Weather protection does not fully meet the standards desirable in these unpredictable islands."

However, this problem was purely academic initially as the Courier's entire first production run was already spoken for, bought up by the American importer Continental Motors of Washington D.C. It was not until 1960 that this model was also made available, in kit-car form, to customers in the cold and wet UK, slightly modified, for example, with a curved windshield as opposed to the original, which was simple and straight.

Like Chapman, Nichols used both familiar and unfamiliar components to produce the finished article. Up to the end of 1961 about 700 individualists, who laid particular store by driving a different car from everyone else, took delivery of a very special vehicle in the Mk I and Mk II versions.

The car was built around a tubular frame strengthened with crossbraces, with in-house independent front suspension attached to trapezoidal A-arms using coil springs, and at the rear with a BMC rigid rear axle with coil springs, trailing arms and a Panhard rod. Drum brakes were used at the rear, but disk brakes at the front end were indicative of the new age being ushered in.

The complete chassis weighed a mere 1000 lb (454 kg). That the Elva Courier was a featherweight at only 1554 lb (705 kg) in total was mainly attributable to its plastic body, pleasing and comical in equal measures, and a classic example of the maxim that beauty is in the eye of the beholder. The space available to the driver and passenger was cramped in the extreme. In order to achieve an optimal weight distribution of 53.1 percent at the front and 46.9 percent at the rear, Nichols had positioned the engine as far back as possible. As a result, a significant proportion of the transmission housing intruded into the passenger compartment, at the expense of space for the clutch foot, which had to rest on a ledge provided specifically for this purpose. A certain degree of contortion was required with the gear-shifting hand to reach the shift lever, positioned well to the rear. The trunk,

by contrast, a deep cavern where the spare wheel sat upright at the head end in case of emergencies, was unusually spacious.

The power plants chosen were the BMC B-series engines ranging from 1489cc to 1798cc, which were already performing sterling service in the MGA and MGB. According to *The Autocar*, the newcomer to the market was always nippy, though without quite achieving the magical three-figure top speed of 100 mph (160 kph). It reached its critical engine speed at 5500 rpm, when the valves would begin to bounce unmistakably. Speed was always felt very physically, though when cornering it was more because of high lateral G-force than any tendency toward breakaway. The fan vanes were supplied for self-assembly, the magazine reported, though overheating problems only occurred on London's congested roads. The magazine concluded that the Elva Courier undoubtedly had a brilliant future, despite a few minor glitches.

The Elva Courier's face is dominated by dynamically rounded lines with an intake scooping up the air for the engine from just above the road. The MG engine's sump is slung low so that the hood can also be kept low. The plastic body is made of a single piece and is therefore unusually rigid and robust. Elva drivers don't run with the crowd—an individualism that is emphasized even further by ingredients such as the stone-chip grills over the headlights.

Unfortunately that did not prove to be the case. When the American end of the operation disappeared behind bars in Washington because of certain irregularities, Frank Nichols had already lost some of his enthusiasm for the project, so he sold the rights, and then later his entire company, to his former rival Trojan Ltd in Croydon. Under the management of Trojan Ltd, some 100 further models of a third and fourth generation of the Courier were built with decreasing frequency. The last model was built in 1968, and was accompanied by a sigh of relief.

FRAZER NASH

FRAZER NASH

One look is enough to tell you that the Frazer Nash Mille Miglia is built for racing. An ingenious spaceframe enables its center of gravity, and therefore the entire car, to be kept extremely low. It is clad in an aerodynamic alloy jacket.

Even before the war the creations of Frazer Nash Ltd, established in 1924 by Captain Archibald Goodman Frazer Nash, but under the ownership of the Aldington family since 1926, enjoyed the discreet charm of exclusivity. In the 10 years after 1947 things did not change: a population of only about 100 cars flew the flag for this small company. Nonetheless, London Road in Isleworth, Middlesex was a premier address simply because of the great impression its products made on the racetrack.

All Frazer Nash cars from the post-war period featured two constants of German origin. The chassis, a tubular frame with independent front suspension with A-arms and a transverse leaf spring and live rear axle with longitudinal torsion bars, was designed by former BMW engineer, Dr Fritz Fiedler. He continued his interrupted career in England, as a kind of living reparation payment and human encore for the design plans of the engine for the BMW 328, now owned by H.J. Aldington.

In slightly modified form this found a home under the hoods of Bristols and was also made available to Frazer Nash—a six-cylinder model with side-mounted camshaft and cubic capacity of 1971cc, delivering 110 bhp and even more in various engine tunes, with the relevant four-speed

gearbox. The company's various creations took on an individual profile thanks to the different bodies, all in-house designs and sometimes strikingly attractive.

First came the Grand Prix which, despite the hints at the loneliness of the single-seater in its name, was in fact a two-seater. Its similarity to the BMW 328 prototypes with the large vent in the hood, which were successful in the 1940 Mille Miglia that had been downgraded to the Gran Premio Brescia, was no accident: it probably was one of them. After its rebirth as a British car it suffered the fate of the loner whose line dies with him.

It was followed by the High Speed, also known as the Competition, a narrow, cigar-shaped two-seater with close-fitting, motorcycle-type fenders, removable headlights, an exhaust system fitted outside the body, and the spare wheel on the left side of the body, the whole lot tipping the scales at just 1510 lb (685 kg). It was available with spoked or solid wheels and a whole range of gear ratios and rear-axle reduction ratios, the least expensive costing £2237 including purchase tax. Externally only the slightly modified BMW kidney grill revealed its continental origins.

Finishing as runner-up behind a 3.3-liter Bugatti on its debut at Silverstone was just the first entry in a long catalog

MILLE MIGLIA

of sporting success. Following its third place at Le Mans in 1949 with Norman Culpan and H.J. Aldington at the wheel behind the victorious Ferrari Barchetta Tipo 166 driven by Lord Selsden and Luigi Chinetti, the High Speed was renamed the Le Mans Replica. This model achieved 25 sales and dominated the 2-liter class on British tracks. Yet it also had greater ambitions further afield: driving the nimble Frazer Nash, Stirling Moss won the British Empire Trophy in 1951 while Franco Cortese was victorious in the Targa Florio of the same year, the first win by a British car since the inception of the Madonie race 50 years previously.

But the real proof of the Le Mans Replica's versatility was demonstrated in 1952 with victories in the Sebring 12 Hours, the Rallye Soleil, and the Rallye Aix–Madrid–Aix. Its endurance capabilities had already been demonstrated by Anthony Crook at Montlhéry in France in November 1951 when he covered 200 miles (320 km) at an average speed of 120 mph (193 kph). An absolutely standard, much-used and somewhat flogged car later managed 0–60 mph (up to 100 kph) in less than eight seconds and reached a speed of 115 mph (185 kph) at 5500 rpm. The reporter warned that nothing much happened below 3700 rpm and that it was important to make good use of the gears.

The Mille Miglia type, introduced in 1950, was merely a more aerodynamically tweaked version of the Le Mans Replica. A Formula Two model was also based on this, although it was clearly overshadowed by the Cooper Bristols.

1952 saw a revised version make its appearance at Earl's Court, which was a good 110 lb (50 kg) lighter, principally because of its slimmed-down 200-series chassis, and boosted to 132 bhp. In race trim, such as Ken Wharton's 1953 car, it even had a De Dion axle. Eight Mk II models were built in two years, while an elegant coupé named Le Mans in a tiny production run of nine units closed this particular chapter in Frazer Nash's company history in 1953.

However, the speedy racers from Isleworth carried on winning for a little longer yet, such as in 1954 in the Coupe des Alpes with O'Hara Moore and John Gott—just because it had become something of a habit.

Following pages: The Grand Prix, High Speed, Le Mans Replica, and Mille Miglia models are variations on a theme. They all contribute to the good name of Frazer Nash in motor sport. One shared feature is the Bristol 2-liter straight-six in a variety of tunes.

GINETTA G4

As owners of an agricultural engineering factory in Woodbridge, Suffolk, the Walklett brothers—Bob, Douglas, Ivor, and Trevor—should by rights have been caught up in the minutiae of everyday life. Despite or perhaps precisely because of this, they decided in the mid-1950s to introduce a little light in the form of a special based on the Wolseley Hornet. The use of their own ingredients justified a new name: Ginetta. Quite how this name originated is a family secret that has not been revealed to this day. The model designation G1 essentially represented the start of an automotive Köchel index for the Walkletts' handiwork, albeit with gaps and inconsistencies, as we shall see.

1957 saw their first car in kit form—the G2—go on sale, and by 1962 things were going so well that the Walkletts were able to give up the agricultural engineering day job and concentrate purely on the Ginetta side of the business at their new premises in Witham, Essex. They complemented each other perfectly: Ivor designed the cars, Trevor styled them, Douglas managed the factory, and Bob was responsible for the business side. The four obviously had the knack: unlike comparable manufacturers Ginetta Cars Ltd never experienced financial difficulties.

The G4, introduced to a knowledgeable public at the Racing Car Show in London in January 1961, sold more than 500 times and was the small company's first model to significantly raise its profile. As a kit car, which it was claimed could be assembled in a good 40 hours, the price announced at the show was £499—the same as for a Mini. Everything else about it was right too, starting with its graceful appeal. The most striking thing about the G4 was its pleasing exterior which featured curvaceous front and rear ends and an oval air inlet with which it sniffed the road like a racing car. Its rear end was reminiscent of the Lotus Eleven. The drawback of a tiny trunk was countered in 1963 in a second series that offered a longer, beautifully styled rear, though initially only as an optional extra for the princely sum of £15, and also a hardtop, at a cost of around £50.

Particularly when this was in place, the Ginetta was not the easiest of cars to get into. Although the spaceframe over which its fiberglass body was stretched reached its lowest point in the door region, the remaining opening was still so tight that the driver needed the suppleness of youth to be able to take his place behind the series-fitted, aluminum-spoked leather steering wheel. Once in place, it's fair to say it was more of a lying than a sitting position on a thin foam cushion with a rudimentary backrest. Lateral movement was prevented by the door sill and the wide transmission tunnel which ensured that this was the automotive equivalent of a twin, rather than a double, room.

But who cared? The Ginetta G4 was one of those cars that demanded the driver's absolutely undivided attention.

On the road it repaid this with mischievous driver enjoyment, and on the track with countless successes. It clung to the road like a leech, enthusiastic reviewers joyously reported, with a live rear axle with trailing arms and additional guidance from an A-shaped sway bar and independent front suspension with A-arms. The latter became an option at the rear, too, from 1964 onwards, following the example set by the G4R (for Racing), as did disk brakes all round.

A weight saving of 40 lb (18 kg) was achieved over the Series II model by replacing the Ford rear axle used previously, with one from BMC. With a curb weight of only 952 lb (432 kg) the Ginetta G4 really was a featherweight, so that even with the apparently minimal 39.5 bhp of the Ford four-cylinder 997cc 105E engine it offered exciting performance. A final gear

reduction of 4.2:1 enabled a top speed of around 92 mph (almost 150 kph) and a 0–60 mph (up to 100 kph) time of 13.8 seconds. Yet its fuel consumption was miserly, even by today's standards: the factory promised an average consumption of no less than US 36 mpg (imperial 43 mpg or 6.5 liters/100 km) with moderately careful use of the accelerator. Test reports such as those in the respected publication *Motor Sport* in 1964 warned, however, that the gearing in the four-speed gearbox supplied as standard—in which only first gear was not synchronized—was too wide. This came from Ford like numerous other possible power plants, for example the engine used in the Cortina GT with 1498cc and up to 95 bhp from 1963 onwards.

By the time of the third specification dating from 1966 the original concept had been thoroughly rationalized. Its

square-section frame was stiffer and easier to manufacture. The windshield was raked at a greater angle to the wind; at the same time new pop-up headlights ensured a more streamlined design, though the delicate front bumpers offered inadequate protection. Nonetheless, two years later the Ginetta G4 fell Sleeping Beauty-like into a fountain of youth, from which Prince Charming awoke it with a kiss only at the start of the 1980s.

Its predecessors were targeted at enthusiasts who wished to build their own car and travel from A to B in economical yet enjoyable style. The Ginetta G4 is now aimed at the would-be racer, who also wants his car parked outside the office during the week. Where form follows function so rigorously, good looks are an automatic feature.

The hood can be tipped forward in its entirety. This means that smooth curves rule the day, uninterrupted by annoying joins. The gentle swing of the hips seen on the car body over the rear wheels is also a reminder of the female form. The rocker cover with the Ginetta nameplate on the Ford Cortina unit is a rarity.

GINETTA G27

There's no denying that you have to have a certain *je ne sais quoi*—and in spades, at that—to become your successor's successor. However, the Ginetta G4, the star of the 1961 Racing Car Show in London's Horticultural Halls, showed that from the very beginning. In 1968 it had to give way to the G15, the minor marque's second major success. 13 years later, however, progress took the form of a return to a legend: the last MGs were leaving the production lines in Abingdon, so the time and the market were ripe for a nimble sports car set below the price level of the Fiat X1/9 or the Triumph TR7.

However, it was not a completely unchanged G4 that resumed its journey through the remainder of the millennium and beyond. Although it was intended more for the road than the racetrack, a rollover bar connected to the windshield via a T-junction with an additional strut was fitted as standard. The rear fenders were slightly leveled, and the

headlights were raised to the 24 inches (610 mm) required by law.

The fact that the body panels were now bolted rather than bonded over the featherweight roadster's spaceframe simplified repairs after those little incidents of the type that always happened but never really should. Ginetta's advertising claimed, in a fit of touchingly innocent faith, that the G4 could be built in a weekend.

As of old, the spacious hood concealed a choice of Ford power units, in a crossflow configuration or with overhead camshaft. Their exhaust emissions exited through the sill below the driver's door with a harsh roar that rendered communication within the cramped passenger compartment extremely difficult and became deafening on extended journeys. The front suspension, using A-arms, was borrowed from Triumph, while the rear—a rigid axle using four trailing arms and a Panhard rod—came from Ford.

And this was where the work on a racing version for the 750 Motor Club Race Championship started. A rigidly installed differential offering a whole range of different transmission ratios was sourced from Jaguar, as were the rear disk brakes, propshafts, and hub carriers on in-house trailing arms and wishbones. The chassis was correspondingly reinforced.

At this stage the Walklett brothers, ably assisted on the secretarial side by their sister Dorothy, were still at the reins of the company, which they then sold for £2 million in 1988. This much innovation, they felt, deserved a name of its own. And so, from 1984 onwards, the G4 took a quantum leap and became the G27.

However, the new owners—Martin Phaff, Mike Modiri, and Stuart Hobson—decided to put an end for the moment to the costly racing side of the business and instead to incorporate all the experience gained there into the road-going G27 kit car. How to convert the kit into a car that could take to the road was contained in a comprehensive and detailed manual that came with the consignment from Witham.

All this happened in 1990, while the next move four years later was to use the front suspension of the Ford Sierra together with the Escort rear axle, accompanied by some vigorous restyling of the composite cult object by analogy with the dashing lines of the Ginetta G33. The much-criticized roof T had now gone, while the sporty nature of the third-series G27 was emphasized by means of covered head restraints. At the same time the joy of competition was rediscovered as the aging youngster found itself racing exclusively against its peers in the Bridgestone Ginetta Championship on British tracks.

Yet sports cars of the Ginetta school were under threat since the traditional configuration of front-mounted engine and rear-wheel drive was becoming obsolete. Among the usual organ donors front-wheel drive cars were winning out, and a longitudinal transmission and rigid axle were suddenly showing their age.

In this precarious situation the Ginetta demonstrated the development reserves that it possessed: it was converted to independent suspension at the rear too, by incorporating appropriate components from the Ford Sierra in the bowels of the car. This was announced in January 1998, together with a raft of changes to the styling, higher front indicators and integral headlamps, a pronounced bulge on the hood to ensure sufficient headspace for engines designed with the latest emissions regulations in mind, exterior door handles, and differently shaped taillights.

However, there was as usual the difficulty of choosing from engines of up to 150 bhp, but also between the new running gear design at the rear and the traditional rigid axle with which the G27 was fitted in the Bridgestone series. Despite all the changes, owners remained in an exclusive minority: up to November 2000 a mere 282 cars in the various specifications had been sold.

The Ginetta G27 has been resurrecting echoes of the past since 1985, particularly from its G4 predecessor. In the latest metamorphosis, dating from 1998, the timelessness of the concept has been freed from the influences of past fashion up to a point. It, too, is a split personality, a jack of all trades. In the cockpit shown here the sporty character dominates.

GINETTA CARS LIMITED

KEEPING IT SIMPLE

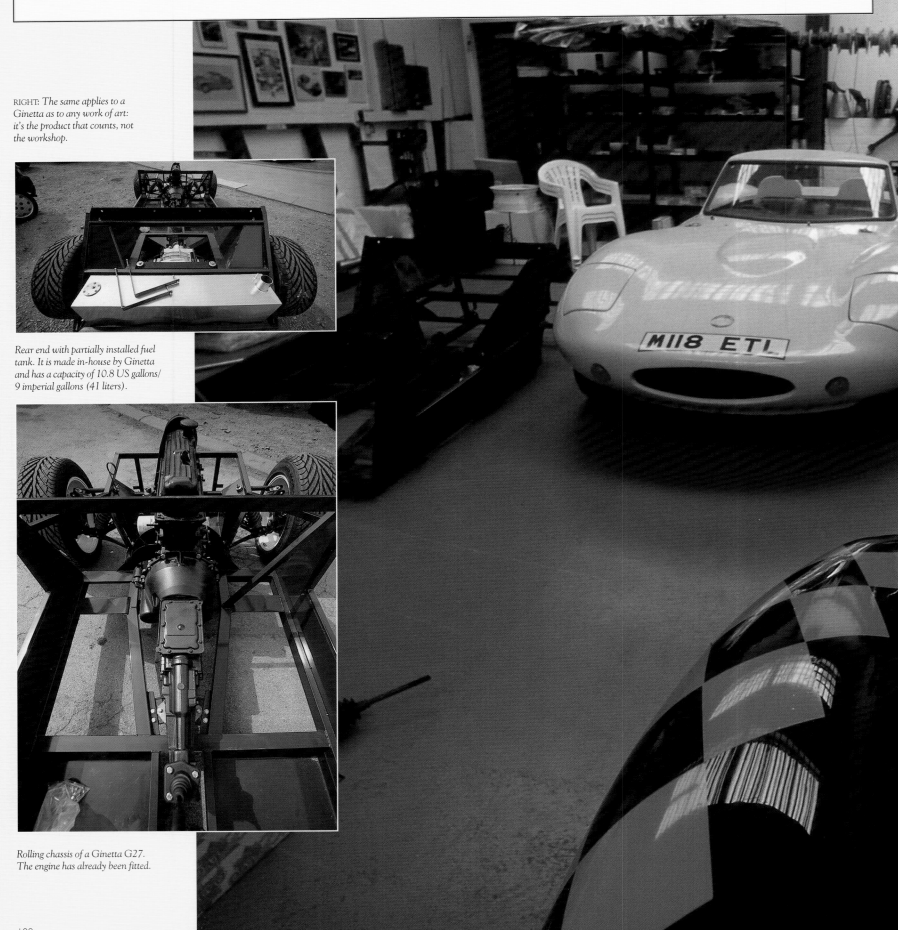

RIGHT: *The same applies to a Ginetta as to any work of art: it's the product that counts, not the workshop.*

Rear end with partially installed fuel tank. It is made in-house by Ginetta and has a capacity of 10.8 US gallons/ 9 imperial gallons (41 liters).

Rolling chassis of a Ginetta G27. The engine has already been fitted.

M118 ETL

Hood of a 2001 model G27, recognizable by the headlight openings.

Main body section from the front. The footwells have been removed for conversion to left-hand drive.

The mating of the bodywork and chassis is already underway …

… and is now complete. The Ginetta has precious little bodywork protection against front or rear-end collisions.

HEALEY SILVERSTONE

Donald Mitchell Healey, born in 1898, known by his friends for reasons of linguistic brevity as D.M.H. (this sort of treatment is always a sign of popularity) was an unusual man. In World War I, D.M.H. served his king and country well as an RAF pilot. Despite being invalided out as a result of an airplane crash, he enjoyed a wild career as a racing and rally driver, culminating in his victory in the 1931 Monte Carlo Rally in a 4.5-liter Invicta.

The cars that left the Donald Healey Motor Co, which the active entrepreneur had set up in Warwick in 1946 with £50,000 start-up capital, were also unusual. The first Healey sports car was rolled out on its narrow disc wheels that same year, with a highly-tuned version of the 2443cc Riley four-cylinder type 16, delivering 100 bhp, under the hood. The chassis consisted of two straight box-section beams with transverse beams, and independent front suspension incorporating trailing arms and coil springs—also used at the rear where there was the usual rigid axle. The in-house displeasure toward a prototype because of the inevitability of having to use poor materials in the immediate post-war period was reflected in the car's nickname, "The Horror."

D.M.H. tested "The Horror" and later derivatives personally at the airfield at nearby RAF Honiley. In order to save weight, but also because of a sheer lack of steel, the body consisted of a hardwood frame with sheet metal panels made of an aluminum/magnesium alloy. Healey stalwart Ben Bowden, it is rumored, designed it on his living room wall. Peter Shelton, an employee at the Westland coachbuilders, completed the body of the first four-seater roadster after it had received its aerodynamic fine-tuning in the wind tunnel of the Armstrong-Whitworth aviation company.

Since D.M.H. was also concerned with meters and seconds in private, he preferred to let the numbers speak for themselves. Sport and records were what mattered above all else: on the highway near Como, Italy, the car reached 104 mph (168 kph), and no less than 110 mph (178 kph) on the Belgian highway between Jabbeke und Aeltre, despite the poor quality of the gasoline used. And that, Healey's advertising proudly proclaimed, made it the fastest production car in the world.

A sports saloon was also announced soon after, but production was slow to get going, since there was a constant shortage of the necessary materials.

In 1948 the existing small range of models was joined by the progressively styled Sportsmobile luxury soft top. A year later the Healey Silverstone arrived, the pinnacle of the company's models up to that time, rough yet elegant in equal measure, a roadster for the open road and the racetrack with separate mudguards and closely positioned headlights behind the radiator grill. The production run of the Len Hodge-designed car was 105 units and its windshield could be partially retracted below the upper edge of the hood for racing purposes. The spare wheel was housed in a horizontal opening in the alloy body where it proved an effective bumper in emergencies. The Healey Silverstone's power plant, still the proven Riley 2.4-liter, was moved 8 inches (203 mm) to the rear, with the resulting improved weight distribution helping the Silverstone to achieve its widely lauded roadholding.

Aerodynamically, however, it was not the best, and so, despite being up to 507 lb (230 kg) lighter than the company's other models, it failed to break the 100 mph (160 kph) barrier. Nonetheless, its racing performance was as good as would be expected from a car of its name, particularly in the US, where Briggs Cunningham, for example, bought two, in one of which he fitted Cadillac's new V8 motor. However, the 18-year-old Tony Brooks, later a star driver for Aston Martin, Vanwall, and Ferrari, talked his mother into believing this was an ideal car to buy, but then subjected it to his own particular form of rough treatment.

It wasn't cheap: designed from the very outset so that it would remain below the £1000 barrier, above which purchase tax was doubled at that time in the UK, it cost £975 plus £271 in tax.

In 1950 the Silverstone was the only model to fly the flag for the Healey name. In the previous year D.M.H. had agreed a joint venture in the US with Nash director George Mason. The first joint product bearing the Nash-Healey name was a Silverstone chassis with a straight-six provided by the American partner. A prototype was driven in the 1950 Mille Miglia. Who was at the wheel? Why, both Donald Mitchell Healey and his son Geoffrey.

The Healey Silverstone shown here can look back over half a century of eventful motoring history. At the Silverstone International Trophy in August 1949 it was co-winner of the team prize and husband and wife team Charles and Jean Mortimer entered a number of British races in it in 1950 before embarking on the long journey to Australia. Not until 2000 did its current owner bring it back to Europe. Who knows whether it will ever be allowed to retire!

Despite its misleading registration plate (German for grandpa!), the Silverstone was a speed machine that meant business. The model on which it was based—a slim body with four motorcyle-style wheel guards—was pretty common currency, but the Silverstone was immediately identifiable by its closely positioned headlights located behind the vertical bars of the grill and partly exposed spare wheel sandwiched like a hamburger between two halves of a bun.

H.R.G. 1500

Messrs E.A. Halford, G.H. Robins, and H.R. Godfrey were all devoted to the car and loved speed. So it was they joined forces in 1935 in a concerted action to design a car to rival the one Godfrey had already produced in 1910 with his then partner Archibald Goodman Frazer Nash, known as the GN (for Godfrey-Nash). The statement of intent was also maintained: they were designing a car "by enthusiasts for the enthusiast." A prototype emerged that same year.

The unadorned H.R.G. logo, made up of the trio's surname initials or perhaps simply the initials of the company's driving force, Henry Ronald Godfrey, was eerily symbolic of the conservative product itself. The policy of rejecting all experimentation is evidenced by an age-old ladder frame, which had a tendency to flex in response to the unevenness of the road—a highly desirable quality for competition cars of the time—and the suspension, which consisted of a beam axle with quarter-elliptic springs at the front and a live axle with semi-elliptic springs at the rear.

It was important for the driver of an H.R.G. not to have too sensitive a rear end of his own. Every piece of grit on the road was transmitted directly to the occupants as if the car had been kicked by a horse. This, in combination with the flexibility of the floor structure, meant that the bodywork occasionally showed evidence of fatigue, as seen, for example, in the car that finished as runner-up in its class in the 1937 Le Mans 24 Hours race. The narrow and drafty body, whose total simplicity was what made it so attractive, only offered cramped space for two. The comfort of a heater was one that the occupants had to do without, nor would it have been appropriate to the uncompromisingly sporty nature of the H.R.G.

In the 20 years over which it was manufactured—during which 241 H.R.G.s were produced—it changed very little. After brief concessions to the *zeitgeist* such as the Aerodynamic model in 1946 and 1947, the powers-that-be at H.R.G. in Tolworth near Kingston, Surrey, England, reverted almost in shock to their tried-and-tested design.

Although by no means generously powered, these cars, which were expensively built by hand and only to order by the tiny factory, quickly gained a reputation for being successful and capable multi-purpose vehicles for the road, racetrack, and even off-road. They were initially fitted with Meadows engines. Very soon, however, a steady relationship was established with Singer, whose standard engines were lavishly revamped in Tolworth from 1939 onwards. For example, the displacement was changed, and steel crankshafts, different conrods and racing pistons, higher-performance camshafts and larger valves were used. The normal engines were of 1074cc and 40 bhp or 1496cc and 61 bhp, each with an overhead camshaft and two SU downdraft carburetors. Since the larger engine was considerably more powerful but hardly any more expensive, it is a wonder that anyone opted for the other.

From 1950 onwards the H.R.G. was only available with the 1.5-liter engine. 1956, when only five units were built in the year, saw the end of production, as the pre-war model had become a veritable antique. Nevertheless, it remained a successful competition car.

In the early 1950s people looked back nostalgically to the post-war enthusiasm of 1946 and 1947 when demand was high and sales reached some 70 units, which resulted in the

Tolworth-based company being stretched in both staffing and financial terms. This period also saw the manufacture of the 30 H.R.G. Aerodynamics that had a half-heartedly streamlined body made by the coachbuilding company, Fox & Nicholl, with fully-enveloped rear wheels and headlights bulging from the front fenders as if on stalks. Almost all were open-top models. A solitary coupé version with Ray Barrington Brock at the wheel delivered some wonderful racing successes.

Three 1500 Lightweight models, modified and made even lighter by the future Aston Martin racing director John Wyer at Monaco Motors in Watford, won their classes at the 1949 Le Mans and Spa 24-Hours races. However, the cars were in a lamentable state by the end of the events because of the frailness and weakness of their chassis.

Sales of the radically new 1500 Mk II dating from 1955, with independent suspension all round, Palmer disc brakes from the aviation industry and double overhead camshafts in the aluminum H.R.G. cylinder head, could be counted on the fingers of one hand. In the age of looming mass production H.R.G. Engineering's creations were full of character but were fighting a lost cause.

The designers of the H.R.G. had a clear concept in mind: a vehicle with excellent roadholding and accurate steering suitable for all kinds of racing. The result was a simple two-seater of exceptional user-friendliness. Removing just six screws allows the body to be lifted off the chassis and wings, and lamps and other accessories can also be swiftly removed. The two spare wheels attached to the rear of the car were items of special equipment and offered additional protection against collisions.

The creators of the H.R.G. placed particular emphasis on the full stops between the initials of the marque name. Enthusiasts, on the other hand, cared little for such niceties and rechristened the car the "Hurg." In order to achieve better weight distribution, the Singer engine was moved significantly further back and for homologation purposes the capacity of the original power unit was reduced slightly—to just under 1500cc—through the fitting of a large Laystall crankshaft.

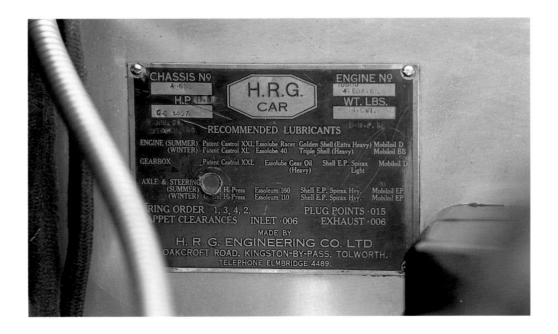

SS1 & JAGUAR SS100

William Lyons' SS1 sports saloon was not yet the Jaguar, but with its long hood and short passenger compartment it started a trend and a tradition that are still evident in the big cat marque today. Typical of this era was the short, square trunk with the spare wheel attached to it in the gap between trunk and bumper. But Lyons had also responded to existing trends, for similar stylistic features were typical of the continental coachbuilders Van Vooren and Figoni, and their British counterpart Avon Bodies.

For long stretches the history of the Jaguar marque is also a history of the basic geology of the British motor industry. And it shows how much, despite an individual's old age, a single man can achieve—men such as Henry Ford, Ettore Bugatti, and William Lyons.

Ambitious, energetic, creative, and with a winning manner, William Lyons entered the flourishing combination business shortly before his 21st birthday in September 1922 in Blackpool, where he founded the Swallow Sidecar Company. From 1927 he freed a number of Austin Sevens from the monotony of big series production by giving them extravagantly rounded special two-seater bodywork. Following its move to Coventry in 1929 his Swallow Coachbuilding Company also clothed chassis by Fiat, Swift, and Standard in tailor-made robes.

But Lyons was aiming higher. In June 1931 striking advertisements in the British motor press announced two coupés of outstanding beauty. They became an event at the London Motor Show in the fall of that year, known as the SS1 and SS2. They also marked the birth of the slogan "value for money," for instead of the generally expected £1000 the SS1 cost only £310. It was the first proof of Lyons' design philosophy—low, sporty, and powerful, with a long bonnet, a low center of gravity, and well balanced weight. The SS stood for Standard-Swallow, for the fine pair were based on components from the Standard Motor Company, like a chassis specially commissioned by Lyons and a four-cylinder 1004cc engine or a six-cylinder of 2045cc.

Among the many vehicles with which Lyons made a name for himself in the next few years the SS90 of 1935

stands out. It was a roadster with a 2.7-liter engine. In the same year the company was changed to a joint stock company, SS Cars Ltd.

A few days before the London Motor Show of 1935 Lyons achieved a typical PR coup in London's Mayfair Hotel. Working with Harry Weslake, the highly gifted cylinder head engineer in Rye, Swallow engine expert William Heynes had tuned the SS1 from 75 to 90 bhp, and with even higher compression, to 102 bhp. He was also responsible for a new chassis, a box frame taken under the axles through dual right-angled shafts, and with cruciform diagonal struts and rigid axles on semi-elliptical springs in front and behind.

This creation was crowned with an elegant limousine body with four doors and a long hood with the spare wheels mounted on its sides—not dissimilar to the contemporary Bentley. All this intense innovation needed a new name: they voted for Jaguar, the suggestion of noiseless movement and the suppleness of the big cat.

And so it was the 2.5-liter SS Jaguar Saloon that was unveiled in the Mayfair Hotel to compliments, food, and drinks. Its 2663cc had been rounded down to achieve a neater number. Questions to the assembled journalists on what the gleaming exhibit should cost elicited an average estimate of £632. In fact, the Jaguar cost £395, as much as the SS100 that replaced the SS90 in 1936. It had 102 bhp and was the apotheosis of Lyons' creations before the war, a dream car for later generations of lovers of classic cars. A test report in *The Autocar* of July 9, 1937 confirmed its responsiveness, and it did indeed prove its worth in racing and rallies. The motor journalist Tom Wisdom, for example, and his wife Elsie, won the Alpine Cup in 1936, and a three-team group won the team prize at the RAC Rally a year later, where a privately-entered SS100 scored the overall victory. At the end of September 1937 the company equipped the model with an engine of 3485cc and 125 bhp, pricing it only

£50 more than the 2.5-liter version, which remained in the range. The Jaguar only took 10.5 seconds to reach 60 mph (100 kph), and could touch the psychological 100 mph (160 kph) barrier (in its issue of September 9, 1938 *The Autocar* recorded 101.12), so living up to its name. A total of 309 of the two variants were made.

A single coupé, designed by William Lyons personally and shown at Earl's Court in 1938, never went into series production, for beside all the other, more serious damage it did, World War II put an abrupt end to the brilliant career of the Jaguar SS100.

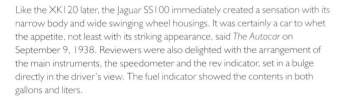

Like the XK120 later, the Jaguar SS100 immediately created a sensation with its narrow body and wide swinging wheel housings. It was certainly a car to whet the appetite, not least with its striking appearance, said *The Autocar* on September 9, 1938. Reviewers were also delighted with the arrangement of the main instruments, the speedometer and the rev indicator, set in a bulge directly in the driver's view. The fuel indicator showed the contents in both gallons and liters.

Contemporaries like the tester of *The Autocar* believed they would get a regular thrust in the back when accelerating, particularly in third gear, with the 3.5-liter engine that was subsequently added to the SS100 of 1936 shown here. Otherwise they could roll along happily without arousing any unseemly attention. As the hood fitted closely over the six-cylinder engine you had to lift one wing to check the oil, and the other to fill the tank.

JAGUAR

The Jaguar XK120 came, was seen, and conquered all when the model's bronze-colored prototype was unveiled at the London Motor Show on October 27, 1948. According to American motoring journalist Ken Purdy, its competitors unloaded their vehicles, saw the Jaguar and despaired. The car did indeed destroy a number of manufacturers' dreams, especially as it was offered for sale at the extraordinarily low price of £998.

But it was only designed to serve as a stopgap, a rush job of 240 aluminum-bodied examples, as steel was still rare and expensive during those lean post-war years. The company had fallen behind with the bodywork of the planned Mark VII Saloon, but the chassis, copyrighted by William Heynes, and a power unit developed by Walter Hassan—two of three of the ingredients for an excellent sports car—were ready and waiting to be used.

The chassis, shortened and slightly modified for its new use, was a longitudinal box frame with crossmember, independent front suspension consisting of wishbones and longitudinal torsion bars, and a rigid axle suspended by semi-elliptic leaf springs at the rear. The engine was a 3442cc, twin-overhead-cam V6 delivering 162 bhp, and in a Special Equipment variant, 180 bhp.

The boss himself was responsible for the bodywork. With a sure sense of style, Bill Lyons designed the shell in photofit manner at Jaguar's Foleshill works. Individual sections were substituted in turn until they blended together to form a harmonious whole. That form does not always follow function—the cabin is relatively cramped and there is not a lot of room for luggage—is readily forgiven, however, because of the XK120's sheer, irresistible charm.

And besides, the car was really convincing on performance: on May 30, 1949 Lyons gave 20 hand-picked British motoring journalists the privilege of seeing works test driver Ron Sutton putting the vehicle (with folded down windshield) through its paces on the closed-off Belgian highway between Jabbeke and Aeltre. He surpassed the official top speed of 120 mph (193 kph) by some distance, achieving 132.596 mph (213.4 kph).

Countless racing victories were reflected in what was building into a huge sales success and vice versa. Ian Appleyard won the 1951 Tulip and 1951 and 1952 Alpine Rallies at the wheel of XK120 with registration NUB 120

XK120

(with Lyons' daughter Pat as co-pilot). 1951 also saw Peter Whitehead and Peter Walker inaugurate a series of five Jaguar wins at Le Mans during the 1950s (1951, 1953, 1955, 1956, and 1957) under the direction of legendary race manager "Lofty" England. Their car was a C-Type that was mechanically almost identical to the basic model, the main difference being a tubular frame designed by Bob Knight.

The first XK120 to be sold to a customer left the factory on July 21, 1949. By the time the last "Series 0" car was shipped to Singapore on May 1, 1950, the Pressed Steel Company had already started production of steel bodies. The doors, hood and trunk lid were the only parts left unchanged and continued to be made of alloy. The XK120 Super Sports, to give it its official name, understeered slightly and at the limit its rear end had a tendency to swing out, without, however, overtaxing the average driver too much. A more serious defect was that its Lockheed brakes could have problems bringing the elegant 2921 lb (1325 kg) beast of prey to a stop, and so Jaguar pioneered the use of Dunlop disc brakes (previously only used in airplanes), introducing them on its 1953 Le Mans winner. The production model's fittings and equipment were luxuriant and extensive. Broad and soft two-tone leather seats ensured a high level of comfort and on the other side of the four-spoke Bluemel steering wheel, an array of—in part very large—instruments kept the driver informed about the condition of the vehicle. In 1945 the initials SS, with their negative associations, were dropped and the model name Jaguar, which by contrast enjoyed distinctly positive connotations, was adopted as the company title.

In March 1951 the range was extended through the addition of a fixed-head coupé not dissimilar to the one-off model designed by Bill Lyons over the chassis of the SS100 for the London Motor Show. This was followed in 1953 by an equally impressive drophead coupé with winterproof top and wind-up windows for all those not wishing to take their car off the road during the cold season. 1769 of this model were built, making it the rarest of the XK120s, while the roadster, 7631 units of which were sold, became the bestseller of the series, considerably outselling the fixed-head coupé (2678 units).

The Jaguar XK120, shown here with its door invitingly open, has a strong appeal for driver and passenger alike. Space behind the two-piece windscreen is relatively restricted, however. The rear-view mirror in this example has a long stalk in contrast to the original short one, an indication that the model underwent continuous development.

A roadster of the first order, shown here wearing fashionable whitewall tires. In fine weather, or indeed any other kind owners choose to regard as agreeable, the fabric top disappears into a space behind the seat and above the battery compartment. Whoever fitted the rear overriders the wrong way round here either wishes to be different or does not know his car very well.

JAGUAR XK150

The third chapter in the XK saga begins in May 1957, its protagonist being the XK150, which first appeared in 2+2-seat coupé and cabriolet versions. In true prima donna fashion, the roadster kept people waiting a while longer—until March 1958. This beautiful trio replaced the XK140, 8884 of which were produced, a lightly reworked version of its predecessor that sported stronger fenders, fewer grill bars and more interior space: the engine was moved forward three inches, which meant that the fixed-head and drophead coupé versions could be given fold-away rear seats for occasional use.

Changes introduced for the XK150 were far more substantial, thanks largely to the fact that Jaguar had announced a reduction in its racing activities during the 1957 season. There was spare capacity and a small army of development engineers had rolled up their sleeves enthusiastically in readiness. The main selling point of the new model was its all-round Dunlop disk brakes, an eagerly awaited improvement. In the two previous models, the last few meters of

any emergency braking procedure had been an unnerving experience, especially as their rear drum brakes had a tendency to overheat. Thorough testing was carried out at an early stage: a prototype was accelerated to 100 mph (160 kph) 30 times at intervals of a minute and then brought to a crashing halt. And then there was the 24-hour laboratory of Le Mans.

The main subject of attention was the car's exterior. A virtue was made of financial necessity by combining existing elements in a new way. The jaunty kink of the hips gave way to a higher, more gently curving waistline.

The old-fashioned two-piece windshield with square-edged panes was substituted by a fashionable wraparound windshield with far more efficient wipers. As a way of visually promoting Jaguar's corporate identity, the sports car was given a modified version of the Mk 1 sedan's radiator grill. The curving bottom of the grill fits into a recess in the front fender. In consideration of the uncouth manners of certain road users in the USA, an important export market, both

front and rear fenders adopted a more robust design with strong overriders.

Most XK150s left the factory building (now on Browns Lane in the heart of Coventry) in a Special Equipment version, in other words with wire wheels sporting a two-winged central spinner and featuring a 210 bhp version of the long-stroke engine equipped with the so-called B-type cylinder head. More and more customers were opting either for the overdrive version of the standard Moss four-speed transmission, which improved the fuel consumption of the thirsty six-cylinder engine somewhat, or for a Borg-Warner automatic, which was particularly popular in the North American market. Identifiable from the bell-like housings of its three horizontal SU carburetors, the S-type engine made its appearance at the same time as the third of the trio of XK150 models, and in fact was only available (and only in a manual version) in the roadster. Its 253 bhp was largely the brainchild of the wise and experienced Harry Weslake, who, from barrack-like premises in Rye in the south of England, conjured horsepower from cold metal like a magician would rabbits from a hat.

The 1960 range, announced not long after, included a larger, 3781cc power unit, available in a standard version (with B-type cylinder head) delivering 220 bhp as well as in the Weslake version, which at 265 bhp was already becoming a major player in the tumultuous and prestigious battle for the status that came with high performance. This was clearly no dressed up figure, as Jaguar's horses were standing magnificently by. In 1960, John Bolster, editor of English racing magazine *Autosport*, reported that this model had reached 100 mph (160 kph) in 19 seconds, complaining at the same time, though, about the uninhibited fuel consumption to which such excesses gave rise.

True to the philosophy of company boss Sir William Lyons (Queen Elizabeth II had knighted the popular self-taught industrialist in 1956), however, the English wildcat was extremely gentle on the purchaser's pocket. The 1960 coupé cost around half the price of an Aston Martin DB4 and rather less than half that of a Ferrari 250 Berlinetta SWB. Neither did this go unnoticed by the public, as Jaguar's sales surpassed those of its Feltham- and Modena-based competitors by some considerable way. In the four years up to 1960 it shifted 2256 roadsters, 2671 drophead, and 4462 fixed-head coupés. They remain a feast for the eyes today.

The big cat getting ready to leap on the hood of this example may convey a sense of latent aggressiveness, but the Jaguar XK150 coupé was also a thoroughly civilized tourer. A new feature was its leather dash with instrument panel in a contrasting color.

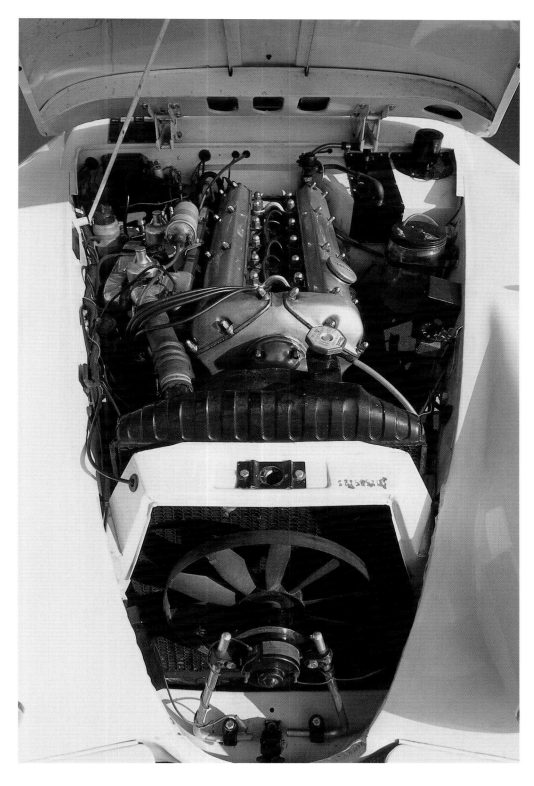

The Jaguar XK's facelift made a virtue of necessity. As a result of cost-saving modifications to its fenders, the XK150 lost some of the swing of its hips, gaining a fresh new look at the same time. Its hood followed the design of the XK140, and other than for the addition of disc brakes, its chassis also remained unchanged. The engine compartment remained just as tight a squeeze as before.

JAGUAR XKSS

It was the fastest and safest road-going sports car of its time, but at £3878 not the most expensive. It could also boast the very best pedigree, having four Le Mans winners in the family. The idea behind it is thought to have originated with Duncan Hamilton, the bearded star tamer of the fleet-footed big cats.

In 1956, Hamilton gave his 1954-vintage works car, registration number OKV 1, a thin veneer of civilization in the form of a windshield and weather protection with a view to using it for the occasional nostalgic excursion.

The idea was taken up enthusiastically at Browns Lane in Coventry. While the D-Type was being homologated for racing, a series of specimen models had to be shown and so there was always a quantity of parts and half-finished vehicles lying around unused. To some degree the company had its eye on the SCCA (Sports Car Club of America) scene. In late 1956 a miniature series of 16 XKSSs was got ready, but the project was finished off in mid-February 1957 by a devastating fire at the factory.

The car incorporated much of the existing fabric of the D-Type—its aluminum monocoque construction, for example, with front sub-frame of square-section tubing, its servo-assisted Dunlop disc brakes all round and its suspension, consisting of wishbones and longitudinal torsion bars at the front and a rigid axle on trailing links with diagonal torsion bars and a triangular stabilizer bracket at the rear. The power unit that held court beneath the long hood was also left fundamentally unchanged. This was a 3442cc in-line six-cylinder unit with twin overhead camshafts and a dry sump lubrication system whose very real and voracious 250 bhp was fed by three Weber 45 DCO carburetors. Its emissions escaped noisily through a double exhaust outlet positioned just in front of the left-hand rear wheel, generating an uncomfortable amount of heat as they did so. That this car was engendered on the battlefield of the racetrack can be seen from its enormous 44-gallon (168-liter) gas tank. Inevitably this meant the SS driver had to do without the luxury of a trunk. A toothbrush could, at a pinch, be secured in a chrome-plated rack supplied for this or similar purpose in front.

Other small measures were taken to prepare the model for life on public roads. These included the provision of a small door giving the copilot (now passenger) access to the cockpit and the disappearance of the bulkhead between the vehicle's two occupants. The filigree side pillars of the curved windshield are held in place by means of specially designed body-color alloy panels anchored into the bodywork. A short mohair top might provide rudimentary protection against foul weather but certainly not against the cocktail of noise that provided the acoustic background to an outing in an XKSS. This was made up of the roar of the engine, the rush of the wind and the

Preceding pages: the XKSS owed its existence to a decree by racing's ruling body that the D-Type racing car had to be supported by a production series. This gave rise to a road-going version of the D-Type with panoramic windshield, passenger door, fabric top, efficient shock absorbers that obeyed the letter rather than the spirit of the law and a luggage rack. Malcolm Sayer's beautiful basic shape, tested in the wind tunnel, remained unchanged.

whining of the Dunlop R1 racing tires. The bumpers were of pretty well symbolic value only as they were hardly up to the task of protecting the car against substantial knocks.

The interior was done out in leather. Although the bucket seats were comfortable, supporting the body particularly well in the shoulder area, neither they nor the steering wheel were adjustable. Erring on the side of caution, three gentlemen of differing stature and a lady had been invited to try out the seats during the fast roadster's development and thus a universally acceptable seating position was established. The large speedometer and tachometer are positioned horizontally to the left of the steering column and the small oil pressure and water temperature dials vertically on the right.

Road & Track recorded the 2020 lb (916 kg) stripling notching up 0–60 mph (up to 100 kph) in 5.2 seconds and 0–100 mph (up to 160 kph) in a mere 13.2 seconds— sensational speeds for 1957. By his own admission, the lucky editor of *The Autocar* of May 3 the same year ran out of superlatives for the car. Short legs were recommended for a journey of any duration in the cramped passenger seat, he wrote, but the lower limbs of the many people wanting to accompany him at all costs on the test drive suddenly seemed to shrink miraculously. The writer was impressed by the sensitive steering in bends, which, as in a true racing car, added to the driving pleasure, but noted that the steering needed constant correction on the straight, particularly on a poor surface. At 4000 rpm, he reported, such enormous thrust kicked in that the occupants felt as if they were riding in a rocket sled rather than a car. And the reporter must have really been putting his foot down as he notes that enemy vehicles appeared on the horizon, were overtaken and disappeared into the rear-view mirror in the twinkling of an eye. His article went on to mention his feeling of extreme security in the warm pocket of air the car carried along with it while the sharp, cold wind whistled past outside. The car forgave mistakes like a good chum, he observed, even helping the driver to iron them out.

What a pity that the XKSS, like all really good friends, is such a rarity.

Naturally the XKSS makes no secret of its racing origins: indications of these are its barely tamed power unit, its side-mounted exhaust and its easy-lock filler cap located in an accessible position, as can be seen on the vehicle depicted here. Starting life as a 1955 D-Type, it was later converted for use on the public roads. Its owner is guaranteed a huge amount of interest from the general public.

JAGUAR E-TYPE

The XK150 legend had started to acquire a distinct patina of venerable old age by the time a new era dawned with the launch of the E-Type at the 1961 Geneva Motor Show. The Coventry big cat had remained hidden in an enormous box until the moment of its unveiling, when the covering was raised high to spontaneous applause. Apart from a certain distant resemblance to the D-Type and the XKSS, the slender lines of the novice, an ellipse-based design by Jaguar's aerodynamicist, Malcolm Sayer, and company boss Sir William Lyons, were uncompromising. Although scientific knowledge played a part in its conception, practical considerations were boldly subordinated to aesthetic ones. The long engine cover thus by no means ends where the car's occupants cease to be able to see it, resulting in numerous costly bumps. And the seating position seemed to have been designed around the needs of the Jaguar test driver Norman Dewis who was only 5ft 4 in (1.63 m) tall. Furthermore, while the left-hinged trunk lid opens to reveal a generous amount of luggage space in the fixed-head version, those traveling in the open-top model have to severely restrict what they take with them. In order to prove that the new exhibit was no toothless tiger, a second vehicle was standing by to take people on a (fast) trip round the block.

The E-Type's part-monocoque bodywork was extremely rigid, especially in the coupé version, which at £2197 (new) cost around a hundred pounds more than the roadster. The front and rear sections, which are of around the same length, are joined together in eight places. Where they meet, the rear monocoque merges into a tubular frame. Past also meets present in the car's all-round independent suspension: in front, wishbones and longitudinal torsion bars, as on the XK series and in the D-Type; to the rear, radius arms, tubular lower wishbones, driveshaft links, and double coil springs in a system based on the 1960 Grand Prix Lotus 16.

Another tried and tested feature was the occupant of the engine compartment of the first 15,496 Series 1 E-Types sold up to 1964: Harry Weslake's version of Jaguar's 3781cc six-cylinder engine. The 265 bhp officially claimed for the car was a blatant case of very un-British PR exaggeration:

220, it was rumored, would be nearer the mark. One almost anachronistic element was the car's scratchy four-speed transmission, and its Dunlop disc brakes, once the *non plus ultra* of deceleration, had their work cut out with the E-Type's top speed of 150 mph (240 kph).

A number of defects of this kind were eliminated in the second generation of E-Types, which went on to sell 41,724 units between October 1964, when the cubic capacity of the twin-cam power unit was increased, and the introduction of Series 3. This increase took the engine up to 4235cc, a statistic emblazoned in chrome below the company logo on the trunk. While torque was increased, power remained the same. More powerful servo assistance took some heat out of the brake problem and a new gearbox, designed by Jaguar, rendered all criticism of its predecessor meaningless at a stroke. In March 1966 the demand for a 2+2 model was met when wheelbase was increased from 96 inches (2438 mm) to 104 inches (2667 mm), the curving roof raised by 2 inches (50 mm) and the doors widened. Not only did some rather basic rear seating result from these modifications, but also the chance to offer customers optional automatic transmission in the form of a Borg-Warner unit.

The Series 2 E-Type was launched on home soil (at the Earl's Court Motor Show) in October 1968. It can be recognized from its wider air intake opening, higher, full-width fenders, a steering column lock, larger indicators and sidelights, its headlamps that have been moved two inches further forward and exposed from beneath their Triplex covers, and purposeful Lockheed disc brakes. Many of these changes were designed to force the car through the needle of restrictive US motoring legislation. Its power unit was cleaned up and even sagged to a feeble 171 bhp on certain models.

By way of temporary relief from all this economically motivated adherence to the regulations, let us huddle together conspiratorially for a moment and remember the twelve lightweight (aluminum) E-Types delivered between March 1963 and January 1964 that produced 344 bhp. It was in one of these that German Jaguar importer and racing driver Peter Lindner, who took possession of his silver-gray coupé on May 7, 1963, famously gave a Ferrari 250 GTO a run for its money on the Nürburgring the same year.

Most observers agree that the E-Type's silhouette borders on perfection. Yet it was modified in numerous small ways over time, as illustrated by the headlamps of this 1967 "Series 1½" model, whose cowls were removed. The number plate was generally positioned below the air intake opening on export models and above it on those destined for the UK market.

The interior of the 4.2 version, which came out in 1964, offered broader, more comfortable seats. While its instruments retained the same arrangement as before, the aluminum dash panels trimmed in the same color as the seats were consigned to the past. A glove box was fitted into the space between the seats. The large steering wheel with polished wooden rim and three spokes with sporty drilling was also retained.

JAGUAR E-TYPE V12

There's no doubt that at its premiere it was the E-Type's irresistible exterior that captivated the crowds. The appeal of its third metamorphosis, however, unveiled almost exactly a decade later at the New York Car Show in March 1971, only became apparent when one took a look beneath its long hood, an act that caused many a double take. There, as auto poet Ken Purdy put it in his *Book of Automobiles*, one was met by a sight with the power to move a heart of stone.

Planted firmly among the roughly finished sections of the front tubular framework lurked a compact V12, a collaboration between William Heynes (who had been with the company since 1943 and had almost become part of the fixtures and fittings), chief engineer Claude Bailey, chief designer Harry Mundy, and Walter Hassan. Hassan found himself unexpectedly back on board in 1963 when Jaguar swallowed up renowned racing engine manufacturer Coventry Climax whom he had joined in 1953.

The two elderly gentlemen William Heynes and William Lyons had in a certain sense cast a light metal memorial to

themselves in the form of this 5.5-liter (5343cc) power unit with single overhead camshaft and transistor ignition system that was barely any heavier than its six-cylinder predecessor, which had enjoyed such a long and honorable life. Heynes had gone into well-deserved retirement in 1969 and Lyons was preparing to do the same in 1972. This illustrious engine owes its existence to the fact that during the mid-1960s, Jaguar flirted with the idea of making a Le Mans comeback. First of all it had to be tamed for public consumption. To this end it was stripped of around half its horsepower and two of its camshafts. As the planned fuel injection system was not ready in time, its fuel-air mixture was regulated by four horizontal Zenith carburetors. The development of this engine sheds an interesting light on a certain aspect of British culture in general and car culture in particular: while certain competitors from beyond the Alps prattle and rasp in rather proletarian but effective fashion, proclaiming their presence loudly and leaving you in no doubt as to what you are dealing with—a host of mechanical parts cooperating with

each other at volume and not always in perfect harmony—Jaguar's V12 performs its duties with all the discretion of an English film butler but with no less vigor than the spirited machines from the south. And far more cheaply: once again Sir William won the half price battle, marvels Ken Purdy. For the purchase price of a car of similar performance and status, he enthuses, you could buy two 12-cylinder Jags at $7300 each and still have change for a dune buggy and a decent bicycle.

In actual fact the magic of twelve cylinders gave the E-Type a much-needed injection of new blood, helping the old campaigner back to its feet and up to sales of 15,287 by mid-September 1974. Like all distinctive designs, however, time and familiarity took their inevitable toll of the E-Type. The gradual advances and developments achieved over the years were not reflected in any significant increase in sales figures. There were now only two models available, the 2+2 coupé and the roadster (always known in Britain as the Open Tourer Sports or OTS), each with a wheelbase of 104 inches (2667 mm). A fiberglass hard top was reintroduced for the open version, and additional luggage space was now provided in a space behind the seats that was taken up in the fixed-hood variant by seating for two small children—or a single supple adult particularly well disposed toward the car.

A number of cosmetic changes suited the car less well: an enlarged air intake with wide-mesh grill below which was sited an ugly scoop designed to increase the inflow of air even further, more emphatically flared front wheel arches whose purpose was to accommodate a wider track and broader tires, lever-off hub caps as standard and even—from 1974—rubber-faced overriders for export to North America.

In the US the writing then appeared on the wall for the aging star, 87 percent of whose production was for export. An article in respected *Road & Track* magazine amounted to an obituary. The E-Type's agony was prolonged one last time with the launch of a swift advertising campaign, but when its demise eventually became inevitable, Bill Lyons (ever a friend of spectacular PR stunts), in a darkly symbolic gesture, announced a special commemorative edition of 50 black roadsters. Only one, in response to the wishes of purchaser Robert Danny, was given a different color—green, the color of hope.

The new look of the V12 E-Type was not to everyone's taste. The changes included a wide-spaced grill with four vertical bars above an unattractive air scoop whose job was to prevent the Jaguar overheating in traffic. The rectangular grill on the trunk door provided an additional air outlet and was designed to improve ventilation.

Normally a vision of seductive sleekness, the Jaguar E-Type V12 2+2 coupé becomes something of a monstrosity when all its doors and hood are opened. Just one simple symbol beneath the manufacturer's name on the back betrays its identity and reveals the formidable source of power, the first of the marque to be given an aluminum block that lurks beneath the integral front section of the car. Steel wheels have become standard.

JAGUAR XJ-S

For any journalists present who remembered the launch of the E-Type in Geneva in 1961, the unveiling of the XJ-S by Jaeger models at the Frankfurt Motor Show in September 1975 would have provided a complete contrast to the earlier debut, for it met with a crowd of long faces. Where the E-Type won over all those present with its blatant sportiness, the newcomer revealed no more than a couple of sporting characteristics; where the earlier model seduced with its spirited and coherent lines, this one seemed no more than a patchwork of ideas and disparate elements; where the former tapped new sales markets as a result of its astonishingly reasonable price while also retaining older customers, the latter, with its initial price ticket of £8900, was in the same price category as a Ferrari 308. Nevertheless, in terms of sales it significantly outperformed its much-loved predecessor: over the 21 years it remained in production, up to April 4, 1996, 112,052 units were manufactured, 50,316 of which were exported to the US.

The XJ-S was a large car, a lavishly equipped 'grand tourer' hardly any shorter, a tiny bit wider and significantly lower than the XJ sedan from which it was derived. The basic design grew out of the proven love of clear lines of former Jaguar boss Bill Lyons, with aerodynamics input from Malcolm Sayers. Its bodyshell rests on the XJ chassis, but with the wheelbase reduced from 112 inches (2865 mm) to 101 inches (2591 mm). The front suspension features independent wishbones; the rear suspension (also independent), forked arms on supporting half axles, trailing links, and double telescopic shock absorbers. Space under the hood, which falls away only gently, is extremely tight. It is home to the regal 5343cc 289 bhp V12 power unit (and its attendants) that contributes more than anything else to making a Jag that bit special, a duty it discharges smoothly, silkily, and almost noiselessly. This engine did not always hit it off with the highly popular Borg-Warner transmission unit, a problem only ironed out when the latter was replaced by General Motors' Turbo Hydramatic system in spring 1977.

Under the leadership of John Egan, given the task in 1980 of reprivatizing Jaguar, which had become a British Leyland subsidiary, and restoring it to its former glory, the XJ-S

Due to its imposing size and the abundance of comforts provided, the XJ-S occupied a niche somewhere between sports car and luxurious tourer—a true exponent of *Gran Turismo*, particularly as the considerable expense it entailed served to transport just two people.

underwent extensive improvements to its specifications. In July 1981 the HE (standing for High Efficiency) 5.3-liter V12 coupé was announced, with an engine whose fuel consumption, output and emissions had all been improved with the help of Swiss engineer Michael May.

At the same time, Jaguar engineers Jim Randle and Trevor Crisp revealed a new six-cylinder engine that had been developed with a budget of £21 million. This was a 3.6-liter unit based on four-valve technology that delivered 225 bhp. In September 1983, in keeping with company custom, the new unit was initially introduced in a car with relatively restricted sales, the XJ-S coupé, as well as in a new 'cabriolet' model (really a targa with wide, heavy-looking roll bars), the first open-top Jaguar since the E-Type.

In July 1985, a V12 version of the "cabriolet," the XJ-SC HE, was also released onto the roads of Marbella, Morcote and Monterey. But there was already pressure from potential customers to do away with the hybrid cabriolet in favor of a proper open-top model without roll bars, a desire that was acceded to in April 1988 with the V12 convertible whose stiff, electrically operated winterproof top could be opened or closed in 12 seconds.

In spring 1990, Jaguar became an elite subsidiary of Ford, retaining extensive autonomy over its models. This coincided with the end of John Egan's leadership. Under his successors William J. Hayden and from 1992 Nick Scheele, the XJ-S went through further metamorphoses. On May 1, 1991 the

results of a thorough facelift were unveiled: of a total of 490 bodywork panels, 180, chiefly in the roof, door, trunk and rear wing areas, were replaced, and alterations made to the interior as well. Also at this time, a 4-liter variant of the six-cylinder power unit was introduced into the coupé and in May 1992 into the convertible too. This engine was designed to run on lead-free fuel and suffered slightly for this with performance remaining about the same. A year later the range reached its pinnacle with the XJ-S V12 6.0 coupé and corresponding 2+2 convertible. Like the two 4-liter versions, these were available with body-color fenders and attractive alloy wheels.

Meanwhile, preparations were being made for the end of the XJ-S. As with the E-Type, this did not come completely out of the blue, but in the form of a celebration model to mark the company's 60th birthday, a six-cylinder version with lavish fittings and featuring all the cardinal virtues (grace, pace, and value for money) that had been adopted by highly respected company founder Sir William Lyons, who had died in Wappenbury in February 1985, as his corporate philosophy all those years ago.

Despite numerous specification changes, the distinctive shape of the XJ-S (which was by no means to everyone's taste) survived for many years without any major remodeling.

A fully open version of the XJ-S did not appear until spring 1988, when it became an immediate success. The convertible was equipped with a high-quality fabric top developed by Karmann in Osnabrück, Germany, with electric opening and closing. Originally it was only available with the whispering 5.3-liter V12 engine, whose already impeccable manners were refined even further by painstaking improvements to its chassis mounting.

Allowing light, air, and sunshine into the XJ-S also did wonders for the car's external appearance. One could willingly forgive it, therefore, for the extra 220 lb (100 kg) in weight it put on, not least as a result of necessary reinforcements to the shell. 108 panels had to be newly designed and 48 modified—a third of the total number of body components. The door is shown open here in invitation.

JAGUAR XJ220

In 1981, with his well-deserved retirement already looming on the horizon, Engineering Director Jim Randle allowed himself to indulge in a lifetime dream: to create a supercar away from the rigid practical constraints of series production and the red pen of the cost accountants. At the end of 1984 he gathered around him a troop of determined enthusiasts willing to work out of hours who soon came to be known as The Saturday Club.

When the big cat baptized XJ220 was revealed to the public at the Birmingham Motor Show in 1988—like the XK120 40 years before in London—it still corresponded largely to Randle's bold vision, which was to house Jaguar's own long-serving 12-cylinder engine behind the cabin, stark naked under an enormous glass cover, now driving not only the rear wheels but the front axle too, as with the Bugatti EB110.

The V12 combined with an all-wheel drive mechanism would have exceeded the project's tight budget as well as any reasonable weight limits and yet the project was not simply dismissed as an unfulfillable dream. A small series of 350 units was planned and immediately, following the announcement, set in motion behind closed doors. The car would eventually see the pale light of day in a factory specially set up for the purpose in Bloxham, Oxfordshire, after Tom Walkinshaw, chief of Jaguar's racing arm, had turned the concept inside out. All that remained unchanged was the aluminum-clad outline, eight inches (210 mm) shorter than the prototype, but still an impressive 194 inches (4930 mm) long. A luxury liner of the first order was transformed into a

With an aluminum exterior made by Abbey panels in Coventry, at around 192 inches (5000 mm), this ultra-flat machine from Bloxham is not only enormously long, but also exceptionally stable.

road-going racing car whose blood relationship with Jaguar's C-Type racers is written all over its face despite the fact that those who climb inside (through doors that only open to a very narrow angle) are met by an array of familiar Jaguar instruments and the bewitching smell of Connolly leather.

In front of the rear axle, which drives the rear wheels only, rages a V6 engine of just 3.5 liters (but boosted by two turbochargers) that had already proven its worth on the racetrack. The 549 bhp it delivers at 7200 rpm guarantees the Jaguar a place in the highest performance category. German magazine *auto motor and sport* diagnosed a split personality when it tested the car on September 9, 1994: beneath the civilized exterior of Dr. Jekyll lurks the monstrous Mr. Hyde.

Upon turning the ignition key, wrote the author, the fuel pumps begin to buzz like a swarm of wasps and the needles of the dials remain at rest briefly before springing into life at the very moment a large red button to the right of the steering column lights up. One short push and the engine willingly starts. The cacophony of noise while the engine is idling is initially alarming, as if some imminent mechanical defect were being announced. Gearwheels can be heard meshing, the clutch rattles and the transmission imitates a clapped-out coffee grinder. This discordant mechanical concert, accompanied by the sound of the power unit straining at its mountings, the groaning of the bodywork, the banging and creaking of the chassis (which is as wide as that of a truck, with a turning circle of around 600 inches (15,000 mm)) persists until 2000 rpm is reached.

When a prototype was test crashed into a concrete block at 30 mph (48 kph), the steering wheel was forced a mere half an inch (13 mm) backwards and the headlamps escaped unscathed. The roof, based on a steel cage construction, is able to withstand a weight of 10 tons/tonnes.

During the design of the breathtakingly fast piece of sculpture known as the Jaguar XJ220, all the aerodynamic stops were pulled out. Nevertheless a rear spoiler was still found necessary as there is more to the supercharged V6 power unit (which seems slightly lost under the large rear canopy in the middle of the trunk area) than meets the eye. This is an engine with the power to rekindle hell.

You have to ask yourself why anyone would want to spend around £195,000 ($345,000) on such an instrument of torture. At 3500 rpm the two turbochargers start to unleash their full power in the twinkling of an eye and back-bending amounts of thrust set in through all five gears, propelling the XJ220 to speeds that should be reserved for the Hunaudières straight at Le Mans.

The car's suspension, based on double wishbones and inner coil springs, would also, no doubt, be more at home at the French temple of 24-hour racing. Strong biceps are the order of the day as servo-assisted steering is not provided, and anyone hoping to tame this big cat will also need strong calf muscles to operate the vehicle's powerful disc brakes. This Jaguar stands for no nonsense and will only give of

its best in expert hands. In tire tests carried out on the Nürburgring in May 1991, prototype 005 achieved the fastest lap time ever recorded there by a road car. The XJ220's debut appearance in its final form was at the Geneva Motor Show in 1992, and the first ten cars were delivered on schedule in June and July of that year.

Hopes of major financial success (as achieved by the Ferrari F40, for example) were cruelly thwarted when the completely overheated supercar market suddenly collapsed. Many customers even forfeited their £50,000 deposits in order to avoid having to pay the rest of the purchase price—a Van Gogh, after all, makes a far better investment.

JAGUAR XK8

The brief was unequivocal yet still left scope for freedom: the new Jaguar sports car had to resurrect memories of its illustrious predecessors, incorporate the new eight-cylinder power unit known as the AJ-V8 alongside a host of high-tech features, display Jaguar's customary refined English manners and last but not least compete with the Mercedes SL series on price.

This was 1993; completion of the project was announced by Nick Scheele just 30 months later. The finished project was launched in spring 1996—the coupé at the Geneva Motor Show and the cabriolet the next month at the New York Auto Show. Prizes and honors immediately poured in and the intended nostalgia effect also came into play. Designer Geoffrey Lawson put it in a nutshell: with its

flowing lines, sensuous curves and substantial proportions, the XK8, he claimed, was following on in the tradition of the E-Type and XJ220. Echoes of the C-Type, D-Type, and XK120 were also quite intentional, no doubt, while the beau of Browns Lane managed to dissociate itself completely (a sign of the generation gap?) from its angular predecessor the XJ-S.

The extravagant luxuries designed to lure potential purchasers away from Stuttgart-based competitor Mercedes include the beautiful scent of fine leather and highly polished veneer of walnut or dark-stained bird's eye maple that adorn the dashboard and parts of the center console and steering wheel. The amount of space provided in the rear seating compartment, on the other hand, is derisory: in order to get

into the back at all an adult male of average European build must roll himself up into a ball like a high diver before stretching out again for the final plunge.

Generally, however, the dimensions of the XK8 look impressive, although at 186 inches (4760 mm) it is a hand's width shorter than the XJ-S, on whose floorpan and wheelbase Lawson's elegant solution rests. In terms of dynamic performance, this Jag by far outdoes the XJ-S thanks to double wishbones and an aluminum suspension subframe in front, lower wishbones and co-supporting half axles to the rear and a new variable ratio power steering system. Only purchasers of the coupé version are able to enjoy the pleasures of larger (18-inch/457-mm) wheels, harder springing, and electronically adjustable shock absorbers, introduced by

Outward indications of the prestigious supercharged variant, the XKR, are highly discreet: a chromed grill covering the aperture of the air intake, horizontal louvers on the hood, a logo to the right-hand side of the trunk and special inlays in the front badge and on the rudimentary running boards.

Jaguar under the catchy and appropriate label CATS (Computer Active Technology Suspension).

Also at the cutting edge of technology is the XK8's high-torque engine, the best V8 in the four-liter class according to Jaguar's usual self-adulatory advertising, weighing in at just 441 lb (200 kg) and manufactured in a brand new factory in Bridgend, south Wales. In order to ensure harmonious symbiosis, it has been mated here with five-speed automatic ZF transmission featuring two modes and the usual, though here significantly more precise, J-gate shifter: right for automatic and left for manual selection of stages two to four.

The XK8 recipe has proved consistent with the past in another important respect too: at around £55,000 (in 1997), the convertible cost around 5 percent less than a Mercedes SL 320 and around 40 percent less than a Ferrari 355 Spider—just as late Jaguar founder Sir William Lyons would

have wanted. The car sold 14,269 units in 1997, more than half of them (7223) in the US.

Since the 1998 Geneva Motor Show, anyone who finds this purring 284 bhp cat with a live weight of 3933 lb (1784 kg) rather too tame has been catered for by an addition to the range known as the XKR—a supercharged variant described by Germany's *auto motor und sport* magazine of May 6 that year as a car that accelerates like a fully grown Ferrari, is as beautiful as a Ferrari, but costs only half as much as a Ferrari. In order to boost its power to a rugged 363 bhp, all they had to do at Jaguar was search their own shelves for something suitable—in this case the same unit that was being used to power the XJR sedan. Paired, interestingly enough, with a five-speed automatic transmission from rival Mercedes-Benz, it takes the XK to a new dimension of motoring refinement. Although a self-imposed speed limiter

intervenes at 155 mph (250 kph), this hardly detracts from the exhilaration of reaching 60 mph (100 kph) in a mere 5.5 seconds and 100 mph (160 kph) in 12.4.

This supercharged engine excels through the unexcitable, imperturbable and even manner in which it carries out its work. The main outward signs of its presence in the engine bay (every inch of which is filled) are a chromed mesh grill across the air intake, a new wheel design, a neat rear spoiler and businesslike louvers on the hood, designed to improve both cooling and downward pressure on the front axle.

No doubt about it: the XKR is a car that lives up to even Sir William's high standards.

The supercharged V8 performs its work with unexpected discretion. The only sign of the supercharger's presence is a soft chirping when one puts one's foot down. It is always paired with five-speed automatic transmission whose shifter operates within a U-shaped gate. Among other things, the oval gills in the hood are designed to assist downward pressure on the front axle.

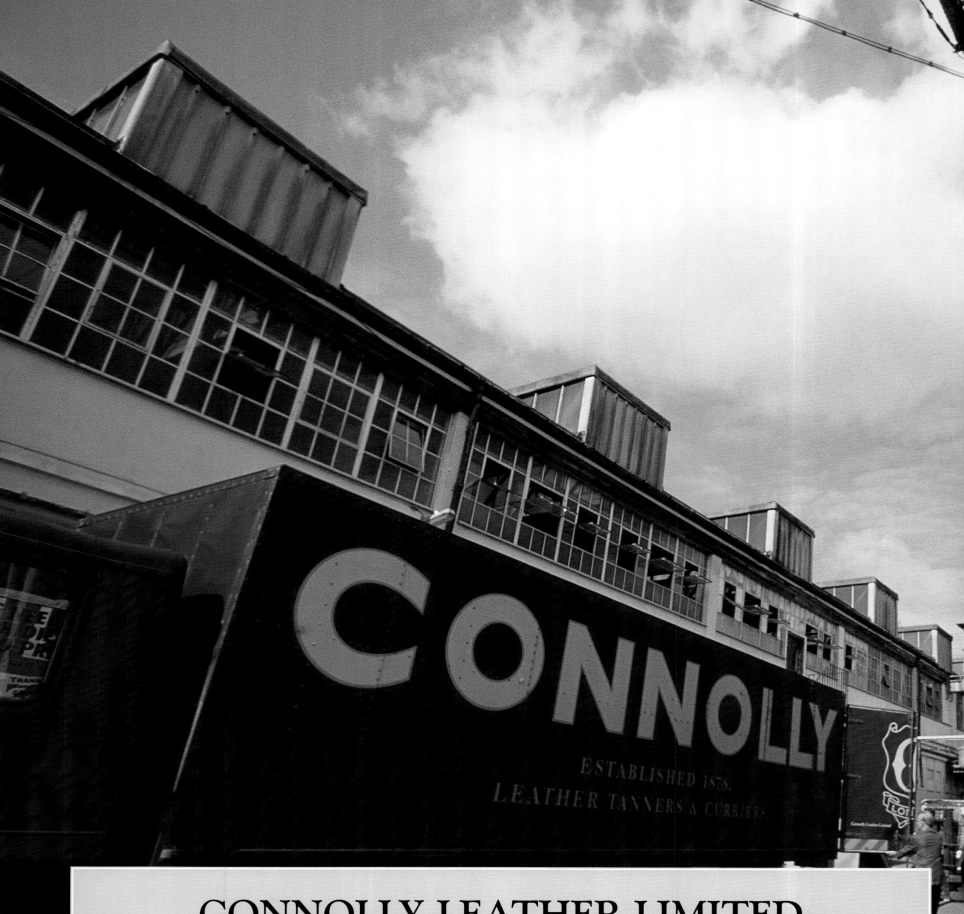

CONNOLLY LEATHER LIMITED

TOP-GRADE LEATHER FOR TOP-GRADE CARS

Hides arriving at the tannery in Canterbury. They still have an unpleasant smell at this stage.

The hides are treated with a lime and sulfide solution to remove salt, hair, and remnants of dung.

Another view of the same process, which is still carried out the way it was when the firm started up.

Hides being split. The grain side is used for upholstery and the underneath for suede.

1. Hides being fed into a machine that will render them soft and supple. The tannery's raw materials requirements depend on a flow of hides from 12–15,000 purebred cows per week.

2. Enormous mangles wring the residual water from the hides and press them smooth. Here we see a hide emerging from a mangle.

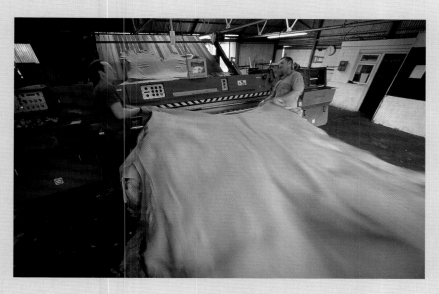

3. Hides being fed into a machine that splits them dry, as opposed to that shown on p.159 which splits them when wet.

4. Checking to ensure that the split hides are of the required thickness. Although we are dealing here with natural products, many customers work to tolerance levels as tight as one tenth of a millimeter.

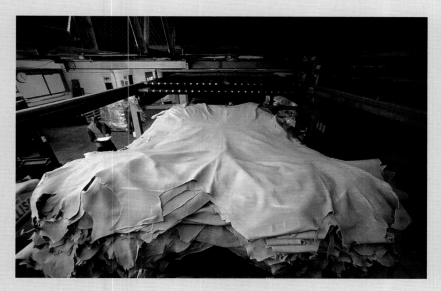

5. An automatic stacking device. In contrast to the early days of the company, many processes are now carried out without human intervention and some are fully computerized.

6. Whatever color they are destined to become, the hides are dyed in special drums. The choice of available colors is extremely wide.

LEFT: Hides emerging from the drums along with the tanning substance. They are blue because they have been treated with chromium. For environmental reasons, this method has now been dropped in favor of conventional methods, and quebracho, mimosa, and beech barks are again being used.

RIGHT: Hides treated with chromium await the dyeing process and final surface finishing.

The same phase with the hides now folded. A pleasant aroma gradually starts to develop.

The hides are loaded up and taken to the trimming station, where they are cut to the required size.

Final checks being carried out for evenness of color and general quality. The best hides come from the north as they tend to be unimpaired by insect bites.

The required thickness of the hides varies according to the use to which they are to be put.

Knives being laid before the individual pieces—destined for car interiors—are cut to shape.

Finished parts awaiting shipment. The supply of prefabricated sets—to Lear, for example, which makes Jaguar seats—is becoming more and more common.

RIGHT: A collection of tools and stamps for the creation of pattern books, leather facings in tables, and gold embossing.

Hides in a dryer after emerging from the final dyeing stage.

Next, they are stored before shipment, and are seen here being checked by Connolly director Anthony Hussey.

Customers will receive these goods in bales. The customers are automotive suppliers who are now more closely involved in the manufacturing process.

Finished leather, resistant to wear and tear, heat and light, being selected for pattern books.

Storage racks in the samples department. For the right price, the perfect color and quality can be found for vintage cars too.

Stamps—those currently in use alongside historical examples. The latter are still occasionally needed to fulfill special requests.

JENSEN 541

Brothers Richard and Alan Jensen no doubt inherited their taste for the unusual along with their determination to do their thing extraordinarily well.

The cars they created in turn attracted some rather unusual customers, among them actor Clark Gable, who in 1934 commissioned a four-seater cabriolet from the still relatively unknown Jensen Motors Ltd based in West Bromwich in the county of Staffordshire.

In 1946 the Jensens unveiled a rather ungainly sports sedan named, somewhat transparently, the PW (standing for Post War). By 1949 this had developed relatively smoothly into the Interceptor, a grand tourer that displayed the pleasing hand of Jensen designer Eric Neale and was powered by the 4-liter, six-cylinder A125 Sheerline in a deal agreed with Austin boss Leonard Lord. The business relationship between the two companies was based on give and take: in return Neale designed the body of the Austin A40 Sports, which promptly rolled off the production line looking like an Interceptor that had shrunk in the wash.

Meanwhile, the West Bromwich company's bread and butter was production of the Healey 100. As this also happened to generate some useful cash flow for the company, plans were laid for another Jensen model, which was to be faster, more attractive and better value than the Interceptor. Richard Jensen came up with the concept and Eric Neale was responsible for the details.

A prototype of the 541 with steel body was presented at the Earl's Court Motor Show in 1953. When production began in 1954 this was replaced by a fiberglass shell with aluminum doors. The fiberglass construction was robust and of high quality and unlike the bodywork of the Daimler SP250, for example, remained in one piece. This was due to a solid backbone that also contributed to a not inconsiderable curb weight of 2911 lb (1320 kg). It rests on a box frame with tubular longitudinal members and crossmembers. The car has independent front suspension consisting of wishbones and coil springs, and a rigid rear axle resting on semi-elliptic springs. Jensen drivers could control the temperature of the 131 bhp, moderately temperamental Austin six-cylinder DS7 power unit by means of a flap in the air intake opening.

In the fall of 1956—in a pioneering move every bit as important as the earlier introduction of servo assistance—the

541 was equipped with Dunlop disc brakes all round. October 1957 saw the introduction of the Jensen 541R, the middle chapter of a three-part saga, whose rugged DS7 was boosted to 150 bhp by two SU semi-downdraft carburetors positioned to the right of the cylinder head, whereas the three horizontal carbs of the basic model were sited on the left. Like its older sibling, the new model was aimed at non-conformist, well-off gentlemen in their mid-fifties who wanted to travel fast, if not exactly sportingly. The main obstacle to the latter, noted contemporary test reports sourly, was the layout of the pedals: the gas pedal was too far from the brake pedal for drivers to be able to gain feet and seconds by "heel and toeing" or to be able to double-declutch during deceleration in order to avoid grinding the badly synchronized Moss transmission. In all other respects the car performed comfortably and discreetly. With the Laycock de Normanville overdrive engaged in top gear, the calm and composed long-stroke power unit under the hood would happily achieve 100 mph (160 kph) at 4000 rpm.

This was also true of the 541S, launched in October 1960, 127 examples of which were eventually built, compared to the 225 of the 541 and 493 of the 541R. The third model in the range was greeted by cries of woe from the purists, however, who accused the company of watering down the original concept.

The 541S indeed delivered around 20 fewer horsepower than the 541R, and even with the most popular automatic transmission option, Hydramatic (also used in the Rolls-Royces of the day), horsepower was lost. This model was, however, almost an inch wider and just over an inch higher than its predecessor, meaning that even adults of slightly larger build could now sit comfortably in the back, although they too were separated from each other by a wide transmission tunnel. This model included many forward-looking features, particularly where safety was concerned—the front seatbelt, the thickly padded underside of the dashboard and the inclusion of a fire extinguisher and first-aid box as standard, for example. The costly air inlet cover was replaced in the 541S by a screen attached to a chain that could be raised or lowered from the driver's seat.

Despite its undisputed qualities, the problem with the Jensen 541 had a name: the Jaguar Mk II. The big cat from Coventry could do everything the 541 could do, and for half the price.

There is nothing of the cheap fix about the striking fiberglass body of the Jensen 541: low, aerodynamic and as a four-seater, spacious. Furthermore, the choice of this light, malleable material in combination with a strong chassis gave the vehicle a long life expectancy. The doors were made of aluminum.

The heavy protuberances above the wheels are a feature of the Jensen. The overall impression of quality is continued inside: full leather furnishings were included in the price. By means of a flap in the air intake opening, drivers could control the running temperature of the car's Austin six-cylinder engine, which is accessible from all sides when the integral hood, hinged to the rear, is raised. The view through the curiously shaped rear window remains unrestricted even with the trunk lid open.

JENSEN-HEALEY

The Jensen-Healey was the fruit of the dedicated labors of men who refused to accept defeat. One such was Donald Mitchell Healey, 17 months older than the century, who had given a lifetime of dedicated service to the automobile and yet was still motivated by a restless creative urge. He had already learned, however, that even legends meet their end sooner or later: in 1967 the production line responsible for the aging Austin-Healey was brought to a standstill and in 1971 the Sprite was also put out to grass by British Leyland.

Another was Kjell Qvale, who was acutely affected by these developments. Based in San Francisco, he supplied the entire American West with the automotive products of the multiple conglomorate, reserving a special fondness for its airy, very British roadsters.

At his instigation, Donald Healey and his son Geoffrey designed a successor to the Austin-Healey. They did not have to cast around long for a production site. Qvale had owned 75 percent of Jensen Motors Ltd in West Bromwich since 1970. The firm now had significant spare capacity as it had been involved in production of both the Austin-Healey and the Sunbeam Tiger, which had also been dropped without replacement in 1967.

Jensen designer Kevin Beattie touched up the original design in places. The outcome was a rather indifferent, angular and smooth body that neither seduces nor offends the eye. Why, wondered many potential customers, should they favor the Jensen-Healey over such neat little movers as the MGB or Triumph TR6? Furthermore, word got out about a number of problems plaguing the newcomer, stemming from a lack of production readiness: on bumpy roads its self-supporting and unusually rust-prone body with Vauxhall Viva-derived suspension—wishbones and coil springs in front, rigid axle with trailing links and coil springs behind—was shaken to its core. The hastily thrown-together plastic dashboard would sigh in tormented accompaniment and the crude top moderated the effects of wet weather rather than properly protecting the car's occupants from them.

The originally planned Vauxhall engine would have needed to sacrifice too much of its power to the rigid North American emissions regulations, and BMW and Ford power plants also considered during the planning phase proved similarly unsuitable. In the end a 2-liter unit from Lotus was selected. Colin Chapman, boss of Jensen's illustrious competitor, released it willingly, particularly as this meant its teething troubles would be sorted out in the Jensen-Healey prior to the engine being fitted into any vehicle emanating from Lotus's Hethel factory.

The gleaming architecture of the compact Lotus creation, developed by old hands Tony Rudd and Ron Burr and featuring four valves per combustion chamber and two overhead camshafts, was extremely impressive. It was originally based on the cast iron lower half of the Vauxhall Viva four-cylinder unit. Following extensive testing, however, the same aluminum alloy was chosen for both lower and upper portions. The resulting engine was gruff of manner and susceptible to expensive infarctions, but was nonetheless remarkably environmentally friendly. With its two Stromberg-Zenith carburetors, the toxins emitted by the US variant were only marginally lower than those emitted by the European

version, which was fed by two dual Stromberg carbs and delivered 140 bhp—just four horsepower more than its North American counterpart.

The Jensen-Healey, the late creation of two gentlemen of advanced years, was unveiled to an impressed public at the Geneva Motor Show in March 1972 and underwent relatively minor improvements in 1973. In 1974 its Chrysler transmission (with overdrive) borrowed from the Rapier model was replaced by a five-speed Getrag transmission. A total of 10,926 cars were sold.

In 1975, the company focused its attention on the Jensen GT built over the same chassis—a less sporty, more comfortable alternative to the spartan, open two-seater. Its shape is reminiscent of both the Volvo 1800 ES estate and domestic rival, the Reliant Scimitar GTE (Grand Touring Estate). Response to the GT was also mixed and with sales of just 473 the new model could do little to revive the fortunes of the small, ailing firm. In 1976 Jensen Motors called it a day, opting for voluntary liquidation, a decision that met with some, if not overwhelming, consternation.

The Jensen-Healey's design was no doubt influenced by the Triumph Stag and Spitfire, but the charm of the latter model failed to rub off on it. In spite of its impressive appearance, its Lotus power plant, shown here in the twin-Stromberg-carburetor version, could be rough and testy. Poor access to the engine made servicing difficult, and the ignition distributor was almost out of reach.

JOWETT JUPITER

The Jowett Jupiter Convertible was originally intended as a light and simple car. While it remained true to the first principle, weighing in at just 1874 lb (850 kg), its progenitors' ambitions for the vehicle were betrayed by their decision to name it after the king of the Greek gods and thus the extensive catalog of British sports cars was further enriched by a highly unusual specimen—just 899 of which were made.

Before it, the Javelin, with which Jowett Cars Ltd of Bradford had announced its return to car-making after the general mobilization of the World War II, had already shown itself to be no ordinary sedan. It had been designed between 1942 and 1944 by Geoffrey Palmer, who was given a pretty free hand by company boss Callcott Reilly and chief engineer Frank Salter. The prototype appeared in 1946 and went into production a year later, featuring six side windows, a light, semi-self-supporting body with streamlined hood and barely protruding wings. Forward of the front axle was the marque's well-known 1.5-liter boxer engine with central camshaft. Each pair of cylinders was fed by its own carburetor.

At Jowett they were convinced that the Javelin's mechanical components would form the ideal basis for a sporty, open-top two-seater. The idea was immediately acted upon, and a chassis was commissioned from English racing car manufacturer ERA, based in Dunstable. ERA called upon Professor Robert Eberan von Eberhorst— who had already performed outstanding work for Auto Union of Germany and Cisitalia (he would later do the same for Aston Martin)—for advice. The respected academic designed a tubular frame based on longitudinal members and a diagonal crossbrace. Front suspension consisted of wishbones of unequal length, and the rear suspension of a rigid axle with torsion bars, trailing links and a Panhard rod.

In fall 1949 a forerunner called the ERA-Javelin made its debut simultaneously at the London Motor Show and in the company's showrooms in the capital. The chassis was offered for sale at £500 with the idea that it could be kitted out by specialist coachbuilders—such as Abbot—as a fixed-top coupé similar to the Aston Martin DB2.

Yet there were still a few things to sort out: among others the frame used by ERA in a small fleet of six test vehicles twisted and had to be scrapped. In March 1950 the company announced details of the production body, which was to be made of aluminum like that of the Javelin. The whole of the front section, including its sweeping wings, could be lifted up as a unit, considerably simplifying the task of servicing, maintaining and repairing the engine. The bench seat could accommodate up to three people. Access to the trunk, for

Having metamorphosed into a car form (aided and abetted by designer Reg Korner), the "ruler of the gods" ended up at a rather short 168 inches (4270 mm) in length, but made up for this by carrying its head high and tapering away attractively toward the rear. The car's front track was just over one and a half inches wider than the rear. A column-mounted gearshift meant that three people could snuggle up on the bench seat. The model designation Mark IA can be made out on the trunk lid.

the purpose of stowing away the tailor-made, standard-equip-ment Revelation luggage set, for example, was from behind the fold-down seat back. The fabric top fastened to the windshield frame in three places.

Good publicity for the start of production was ensured by Tommy Wisdom and T. C. White's class victory and 16th overall place in a Jowett Jupiter at Le Mans in 1950. The following year the car drew further attention to itself by achieving first and second place in the 1.5-liter class and a team win at Monte Carlo, and in 1952 journalist Gordon Wilkins achieved 13th place on the Sarthe circuit in the R1 competition version of the Jupiter, which differed from the version on general sale through its slimmer body and motorcycle-style wings. But for numerous pit stops caused by water and sand in the engine, an even better finish might have been possible. An initial test report published in The Autocar of December 1, 1950 emphasizes the car's suitability for both town and country and praises the absence of uncouth, self-advertising engine noise. A Jupiter Mark IA followed in 1953, bringing with it improvements to the engine, a revised exterior, an externally accessible trunk and greater comfort (the car already featured a dashboard of

polished high-grade veneer in the best English tradition). At the end of the year the appearance of the Jupiter R4—a sporty roadster not dissimilar to the Ferrari Barchetta whose body, made of a combination of sheet steel and plastic resin, rested on an abbreviated chassis with rear semi-elliptic springs—seemed to be the harbinger of a more secure future for the marque.

Appearances, though, were deceptive. The small manu-facturer was beset by severe financial difficulties. By the end of 1952 the company was £285,363 in the red, meaning that the small profit of £25,971 it turned in during the following year was a mere drop in the ocean. Furthermore, an impor-tant business partner, coachbuilder Fisher and Ludlow, was swallowed up by the British Motor Corporation, and exports, in particular those to the US, started to dry up as a result of competition from vehicles such as the Porsche 356A. The fate of Jowett Cars Ltd was sealed when its factory passed into the hands of the International Harvester Company in July 1954.

The whole of the Jowett Jupiter's sweeping front section could be raised, revealing and providing access to the car's four-cylinder boxer engine and front suspension, which consisted of wishbones, longitudinal torsion bars and an anti-roll bar. By 1954 its initially pretty unreliable power plant had overcome most of its teething problems and was beginning to prove its worth in terms of reliability.

LEA-FRANCIS
2½-LITER SPORTS

In August 1895 Richard Henry Lea and Graham Inglesby Francis formed a company whose clear goal was to manufacture a high-quality vehicle that would cause a sensation in the bicycle industry. And indeed their hand-made velocipedes, the Tourer and Light Tourer, stood out not only for their superb craftsmanship, but also for the ingenuity and imaginativeness that went into them. Their handlebars, for example, contained a tool kit and small oil can and the firm soon began selling models with two- and three-speed hub gears.

The same approach to quality characterized the cars produced by Lea-Francis Ltd, based first of all in Lower Ford Street and subsequently in Much Park Street, in Coventry. Nonetheless, their car production, launched by the first of three three-cylinder prototypes in 1903, got under way only after a hesitant, stuttering start, and would be interrupted by long creative pauses. The company attracted attention above all with minor marvels such as the Hyper, produced between 1928 and 1931. This was the first British production car to boast a supercharger and it managed to score a couple of decent racing victories.

The Twelve, which went on sale on January 23, 1946, was an unashamedly pre-war product. Its lively and appealing 1496cc four-cylinder engine was developed by Hugh Rose, formerly with Riley. Notable features include twin camshafts located high up on the sides of the engine block, and correspondingly short pushrods. The sports version, for which the wheelbase of the existing chassis (with rigid axle and semi-elliptic leaf springs) was reduced by twelve inches, was less reliant upon the company's own pre-war models. A prototype, developed by the company's service department and kitted out with an open two-seater body by coachbuilders Abbey Panels, was ready by July 1947. A further prototype, completed two months later, included a number of modifications, including a new grill and lower windshield.

The company opened in 1948 with a production version of the Twelve based on these two prototypes, before proceeding to build 88 Fourteens, which had a 1767cc engine delivering 72 bhp. A total of 136 were produced by the end of the following year. The exterior of the Fourteen combined old and new elements in a unique but by no means unattractive way.

Not every design idea was seen through to its logical conclusion, and thus the streamlined front, with headlamps positioned on the ends of the wings, did not sit particularly happily with the conventionally shaped hood. One aspect of the car that was definitely lacking was the poor protection it provided against the notoriously treacherous English weather—a Spartan tent roof. But the Fourteen was maneuverable and enjoyable to drive and its engine a gift to the tuner—to such an extent, in fact, that it was adopted by the Connaught racing team. "A well constructed and exciting English car," is how *The Autocar* magazine greeted the new model, indicating that it was miles ahead of all its competitors—other than H.R.G. perhaps. With respect to the already excellent roadholding of the unconventional tourer, its independent front suspension (double wishbones with lower torsion bars) displayed little further progress from fall 1948 onwards.

Hugh Rose had begun work sublimating the Twelve engine into a 2½-liter Eighteen back in September 1946. In doing so he also took into account the need for profitability and practicality and one feature of the new engine was that it was easier to assemble. In May 1948 the new unit found itself beneath the hood of a wolf in sheep's clothing in the form of the Fourteen Sports. The final extension to the range, the 2½-liter Sports (whose motto in the company brochure was: "a fast car that is fascinating to handle"), was launched in 1950. Just 78 were made. Upon closer inspection it became clear that this Lea-Francis sports model had put on a bit of weight all round, but without any fundamental transformation of its overall proportions and ample curves. The generously proportioned leather *fauteuils* that afforded the driver and passenger such a comfortable ride were supplemented by an extra seat adequate for those of modest build, the doors were now hinged at the front and none too reliable wind-up windows provided basic protection for the occupants.

As the company was unable to raise the funds required to finance the development of a new model, a decline in the sales of the 2½-liter Sports signaled the end of Lea-Francis Cars Ltd as a serious automobile manufacturer. The last two examples of the 2½-liter Sports, dating from 1953, glow like taillights disappearing into the dark of the past. Both have survived: one remained in the factory until 1959 before being hastily auctioned off when the company turned in a loss of £56,121 for the preceding financial year; the other, serving as a reminder of past glories, is still performing reliably to this day, in Sri Lanka.

Great events sometimes cast their shadows before them. Though it had undeniable appeal, the Lea-Francis 2½-liter Sports was essentially a nostalgic product and, despite attracting a favorable response when it was launched, demand quickly subsided.

The basic shape of the Sports was dictated by a prototype built immediately before the war: a narrow body tapering strongly toward the front, emphatic wings, a wasp waist, a hint of streamlining to the front and a return to older styles at the rear, where the spare wheel is stored under a smooth cover.

377 YNN

The first 2½-liter engine from Lea-Francis was manufactured in September 1947 and, as expected, produced good torque. The first Sports to be given this particular power plant (chassis number 5026) appeared in 1949 and was exhibited at Earl's Court and Kelvin Hall that year. The fact that it was an exhibit did not earn the car any special privileges, however: in 1950 the debutant was put through its paces in production sports car racing with Ken Rose at the wheel.

The Hyper, forerunner of the later Lea-Francis sports models, appeared in 1927 in two-seater, four-seater, and Sportsman's coupé versions, all featuring the supercharged 1496cc power unit. The name Hyper was chosen as an alternative to well-worn designations such as Super Sports or Special Sports. It was certainly fast: the model shown here completed the Brooklands Double Twelve and 500 Mile races in 1930 with a top speed of 113 mph (181.5 kph).

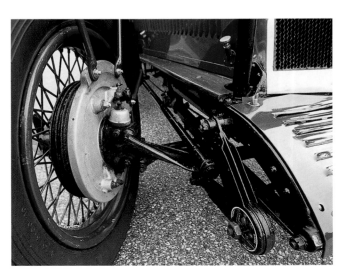

LOTUS ELITE

By the latter half of the 1950s, Lotus boss Colin Chapman already enjoyed a reputation in the pit and the paddock areas that would be substantiated over the coming decades by his daring constructions: as an inspirational, innovative and forward-looking designer of racing and sports cars. Although it was his fellow countryman, John Cooper, who brought about the rear engine revolution in racing car construction, it took Chapman to exploit this to its full extent and produce such svelte featherweight examples. He was an inventor in the best sense of the word, who liked to receive his flashes of inspiration in the seclusion of his bathtub.

Everyone was on tenterhooks waiting for the road-going Grand Touring car he had promised. So the London Motor Show, opened by Prime Minister Harold Macmillan on October 16, 1957, saw many visitors making a beeline for the stand of the tiny North London manufacturer. And there it crouched, in the artificial light of the show, the Lotus Elite, hastily assembled and still untested. And when, a couple of days later, Princess Margaret turned up accompanied by her mother and wanted to sit in it, she discovered that both doors were locked, with the key

still in the ignition. Nevertheless, the exhibit was something totally special, a two-seater coupé with a monocoque construction made of layers of fiberglass and polyester, with metal reinforcements at a few vital points, such as the door hinges, the strongly raked windscreen, and the pick-up points for the suspension. The body consisted of three sections bonded together: the floorpan, the actual load-bearing superstructure, and the outer coupé body. The shape came from the drawing boards of Peter Kirwin-Taylor and John Frayling, and aeronautical engineer Frank Costin refined the aerodynamics before Colin Chapman gave the final nod of approval.

The spare wheel was mounted upright directly behind the two nicely shaped bucket seats. The side windows were fixed, so interior ventilation was provided by the small hinged quarter-windows. As expected, the Elite proved to be something of a lightweight, weighing no more than 635 kg (1480 lbs) when fully tanked with 14 gallons (63 liters). Motor racing influences were discernible on all sides. The suspension resembled that of the Formula 2 Lotus 12: double wishbones with coil springs and telescopic dampers at the

front, and a combination at the rear of Chapman struts, radius arms and driveshafts providing the lateral links. Girling disk brakes on all corners suggested impressive stopping power.

With the FWE incarnation of the Coventry Climax FWA engine, which had originally been devised for a fire pump, a tamed racing engine was able to give remarkable performance thanks to the car's exceptional power-to-weight ratio. Weighing approximately 220 lb (100 kg), the engine itself made an important contribution. Countless tuning trims were available. In the first series up till 1960, the 1216cc engine produced 76 bhp, later boosted to 85 bhp when fed by two SU carburetors. At the same time a ZF gearbox replaced the original unit from BMC, pushing up the price tag considerably.

"Car of the Year?" asked the renowned American magazine *Road & Track* as early as January 1958. And the British publication *Sports Car & Lotus Owner* asserted in November of that year that it clung to the road like a leech, and that it was almost impossible to make the tail break away in the dry. Such merits doubtless placed considerable demands on the owner's sense of responsibility.

They also predestined the little Lotus for a place in motor racing. It was a born winner, a revolutionary newcomer à la

Chapman in the 1.3-liter GT class. It virtually took a season ticket out for the Le Mans title—winning every year from 1959 through 1964. Even jazz trombonist and hobby racer Chris Barber tried his hand at driving the Elite as part of the supporting program to the 1962 German Grand Prix at the Nürburgring circuit.

Only after Lotus Cars Ltd moved to Delamere Road in Cheshunt, Hertfordshire, in June 1959 did production of the Lotus Elite really get cracking. In addition to a run of 998 cars came many more supplied in kit form, which were sent to customers by a rail freight agency to be assembled in the homely atmosphere of their own garages. In this way they avoided paying purchase tax. However, production petered out in September 1963. Competition from cheaper mass-production sports cars, such as the Porsche 356B or the Alfa Giulietta, better tailored to everyday use, had grown too strong, and production of the Elite had proved to be too expensive. And the unusual material employed in the Elite's bodywork showed early signs of fatigue: after only a short while the heavy doors, for instance, would hang at an angle from their hinges.

Nevertheless, it was a pioneering venture that demonstrated a fresh spirit of enterprise, and the model has remained a classic.

The clean body lines of the hip-high coupé are an amalgamation of aerodynamics and aesthetics. They owe much to motor racing, as does the car as a whole. Visibility is excellent, and the wide doors with windows that cut into the roof structure allow comfortable access to the passenger compartment.

High standards far removed from any Spartan expectations likewise await the Lotus driver inside. The commodious bucket seats testify to the careful workmanship, as does the trim as a whole. Not only have door pockets and a storage tray been provided, there is even an ashtray on the transmission tunnel that clearly divides the two sides of the interior. Always in the driver's ear: the Coventry Climax engine, although slightly quieter from 1959 onwards.

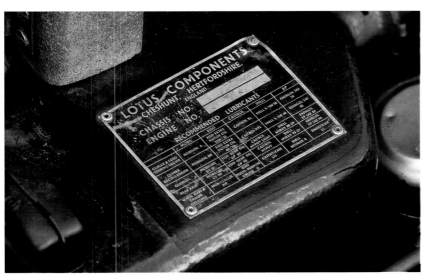

The Elite's alter-ego as a lively GT car shortened the step back to motor sport, from where the design actually emanated. The aggressive color scheme underlines the fact that this Elite had come to do battle. A lower center of gravity and sports suspension produced unusually good roadholding for its day. The protruding filler neck on the right, topped with a quick-release cap, allowed the tank to be filled in a flash.

Instead of paying attention to his lessons at high school as he should have, Anthony Colin Bruce Chapman, born on May 19, 1928 in Richmond-upon-Thames, already had his mind on other things: on one day presenting the world with the quintessence of the car, a "motorcycle on four wheels" for the student and his girlfriend, who wanted to snuggle up close to him.

The future mastermind of the Grand Prix racing world took a first step in this direction in the form of the Lotus VI, with its tubular frame clad in a glittering sheath of unpainted aluminum and two makeshift seats, which between 1952 and 1956 came to be thinly scattered among the freewheeling populace in a total run of 100 cars. Lotus Engineering Co Ltd first took a more serious turn in 1957, when, at 7 Tottenham Lane, Hornsey, London N8, they began to forge and weld a legend: the Seven. This was a driving machine for hardened, inveterate enthusiasts with limited finances, and simultaneously a car blessed with a whiff of immortality, as time was to show. It was unveiled at the London Motor Show in October of that year, where it shared its premiere with the Elite.

The Seven was often supplied as a kit in order to spare the customer the purchase tax. The fame of founding father Chapman was rising steadily, so a suitably snappy slogan was thought up for the mail order article: "He designed it, you build it."

There was plenty to do, though. As a rule it took 60 hours of diligent DIY before the vehicle was ready for the road, not forgetting a few impatient night shifts. Everything had to be unpacked, a plan of action hatched, and countless parts fitted together: from the multi-tubular spaceframe, which together with the floor panels, the tunnel for the propeller shaft and the aluminum side panels formed a semi-monocoque, to the bright shiny aluminum body, with its cycle-type wings and lights, to the suspension—front wishbones and coil spring/damper units, a live back axle located by twin trailing arms—and the four drum brakes, and finally the engine and transmission of one's choice, not infrequently purchased elsewhere by the customers.

Over its long career, the Seven's sleek nose housed the occasional six-cylinder, but in the main countless four-cylinder engines, ranging from the 998cc BMC A-series or the 1172cc Ford 100E with 40 bhp at the very start, to the Lotus dohc engine with 1558cc in the Super Seven Twin Cam of the Series III from 1968 onwards, to a Holbay engine version that punched out 125 bhp and really showed the driver what's what. A featherweight of just 725 lb (336 kg),

The Lotus Seven Series III Twin Cam was produced for just eight months in 1968, as an interim model between the Series II and a planned Series IV that was to introduce radical changes. Its brief existence came during a period of crisis, following the death of Team Lotus driver Jim Clark in April of that year during a Formula 2 race at Hockenheim. But it was to live on under a new badge as the Caterham Seven from 1973 onwards.

The twin-camshaft engine of the Ford Lotus Cortina draws in air through the louvers in the Seven's narrow hood. Additionally, the model is recognizable by its broad rear fenders with their neater curves over the wheels, and seat belt mounts. The dash was also redesigned, with the smaller dials for oil pressure, fuel gauge, and water temperature, separate from the main tachometer and speedometer instruments.

right from the first version the Seven was a lively little creature. And since the Spartan roadster, which from looks alone is a racer beneath just a thin varnish of civilization, sticks to the road like a barnacle to a ship, there is scarcely a better instrument for club events when finances are tight.

Under the aegis of Colin Chapman, four generations of the Seven followed each other, production comprising roughly 242, 1350, 350, and 1000 units, respectively. The Series II, built between 1960 and 1968, soon sported the glassfiber fenders of the original export model, the Seven American, and from 1963 disc brakes at the front. One model with the license plate KAR 120C even made its name on television: millions of viewers saw it every week in the opening scene of the series *The Prisoner*, in which Patrick McGoohan dashed along the strangely empty streets of London toward ever new adventures. The Series III, up to 1970, proved more compliant, but without relinquishing the macho feeling of raw power, and had an increased track width at the rear thanks to the Ford Escort rear axle that had

been detailed to its service. The Seven of the Series IV, until 1973, had smoother, all-fiberglass bodywork, and since it also offered more comfort it was scornfully referred to as the "soft" Seven. It was considered an abomination in the eyes of purists, but nevertheless it became a good seller.

The introduction of VAT in place of purchase tax tolled the death knell for the kit car. Apart from which, the Seven was no longer conducive to the changing image of Lotus Cars Ltd, which had moved in 1959 to Cheshunt, then late in 1966 to Hethel, Norfolk, as a producer of sports cars in the upper price and performance brackets. As a result, in May 1973 Colin Chapman disposed of the production rights to Caterham Car Sales, in Surrey. After just 38 units, the Surrey venture stopped manufacturing the Series IV Seven and resurrected its more rugged predecessor.

Like a motorcycle, it had come to serve in the meantime as a second car, in contrast to its original vocation, and it is no secret that one can take more pleasure in suffering in a vehicle like that.

LOTUS ELAN

The Elan was premiered at the London Motor Show at Earl's Court in October 1962, the year before the first World Championship was won by a Formula 1 Lotus with Jim Clark at the wheel. That was eloquent testimony to young entrepreneur Colin Chapman's mental agility and his capacity to learn, an impression that was to be shored up by fast and intensive model updates.

Unlike the Elite, which was built upon the dubious rigidity of a glassfiber monocoque, the Elan had plenty of backbone, quite literally: a massive X-shaped structure of sheet steel, drilled at the sides and six times as stiff as the spaceframe of the previous Lotus Grand Prix winner, while simultaneously 75 lb (34 kg) lighter. The man responsible for this was Ron Hickman, while the initial ideas came from Chapman himself.

Straddling this powerful frame and attached to it at 16 points was the Elan's bodywork of reinforced polyester. It formed a single unit, albeit with a complex shape, to which doors and hoods had then been added. The lid on the engine bay could be completely removed in 10 seconds.

And it was designed to move with the times: its wrap-around bumpers that extended to the wheel cutouts were filled with polyurethane foam. They could take considerable punishment if it came to it, although that was nevertheless something better avoided, while the retractable headlights were to remain one of the Elan's weak points. The ingenious control mechanism—each light having a vacuum cylinder connected to a central vacuum reservoir from which the air is evacuated by the exhaust manifold—had a tendency to give up the ghost.

Anchored in the forked ends of the cruciform frame were the engine and the gearbox, as well as pick-up points for the suspension. Hollow half-shafts transmitted the drive via rubber doughnut universal joints—which were known for their tendency to wind up and unwind—and located immediately outboard of them were the disc brakes. The rear independent suspension was characterized by extremely wide-based wishbones with low-sited pivot points, while the Armstrong coil spring/shock absorbers were mounted unusually high—as in the Elite. The front suspension

comprised compact upper and lower wishbones with similar coil/shock struts to those at the rear, the only difference being that the brakes were located outboard, within the light, but robust, Lotus-produced steel wheel rims.

The four-cylinder engine had been shifted right back in order to achieve optimal distribution of the vehicle's weight of approximately 1300 lb (590 kg). The engine was developed by Harry Mundy, technical editor of the magazine *Autocar* and a shrewdly practical man, and consisted up to the waistline of the Ford 116E unit from the Cortina, topped by Mundy's new twin-overhead-camshaft cylinder head.

The original version, of 1498cc and 100 bhp, was enlarged in May 1963 to 1558cc and it then produced 105 bhp. The 22 Elans which had been fitted with the original engine were then recalled, to be supplied with the larger one.

November 1964 saw the introduction of the Elan Series 2, with larger front brake callipers, oval-shaped taillight clusters, a wood veneer dash and knock-on wheels as an optional extra. The next stage in the development, the S3, which became available from September 1965, was first introduced as a comfortable coupé, and not until June 1966 was it joined by the convertible, with chrome-framed side windows, as in the hardtop version. From January of that year there was also the S/E (Special Equipment) version with 115 bhp, knock-on

wheels and servo-assisted brakes. The Series 4 Elans, produced from March 1968 onwards, could be recognized by the bulges over the wheel cutouts, designed to give the low-profile tires a bit of elbow room, a hump on the hood, and a larger lamp assembly at the rear.

The build quality, which at first was somewhat lacking in this model series, reached its zenith in the Elan Sprint, which was launched in February 1971, and was claimed to have 126 bhp. It was announced in Cheshunt as being 25 percent more powerful than its predecessor, but the inconsistency was immediately explained in rather sheepish tones: a mistake had been made and the more liberal SAE gross unit of measure used; in fact it only delivered 101 SAE net bhp. The words "Big Valve" were written on top of the ribbed camshaft cover, a pointer to the larger intake valves which racing engineer Tony Rudd used to pep up the Lotus engine. Differential and drive shafts were reinforced accordingly.

Apart from which, the vehicle did full justice to its name: *Motor* was pleased to note on March 6, 1970 that it knew of no other production car with 1.6-liter displacement that could accelerate to 60 mph (100 kph) in just 6.7 seconds. The magazine closed its report with the words: "We are most impressed."

The long career of the Lotus Elan ended in August 1973, after a run of 12,224, some of them supplied as kit cars.

In many ways as a contrast to the Elite, initially the Elan was only available as a convertible with the clear shape, free of all frills and fancies, that made it such a hit with the public. The introduction of a backbone chassis allowed the top to be opened up. It looks larger in pictures than it really is, but slightly smaller from behind the wheel. Wide doors allow easy entry.

The Lotus Elan 1600 power plant was by and large Lotus-made, using a Ford block beneath a cylinder head in which two camshafts put the valves to work, as in the Lotus Cortina. It is easy to get at. The chopped tail is like that of the Elite.

The headlights—a real innovation at that time—could be popped up or put to bed by means of a vacuum, which was faster than contemporary electrical mechanisms, but also prone to malfunction.

LOTUS EUROPA

Two years lapsed between the conception and realization of the Europa, which was launched in 1966 and put into production at the new Lotus works at Hethel. Derek Sleath headed the small team responsible for the commission, and John Frayling, of Elan coupé fame, attended to the styling. Colin Chapman viewed the hip-high two-seater sportster as something for Lotus fans who enjoyed the idea of having the power plant breathing down their necks, rather like superstar Jim Clark, the 1963 and '65 World Champion driving mid-engined Lotuses.

The name Europa indicated that the model was chiefly intended as an export article. Chapman also wanted to demonstrate that he had certainly not been reduced to being a satellite circling the fixed star Ford, and he picked La Régie Renault as his partner. The go-between in the negotiations was Grand Prix journalist Jabby Crombac,

so that the driver didn't set off with four reverse gears and one low-ratio forwards.

Rear suspension was a Lotus-made construction, consisting of coil springs, long trailing arms, bottom links located on the gearbox and fixed-length drive-shafts. The rear wheels were fitted with drum brakes, while those at the front—suspended by double wishbones surrounding coil spring/damper units—had disc brakes. Initially the polyester body and steel chassis formed an indivisible whole of enormous stiffness, and the curved side windows were fixed, which prompted Europa biographer John Bolster to wonder: "How could one ask the way, rebuke another motorist, or explain to a policeman that one hadn't done it?"

Both shortcomings were ironed out in the Series 2 introduced in April 1968: the superstructure could be removed in order to facilitate repairs, and power windows allowed the necessary oxygen to stream in from the left and right, as required. And while previously one tank of very modest proportions had made the Europa a frequent visitor to the gas station, the new model had two with separate filler necks, which allowed a larger cruising range. The introduction of the Twin Cam in 1971 saw the Gallic guest being shown the door. Waiting now to let rip behind the occupants was a Lotus-Ford unit like that in the Elan, with a twin-overhead-camshaft cylinder head perched on a cast-iron block. The roof-high fins either side of the engine cover, which in any case were of more optical than aerodynamic value, were trimmed down, but they continued to impede visibility to the rear corners, especially in town traffic. The eight-spoke wheels fitted to this model were not exactly a great aesthetic leap forward. In September 1972, the evolution of the model series culminated in the Europa Special with the 126 bhp "Big Valve" engine and a Renault five-speed transmission, initially as an option but later as standard. The hottest version of all, the Lotus 47, looked superficially similar, but it was completely different beneath the skin, being a pure race car. A total of 9230 Europas were built, many of them by do-it-yourselfers; the S2, for instance, cost £2471 ready to drive but only £2044 in kit form—more expensive, however, than the Elan kit, which the Europa had been intended to undercut significantly in price. The vehicle was never to achieve the same popularity among the testers as the more engaging Elan. Its critics picked above all on the tunnel vision it provided to the rear. It was also accused of leaping about like a frog on poor roads, and complaints were made that the clutch was too heavy and sluggish due to the long transmission cable, while gear changes were doughy and lacked accuracy. A remedy was later found for this, and even the animated utterances of the exhaust gave no more reason for complaint after the entry of the Lotus-assembled Twin Cam engine. And thus the Lotus Europa became a seemingly successful experiment that was, in fact, a failure.

Amid the wealth of radical solutions offered by the Lotus Europa, two things in particular stand out: its diminutive size and its shape, which flies in the face of convention, both as a whole as well as in the details. At the same time, other elements are clearly off the peg: the rear bumper, for instance, comes from the Ford Cortina, and is bolted directly to the polyester body.

who was a good friend of Clark, and had always been close to the House of Lotus. Legend has it that the deal was arranged between Crombac and Renault PR boss Robert Sicot at a meeting in a swish restaurant, and that for simplicity's sake the technical drawings were produced on the tablecloth.

As in the Elan, the frame consisted of a massive steel backbone, this time fanning out into a T at the front, while nestling in the Y at the rear was the compact engine (four cylinder, 1470cc, 82 bhp) and gearbox unit. A crossmember right at the back supported the rear end of the transmission. This was made of light alloy, as was the front-wheel-drive Renault 16 engine, and since the entire drive train could be swung around 180 degrees, the same arrangement was achieved as is found in contemporary Formula 1 single-seaters. The differential, however, had to be slightly modified

Engine and transmission from the Renault 16 have been swung through 180 degrees and placed behind the cockpit, which radiates a solid, sporty atmosphere. The small gearshift rests nicely in the hand, and an average-sized passenger can sit comfortably with arms outstretched in the beautifully shaped bucket seats. The "plateau" covering the engine compartment ends in a spoiler ridge, but visibility through the letterbox rear windshield is limited.

LOTUS ELAN +2

After four years in the planning, its launch in June 1967 was a major event: enter the Elan +2, later called simply the +2 or Plus 2. In the new, spick and span, ultra-modern Lotus works in Hethel, Norfolk, the wheelbase of the normal Elan was lengthened by 12.6 inches (320 mm) and the track width increased by 7 inches (178 mm). The upshot was more elbow room and two seats at the back, meaning that the heads of young families no longer needed to take the cold plunge and buy a saloon.

Despite unmistakable similarities in its lines with the two-seater, the +2 turned out be a truly individual car, and in the opinion of many, more beautiful than the original. The points the two cars had in common included major features like the polyester body mounted on the X-shaped steel frame structure, which was also used to reinforce such strategic points as the door openings. The thickness of the polyester body varied from 0.125 to as much as 0.25 inches (3.17 to 6.35 mm) for the highest stressed areas, such as parts of the floor and the edges of the wheel cutouts.

The two models also shared the concealed headlamps, which could barely withstand the wind blast at high speeds due to their rather feeble vacuum mechanism. Also identical was the drive train with the 1558cc twin-cam engine delivering 118 bhp, which astonishingly enough allowed the +2 to more or less match its more than 330 lb (150 kg) lighter sister in both top speed and acceleration, while the wider track allowed the +2 to actually improve on a standard of roadholding that Elan owners already considered to be exemplary. John Bolster, writing in the April 5, 1968 issue of *Autosport*, praised the test car as being the ideal solution for the man who was keen to have a road car with the driving characteristics of a Grand Prix vehicle. The number of interchangeable elements between the two Elans was relatively small; for example, the +2's doors were more smoothly curved at the leading edge, forward of the A-pillars.

The somewhat complicated nomenclature of the 2+2-seater reflects not only a policy of careful model improvement, but also the evolution of an ambition: Colin Chapman was bent on moving up-market. As an indication of this, beginning with the +2S launched October 1968—its predecessor remained in production until December 1969—the model was no longer available in kit form. The new version, identifiable, like the contemporary two-seater Elan Series 4, by a hump on the hood, pampered a steadily

Despite unmistakable family resemblances, the Elan coupé differs from the +2 in a number of areas. These include the shape of the door openings, as well as the arrangement of the turn signal lights and sidelights at the front. In the two-seater they are positioned under the bumper, in the four-seater above it.

transforming clientele with increased luxury and comfort, as well as with additional fittings, such as the foglamps. But the fun behind the wheel remained the same: although, according to *Autosport* technical editor John Bolster, its direct steering never left the driver in any doubt about the condition of the road surface, the Lotus inspired immediate confidence. He added that one could hit the curves without hesitating—or the car complaining—and that the engine was remarkably flexible and amenable, and wouldn't even object to sustained dawdling. The +2S was replaced in February 1971 by the +2S 130 "Big Valve" which had an engine tweaked by Tony Rudd to deliver 126 bhp, and was recognizable by its silver-painted roof.

The final metamorphosis came in October 1972 in the shape of the +2S 130/5. The extra, stuck-on number pointed to the inclusion—as in the last four or five Elan Sprints built—of a five-speed transmission, which already anticipated future generations of 2-liter Lotuses like the Elite or Eclat. The vehicle was a hardy creature right from the word "go."

At first the driver would find gearchanges very heavy and operation far from precise. Above all it was reluctant to slip into fifth gear, and then all the more unwilling when one tried to disengage it again. But one soon got the hang of it, making gearchanges a small sensual delight. Top gear was effectively an overdrive. A lot of customers had been waiting for this, especially on the European continent, where drivers still had the freedom to drive at full-throttle, whereas British motorways had long since been demoted to permanent crawler lanes by the 70 mph (113 kph) speed limit. Driving at 120 mph (193 kph) in fourth gear, the needle of the tacho already risked straying into the red zone, but the same speed in fifth spared the engine by all of 1400 rpm, as well as the Lotus driver's hearing and his gas budget.

The +2 outlived the Elan two-seater by a year, and reached a run of 3300. In 1974, new horizons were beckoning in Hethel, but tougher safety regulations were also in the offing, along with costly crash tests. And people are naturally loath to expose the classic models to such unsavory customs.

One of the merits of the Elan +2 is its roomier luggage compartment, due to the fact that the "Family Elan" is broader in the beam. A more comprehensively equipped dashboard with two additional instruments at the center also makes concessions to the driver's thirst for information, even though they are all monitoring exactly the same engine as in the coupé. The 10-spoke wheels come from Lotus itself.

LOTUS ELITE & ECLAT

In May 1974, Lotus saw the rebirth of the Elite, which had passed away in 1963. But the only similarities were in the name and the composite construction of its body. Otherwise, this unusually shaped four-seater was aimed by Colin Chapman at finally dispelling the odor of the "poor people's kit car maker" from his premises and setting his sails for the rich pickings still to be found after the oil crisis of 1974.

The interior design of the Elite, with its functional, ergonomic and distinctly non-English dash design, came from Giorgetto Giugiaro's beauty parlor Ital Design, while an in-house team assumed responsibility for the silhouette. But at the same time they were quite receptive to new, outside influences, as shown by echoes of the Mercedes 350 SLC, for instance, or of the Lamborghini Espada. There were also precedents for the slender-framed rear window that simultaneously served as a tailgate—which incidentally could be held in any desired position by means of gas cylinders—namely the Volvo 1800 ES or the Reliant Scimitar GTE. A striking detail here was the low-set window line that slanted downwards behind the A-pillar and rose again before the C-pillar, and allowed an all-round view that had been something of a problem in the original Elite, and decidedly so in the Europa. The strongly raked front windshield was made of Glaverbel glass from Belgium that was 0.16 inches (4 mm) thick.

Originally a self-supporting glassfiber body was planned for the vehicle, but later it was decided to give it a sturdy foundation in the shape of a backbone chassis. To increase passive safety—particularly with an eye on the North American market—steel reinforcements were worked into the doors and an integral rollbar structure into the roof, as well as into the bumpers, which apparently would take a bump at up to 5 mph (8 kph) without damage.

Set between the front chassis extensions at an angle of 45 degrees to the left was the selfsame 2-liter four-cylinder engine with twin overhead cams and 155 bhp that had let rip during its tearaway youth in the Jensen-Healey. It remained an uncouth creature, particularly when approaching the limit above 7000 rpm. Typical of Lotus, all four wheels were independently suspended, with wishbones at the front, and long trailing arms, wishbones and fixed-length drive-shafts at

As with the Europa, the second-generation four-seater Lotus Elite stirred up controversy over the two kinks in its silhouette line at the rear, and over the upward tapering line of the window area. But there was no argument about the fact that the small surface area at the front and a drag coefficient of 0.3 gave it the best figures in every league—the result of industrious work in the wind tunnel. The rear window simultaneously acts as access to the luggage compartment, which is separated from the passenger cell by a glass pane.

the back—where a set of drum brakes recalled the good old days. A layout like that of the Grand Prix racers, such as Chapman would have preferred, would have compromised the rear-seat passenger space.

This is precisely what occurred in the 2+2-seat fastback coupé, which in most ways was very similar apart from the low-sweeping roofline, and which flanked the Elite at the London Motor Show in 1975. Its name was the Eclat.

Both models were followed in June 1980 by the so-called Series 2.2, which boasted power plants bored to 2174cc that delivered 160 bhp, and was recognizable by its fixed skirts, which protruded at the sides, and continued the line formed by the groove between the front spoiler and the body. The taillights were now grouped in larger units, and the halogen headlamps were no longer popped up and retracted by vacuum power, but by electric motors. Both were offered in a Riviera edition with sunroof. Furthermore, the trim versions were distinguished by cleverly thought-out designations: the basic Elite was the 501, a deluxe version with air-conditioning and upmarket stereo the 502, the most Spartan Eclat variant the 521, and so on.

The July 1974 issue of *Wheels* tested the Elite 502 and deemed it a comparatively exotic rival to the Porsche 911. But the lavishly upholstered leather seating, which provided the passengers with commodious individual seats either side of the central spine, together with the overall air of luxury about the test car, was sensed as something of an affront to those purists who still associated Lotus with the comfort of a bed of nails.

The punning title of an article in the 5 June 1975 issue of *Autosport* was "A Lotus for the Elite," which referred to the 503 and suggested that Hethel had been learning a lot from motor racing. The Lotus was seen as quite capable of taking on competitors like the roughly equal-priced Mercedes 350 SL, even though it had only four cylinders to its name; against that, it was seen as having an incredibly aerodynamic shape and exemplary handling, "typical of products of the marque." And the fact that the body was still made of glassfiber offered, in their opinion, one big advantage: the car didn't rust.

This was a point with which the 2531 Elite owners (up until 1983) and 1522 Eclat purchasers (manufactured up to 1985) would unreservedly agree.

The gain in storage space in the second-series Lotus Eclat has been at the cost of passenger headroom, because shortly behind the B-pillar the roofline sweeps down into the fastback. Now flush beneath the rear window is a trunk lid of glassfiber. Once deemed an uncouth youth, the majority of the testers now felt that the six-valve engine beneath the hood had outgrown its awkward phase.

LOTUS ESPRIT

Like the Aston Martin DB5, the Lotus Esprit made a name for itself as a four-wheeled film extra. In the James Bond epic *The Spy Who Loved Me*, for instance, where it sank into the crystal-clear waters of Coral Harbour, Nassau, with the amphibious 007 at the wheel, only to continue its journey at 15 knots underwater. Or in the sex-and-crime shocker *Basic Instinct*, where it demonstrated astonishing driving properties on the damp tarmac of the big, night-time city, as well as the remarkable sturdiness of its composite body when it landed on its roof.

It began its career as a style study by Giorgetto Giugiaro shown at the Turin Salon in 1972. Not that the Italian maestro had come up with a new trend here; he simply

reshuffled the typical components of a super sports car and launched one of those barstool-high wedges at the onrushing wind that basically make the presence of other passengers superfluous. It first went on sale in June 1976. As in the Elan, Europa and second-generation Elite, the dashing body straddled a backbone chassis-frame made of sheet steel. The suspension of the Esprit was the same as in the two sister models, the Elite and Eclat.

It also shared with them the engine that assumed monoculture status at Lotus: a 2-liter job with twin overhead cams and four valves per cylinder, banked at 45 degrees to the exhaust outlet side, and coupled with the five-speed transmission from the Citroën SM, but installed behind the

passengers' backs. Although it had already achieved a great deal of maturity, this small, complex machine demonstrated vociferously that a lot of its mechanical parts did not always work together in perfect harmony. Testers complained that at certain speed ranges deafening vibrations would make the vehicle body quaver like a violin—not to mention the driver's body. The top speed of 138 mph (222 kph) promised by the company seemed to be more a product of its imagination. *Autocar* at any rate reported 124 mph (200 kph) at the very most.

The futuristic flair of the interior in the first series rubbed purists up the wrong way, but concessions were made in the second series launched in June 1978, above all in the form of

The Lotus Esprit Series 3 of 1981 differed from its predecessors by its new shaped, color-matched rocker panels, bumpers that snuggled around the corners of the body, less obtrusive "ears" behind the side windows, and new wheels—here with the optional BBS rims. The word "Lotus" has been stamped into the rear bumper in large letters, so that other, unsuspecting road users learn who or what has just overtaken them.

The seats on the left and right of the powerfully shaped center tunnel envelop their occupants with soft crumply coziness, but also give firm support. The twin-spoke Momo steering wheel was now standard, and the handbrake had been allotted a place directly in front of the driver's seat by the door sill. The space inside is tight, as if every Lotus had been devised around the dimensions of the slimly-built Grand Prix driver and Chapman confidant Jim Clark. The 2.2-liter type 912 engine was used in all of the marque's road models from the summer of 1980 onwards.

instruments comprising more conventional elements. The front spoiler wrapped around to the front wheel cutouts. New taillight units also included fog lamps, and the almost vertical pane separating the passenger compartment from the engine was more strongly raked in order to eliminate reflections. On top of which, ventilation was improved in the passenger compartment with air inlets directly behind the rear side windows. A "noisy thoroughbred" was the verdict on the Esprit S2 in *Autocar*, January 20, 1979, which also complained about the fact that the armrests couldn't be adjusted in a car costing £11,754. In one of the occasional special editions, the vehicle was presented in the black-and-gold livery of the Formula 1 sponsor JPS (John Player Special), as in the model handed over to Lotus' 1978 World Champion Mario Andretti.

In the next model development, the 2.2 from 1982, the Esprit joined in the general Lotus upgrade to 2.2 liters and 162 bhp, and the Series 3 a year later included the improvements that had already been made in the 1980 turbo version.

1987 was an incredibly important year in the history of both the model and the company: Lotus took in £2,000,000 for its new owner, General Motors. Since Giugiaro's razor-sharp design was no longer up with the times, it was given a brisk revamp by a team led by Peter Stevens, under the supervision of Lotus chief engineer Colin Spooner. Some 15 months lapsed between plan and completion. Smoother, more rounded, and with that more sensuous appearance, suddenly the Esprit looked once more up to date. And although not a single element of the body—essentially two halves of glassfiber bonded together and reinforced with Kevlar—remained unchanged, astonishingly the overall look was retained.

Coupled with the Renault GTA transaxle, the engine now unleashed 172 bhp and allowed exactly the originally announced 138 mph (222 kph) to be reached. It meant, however, that the Esprit S4 lost some of its spriteliness, because it was now more than 220 lb (100 kg) heavier; 0–60 mph (up to 100 kph) in 6.7 seconds was nevertheless a presentable figure for a normally aspirated 2.2-liter engine.

After 2919 sales, production of the Lotus Esprit dried up—bringing to an end a brainchild of Colin Chapman that not only floated above the waters, but wasn't afraid to plunge into them.

LOTUS ESPRIT TURBO

Old King Esprit was still alive as the new sovereign, the Esprit Turbo, began its reign. It has taken Lotus through thick and thin, and was still with us in 2004.

The Turbo mounted its throne at a monumental party which the marque's new Formula 1 sponsor, Essex Petroleum, threw in February 1980 at the Royal Albert Hall in London. It did not go on sale until August, and at first only as a limited edition of 100 available solely until March 1981, finished in the sponsor's livery: metallic blue, red, and silver.

As part of a policy to generate more power, a project group headed by Lotus manager Mike Kimberley and technical director Tony Rudd had got to grips with the standard 2.2 engine, and empowered it with a further 50 bhp by means of a Garrett AiResearch T3 turbocharger. Part of the heat it developed was evacuated via a descending flight of louvers. Apart from which, couturier Giorgetto Giugiaro had placed his nine-year-old concept in line with the Esprit Turbo's 210 bhp by adding, among other things, more powerful bumpers, efficient spoilers fore and aft, and sweeping side skirts, as well as larger wheels, a stiffer frame, and modified rear suspension.

The next stage, the HC model (for High Compression) was revealed in March 1986, and came with further 5 bhp and extra space, and the turbocharged version in 1987 also came newly decked out in the flatteringly tailored composite outfit from Peter Stevens—without the slatting over the engine. From May 1989 the SE was offered as an alternative to the HC. Squatting piggyback on the engine was an intercooler that reduced heat levels, which had been a notorious weak point in the model, which in this variant delivered 264 bhp. The designation "turbo" was officially dropped in 1990.

An indication of the unremitting evolution that this new-style Esprit underwent can be seen in the power steering that was introduced 1993 as standard in the Series 4 to reduce the work required of the reclining driver. By 1994 there was now an engine producing 300 bhp inside the new S4S, which was recognizable from its larger-sized wheels. On March 1, 1996, journalists were given a first glimpse of the racing Esprit GTI at the Circuit Paul Ricard, in the South of France. Sitting in its tail was a power plant that delivered the enormous thrust

for which the Turbo had always been intended. The veil of mystery that still surrounded it was finally lifted four days later on the opening of the Geneva Salon.

Gone were the days when testers passed the stereotype verdict on Lotus that it was strong, fast and beautiful, but sadly had only four cylinders. For now a stylish nameplate on the Esprit's tail proclaimed the power of a twin-turbo V8, whose exceptionally compact dimensions would never have led one to expect a displacement of 3.5 liters, the muscle of 354 bhp, and a top speed of 175 mph (282 kph). The aluminum alloy engine—tastefully presented in wrinkle finish—took up less space than the customary four-cylinder in-line engine. Four camshafts controlled the concerted action of 32 valves, while two small Garrett turbochargers ensured a volumetric efficiency of over 100 bhp per liter displacement, a flat torque band, and almost lag-free acceleration. At the same time, the customer was spared the angry rumble of conventional V8s, for while normally one cylinder fires at every 90-degree turn of the crankshaft, in the Lotus version two fire at every 180-degree turn, meaning that the shrill whine of the starter is followed by a rather wailing sound. According to Götz Leyrer, in issue 20 of the German magazine *auto motor und sport* in 1996, the Esprit V8 had essentially remained the archetypal exotic it always was,

adding that dyed-in-the-wool fans still had to endure a lot of trouble, if not grotesque contortions, when getting in, along with tiny pedals that bored sharply into the soles of the feet, and a sloppy standard of fit and finish. The four-cylinder models nevertheless remained, and in October 1996 the V8 was flanked at the Paris Salon by the GT3, a lightweight with 2-liter capacity and intercooler that produced 240 bhp.

And there was no need to worry about the continued existence of the Lotus Ltd Group: at the end of that same month, Malaysian multinational Hicom announced that it had acquired the majority shareholding. In 1997, the V8 was given a new interior design, and with it a somewhat simpler version, the V8 GT, hit the market. Lotus' last word for the time being in Esprit matters is the Sport 350, lighter and with larger brakes, which went on offer in 1998 in a limited edition.

And as with its earlier relatives, the driver does not simply motor along in it, because there is always something happening. Some sensations never grow old.

In October 1987, the first-generation Esprit with its rather crisp lines from the pen of Giorgetto Giugiaro was put out to grass in Hethel, and replaced by a more rounded and obliging version devised by Peter Stevens. Not a panel nor a glass surface has been left unchanged, yet its profile remains in principle the same. Over the years that followed, the tail of the turbo was also to be graced with a variety of spoilers.

Initially the new species of the Lotus Esprit Turbo is chiefly recognizable by its nameplate and a different rear lower body molding and cooling grill arrangement beneath the rear bumper. Additional revisions were made to the surgically rejuvenated Esprit (Lotus code X180), such as the layout of the instrument binnacle behind the meaty steering wheel, and the engine, fed by means of a Lotus/Delco multi-point injection unit. The transmission was now from Renault.

LOTUS ELAN

Lotus is not only known for economy in its weights and measures, but also in its choice of names, particularly when they have such a positive ring to them hailing from a glorious past, such as the name Elan. The decision was made in the late 1980s to revive the legend. The yardstick for the new version was correspondingly high.

In October 1989, the second-generation Elan designed by Peter Stevens was unveiled at the London Motorfair. And there can be no doubt about it, like its illustrious ancestor it embodied many articles of faith from the creed of founding father Colin Chapman: a galvanized steel backbone chassis-frame, forming a metal spine passing lengthways through the floor to bear the body, powertrain, a small aluminum subframe and the suspension units, was still regarded as a contemporary solution by the folks at Hethel. This backbone principle, combined with an open, non-structural fiber-reinforced plastic body, produced enormous torsional stiffness. The word glassfiber had long since been banished from the Lotus vocabulary due to the strong whiff of DIY that surrounded it; as early as 1982 the press department kindly requested that in future, journalists the world over should use the word "composite."

Also completely in keeping with the departed Elan of 1982, the suspension was as fine as could be, with double wishbones front and back, coil springs, tube shock absorbers and anti-roll bars. This was the necessary prerequisite for Lotus boss Mike Kimberley's minimalist agenda: this had to be the fastest A to B car on the roads. The punchy format of the resurrected model was likewise in the best Lotus tradition: approximately 150 × 67 inches (3500 × 1730 mm) it is as short as a Honda CRX and as wide as a Porsche 944. Which more or less wraps up the similarities between the Elan (old) and the Elan (new).

The differences—a wholesale slaughter of sacred cows—began with the target group: the market, as Kimberley forthrightly asserted, had changed. The age group he was now aiming at consisted of upward movers from the GTI class. The differences continued in the power plant, a trans-versely mounted 16-valve engine with 1588cc, which in normally aspirated form produced 130 bhp at 7200 rpm, and 165 bhp at 6000 rpm in the version with turbo and intercooling. Although the letters "LOTUS" were emblazoned in red on the cylinder cover, they had been placed behind the metal-color nameplate of the engine supplier Isuzu, of which Lotus' owners, General Motors, owned a 41.6 percent share. Although this Japanese import responded willingly to the accelerator, it lacked passionate spontaneity and sporty vocals, the latter consisting principally of a strained boom.

The differences were by no means restricted to the drive unit: the driveshafts followed an elegantly short route to the front wheels from the differential, which was integrated with the gearbox and engine, without this producing even the slightest problems in face of the manifest power of this mere 2249 lb (1020 kg) lightweight.

The US version of the Elan pointed a longer nose into the wind, complete with a stronger bumper—a modification that many felt went nicely with the model's looks. In 1991 it received the British Design Council Award. Later that same year, the Lotus stand at the IAA in Frankfurt sported a futuristic concept car, a speedster called the M200 based on

the Elan. Then the 1992 version responded to flagging sales and production by offering an optional hardtop.

Despite this, a limited new edition of 800 was produced in winter 1993/94, with 16-inch (406.4-mm) wheels and further improved suspension, and was launched at the Geneva Salon in spring. March 1995 saw just such an Elan S2 come off the assembly line as Lotus number 50,000, and with the assistance of the British tabloid *The Sun* and film star Britt Ekland, it fetched £65,000 at a charity auction.

Five months later the curtain was lowered on this act. Number 800 of the S2, the 4655th Elan in all of the second generation, was retained by Lotus—for exhibition purposes

and as a souvenir of a project that never delivered what it seemed to promise. Not forgetting a contemporary curiosity: while the Mazda MX-5, an almost unconcealed plagiarism of the original Elan at half the price, became a bestseller, Lotus resorted to Japanese components in its own reprise of the model...

The second-generation Elan, designed by Peter Stevens, slices through the air like a rounded-off wedge, as smooth and slippery as a well-used piece of soap, with only the tiniest of overhangs. The resoluteness of its line is even reflected in the rear spoiler, which performs its aerodynamic mission firmly integrated in the trunk lid. The Elan's backbone chassis together with the fiber-reinforced composite body ensures great torsional stiffness.

Without doubt the Elan of the 1960s gave the Japanese a lot of design stimulus. When the belated comeback was on the verge of arrival, the Land of the Rising Sun gave its thanks in the form of a meaty present: concealed beneath a wealth of names is a dowry from Isuzu, a powerful, revvy engine without any long-winded lag in the turbo department.

The cockpit is wide, homely, yet nevertheless sporty. Switches and instruments were sourced from Opel's shelves.

LOTUS ELISE

The Elise's debut at the IAA in Frankfurt in September 1995 threw out a last lifeline just as the power plants at Lotus Cars Ltd, in Potash Lane, Hethel, began to splutter and fail: harbinger of hope had been the Elan, but it proved a flop, and at that moment the new parent, Bugatti Industries, which bought the small sports car concern from General Motors in 1993 for £25,000,000, went into receivership.

Company founder Colin Chapman, whose only answer to lightness was even more lightness, would have been as pleased as punch with the 147 inch long and 48 inch tall (3726 × 1200 mm) open-top mid-engined "mini," whose mouth creases at the corners of the air intake in what seems like a mischievous little smile. Its monocoque, made of bonded aluminum extrusions, together with its composite-material bodywork, reduced the weight to 1616 lb (733 kg) fully tanked with 40 liters of fuel. The chassis weighed a mere 150 lb (68 kg), the front part of the bodywork 29 lb (13.3 kg), and the rear 55 lb (25 kg). The inside of the Elise likewise had the severe minimalism and spatial economy of an egg: surrounded by fully exposed aluminum alloy, with a juicy little Nardi steering wheel in front and a couple of meager-sized instruments, pampered by three Peugeot pushbuttons and two small control stalks, and expressly admonished not to smoke by the absence of an ashtray, the driver was offered a driving experience reduced to the essentials, without any frills and fancies. Despite this, the Elise was not some new fashionable roadster, for behind the commodious seats was a beefy rollover bar and a proper rear window. A tiny luggage compartment cramped any desire to lug too much junk around. But if the driver did decide to take a pullover along, he or she would find it nice and warm when they put it on, because the trunk was located behind the engine and over the exhaust.

Typical in-house motor racing influences could be seen on all sides. As in the design of the suspension: double wishbones at the front, with coil springs over damper units. The latter were also to be found at the back, where five-spoke 7J × 16 format wheels (front 5½J × 15) were located by a lower wishbone and an upper lateral arm. The lack of power steering increased the driver's feeling of intimacy with the road, which the Lotus bit into with glee. It could be taken through every kind of curve with the greatest of ease, and only very late on did oversteering reveal that 60 percent of its weight rested on its rear axle. The fact that the MGF's four cylinders set behind the passengers only released 120 bhp might sound uninspiring at first. But since every horsepower

The Elise has undergone a striking transformation that brings it up to the times, and varies the classic Lotus themes of lightweight construction and functional compactness, while remaining rather broad in the beam. The figure two dominates below the rear spoiler: two pairs of rear lights, two radiator inlets with cat's eyes set in the corners, and likewise twin tailpipes that point at the opponent coming up from the rear like a machine gun.

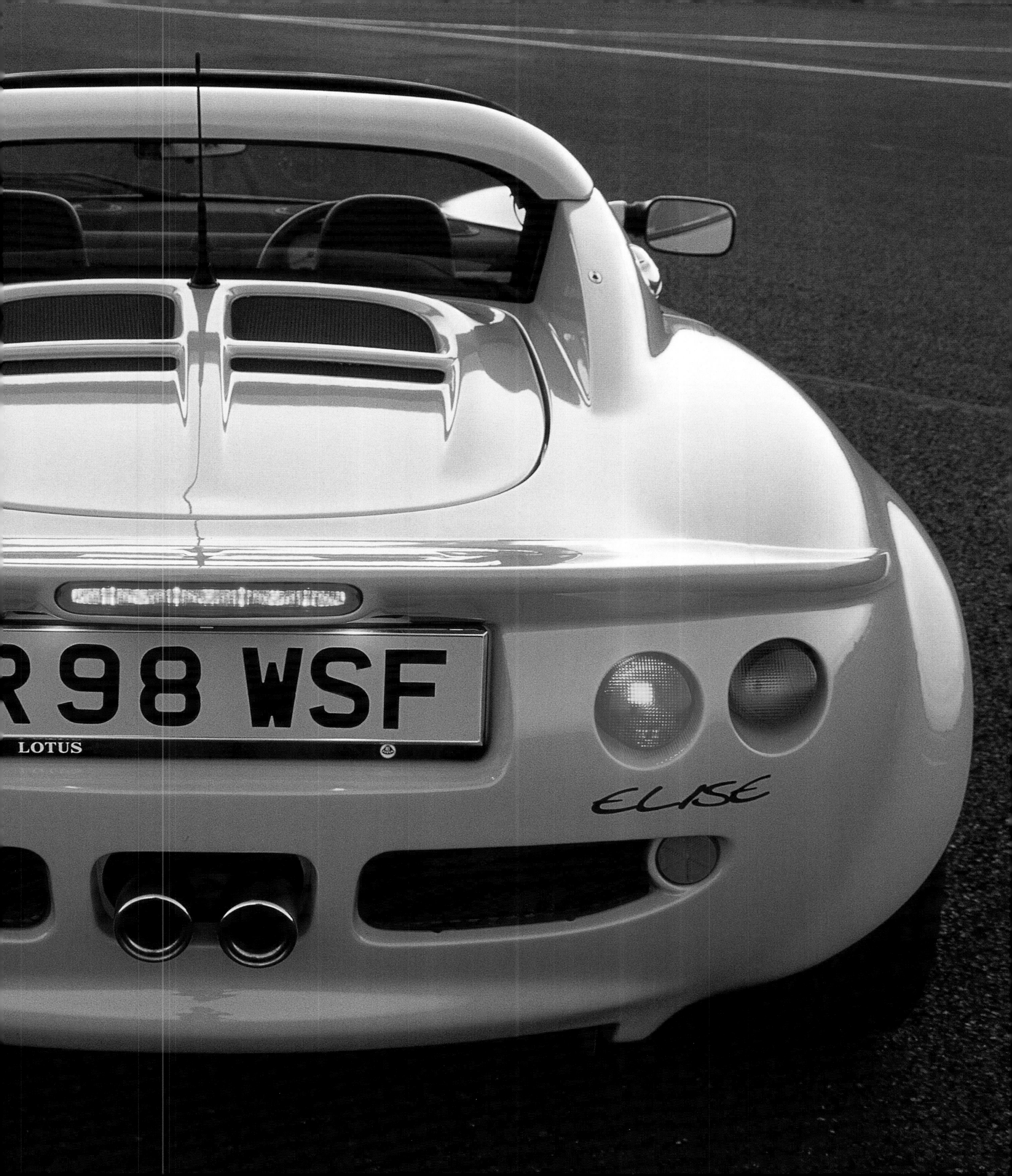
R98 WSF
LOTUS
ELISE

used in making this car move counted—just like every tenth of a second in Formula 1—the Elise gave a very spirited and tempestuous performance. The spurt from 0 to 60 mph (up to 100 kph) took just 6.5 seconds, and while there was a comparative lull when driving along city roads, at the top speed of 126 mph (202 kph) the wind blast coming into the cockpit was simply brutal.

Since 1997, the Elise has also been available with a scanty-fitting hardtop. 1998 became the key year in the life of the model. In the UK it was awarded Millennium Product status by the Design Council, and the Birmingham Motor Show that fall saw the unveiling of the Elise Sport 135. It was envisaged as a limited edition of 50, but every conceivable part was available to retro-fit the normal Elise. Simultaneously, the Lotus 340 R, a weirdly shaped road-capable competition car with 179 bhp constructed on the basis of the Elise, was launched to sound out the market. The experiment paid off: a year later Lotus set about spreading the former concept car among the paying customers in an edition of 340. In November, the 50th anniversary edition of the Elise brought home the fact that Lotus had outlived its midlife crisis with élan, albeit without the Elan.

March 1999 saw a new addition to the family when the Lotus presented the Elise 111s at the Geneva Motor Show, a toy to appeal to the boy in the man, 25 bhp more powerful and,

inevitably, somewhat pricier than the original, and now with an elegantly shaped rear spoiler. Hidden beneath its unconventional garb was the VVC engine from the Rover K-series, which, unlike the standard power plant of the same capacity, had variable valve timing. It injected even more pep into the 111s, reducing the sprint from 0 to 60 mph (up to 100 kph) by half a second, and increasing top speed by 7 mph (11 kph), so adding new dimensions to the performance that was also assisted by a closer-ratio gearbox. No wonder, for the basic model had to shift 12.3 lb (5.6 kg) with each horsepower, the more powerful version a mere 10.8 lb (4.9 kg). And that's not the end of it: with the next model development, the Sport 160, launched on February 1, 2000, everything that defined the Elan had been taken to the extreme.

The snappy little racer was soon regarded as easier going in its most recent metamorphosis from the fall of 2001, despite its belligerently chubby cheeks; while admittedly a wolf in sheep's clothing, it is one that has learned a few lessons from its forebears. The cockpit is also new, and the wheels have grown from 16 to 17 inches (406 to 432 mm). In keeping with the times, the men at Hethel have kept anything looking like fabric away from the top: the customer gets virtually two cars, because when not required the two sections of the reworked hardtop can be swiveled upwards, released and stored without problem in the rear. But that smile is still there.

In the event of a rollover it's comforting to know there's a sturdy rollbar up above. The cockpit, fronted by the sharply raked windshield, is as tight as a monk's cell and offers thriftily-sized and well separated seats for two. For the person behind the wheel, the Elise reduces movement to driving and nothing else—just as its owners want.

LOTUS EXIGE

Obviously the name is linked with the French verb *exiger*, meaning to demand or insist. And truly the Lotus Exige, which was unveiled in the spring of 2000 in fitting style on the undulating course at Brands Hatch in Kent, is *très* demanding. Located in the border zone between two worlds, it is a road-going vehicle based on the Elise Sport racing car, which is waiting to become the next cult object for those hard-boiled individualists who have always made up the ranks of Lotus owners.

Because a deeper acquaintanceship with it begins with having to forego an air conditioner, which would certainly not be amiss in the claustrophobic, sweaty confines of its interior, dispense with power steering and a radio, and do without softy, lily-livered paraphernalia like ABS and brake boosters. Instead, the Exige imperiously demands youthful agility before one can even begin to lead it to its chosen destiny. Clambering aboard requires a carefully studied choreographic procedure. After performing a tense balancing act, the right foot can be thrust deep down inside to the frugal pedals; the driver's backside then follows the law of gravity until it is in front of the door sill, which stands tall and angular in the way, then describes a semi-circular movement in order to surmount the obstacle, and finally slumps down into the deep-set, firmly bolted seat. The other leg, which is still outside, is quickly drawn in and suddenly one is faced by a fat-rimmed but tiny steering wheel; staring behind it are the two most important dials, looking pale but not uninteresting. It's easier for the neighbor for there is no steering wheel to combat, but he or she, too, is surrounded by aluminum pressings that pass along the length of the vehicle like girders. Alcantara in the four

Naturally it has that certain similarity to its brother (or sister?) Elise. But already the Lotus Exige's outward appearance is more aggressive as a result of the rear wing on its skeletal struts and its wider track. It is clearly a fighter, a lonesome racer that has strayed onto the public thoroughfares, for it rarely follows the pack.

available colors—black, blue, red, and silver—covers the bare essentials.

But before the heavy buckle of the harness system has snapped into place with a solid metallic clunk, the driver has already succumbed to the rough charms of this English street urchin, which entices with sweet promises and rewards with pure fun. This begins with its outside appearance, which demonstrates an accomplished mixture of function and show, as in the belligerently styled glassfiber-reinforced composite bodywork. The deep-set front air splitter, with its high-set accomplice at the rear, produces the harmonious downforce characteristics of 77 lb (35 kg) at the front and 99 lb (45 kg) at the back at 100 mph (160 kph). A horizontal scoop on top of the roof slurps cooling air into the engine bay; the heat is extracted via a tailgate exit duct set at the center, as are the twin pipes for the Exige's exhaust gases. A dark-tinted dome of polycarbonate above the luggage locker allows rudimentary vision to the rear.

Lotus already moved on from the unit-construction fiberglass body after the first-generation Elite, so the Exige's body rests on a chassis made of epoxy-bonded aluminum extrusions with an integral steel roll bar structure. The suspension units for the matt black Lotus alloy wheels, with their low-profile, super-gripping soft tires from Yokohama, are the pure embodiment of racing: double wishbones with coil springs and monotube dampers front and back, with an adjustable anti-roll bar at the front.

In civilian life, the 1.8-liter four-pot engine of the mere 46-inch (1175-mm) tall coupé can also be found in such mild-mannered limousines as the Rover 75. Not only did it forget all of its manners on the way to the engine compartment, it also put on an extra 179 bhp of muscle. Thus in alliance with the vehicle's mere 1735 lbs (787-kg) curb weight, the upright citizen mutated into a firebrand, which can hurl the Lotus along with two breathless occupants to 60 mph (up to 100 kph) in under 5 seconds. It always makes itself heard, objects to cold starting with a wheeze and a cough, then rising to a hoarse rasp under the right working conditions, until at 5000 rpm an acoustic inferno reduces conversation between the occupants to a series of monosyllabic shouts.

But in any case, the driver's attention has long since focused exclusively on the Exige—at least when well away from the large, crowded roads. For the Lotus Exige lusts for the wild freedom of the mountains or foothills at the crack of dawn or at dusk, when one is alone with oneself, the car, and the tarmac. Then it keeps the promises described in its specs: lively like quicksilver, an oversized go-kart, a Formula car for two, scantily dressed to permit everyday encounters.

Nearly £30,000 had to be handed over in the fall of 2000 for this automotive abstraction, a resounding slap in the face of the cold calculating family father, but a special bargain for the playful *Homo ludens*, whom the Dutch cultural theorist Johan Huizinga divined in us all in his book of that name.

The observer is confused by the jagged body architecture, with its yawning lairs and grottoes, its precipitous elevations, like the stack which forces fresh air down to the four-cylinder engine that is waiting, stark-naked, under its acrylic glass lid. The inside is claustrophobically cramped, and even boarding requires youthful dexterity and choreographic finesse.

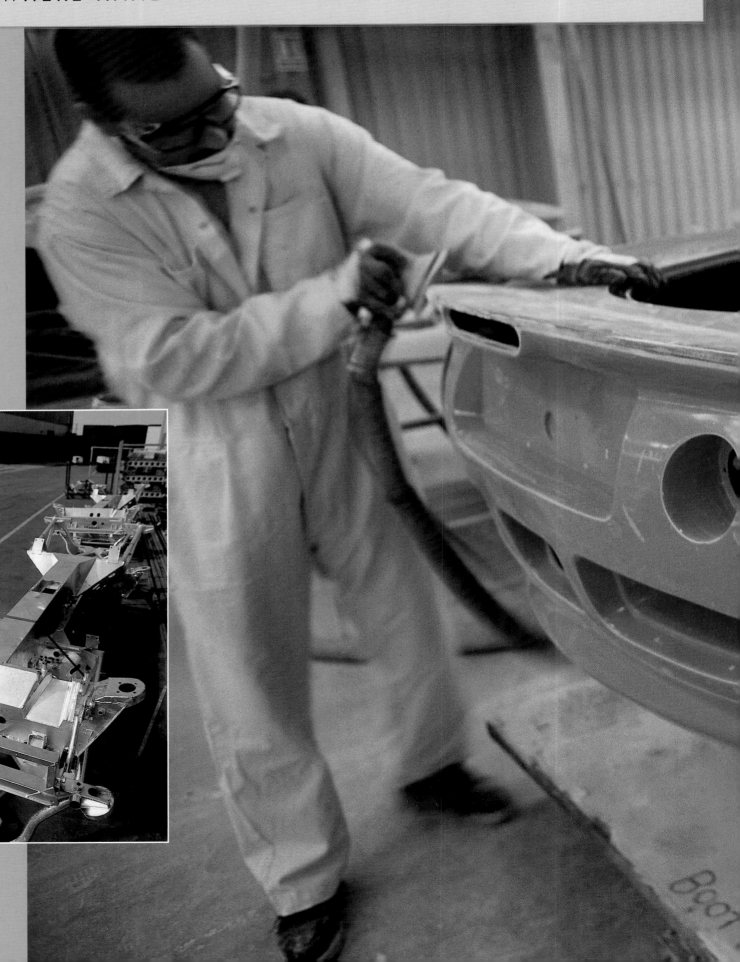

LOTUS CARS LIMITED
WHERE HAND MANUFACTURE STILL COUNTS

RIGHT: *The body of an Elise—still in the color of its basic material, GRP (glassfiber-reinforced polyester)—receives the finishing touch. The main work is done, however, by two robots with a powerful water jet.*

The backbone of an Elise Mark I. The sheet metal parts come from specialists from Scandinavia Nord Hydro.

228

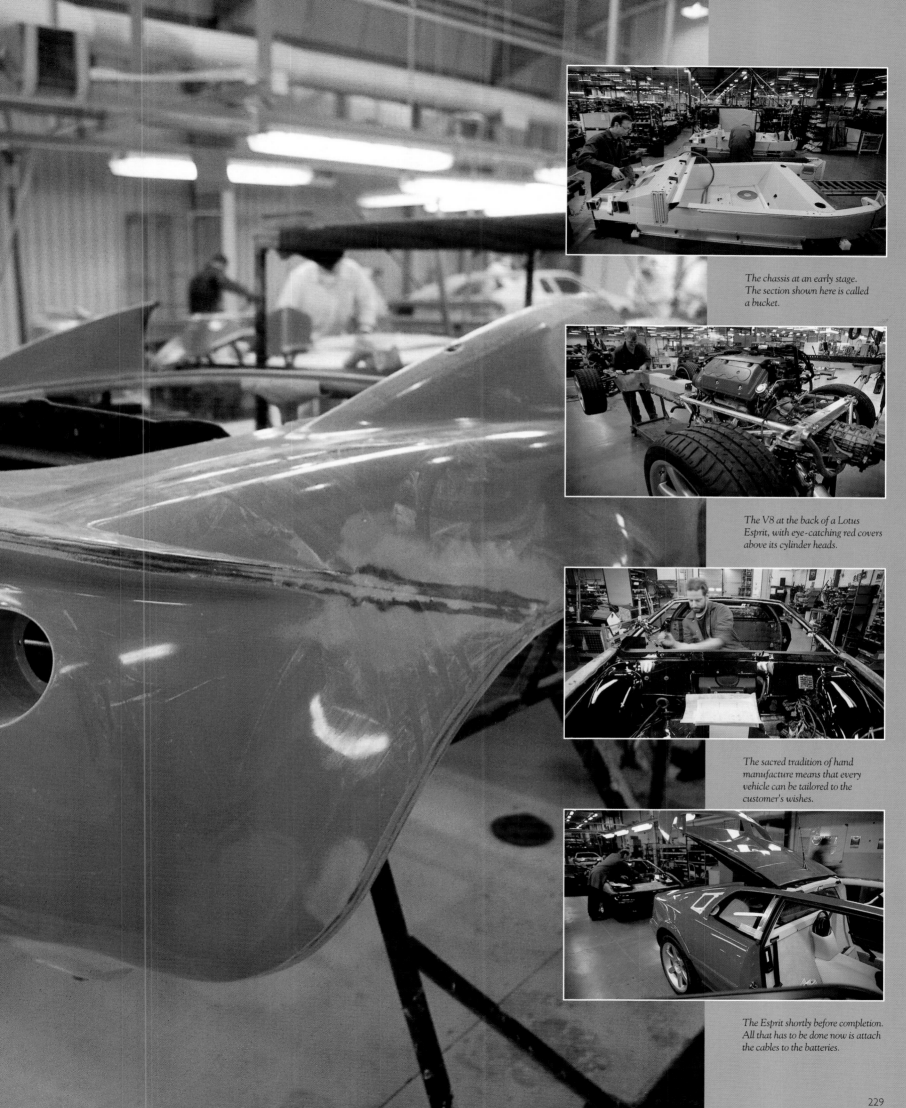

The chassis at an early stage. The section shown here is called a bucket.

The V8 at the back of a Lotus Esprit, with eye-catching red covers above its cylinder heads.

The sacred tradition of hand manufacture means that every vehicle can be tailored to the customer's wishes.

The Esprit shortly before completion. All that has to be done now is attach the cables to the batteries.

MARCOS GT

Engineer Jem Marsh and aerodynamicist Frank Costin were not people who believed in doing things by halves. Only once did they make an exception, when in 1959 they took the first three letters of their two surnames to create a word that had a pleasingly Greek ring to it.

Marcos was to be the name of a Gran Turismo with a displacement of one and a half liters. The intention was to place it in a small but receptive market niche in the manner of Colin Chapman, as a "dry Lotus Seven," as Jem Marsh described it.

The name of Marcos proved considerably more resilient than the joint venture the two men set up. Costin left the small company in Bradford-on-Avon after only the first six vehicles had been made, but not before leaving his indelible mark on the project. Formerly responsible in the 1950s for streamlined car bodies at Lotus, Lister and Vanwall, his time

working at de Havilland enabled him to draw liberally on a rich store of experience in aeronautical construction. Consequently the glassfiber body of his unusual creation was based on a semi-monocoque made of spruce and laminated wood bonded with Aerolite 300, onto which the suspension elements were directly located. This natural material lent itself well to the purpose, being sturdy, non-corrosive, water-resistant and fireproof, and was deliberately abused in the prototypes in order to prove as much.

The sheer hideousness of the first Marcos did not prevent it from enjoying a long series of sports successes, not least because future greats such as Jackie Stewart, Derek Bell, and Jonathan Palmer were to cut their teeth and win their first spurs with products of this marque. Costin's successors, Dennis and Peter, kept to the woodwork in their concept for the Model 1800 from 1964. The only difference was that

their chassis was surmounted by a still highly individual but now pleasingly shaped, broad, low fastback structure originally intended as a stopgap measure. The model designation referred to the 1780cc of its four-cylinder Volvo engine, which produced 114 bhp. It was located on a tubular steel subframe, as was the four-speed transmission with overdrive from Laycock de Normanville, and also the front suspension comprising unequal-length wishbones and coil springs. A layout at the rear similar to the De Dion configuration was finally rejected in favor of a well-located live axle with coil springs, radius arms and a Panhard rod when better-priced 1499cc and 1650cc engines from Ford came to replace the complacent Volvo unit.

The model year 1970 saw that seemingly indispensable article of faith, the wooden underbody, struck from the Marcos catechism. There had been mounting obstacles to it

The space beneath the unmistakable Marcos hunch never seemed suited to more than a long weekend break, all the more so since the tank in front and the spare wheel beneath the flat luggage compartment had their own claims to it. The sharp Kamm tail contrasts strongly with all the curves in front. Not too much reliance should be placed on the bumpers when encountering the enemy or parking in the American style. The structure of the Marcos is sturdy enough for a sunroof.

Power for the 1800 came from Volvo. The sterling four-cylinder engine from the Swedish manufacturer certainly made a sports car of the light, 1455-lb (660-kg) glassfiber coupé without needing to get het-up about racing-style engine speeds or a strained, blaring sound. The instrument panel of the GT 1800 provided all the information you could want. Since there was little width for elbows, a driving position with arms stretched to the fore was the driver's stance of choice.

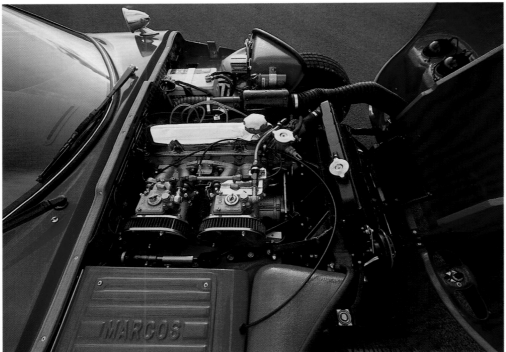

on the American market, and increasing complaints from customers that in some circumstances the Marcos was virtually irreparable after an accident. The Adams Brothers came up with a frame made of square-section tubes weighing just 132 lb (60 kg), over which the coupé's polyester jacket could be slipped and attached at 47 points. This simultaneously brought a saving of 15 working hours in the manufacture of each car.

Chassis and bodywork remained the constants, while tenants under the long, finely tapering hood came and went. At the London Motor Show in the fall of 1968 it was a 2994cc V6 from Ford, and a year later there followed a surprising 1996cc V4 from the same supplier. From time to time the car was even visited by the 2498cc six-cylinder in-line engine of the Triumph TR6. Another 3-liter version that came out in 1970 proved to be a bestseller with a run of 250: its front end housed a voluminous, weighty Volvo engine of the same ilk that harnessed 130 well-trained bhp. Although it made the Marcos distinctly nose-heavy, no objections were made to its introduction to the USA, unlike the various

Ford power plants whose attempts at US naturalization were thwarted by ever-tightening regulations on safety and emissions.

Ultimately Marcos was to meet the same fate, just when the company had decided to move, lock, stock and barrel from Bradford-on-Avon to a new production center in nearby Westbury. The order books were full. Between six and ten units could—so it seemed—be readied for the road each week, but the relocation process interrupted production for too long, in addition to which came problems with the North American importer. Then, for a variety of other reasons, the market there began to crumble. In 1972 Marcos Cars Ltd closed the gates which had seen 780 Marcos GTs roll through them over the years.

But anyone who knew Jem Marsh realized that he was unlikely to retire with the slippers and pipe brigade.

MARCOS MANTARA

The connecting link between the Marcos Mantula, Mantara, and Mantis models was not merely the consistency in the opening four letters of their names. They also progressively departed from Dennis Adams's original design for the Model 1800 in 1964. The visual gains were certainly not achieved by refining a classic-based form. On the contrary, the Marcos models of the 1980s and 1990s tended toward aggressive machismo, as was also reflected in their increasingly lavish power units.

After the closure of the small company in Westbury, Jem Marsh saw chiefly to the maintenance, care, and restoration of the existing Marcos cars. However, he was not one to remain satisfied by simply looking in the rearview mirror. In 1976 he reacquired the rights to the name and the molds, and in 1981 he stoked the marque out of its slumber.

A first milestone came in 1984 with the Mantula, which had sold around 320 examples by 1992 (20 fully assembled models and some 300 as kits).

The power plant was supplied by Rover: the compact aluminum 3.5-liter V8, also put to work in the Morgan Plus 8, was a gift from the gods to the British sports car industry—as William Kimberley so admiringly put it in the September 1993 issue of the flag-waving publication *British Cars*. It gave the Marcos such propulsion that the front section had to be reworked to contend with lift experienced at high velocity. *Autocar* magazine, for instance, recorded a top speed of 137.3 mph (221 kph) in its March 1987 issue. The year before that Marsh had placed a Spyder beside the coupé. Both versions underwent a thorough revision in 1989, when 7-inch (178-mm) wide wheels were installed with

independent suspension based on double wishbones and inboard disc brakes. In turn this produced more luggage space—mockers suggested this reflected the personal interests of the company boss, who had recently taken up golf and wanted to transport a full set of equipment. By now the car came with a 3.9-liter engine, but that did not prevent a 2-liter version from appearing in 1990 in order to avoid the harsh Italian taxes imposed on cars with larger cylinder displacements.

The title of the report in *British Cars* mentioned above was "Evolution by Design," and it focused on the Mantara, which replaced the Mantula in 1993. The author felt that it was bound to put off the purists as a result of the rampant growth of its fenders, deep cutaway engine hood, and the abolition of the Perspex covers over the twin headlights,

One look at the face of the Marcos Mantara Spyder is enough to show that this car is not to be played with. It belongs to the tradition of surly muscle cars once established by the AC Cobra and Chevrolet Corvette. Bumps and bulges on every surface—all convex, mark you—testify to a bodybuilding course designed for sheer machismo.

The Rover V8 beneath the enormous hood ensures that the Mantara's outward appearance is not reduced to empty promises and hollow threats. There is no need for it to be revved to astronomical heights; thanks to its massive torque it does its work with a metaphorical flick of the wrist. The vast performance is also announced by the sound of the exhaust.

which had been reduced to an optional extra. But sitting inside it was akin to being a Frankfurter in a hot-dog bun, bedded down between the enveloping door linings and the juicy transmission tunnel. And that was vital, even when driving the weaker of the two engines on offer, with its 4-liter displacement, catalytic converter and 190 bhp output. The seats, incidentally, were non-adjustable; instead the pedals could be moved by means of an electric motor. The stronger, less detoxified of the two power plants, developed by JE Engineering in Coventry, released all of 302 bhp from its 4.5 liters. This is evidently what is referred to in an advert that Marcos Cars occasionally inserted in special-interest magazines, with its enticing imperative: "Let your nearest dealer transport you to a different world."

Things evidently move fast in this promised new world: with astonishing exactitude, the factory gave the time for the accelerative spurt to 60 mph (up to 100 kph) as a mere 4.65 seconds. This was in fact bettered by the Mantara LM500, which had a 5-liter engine based on the Rover V8 delivering 420 bhp, unveiled at the 1993 Motor Show.

By 1995 the LM600 model was spurred on to its exceptional performance by a 6-liter Chevy V8 engine. This muscle-packed Marcos allowed Chris Hodgetts to come away with the UK GT title that year, and the company to try its luck once more at Le Mans after a break of three decades.

At the same time, the 180-odd Mantara buyers up till 1998 formed an exclusive minority with a marked sense of their own identity, not to mention a streak of fanaticism. Their relationship to their cars made it easy for them to view these four-wheeled friends almost as kindred spirits, and this is even encouraged by the Marcos designations.

The successor to the Mantara was called the Mantis, armed with a 4.6-liter V8 from Ford that delivered 325 bhp and over 155 mph (250 kph)—that could even be further increased by a turbocharger.

The dictionary entry for the word Mantis provides not only the famed praying insect, a member of the *Mantidae* family, but interestingly also describes "a person who enters an oracular state of religious madness."

The back curves up like a duck's tail feathers—a greeting from the Marcos of the 1960s and from the Mantula. Not too much luggage space can be expected here. Driver's seat and steering wheel are immovable, so the correct position has to be achieved by adjusting the pedals by electric motor.

Designer Leigh Adams equipped the Marcos Mantis with more curves and bulges than the Michelin Man, taking motifs to the extreme that had already been touched on in the Mantara. Occasionally this leads to forms that fail to follow function, which are merely decorative: although the side air inlets before the rear wheels are made of carbon fiber, they are simply there for adornment.

The horizontally placed radiator inhales its life-giving air through the Mantis's nose and exhales it through two enormous outlets in the engine hood. The wing mounted on the trunk lid is not part of the standard fittings and is aerodynamically unnecessary, but does add to the Mantis's virile appeal.

McLAREN F1

The McLaren F1 is a superlative, indeed the sum of hundreds of superlatives, a king among kings, and in a league with the Bugatti EB110, the Ferrari F40, and the Lamborghini Diablo—none of which are actually a patch on it.

Whereas other British sports cars manage to make a name for themselves despite coming from poor homes, the McLaren is what it is because it comes from a rich one. After all, it costs £540,000 (US $873,000)—more than the sum of all its English classmates. It is no surprise then that this acted as a form of natural selection among potential customers. A pre-selection process was already created by the time and place set for the presentation: the distinguished Country Club in Monaco on the Thursday before the 1992 Grand Prix.

The sensation was programmed from the very start. Taking this as his agenda, McLaren boss Ron Dennis, in consultation with his partner Mansour Ojjeh, engaged the former Brabham constructor Gordon Murray. The mustachioed South African was the mind behind such strokes of genius as the "vacuum cleaner" BT46B—which in 1978 set the track victoriously ablaze for Niki Lauda in the

Swedish Grand Prix—and the BT52, Nelson Piquet's World Championship wheels in 1983. Money was not an obstacle—Murray didn't have to give a moment's thought about the costs of the McLaren F1 project.

His task was to develop the overall concept, while styling details were seen to by Peter Stevens, who joined the roster with a successful track record at Lotus and JaguarSport. Formula One was the constant force behind the principles, materials and procedures involved. The monocoque was made of carbon fiber, the black gold of a new *fin de siècle*, with sandwich-like inserts made of aluminum and Nomex. It seems to have been made for all eternity: a collision at 31 mph (50 kph) leaves the adamantine passenger cell unscathed. The maltreated test vehicle could even have been driven back from the factory in Woking, Surrey. Downforce is not produced by visually off-putting wings, but by the ground effects created by a flat floor terminating in a diffuser.

Undiluted racing car technology was also manifested in the suspension; twin wishbones all round with inboard spring shocks that were activated by pushrods and rocker arms,

pivoted at the front on an aluminum subframe, and at the rear on the transaxle, which is supported on the rear extensions of the body structure.

One of the goals that Murray set himself was a dry weight 2205 lb (1000 kg). On the way there he haggled over every pound, such as when he refused a 37.5-lb (17-kg) CD stereo system offered by Kenwood, only accepting it once it had been slimmed down to half its weight. The finished vehicle weighed more than 2500 lbs (1134 kg), but that could be made up for by the ebullient engine performance.

The F1 had to have 550 bhp, according to another of Murray's parameters. His search for this proved successful when he turned to BMW Motorsport GmbH, a trusty partner since the six-year-long joint venture between Brabham and BMW that began in 1982. The V12, with a displacement of 6.1 liters, and 48 valves, was only 23 inches (600 mm) in length and 586 lb (266 kg) in weight; his old friend Paul Rosche pulled it out of his sleeve in the twinkling of an eye, and it cranked out 627 bhp. It was coupled with a short, light, transverse six-speed transmission, hand-operated in the good old style. The nit-picking attention that went into the details of the F1 was lavished, for instance, on its cunningly operated detoxifying exhaust unit with four catalytic converters. Simultaneously, it served as a deformable element in the rear impact protection system, a clever move given the enormous

Brembo brake discs that filled out the 17-inch (432-mm) magnesium wheel rims. A step on the center pedal raises a small spoiler that serves a dual purpose: the center of aerodynamic pressure is shifted backwards, while simultaneously two ducts are uncovered that suck in cold air to cool the rear brakes.

The McLaren F1 is just the vehicle for a happy *ménage à trois*, because three occupants can sit in it side by side. The two corner seats are considerably easier to reach than the driver's center seat once the massive gullwing doors have been opened. It requires great dexterity and a choreographic routine that takes two pages to describe in the F1's beautiful handbook. The personality of this extraordinary car would require more than two pages, though, to do justice to its Janus nature: peaceable purring compliance in town traffic and roaring impetuousness on its happy racetrack hunting grounds, as demonstrated by its 1995 victory at Le Mans. Its acceleration of 6.3 seconds from 0 to 100 mph (up to 160 kph) is more than a passenger can be expected to comfortably take, and its top speed disappears at 231 mph (350 kph) in the dark mists of the scarcely feasible.

Not even its fathers are always a match for it: Ron Dennis and BMW chairman Bernd Pischetsrieder had both managed to trash one by early 1998 as a result of obvious driving errors.

The inviting wing-like doors of the McLaren F1 are not there by chance. Gordon Murray and his team first created a wooden dummy with a central seat and filmed different-sized employees entering and exiting before settling on the final form. Even very tall travelers—each vehicle was in any case tailor-made—find optimal proportions inside. Honor where honor is due: the pilot sits slightly further forward than the two side passengers.

The high-placed rearview mirror is equipped with integral warning lights. The OZ wheels of the F1, through which the multi-perforated brake discs are visible, weigh all of 22 lb (10 kg). The roof inlet crosses down to the back and scoops air to the compact V12 motor. The inscriptions on the cylinder head cover bear testament to the joint McLaren/BMW venture.

MG J2

The MG Midget J2 looked so accomplished and so timelessly attractive that it determined the shape and philosophy of the marque's twin-seaters up till 1955, and for a long time actually colored the cliché of what a British sports car should look like. Things couldn't go quick enough for Cecil Kimber, the one-time general manager of Morris's distributor in Oxford, who in 1923 brought the first MG (standing for Morris Garages) into the world, and then became the wilful director when in 1929 the company moved to Abingdon-on-Thames, Oxfordshire.

When finally he dropped the veils on the speedy little Midget in 1932, he did so prematurely in August, and not at the London Motor Show in the fall, as tradition demands. Naturally the J2 was not simply produced in the twinkling of an eye, and was rather the culmination of an evolutionary chain. But anyone wishing to take a closer look at the links must first acclimatize themselves to the merry confusion of letters that fill the MG chronicles. There is the M-Type from 1928, a mere 1102 lb (500 kg) in weight with its twin-seat, fabric-covered—later steel—bodies, which were purchased at six pounds a piece from specialists Carbodies of Coventry. Its engine, with the modest capacity of 847cc, borrowed from the Morris Minor and kept in good spirits by thermosyphon cooling, is a small technological treat, because each of its overhead cams is kept in motion by a bevel gear. With 20 bhp, and later 27 bhp, it egged the car on to 60 mph-plus (over 100 kph), at a very considerate consumption of 35 to 40 miles per gallon. The exhibit at the MG stand at the 1928 London Motor Show in Olympia was the first of a long series of 8500 Midgets up till 1937.

1931 saw the successor model, the C-Type, with a punchy 746cc short-stroke engine that produced 52 bhp (with Powerplus compressor), and 44 bhp when normally aspirated. The tubes of the box-section frame run beneath the rear axle, as was also the case with the 250 D-Types produced from 1932, whose wheelbase was extended from 81 to 86 inches (2060 to 2180 mm). The spoked wheels, with their decorative center-lock hubs, were located on live axles with semi-elliptic leaf-springs at front and rear.

This chassis marks almost the entire extent of the similarities between these newer models and the J2, which was to go on to a total run of 2083 and continue to stir the desires of lively youngsters until 1934.

The price of £199 and 10 shillings marked the beginning of a friendship with an engaging motor whose shape revealed the influences of the company's wide-scale racing activities. Distinctive details included: firmly installed cycle-type wings (although a year later the car was to be adorned with running boards and elegant swept fenders at the rear), the folding front windshield, the twin humps over the dash, and the deep cutaway doors just waiting for a casually draped arm. Then there was the obtusely sloping tail with external 60-liter tank surmounted by the spare wheel.

One curiosity was that it was called a Le Mans tank, although J2s never raced at the course in Sarthes. It stored the lifeblood for the larger of the two engines, which had a reworked cylinder head: intake and exhaust valves, once neighbors, were now placed opposite each other, allowing the 36 strapping bhp to be fed by two SU carburetors. The MG F-Type of 1931 needed all of 1271cc and six cylinders for the same performance.

The J2 proved itself equally on the roads and on the racetrack, and even served as a police car: the Lancashire Constabulary, for instance, ordered six of them for their vigilant officers. It was a member of a small family that also included the J1 as an open four-seater and salonette, along with the J3 and J4 as compressor versions with different tuning levels, all based on the $^3/_4$-liter engine. But together they only made up 424 of a total J population of 2507.

Cecil Kimber stipulated one particular parameter to his employees and the head of the experimental department, Reg Jackson, when coming up with the concept for the J2: the new car had to be able to reach a top speed of 80 mph (129 kph) before it could be handed over to the highly esteemed magazine *The Autocar* for testing. Fact is, the author and racing driver responsible for testing, Sammy Davis, managed to get it up to 82 mph (132 kph). A couple of days later the crankshaft snapped and it was decided at MG to lower the compression and thus raise the life expectancy of the small four-cylinder engine. The result was that letters of complaint from disappointed customers kept coming in for months after: their J2s only managed 70 mph (113 kph)—no more in fact than today's current top speed limit in the United Kingdom. But an impressive speed nonetheless, especially with the front windshield folded down.

The radiator cap on this J2 from 1934 sports a thermometer specially made for it in the USA, in which a liquid column clearly shows the driver cold, medium and dangerous areas—a popular safety measure at the time.

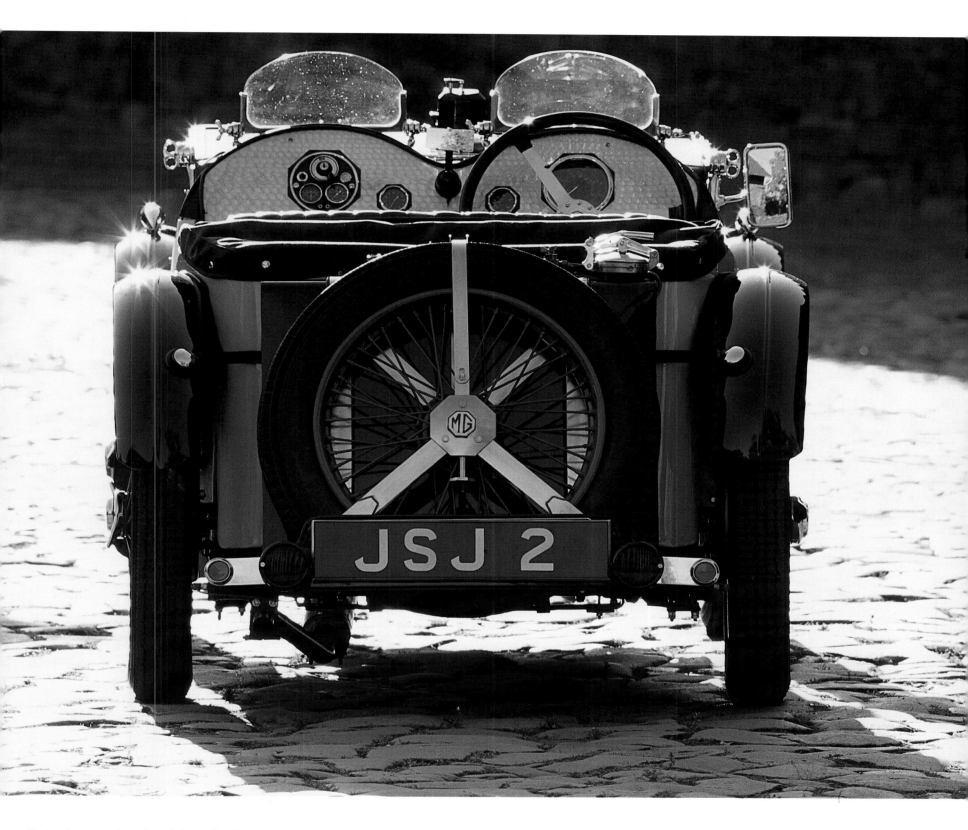

The large instrument clusters beneath the two Brooklands Aero racing windows are astonishingly versatile: the right for speedometer, trip and overall mileage recorders, and tachometer; the left for ignition, light switch, ignition lamp, ammeter, and oil pressure gauge. Plenty of scope for the occasional malfunction!

The tank cap and the system for operating the reserve tank are located directly next to each other. This logical set-up ensures that the J2 pilot never runs out of petrol.

M G

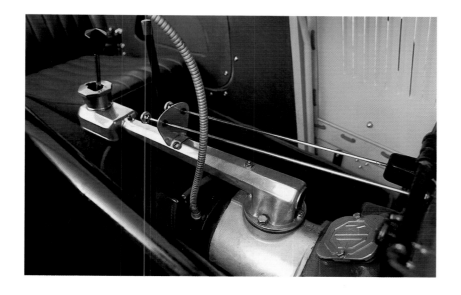

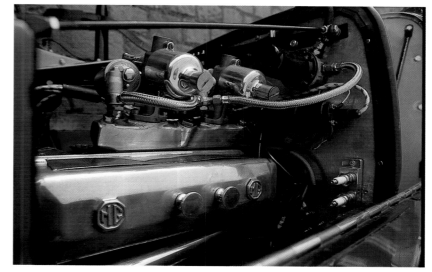

The symbol of MG, the octagon, can be found in every nook and cranny, even for structural purposes, as in the massive rod here that links the exposed stick shift with the switchgear. The thin rods above regulate the idle mixture and the choke.

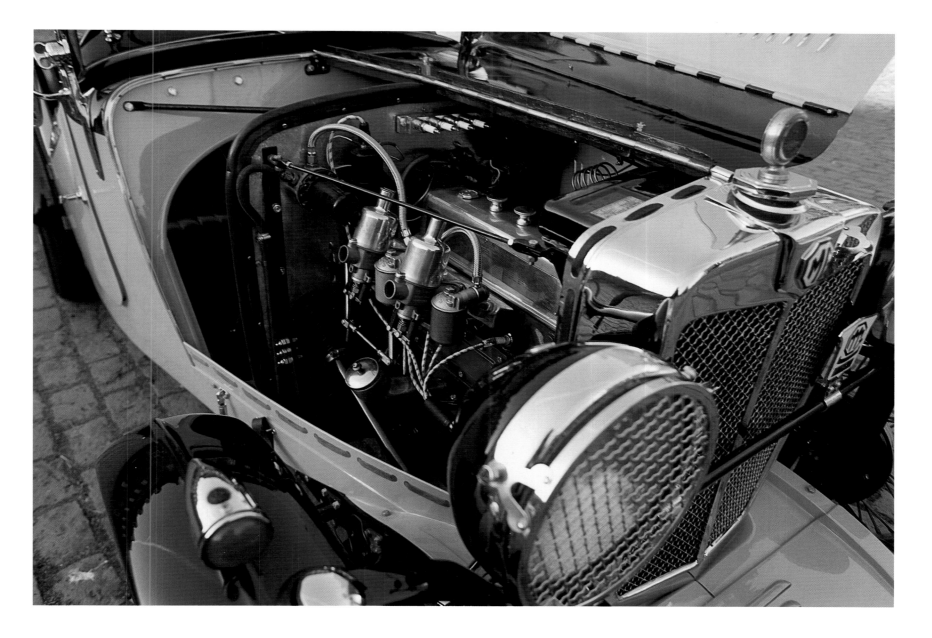

This is an MG PA from 1935, and below is its 847cc engine with overhead cam driven by bevel gear. The badge above the license plate shows that it is number 214 in the Triple M Register, an administrative body set up in 1961 by the British MG Car Club to keep records on pre-war Midgets, Magnas and Magnettes and provide assistance.

MG TA

A bit larger and more grown-up than its Midget ancestor, the MG TA of the mid-1930s founded a long succession of successful T-model generations, right up to the TF. Its top speed of 78 mph (125 kph) may not be particularly exciting, yet it was able to notch up a good many racing successes, above all in trials, where the Cream Crackers—six TAs tuned by the factory and entrusted to the works drivers on a leasing basis—won the much sought-after team award.

At a time when the name MG had become synonymous with the term sports car, personnel shake-ups and reshuffles at the proud small works saw those at the bottom of the pile suddenly rise to the top. On July 1, 1935 William Richard Morris, made Baron Nuffield the year before, sold his MG Car Company Ltd to Morris Motors Ltd. Leonard Lord, governor of Morris, took over command in Abingdon, while Cecil Kimber was unexpectedly toppled to second place as managing director. This was anything but to his liking: his creativity and initiative had flourished from the personal freedom he had enjoyed, and with Lord he had a cool technocrat before him—a writer of prose, not poetry. The cautious co-operation between the two lasted only a short

while: in 1936 Lord put in for a hefty pay rise, only to be fired and replaced by Oliver Boden.

Lord's first step in Abingdon had been to axe the racing department. What formerly was an article of faith for the company was dismissed by him as costly nonsense.

This was followed by such technical extravagances as overhead cams falling victim to his calculations. A typical MG product after the turn-around was the Type SA, also known as the 2-liter—even though the six-cylinder engine under its long hood produced its lithe 73 bhp from a displacement of 2.3 liters. Its valves were driven by pushrods and rocker arms, while the two SU carburetors received their fuel from twin electric pumps of the same make.

The top three gears were already synchronized. Hydraulic shock absorbers to the back and the front likewise pointed to the future, and if the need should arise, the SA—the MG model which with 123 inches (3120 mm) had the longest wheelbase to date—could raise itself up on its own integrated jack. With a strapping 3307-lb (1500-kg) curb weight, it tended to be rather mild-mannered, but could nevertheless clock up 84 mph (135 kph) after a lengthy run-up. Although it had a serious rival in the form of the Jaguar SS 100, by the year 1939 2738 units had rolled out of the small town on the banks of the Thames—as four-seat sports saloons, tourers, and convertibles.

A lot of innovations, such as the hydraulic brakes and a synchromesh transmission in the later models, also found their way into the Midget TA, the successor to the PB, which from mid-1936 was brought to an exceptionally receptive audience in a run of 3003.

One of the most popular and successful small sports cars ever to be offered, it rejoiced under the name *The Light Car*—indeed a worthy appellation. The TA was a lot larger that the marque's previous Midgets, a roomy twin-seater with a 95-inch (2400-mm) wheelbase, more luggage room, and a larger tank. It was almost in danger of poaching sales of the N-Type Magnette, which came further up MG's hierarchy, and which gave similar performance with its six small cylinders. But at £280 it cost considerably more than the £222 of its very reasonably priced rival from the same firm.

The TA was not altogether welcome among purists accustomed to the compact dimensions and lively, responsive engines of its overhead-cam predecessors. The TA engine, which has pushrods and overhead valves, is bland fare by comparison, and the original exhaust unit soon had to be altered: it was simply too quiet for most customers.

Its strengths also proved to be its weaknesses, some of which were echoed in a report by MG employee Reg Jackson, after taking a TA to a dealer in Manchester. During the first half of the trip he thought he would never get accustomed to the car. But on his arrival he said to himself: "Jackson, you've never had a less tiring journey." The reason was the surprising level of comfort afforded by the new car, where its predecessors had virtually beaten their passengers black and blue.

The purists were incensed by the TA, holding the dreary colorlessness of its pushrod engine against it, not to mention its extra 100 lb (around 50 kg) on the scales, its soft suspension, and the fact that it didn't move as crisply or as swiftly as a J2 or PB—preferred at trials on account of their short gearing. MG responded as best it could to all these criticisms: the exhaust system was altered, for instance, to restore the familiar gutsy sound. In the spring of 1939 the Midget was given the short-stroke, four-cylinder 1250cc engine from the Morris Ten M-series, which was able to get up to a top engine speed of 5200 rpm thanks not least to its well-balanced crankshaft. These and other changes also justified a new name—the TB. But as the threat of war drew over the world in the fall of that year, its production came to no more than 379. The TB was, however, to be resurrected after the war as the TC.

For the time being the staff at MG kept their heads above water by taking on occasional contracts—one of them produced frying pans for a local military depot.

Chassis and suspension have scarcely been changed and are in line with the customs of the day: rigid axles, semi-elliptical leaf springs, and friction dampers with Lockheed drum brakes 8 inches (207 mm) in diameter. The new Midget is, however, gentler on its human load than its predecessors – a further bone of contention among the "hardness fundamentalists."

MG TC

Everything spoke against buying one. The MG TC did not even remotely have the qualities of the PB from which it was descended. It was as small and uncomfortable as an artist's garret, only available with right-hand drive, and was as angular as a shoe-box on its thin, spindly spoke wheels. Its antique under-slung box-type frame with rigid axles—even at the front—and semi-elliptic leaf springs that twisted and turned as if made of thin plastic, were an affront to everyone who expected considerate treatment from their car.

There was never a heater. Instead, the two occupants had to provide mutual warmth within the close confines of the cockpit, which at best was a welcome excuse for loving couples—or those intent on becoming that. At any rate, occupants were virtually unprotected from the elements. Together with the wind blast from the front, the high-revving engine thwarted any attempt at genuine dialogue between occupants.

Since avoiding accidents altogether was perhaps the only safety policy, a search for a bumper proved fruitless. In the chief export country, the USA, owners were generally left to see to the maintenance, servicing, and repairs themselves, and often experienced the humiliation of being left standing by common or garden limousines containing families of five, even though they themselves were sitting at the wheel of an exciting sports car. The test car placed at the disposal of the British magazine *The Motor* deigned to claim a top speed of 78 mph (125 kph) when the windshield was down, and a torturous 21.1 seconds to reach 60 mph (100 kph). But the writer was able to find a convenient excuse for this: the miserable quality of the available petrol—a dubious, watery, low-octane cocktail. To cap it all, this stuff remained rationed until June 1950.

And yet there was no better prophylactic against the post-war blues than precisely this hard-as-a-board Midget.

Founding father Cecil Kimber was to build on the enduring charms of nostalgia and bygone days in a clever advertising campaign, featuring, for instance, a dapper Royal Air Force pilot looking wistfully at a neat little fighter plane and saying: "That reminds me of my MG." Kimber packed his bags in November 1941 on account of deep-rooted differences with the directorship of the Nuffield Group.

But his message lived on, and thus in October 1945, five weeks after the end of the war was officially declared, the MG Car Company announced a return to business while others moped over the time needed to hatch their bold new dreams. In Abingdon, just a few miles from the university town of Oxford, a quick decision was made to revamp the TB of 1939 by giving it a few touches to the chassis and body—the passenger cell was widened by 4 inches (102 mm)—and let it rise again as the TC, albeit just in one corner of the machine hall, as it were, and strictly as a "monoculture" until MG was back in pocket again.

This stopgap solution was almost an instant success; 81 units were completed by the end of the year, and over 1500 in 1946. By the time production petered out in 1949, a total of 10,000 MG TCs were scattered around the four corners of the world, driving along dusty unmade roads; 3408 of them had stayed at home, however, even though the internal market had been practically closed by the Minister of Economic Affairs, Sir Stafford Cripps. The other 6592 were exported, 2001 of them to the United States.

It would be hard to estimate the trail-blazing, missionary work accomplished by this patriarchal export object: it founded the Americans' penchant for this species of cute European sports car *per se*, and democratized the racing scene, which previously had been an exclusive preserve from the ground up.

Naturally, calls soon came for more power, which Abingdon responded to with word, deed and even a tuning kit. The modest four-cylinder engine produced up to 97.5 bhp when given a little help from a compressor. Such heroes of the heavy foot as Briggs Cunningham, John Fitch, and Phil Hill drifted inside the TCs to their laurels, and Clark Gable would take his for a spin around Hollywood and the environs, and flash his famous seductive smile from behind the car's voluminous wheel.

Back home, however, in the land from which it came and which it fitted like no other, a young naval officer would arrive from time to time at his girlfriend's home in his MG TC and take her on a trip to the countryside. The family concerned felt rather uncomfortable about this for several reasons. After all, Elizabeth Windsor was one day to become Queen of Great Britain.

The TC has a number of keepsakes from pre-war days, such as the chopped tail, tall, thin wheels, and the long, sweeping front fenders. The convertible top with its spectacle-like rear windows and detachable sides spares the passengers the worst of the weather without making the slightest inroads into the lines of the gritty roadster. Useful luggage space can be found behind the seat.

The two SU carburetors slurp their life-giving air through a large filter that, like other external parts of the engine equipment, is placed up high, keeping it out of the path of road dirt and water. The fact that the speedometer and tachometer are far away from one another demonstrates a love of symmetry rather than practical-mindedness. One thing the TC does not lack is a sufficiency of indications as to its identity.

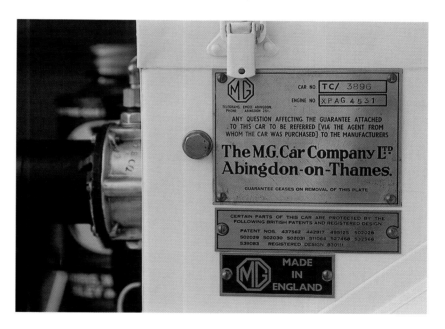

MG TD

Early in summer 1949, the managers of the MG Car Company held a meeting that was to set the course for things to come. It was chaired by Jack Tatlow, former Riley employee and the new boss at MG, who every day covered the 60 miles (100 km) from his home in Coventry to Abingdon without so much as a grumble—indeed, with a growing passion. The only point on the agenda was the request from the North American dealers for a future two-seater, half conservative and half innovative, a TC, as it were, that had attended obedience classes.

The US market was of vital importance. The models up till then had already established a bridgehead there that would allow a minor MG invasion. The new concept was only two weeks in the making and did not cost a jot. Time-tested elements would be blended together—from the TC along with a couple of ingredients from the compact and comfy MG Y limousine of 1947. The latter provided the chassis, although the wheelbase was reduced by 5 inches (127 mm) to 94 inches (2388 mm), and the side pillars of the box-type frame were bent over the rear axle to allow better ground clearance. Disc wheels, only perforated later in the model's career, replaced the spoke wheels. In keeping with the small tourer, the suspension consisted of double wishbones with coils at the front, and according to established tradition, a rigid axle with semi-elliptical leaf springs at the rear. The introduction of rack-and-pinion steering not only allowed the new vehicle to be controlled more precisely, but also the steering wheel to be transferred to the left with considerably more ease: 90 percent of the 29,664 MG TDs made between October 3, 1949 and August 17, 1953 were left-hand drive.

The body lines corresponded by and large with those of its predecessor. Nevertheless, it also underwent some curious changes: a cockpit that was again widened by 4 inches (102 mm), the comparatively compact format of the smaller, broader wheels, the chrome bumpers front and back, all mounted to give the TD a lower-slung and beefier appearance than the spindly pre-war relic, the TC.

Set beneath its boxy engine hood was, as ever, the venerable pushrod four-cylinder engine with its painstakingly measured 54.4 bhp—honest and upright and with a whiff of indestructibility. For those who required more than enduring gentleness, particularly since the TD was 170 lb (77 kg) heavier, an additional £50 (the list price in 1950 was £569 including taxes) would bring them a Mk II version with 57.5 bhp produced by the inclusion of larger valves and SU carburetors of the H4 type, as well as a compression now raised to 8.6:1. On a good day, the car could bring itself to do 82.5 mph (133 kph), although acceleration of 21.3 seconds to 60 mph (100 kph) was little less than an exercise in the old British virtue of patience.

The reception given to the TD was divided. *The Autocar* in 1950 joyfully expressed its thanks that the latest creation from Abingdon still looked like a Midge (the widely accepted nickname for the Midget) and was not the least bit futuristic. *The Motor* was also positive, noting that as with its predecessors, the writer had taken to the TD enthusiastically, and been loathe to leave it, the difference being that now the feelings of anticipation and sorrow were all the stronger. And a brochure published by the company brightly promised the potential customer that even in the densest town traffic a journey in this MG would be a pleasure, because as soon as the road was clear one would leave everyone else standing.

Opinions were, however, far less euphoric among the hardcore enthusiasts, mostly people who already owned a TC: the TD was seen as simply lacking the necessary hardness; the disc wheels did not suit it—compared to previous Midge generations it seemed downright feminine, and it was even described as "like a matron," compared with the slim young things that adorned the covers of the illustrated weeklies.

In 1952, MG employee Syd Enever tested the response to a proposed up-to-date successor, works code EX175. But the prototype failed to curry the favor of Leonard Lord who, with the fusion that year of the Nuffield Group and the Austin Motor company to form BMC (British Motor Corporation), had become the head of MG. Lord had made the snap decision at the London Motor Show to adopt the Healey 100. Next to a rival like that, the MG TD began really to look its age: very old.

Much to the displeasure of conservative and ascetic-minded customers, the fourth scion of the MG-T family rolled up with disc wheels and was even available with left-hand drive. The front fenders had been given a slight downward curve to the front. The TD also differed from its predecessors in that it had a pair of bumpers with massive horns to defend itself against the bumps and jostles of day-to-day traffic. The incessantly gentle nature of the little roadster ensured that the passenger didn't fly into a panic and end up clutching the grab handle provided.

The easy-to-reach spare wheel sits in state on the slab tank outside, which is closed at top-left by a snap-on lid. If desired, the TD could sport yet another wheel at extra price. The lack of a luggage compartment has been alleviated here by the addition of a luggage rack. As a concession to the important North American market, the model has an oil-bath air filter atop its trusty engine.

MG TF

With time, manager John Thornley's complaints to Leonard Lord, boss of MG's parent BMC, became increasingly urgent: they had to go with the times and develop a sports car with a dashing, modern streamlined shape that would almost do honor to the company slogan of "Safety fast." But repeatedly, the petitioner was brusquely brushed aside with the comment that within the multi-faceted combination of companies, with its endless brands and models, MG was to remain the custodian of the classic line.

This policy nearly proved fatal for the men at Abingdon: the export figures for the TD plunged within 12 months to half the volume of the previous year. MG itself began to smell of antiquated business methods, as the guardians of an eternal automotive past.

Thankfully, the company managed to wriggle its way out of this predicament and saw the Midget through fresh therapy that was to completely justify the inclusion of the F in the MG alphabet. The hood was more powerfully raked. The heavy chrome radiator grill faced the oncoming wind at an angle. The front headlights were semi-integrated into the bodywork. The fenders swept out further to the sides than its predecessor's, which the TF outdoes by 4 inches (100 mm) in length while conceding 0.6 inches (16 mm) to it in height.

A frequently expressed wish for the option of spoke wheels was granted after making the necessary changes to the wheel hubs. The time-honored bench seat was replaced by bucket seats. As for the three large instruments tucked beneath the valley between the two striking humps facing the driver and passenger, Thornley's detail designers managed to make a virtue of the conservatism ordained from above. In keeping with a hoary old tradition and analogous to the company logo, they were given an octagonal shape.

But beneath this reworked exterior things remained much as before: independent suspension at the front using unequal-length wishbones and coil springs, and a rigid axle with semi-elliptical leaf springs at the rear. Crouching on the beams of the box-type frame was the so-called competition engine from the TD Mk II, with 1250cc capacity and 57.5 bhp output. A new reduction in final drive ratio saw to it that the engine would be unwilling to exceed 5500 revolutions of the crankshaft per minute in any of the four gears.

In the fall of 1953, the MG TF was submitted to the gaze of the London Motor Show visitors. Its acceptance among the fourth estate depended largely on whether the journalist in question was of a progressive or a nostalgo-conservationist cast of mind: "Mrs Casey's dead cat slightly warmed over," railed Tom McCahill in the US publication *Mechanix Illustrated*, adding "… Only out of supreme arrogance would the manufacturers attempt to keep ramming this old teapot down the throats of American buyers… I personally feel the current management of MG has let me and hundreds of

Headlights integrated between the fenders and the engine, a stronger rake to the radiator grill, a lower contour to the front hood, windshield wipers that have disappeared from view, and a racy outward-curving tail—and with that an aging concept that has been given a new lease of life. The bulges above the instrument panel are covered in leather, and the dials—shaped like MG octagons—are flanked by open glove compartments.

other American MG fans down pretty hard." To make matters worse, a contemporary BMC brochure harked back to the dusty successes of the far-flung past by noting: "Remember how, way back in 1935, George Eyston's team of women drivers in MGs won the Le Mans 24 Hours race?"

The advertising obviously placed matters in a rosier light. An advert from MG dealers SH Arnolt in Chicago wrote exultantly, "New styling, new comfort, new zip, and every inch a thoroughbred!" adding, "You'll want to see, drive, own the new MG Series TF Midget." The Australian magazine *Wheels*, dating from August 1954, noted that the car had "stunning acceleration, top-gear performance and handling," and British writer Gordon Wilkins embarked on a sentimental journey to the Thames backwater of Abingdon, a place of pilgrimage for those who, like him, grew up "between the Kaiser war and the Hitler war." He wrote of how glad he was in view of the TF that everything had remained so gloriously unchanged. The paradox of this car was, for him, that one never grew old inside it, indeed, one did not even appear middle-aged.

In August 1954, George Eyston and Ken Miles managed to set a number of new records in the EX179 over long distances on the Utah salt flats. The normally aspirated engine inside the desert projectile was a slightly larger bored TF engine (with the abbreviation XPEG), which otherwise looked identical from the outside. With a displacement of 1466cc and a reduced output of 65 bhp, it was used to replace the existing engine in the last 3400 of the total run of 9600 standard production Midgets. The reason was not least due to homologation, because the old girl was still being entered for motor races: for years the MGs had been over the limit for the G Class and 250cc beneath the maximum capacity for the F Class up to 1500cc.

Far removed from all contemporary wrangles, the TF is now the most highly-sought Midget of all.

Despite all the revisions in the classicism of the TD, the identity and unmistakable character of the model series has been retained, even if some would regard these innovations as a betrayal of the pure MG doctrine. But even if tastes differ, it is hard to deny that the MG TF was the most beautiful T model to date.

There were new developments under the hood of the last 3400 MG TFs produced, even if they could not be seen: the bore of the trusty pushrod four-cylinder engine was increased from 2.6 to 3 inches (66.5 to 77 mm), giving it a capacity of 1466cc. Already at an earlier date it had had to make a small concession to the flatter silhouette by having its air filters placed on its sides.

And a welcome parting shot: as the spare wheel shows here, spokes are back, even if only as an optional offer that people were keen to take up. Not exactly easy-care compared to the disc wheels of its predecessor, they nevertheless fit harmoniously with the overall appearance of this, the last of its kind.

MGA

The name alone gives symbolic testimony to a new beginning: over its nigh-on 30 years, the MG Car Company had worked its way through all the letters of the alphabet, and now it had returned to the start. At the same time the word Midget was put on ice for the time being: its suggestions of stunted growth were no longer right for this concept.

The first appearances of the MGA superstar at the motor shows in Frankfurt, Paris, and London in 1955 also brought a long and varied story to an end. This model stemmed from early Fifties competition cars and the EX175 prototype at which Leonard Lord had turned up his nose. In June 1954 his lordship at BMC, who treated his minions at Abingdon-on-Thames

somewhat feudally, finally gave his blessing to the project, not least because with an engine and transmission sourced from the shelves of the British Motor Corporation, it complied with the head of the concern's wishes for rationalization.

By the time the MGA had begun to bask in the neon lights of the trade shows, some of the veneer of publicity it had received had already begun to flake off. Already in the June of that year, three works cars had taken part in the Le Mans 24 Hours race, all patriotically decked out in British Racing Green, a cleverly devised coup by which MG director John Thornley made his return to motor racing after many years of abstinence, and simultaneously could help the purists get over the shock of the innovation.

The beautiful garb of the MGA conceals a veritable jigsaw of components. The game starts with the roadster's pushrod engine, which was requisitioned from the BMC B-series. Fed by two SU carburetors, its 1589cc originally provided 68 bhp, and slightly later 72 bhp. The stiff box-section frame with tubular crossmembers was welded together by John Thompson Motor Pressing Ltd, while the sleek bodywork—doors and hood made of light alloy—came from the old MG suppliers Morris Bodies Branch.

Soon an optional removable hardtop ensured improved creature comforts in all weathers. There was some disgust when in October 1956 the open version was presented with a closed-in version at its side, complete with wind-up windows

and panoramic wrap-around windshield and rear window. The pure roadster shape of the MG, as Reinhard Seiffert carped in 1960 in the renowned German magazine *auto motor und sport*, was positively mutilated by a fixed roof shaped like a bowler hat.

Up till 1959, the two versions winged their way, with 58,700 units, to new and quite unexpected sales records. With that the MGA 1500 took its final bow, only to reappear promptly as the MGA 1600 with 1588cc and 80 bhp. The 1600 was recognizable by its new tail lights and Girling disc brakes at the front, where the wheels were suspended on coil springs and double wishbones, while the rear with its live axle and semi-elliptic leaf springs constituted a minor variation of an old familiar theme.

The clean lines of the coupé already intimate that it is more streamlined than the original tourer. Among other elements, the strongly curved windshield and rear window have also been enlisted for aerodynamic purposes, even if at first sight they appear merely to be serving up fashionable trends. Almost the entire bodywork of the open MGA was adopted for the hardtop model, albeit with energetically revamped doors to allow the inclusion, for instance, of wind-up windows.

The door latches of the coupé are both practical and secure. When the car is at rest, they lean against the chrome frame beneath the window. The pane in the rear window would lack stability without the supports on either side. The spoke wheels only came as extras.

Some 31,501 MGA 1600s worldwide had found their way into the hearts of their owners by the time the MK II, with 1622cc and 86 bhp, stepped into its shoes in May 1961. It differed from its predecessor by its recessed radiator grill and yet again revised rear lights. With its final drive reduced from 4.3 to 4.1:1, it now whisked from 0–60 mph (up to 100 kph) in just 13.7 seconds—two prestigious seconds faster than its predecessor. By July 1962 the Mk II had notched up 8,719 sales.

The magic number of 100,000 MGAs was already surpassed in March that same year. A small but select minority among them was formed by the 2111 Twin Cams made between spring 1958 and spring 1960. The basis was the larger off-the-peg B-series engine, but in place of the lateral camshaft it had an intermediate shaft. This activated two overhead camshafts—which lent the model part of its designation—via a double roller chain. With its 97 bhp it managed to sink the 0–60 mph (up to 100 kph) time to less than 10 seconds, but for that it was pretty hard on the fuel

tank, and even demanded high-octane gasoline—by no means commonly available.

Moreover, it responded to any contravention of these demands by burning its pistons. Word quickly got out about this prima donna behavior and proved damaging to the MGA star; not even such winning qualities as disk brakes on all corners or attractive Dunlop center-locking disk wheels saved it from an untimely end. At the same time it became a much sought-after rarity, as were the 395 De Luxe models made between June 1960 and May 1962, a cross between surplus Twin Cam chassis and the normal engines from the 1600 (82 units) and the Mk II (313 units).

How times change: in the old days owning an MG was something special. Yet with the MGA the same could only be achieved by a rare specimen from an enormous production run.

As is often the case with siblings, the MGA coupé lived slightly in the shadow of its older—and more open-hearted—brother. It nevertheless remained in the program until production of the MGA as a whole was discontinued in summer 1962, and used the same engines as the open-top version.

MG MIDGET & AUSTIN-HEALEY SPRITE

They resemble one another like two peas in a pod, are in principle identical, but are nevertheless a little different: the MG Midget was regarded as a touch posher and was slightly more expensive. It can be recognized by the chrome strips on its sides and the vertical slats in its grill, while the wind whistled through the Austin-Healey Sprite via a more lowly sieve.

The twins were delivered from the same conveyor belt under the spacious umbrella of the British Motor Corporation in Abingdon. They were simply presented to the world one month apart—the Sprite in May and the Midget in June, 1961. Together they propagated the idea of a sound and solid people's sports car at an affordable price, in an enormous population of 307,059—226,526 of them with the octagonal MG signet. And one always kept a suspicious eye on the success of the other.

But these fine differences were ultimately thrown to the wind: the two names were melded until the driver was sitting behind the wheel of a "Spridget," in the same way he could enjoy an Oxbridge education.

The Spridget's domain was by no means the highway or motorway: there it would be forced to yield to every even moderately fast-driven middle-class limousine, and even aggressively-driven dwarfs like the Mini Cooper S. Instead it romped around the twisting country lanes and labyrinths of the B-roads, top down beneath a balmy blue sky, preferably hosting a courting couple.

By the early 1970s the word Spridget should have been split into its component parts. Because in much the same way as the Sprite came into the world three years earlier in the shape of the much-loved "frog-eye," it bade farewell to the roads eight years before the MG Midget. The cessation of business relations with Donald Healey in 1971 meant that his name was expunged, then once the remainder of 1022 Austin-Healey Sprites was sold, the model disappeared from the list of the hydra-headed British Leyland Motor Corporation (BLMC), which the Austin-Morris Division had belonged to since 1969.

Up till then the twins had shared their mutual joys and sufferings. The bodywork of the Spridget, which was scarcely or only gradually modified over the years, bore the signature

This portrait of the Midget seems to testify to classical stature and almost mythical greatness. And indeed, the appeal of the little roadster was great.

One doesn't need more from a car, assuming one is young or still young at heart. The 1-liter engine under the hood, which was given a lot of tender loving care, fitted the picture exactly.

of MG head designer Syd Enever. He put the headlights—their exposed position in the frog-eye was a case of one man's meat being another man's poison—back in their traditional place at the tips of the fenders, and with this return to convention brought the car to a wide audience.

He also slimmed down some of the car's inherent chubbiness, and made the luggage compartment accessible from outside—loading the Sprite Mk I from inside had demanded youthful agility and excusable enthusiasm.

At first its chassis was adopted. From October 1962 on, the front drum brakes were replaced by disc brakes, and from Mk III onwards (premiered March 1964) semi-elliptic springs checked the self-steering effect of the rigid live axle, a distinct step forwards from the previous quarter-elliptic leaf springs and twin trailing arms. At the same time, this gentle little nipper proved even more amicable thanks to a larger windshield, wind-up windows and locking door handles on its exterior.

Engine capacity and output grew from an initial 948cc and 46.5 bhp, to 1098cc and 56 bhp from October 1962 (in the Mk III, 3 bhp more), to 1275cc and 65 bhp from October 1966. While the Mk II took things fairly comfortably with a phlegmatic 0-60 mph (up to 100 kph) in 21.6 seconds and a top speed of 85 mph (137 kph), the Mk III stirred itself to 17 seconds and 93 mph (149.7 kph).

The MG Midget Mk IV, from 1972 onwards the only small roadster representing British Leyland, but already on sale since 1969, stood out by dint of its black rocker panel, improved interior appointments, and new Rostyle wheels. In 1972 its rear wheel arches were rounded off—cavalier styling of careful audacity that was to be reversed in the MK V of 1974 and after. Up till now all of the engines were mutations of the venerable BMC A-series, which had already done proud service in the Austin A30 from 1951 on. In 1974 the power plant of the concern's own internal competitor, the Triumph Spitfire, took over under the hood with 1493cc and 65 bhp, bringing its own transmission with it. This allowed something to be realized that previous generations of Spridget drivers could only dream about: the little nipper ran at 100 mph (160 kph), a welcome by-product since the choice of the Triumph machine had chiefly been made with an eye on the rigid USA emissions regulations. The flip side of this orientation to the North American market was hideous black plastic protuberances acting as dubious impact protection fore and aft, which were to mar many a European car during that period.

In 1979 the last genuine small sports car for the time being to have been designed for the working masses was dropped without replacement—an erroneous decision given the new openness that was shortly to follow…

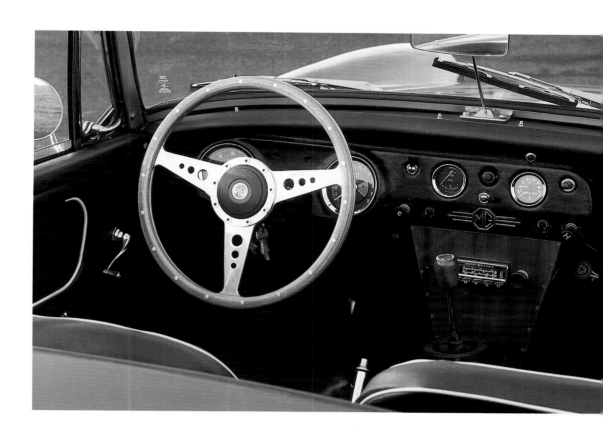

Simple and sparsely populated, the dash nicely fits the attractive sense of economy embodied by the MG Midget. The Mk II version can be recognized by a whiff of comfort, such as in the external door handles and wind-up windows. Even the Spartans sometimes indulged themselves.

MGB

Behind the short abbreviation "MGB" is a success story with stripes on it. It is doubtless good to read that the car universe in general, and MG's company statistics in particular, were enriched by 513,272 sports cars of this name. But the fact that a recipe of refined backwardness had to make do for 19 years led, in the end, to mounting complaints and diminishing sales, particularly since the MG had come to face serious competition over the years, as in the form of the Datsun 240Z. With its final demise on October 22, 1980, the model also took the traditional brand image—MG is synonymous with sports cars—with it into temporary retirement.

Already before the production of the MGA went into the second round in 1959, its fathers at Abingdon were busy chewing over the truism: if you start something, you've got to see it through. The question of price cushioning was quickly resolved: the new car was largely to be based on the large-volume BMC daughters, Austin and Morris. Its bodywork should, like the Midget, emphasize horizontality and be of unitary construction. For a vehicle just a quarter of the normal size they took the record-breaker, the EX181, as their model: that was the vehicle in which Stirling Moss shot across the salt flats of Utah in 1957 at 245 mph (394 kph). Taking this swift, chubby flounder as their point of departure, MG designers Syd Enever and Don Hayter worked in the wind tunnel to create the ultimate roadster form that met the agenda of being timelessly pleasing, even if not being an absolute eye-catcher.

There was not much really new about it. Compared to the MGA, the wheelbase was shortened by 3 inches (77 mm) to 91 inches (2311 mm), and the living quarters were slightly reduced in size. This allowed room for a tight little dungeon behind the seats and slightly more luggage space. Only the hood still consisted of light alloy, and in place of the Perspex sliding side windows it had wind-up windows behind its glass quarter lights. The folding roof came in two comfort levels: the usual makeshift arrangement consisting of a thin plastic mac on a collapsible tubular frame, and a sturdier soft top.

The BMC B-series power plant, now bored to the limits and with a crankshaft supported initially in three, but from September 1964, five bearings, produced 95 bhp: the charm of this MG lay, as with others, not in its excessive potency. It was still only possible to slip it into first gear by accurate double-declutching—an antiquated custom that was only finally done away with in October 1967. The automatic transmission from Borg Warner that was simultaneously offered as an optional extra met with little appreciation and disappeared without a trace in September 1973. With wishbones and coils at the front, and a live axle with semi-elliptical leaf springs at the rear, the suspension was similar to its predecessor, if not identical in all points.

The MGB was launched and enthusiastically received at the London Motor Show in September 1962. And in its first full year of production—1963—its 23,308 units outstripped the entire pre-war MG production of both Oxford and Abingdon combined. In October 1965 the GT arrived as a closed-top counterpart to the roadster, complete with a few splashes of flash southern design from Pininfarina. One attraction was the practical loading hatch at the rear, which once opened was held up automatically.

In 1974 the two models, now advanced to classic status, were subjected to disfiguring surgery in order to boost their position in the USA: hefty bumpers made of black polyurethane increased their "bumpability," but spoilt their appearance, particularly since the body was simultaneously raised by 1.7 inches (45 mm) so that enemy contact would

It is hardly surprising that the MGB immediately won over the viewers at its unveiling in September 1962: clear lines, whose aesthetics would scarcely be touched by the ravages of time, and additionally its reasonable price. The apparent anachronism at the front—a pillar that seems to split the windshield in two—is in fact the rod supporting the rearview mirror. The Rostyle wheels made of pressed steel on the 1967 car shown here first became standard in 1970.

only occur at the appointed places. By this point in time a gently degenerate collateral line of the model series, the MGC, had long since died out. Built between July 1967 and September 1969 in a run of 8999, it blossomed thinly in places obscure. Distinctly nose-heavy with its weighty Austin in-line six-cylinder 3-liter engine, it stood out from the rest by the hunch on its hood, its 15-inch (381-mm) wheels (otherwise 14-inch/356-mm), and torsion bar suspension at the front.

While the MGC is a sought collector's item due to its quirky individualism, the MGB GT V8 attracts the contemporary connoisseur for different reasons. It is as rare as it is accomplished, with its soft, silky purring Rover light alloy V8, which produces 137 bhp with its 3528cc. Confusions and delusions: between April 1973 and September 1976 attempts were made with it to fill a gap in the market—one that didn't even exist! Consequently this branch of the MG family tree likewise withered away after bearing 2591 fruits, every one a coupé. And yet the V8 had been marvelous, with its 124 mph (200 kph) and its perfectly acceptable acceleration of 8.3 seconds to 60 mph (100 kph).

Access to the MGB's four-cylinder engine, and with that its care and maintenance, is considerably easier than with the MGA thanks to its much wider hood. One feature has been adopted from its predecessor in the dash: a light that makes map-reading easier at night. The horn, previously the responsibility of the front passenger, has been moved to the center of the steering wheel. The steering wheel of the roadster shown here is not part of the standard fittings.

A rarity in the guise of an MGB GT: one of the scarce Costello MGB V8s. Ken Costello took an off-the-peg coupé and squeezed a Rover V8 into the engine bay, while leaving the SU carburetors in their normal location, the dale in the V of the cylinder banks. This necessitated a sizeable bump in the hood to allow the engine extra headroom. With 150 bhp and 130 mph (210 kph), the Costello coupé was the speediest of the MGBs—making it a much wanted collector's item.

MGF

At the Birmingham Motor Show in October 1992, MG's owners, the Rover Group, launched the RV8 in order to test public reaction, while simultaneously hoping that the limited edition of 2,000 available till 1995 would whet appetites again for sports cars bearing the traditional octagonal badge. Since the exhibit—a kind of up-to-date MGB roadster—created a quite calculated *déjà vu* effect, the appearance of the MGF at the Geneva Salon in 1995 seemed like its counterpoint—it was indeed the point.

At the heart of the top technology that Rover Special Products marshaled right from 1989 for their Project MGF was the mid-engine concept—a choice item from motor racing. It gave the 154-inch (3910-mm) long vehicle a real pinch of exclusivity compared to the then competition, the front-drive Fiat Barchetta and the conventionally built Mazda MX-5. But it also became an object lesson in the famous disadvantages of this layout. The power plant butts into the passengers' conversations all the time, particularly at high revs, with its insistent, sometimes dominant tones; it bellows like a rutting stag when accelerating from idling, and at the other end of the scale deteriorates into a deafeningly vulgar four-cylinder roar. It tolerates no more than a modest luggage compartment at the rear and chews into heat-sensitive items, assuming it doesn't actually make them melt. It lulls drivers into a false sense of security when taking fast curves, until suddenly they are driving over a limit located in the realms of total uncertainty. On taking the curve too fast, stepping too hard on the gas, or removing one's foot too soon, the tail breaks away without warning, like an unexpected hook from a boxer.

Yet in other models the same light-metal four-valve engine as in the MG, which has a 1795cc displacement and two overhead camshafts and comes from the Rover K-series engine family, is a conscientious and unobtrusive worker. Squeezed sideways into a tiny compartment at the back of the passengers, from whence its 120 or 145 bhp is conveyed with VVC (variable valve control) to the rear wheels via a likewise transverse five-speed gearbox, the mild-mannered device is a rowdy one.

Little similarity can be found to earlier MG models, particularly since a large portion of the F's long period of development lies in Rover's Honda era. Although this has left little more than traces on the mechanical side, there can be no doubt that designer Gerry McGovern worked in distinctly Japanese looks. Apart from which, its somewhat unassuming shape obeys the dictates of the engine in the middle.

The rounded and remarkably short front hood conceals no more than the spare wheel and a couple of ancillary components such as the power brake and ABS units. The beefy tail, on the other hand, already shows in visual terms where the MGF's strengths lie. The car only begins to signalize sportiness behind its seats: the twin exhausts on both sides of the slit rear apron, the side air intake *à la* Ferrari, the bright and shiny tank cap, and wider wheels than those at the front (8 inches (205 mm) instead of 7 inches (185 mm)). It transmits the power of the Rover engine convincingly to the ground with a time of 8.9 seconds for 0–60 mph (up to 100 kph) and a top speed of 126 mph (203 kph). The car that

was tested by German magazine *auto motor und sport* for instance, and received a lengthy report in the January 1996 issue, outstripped the works specs by 0.3 seconds and 10 kph (6.2 mph) respectively.

The interior of the MGF is also subdued, where at most the handsomely shaped cream-colored instruments stand out amidst its all-encompassing shades of black. Ensconsed in the otherwise comfy seat, the driver sits a little too high, so headroom is restricted when the soft-top is closed or the hardtop—available as an extra—is in place. The latter leads to a tangible improvement in the little car's aerodynamics, but on poor roads it announces by means of soft groans that its superstructure is moving. The chassis proves to be surprisingly gentle on the passengers, its double wishbones front and back being damped by Hydragas hydraulic suspension using nitrogen cushions, in which front and rear units are linked with one another along each side of the car.

In 1999 the MGF was given a present to mark the company's 75th anniversary: Steptronic, an electronically-controlled continuously-variable transmission with three programs that allow finger-tip gear shifts.

MG progenitor Cecil Kimber and his successor John Thornley would have gaped in astonishment at all this wealth of innovation: there was no need in their day for fine feeling when driving an MG, it was quite simply a rough critter for rough critters. All of 57,300 customers between 1995 and 1999 allowed themselves to be convinced by the new, mild concept, and the MGF is still far from finished.

The athletic tail tells where the MGF gets its power from. While the front has turned out strangely indifferent, the tail communicates sportiness: the dual exhaust in the slit apron, the air inlets on the sides, the bright, shiny tank cap, and wheels that are 0.8 inches (20 mm) wider than at the front.

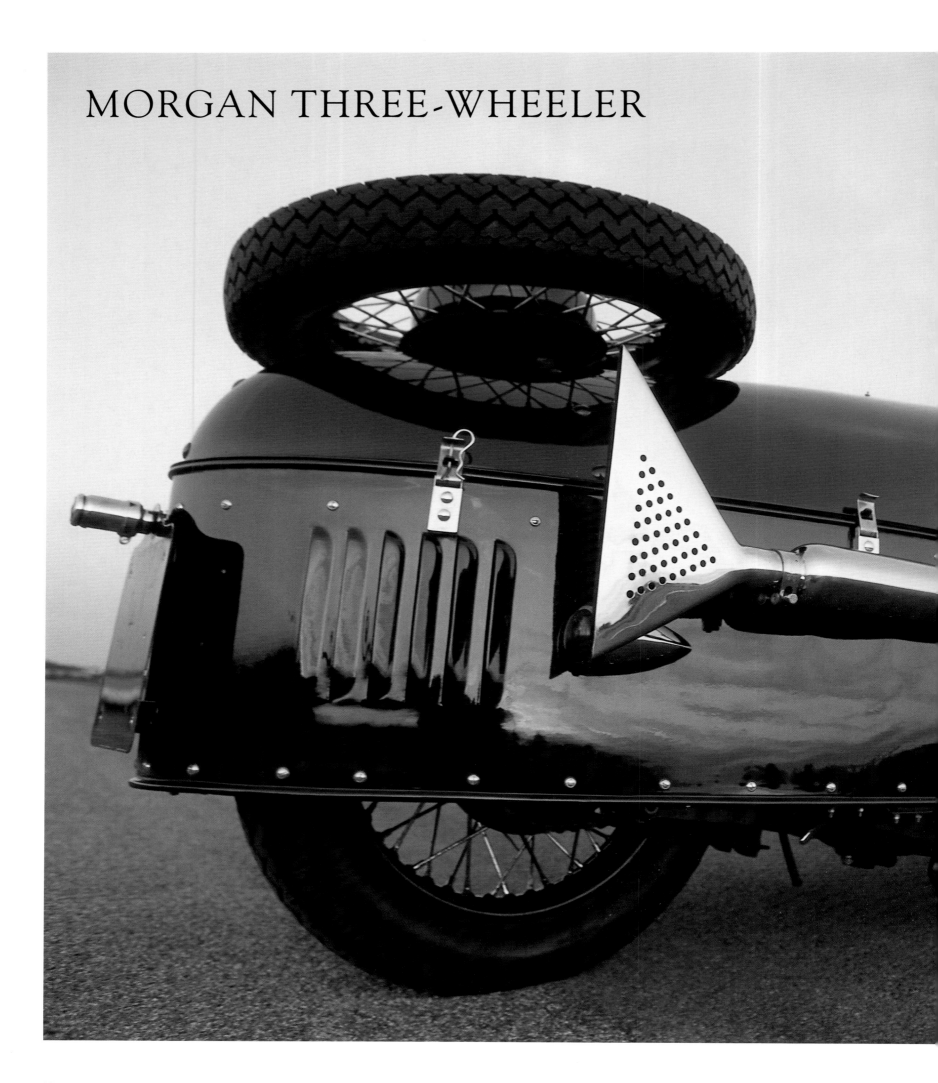

Company founder Henry Frederick Stanley Morgan was fond of declaring that a Rolls-Royce gave almost as good a ride as a Morgan. For his own personal mode of transport, H.F.S. (as this fellow, born in 1881, was frequently referred to for reasons of linguistic economy) generally made do with second-best.

The best initially took the form of a three-wheeler, 40,000 of which were produced in the 42 years between 1909 and 1951. The three-wheeler formed the basis for H.F.S.'s reputation, glory, and wealth. Like his family and the firm that bears his name, H.F.S. was self-sufficient throughout his life, never having to accept either charitable donations or high-interest loans.

The three-wheeler also laid the foundations for a company philosophy as unshakeable as the Ten Commandments. This philosophy is based on a desire to offer a lot for a little. Engineering constants such as an independent front suspension attached to vertical sliding pillars speak of a resolute rejection of rapidly changing fads. A Morgan must be light and compact. The fact that this minimal car, which weighs in at a nimble 770 lb (350 kg), also happens to be as quick as greased lightning, and therefore makes an ideal sports car, seems a mere lucky by-product.

Henry Morgan's first trike was not, however, built by him. Acquired in 1901, the pleasures of his Eagle Tandem could only be shared by means of one person sitting behind the other: the passenger, stowed in front in a wicker basket, was exposed in equal measure to the airstream, dust from the road, and the consequences of any accident. Seven years later H.F.S. built his own three-wheeler runabout—a basic, spartan hybrid between a car and a motorbike—just for fun.

Things started to get serious in 1912. H.F.S. married Hilda Ruth Day (who was to bear him six children), established the Morgan Car Company as a limited company and made his first profit of £1300. The presentation of two of his three-wheelers at the Olympia Motorcycle Show in London met with lively interest and the victory of journalist Gordon McMinnies in the Cycle Car Grand Prix in Amiens in 1913 brought a flood of enquiries, encouraged not least by a detailed account of the great event published by McMinnies himself in the magazine for which he wrote: *The Cyclecar*. The vehicle that had triumphed at Amiens was immediately brought into production as the Grand Prix model and remained in production until 1926. Its succession was taken up by the Aero and Super Sports models, whose trunks terminated in the perfectly positioned spare wheel that acted as a rear fender but could also be seen as both a symbolic crown and the emblematic feature of the series.

Above all, however, consideration was being given to the needs of drivers of limited means. In 1932, for example, the range of models extended from the Family at £95 via the

With a top speed of 81 mph (130 kph), this lively three-wheeler, a 1932 Super Sports Aero, was one of the fastest members of the three-wheeler brigade. Its spare wheel attaches either horizontally or vertically and the splayed exhaust pipe outlet shown here was just one of several available options.

The old-fashioned bulb horn adds an amusing touch to the overall appearance of this early Aero, but is perfectly dispensable: the unmistakable sound of the car's two-cylinder engine is more than enough to draw attention to its approach. Filler caps for oil and gasoline rise up from the hood. Ignition, air and hand throttle can all be regulated or operated from the big steering wheel.

Sports Family and the Sports, all the way to the Super Aero at £145. The acquisition of a Morgan (nicknamed Moggie) is almost always the start of a great love affair: "There is and always has been something altogether delightful about a Morgan… a Morgan is a Morgan and it can be compared to nothing else but another Morgan," eulogized *Light Car* magazine in 1930. This was also the year the irrepressible Gwenda Stewart broke the speed record for three-wheelers in the 1000cc class, achieving 115 mph (185 kph) over the standing-start kilometer. In front of the record-breaking vehicle's front axle rampaged a highly tuned, stark-naked JAP V2 engine, banished from beneath the protective skin of the coachwork like many other motorcycle twin engines used at various times—from manufacturers such as JAP, Anzani, and Matchless, either air or water-cooled, sometimes (in the case of the engines of Swiss manufacturer MAG) displaying four cylinder heads, and with side or overhead valves. In 1933, these engines were joined by the F-type, a Ford four-cylinder engine. This was far more civilized but less lively than its two-cylinder brothers. In the 33 bhp Family Four, it was complemented by a new pressed steel central tubular chassis with a longer wheelbase and increased track width.

Major milestones in the early history of the marque include the company moving into new premises on Pickersleigh Road in the sleepy, conservative retirement town of Malvern Link in the county of Worcestershire (1918). Brakes on all three wheels were introduced as standard in 1926; the introduction of reduction gearing for the steering in 1929, which had previously, due to its brutal directness, been a challenge even for strong men was most welcome. As were the replacement of the car's previous two gears with three, the standardization of the chassis and replacement of the cone friction clutch with leather components with a dry-plate clutch (1931).

In 1935 new tax legislation, which no longer favored the motorcycle-like three-wheeler, took the wind out of the Morgan three-wheeler's sails. In 1936, competition came along from its own manufacturer in the form of the 4/4, which, as its name indicates, boasted four wheels and four cylinders. Hereafter, the road led downhill: production shrank to 137 in 1936 and finally to 39 in 1939, the first year of the war. After 1945, production increased temporarily in response to a demand for inexpensive motor vehicles, but after waiting some considerable time for a buyer to come along, the last three-wheeler, an F Super, finally left the small factory on July 29, 1952.

During its heyday the Super Sports Aero, 40,000 of which were produced, was a common sight, but it now cuts an extremely rare and conspicuous figure on the roads, especially given the general uniformity of cars today. Whenever owners take their vintage racers out for a spin they have no trouble at all finding where they have parked them, which is wherever the crowd of inquisitive onlookers is at its thickest.

It could be said that the Super Sports Aero carries a V-sign on its breast in the form of its water-cooled JAP V2 engine with overhead valves. This engine provides unadulterated motoring pleasure: the immediate surge of power obtained even when accelerating from a speed of 50 mph (80 kph) is a source of endless fascination, reported *Motor Cycle* magazine at the time. The model shown here embodies the sports Morgan of the 1920s and early 1930s.

MORGAN 4/4 SERIES I

In the dying days of 1935, *The Light Car and Cyclecar* magazine landed a New Year scoop. Delighted to have got one over the competition, it reported Henry Frederick Stanley Morgan's start in the London to Exeter Trial on December 28, 1935—in a Morgan four-wheeler. The 4/4 (originally the 4-4) was only unveiled to the public at large at the London and Paris motor shows the following year.

The first production vehicle, with chassis number 3, was delivered to its lucky owner in March 1936. At this very moment, the hands of the company clock on Pickersleigh Road in Malvern Link, England, slowed to a snail's pace. The policy of Morgan Motor Co Ltd—family-owned right up to the present day—has always been to take one small step at a time. This principle has been adhered to by four generations of Morgans during the course of the twentieth century. The times may change, but a Morgan stays more or less the same—a macho car for the masochistic man.

Very soon humorous anecdotes began to circulate, for example that enthusiasts with sensitive behinds could tell which side of a coin they had driven over—heads or tails.

And indeed drivers were punished severely for being bold enough to take any road that was less than perfectly smooth. Neither, of course, could violent downpours be ruled out. Peter, son of company founder H.F.S., declared that to drive a Morgan you have to have a sense of humor and immediately put this to the test by warning that "There are actually more reasons not to buy one than there are to buy one."

Naturally, changes in the reception of its products have worked in the small company's favor. Today, in an age of occasionally stiffly comical retro looks, Morgans are seen as classics; by a stroke of luck a new-old cult car has evolved, revered through cult-like acts. After the war Morgans were regarded for a while as antiquities with rather fossilized features, while originally they had been at the cutting edge. Admittedly their front wheels have independent suspension, but this is based on a sliding pillar system devised by H.F.S. during the reign of King Edward VII (1901–10). The rest of the chassis, however, was conventional through and through: a low-level box frame with crossmembers and a rigid rear axle with underslung semi-elliptic leaf springs.

Various striking characteristics of the car's coachwork, which is constructed over an ash frame, were also forward looking: the long hood punctured by numerous ventilation louvers; the front fenders that curved gently outwards toward the running boards and energetically rounded rear wings. One curiosity that has been retained to the point of eccentricity is that an additional charge is made for external door handles (currently about £65/120 US dollars).

Under the hood a 1122cc Coventry Climax power unit initially gave modest service, chivvied up to 34 bhp by a Solex carburetor and kept to within reasonable running temperatures by a thermo-siphon cooling system. Before starting to be used in Morgans, this engine (90,000 of which had been built) had been cured of any bad habits it might have had. Its Meadows gearbox had four speeds. It was suggested that the new model be named the 4/4/4 (standing for four wheels, four cylinders, and four gears), but this idea was rejected. Only the two top gears had synchromesh—below this drivers had to demonstrate their skill at double-declutching in the manner of their forefathers.

The 4/4 was an immediate sales success. Barely two years after its unveiling at the motor shows, it was joined by another model: an open four-seater with cramped seating space in the rear and a single spare wheel carried on the back instead of the former twin spares. As passengers in the back were seated immediately above the rear axle, they were subjected to bumps of elemental violence from below. The elegant drophead coupé, introduced in 1938, was rather gentler on those who traveled in it, although its rear-hinged and no longer scooped-out doors made it difficult for female occupants to enter or exit the 4/4 in ladylike fashion.

In 1939 Morgan started to offer an alternative power unit for the 4/4. This was a 40 bhp 1267cc Standard engine, a variant of the Flying Ten, which was supplied exclusively to Malvern Link. This was combined with a Moss gearbox.

In 1947, however, the Coventry-based Standard Motor Company informed Morgan that in future it would be limiting production to a 2-liter engine for the Vanguard and various Triumph models. This measure anticipated the end of the Series I Morgan four-wheelers in 1950, without, however, dealing the model a particularly damaging blow. 1436 of the cars had been sold up to this time, 553 of them since the war.

This 1936 4/4, in a no less than pristine state of preservation, is largely the same as the model exhibited at the motor shows of the same year in London and Paris. The two spare wheels, mounted neatly onto the rear of the car, are a reminder of the marque's trial tradition. Punctures were the order of the day on rough surfaces and four tires were now subject to this risk. The double spare solution was retained on the Plus 4 until 1955.

The four-spoke Brooklands steering wheel was offered as an optional extra. The central spinners on the wheels are simply dummies that fasten the hub caps to the rim. In order to ensure even weight distribution, the Coventry Climax engine is supplied with the necessary 12 volts by two six-volt batteries connected in series. Behind them can be seen the rigid axle and shock absorbers.

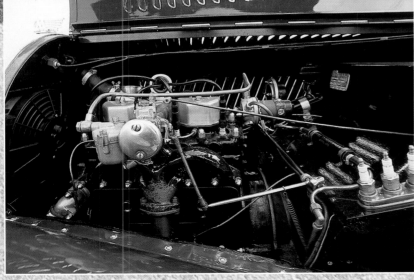

MORGAN

The German playwright Bertolt Brecht declared that his theater was directed at changeable people, those who were both capable and—stirred up and directed from the stage—in a position to put an end to the current lousy state of things. His gaze was set steadfastly on the future.

The Morgan Motor Car Co. Ltd and its clientele would have brought Brecht to the edge of despair. For them the golden age lies firmly in the past. The byword and categorical imperative of the company's unwritten rules is: "Why alter what works perfectly well?" And so Peter Morgan had difficulty persuading his father, H.F.S., that they should use Standard's Vanguard engine when their stock of Flying Ten units from the same manufacturer had been used up. This would mean 2088cc under the hood instead of the 1267cc that had powered their cars hitherto—68 bhp instead of 40 bhp (and thus 70 percent more power, necessitating appropriate changes to the bodywork) and entering races in the same class as the Aston Martin DB2. Without further ado, the younger Morgan fitted one of the 2-liter engines into the existing chassis. A test drive up the steepest hill that could be found in the vicinity of Malvern Link convinced the old man for good: "This is truly wonderful," he muttered, and the Plus 4 was born.

The Vanguard power unit was an extremely versatile engine that even had an agricultural application—serving in Ferguson tractors. In order to provide this engine with the space it needed, the wheelbase was lengthened by four inches. The name Plus 4 also, however, was meant to be a reference to the generous increase in power. The Moss gearbox was re-sited in the middle of the chassis and connected to the clutch housing via a rigid tube in a kind of transaxle construction.

Lubrication of the front suspension involves the active and sensitive intervention of the driver, who is required to give the components a shot of motor oil (by pressing the appropriate button) at intervals of every 100 miles (160 km)

1938 saw the introduction of a model suitable for families and the more convivial of the Morgan's fans—the four-seater. The positioning of the rear accommodation immediately above the back axle does little either for passengers' backbones or the lines of this classic car. Occupants have to do without a trunk. In trials, the co-driver needs to sit in the back in order to achieve the desired weight distribution.

PLUS 4

or so. The chassis and bulkhead were strengthened and the cockpit and track widened a little. A prototype, the progenitor of 5962 two-seaters, four-seaters, and drophead coupés over the next half century, was ready by October 1950, just in time for the London Motor Show.

When the supply of Standard engines started to dwindle, a new and fertile source of power was tapped in 1953 in the form of the Triumph four-cylinder. The TR2 and TR3, TR3A, and TR3B (1992cc offering 90 and 100 bhp respectively) shared the role until 1962, when they were joined by the TR4 and TR4A (2138cc offering 100 and 104 bhp respectively). From November 1960, Girling disc brakes became the norm in front. The main alterations in styling focused initially on the front end of the Plus 4: following an experimental interim solution adopted in 1953, the car was given a continuous valance linking its two front wings, a radiator grill consisting of curved vertical chrome bars, and headlights that are integrated harmoniously into the bodywork in similar fashion to those of the MG TE.

The crowning glory of the range was the Super Sports, which first appeared in 1961 and into which all the marque's competition experience, with drivers of the caliber of Chris Lawrence and Richard Shepherd-Barron at the wheel, was poured. Its lightweight (aluminum) bodywork and 72-spoke wire wheels were standard features. Its engine produced a solid 115 and later 125 bhp. Later versions have a lower front end, a feature adopted as standard in "off the peg" roadsters in 1966.

The Triumph connection ended in 1968, and the Plus 8 immediately came on the scene as the new star in the Morgan firmament. The Plus 4 became redundant and sank into oblivion—until 1985, that is, when it was summoned back to life and fitted with a 2-liter, four-cylinder Fiat engine with twin overhead camshafts combined with a gearbox also from the Italian manufacturer. The Morgans had considered alternatives from Saab and BMW, but these were found wanting.

The curved radiator grill with its vertical bars came into being during the course of a cautious cosmetic revolution in 1953/4, which was also responsible for the design of the headlamps, which grow organically out of the trough between hood and fenders. Before the war and during the immediate post-war period, they were fitted to on the ends of straight tubes.

Occupying the middle ground between the Plus 8 and current 4/4, the new Plus 4 was based on the body of its smaller brother with a wheelbase of 96 inches (2440 mm) (compared to the Plus 8's 98 inches/2496 mm), but borrowed its bigger brother's fenders, which accommodated Cobra wire wheels with generous 195/60 tires. Sales were poor and only 122 cars were sold during the first few years, mainly because die-hard enthusiasts found the origin of the engine hard to swallow. For reasons of rationalization, both models were built on the wider chassis of the eight-cylinder vehicle.

Buy British: from 1988 a powerful 1994cc Rover 16-valve engine lurked beneath the Plus 4's rounded hood. This was steadily developed over the following years, as was also the five-gear transmission (from the same manufacturer) with which it was symbiotically linked. In summer 1997 the concept was pepped up once again with the fitting of the inevitable airbags, longer doors, greater adjustability of the seat, a lower dashboard, and lockable steering wheel.

The death knell sounded for the Morgan Plus 4 in spring 2000, when the supply of suitable clean-burn power units dried up. In fact, the reborn Plus 4 had never really enjoyed a secure place in the Morgan range.

The raised hood of the Plus 4 affords a view of the new occupant that took up residence in spring 1988: a 2-liter 16-valve Rover engine known as the M16i. Even around this time passengers remained exposed not only to the unevenness of the roads, but also, thanks to their high sitting position, the almost unshielded airstream—a defect that was only recently dealt with. Demand for the tourer remained low, however.

MORGAN 4/4 SERIES II AND LATER

With its comparatively powerful engine, the Plus 4 moved very quickly into a higher price category. As a result, the trinity at the head of Morgan Motor Co Ltd, father H.F.S., son Peter, and George Goodall, works manager since the late 1930s, reintroduced the 4/4 in 1955.

With a basic price tag of £638 in Great Britain, it was the least expensive open two-seater at the 1955 London Motor Show. The chassis and overall look were taken from the Plus 4 and thus the headlamps grew naturally out of the trough between the curved radiator grill and the fenders, while the rear, which now carried just one spare wheel, fell away more gently than before.

Other than this, the company's tried and tested solutions were not tampered with. This Morgan too was hand-forged, hand-shaped, and even hand-joined: the car's metal body covers a frame of Belgian ash (screwed onto the low-level box frame), which is almost everlasting and rock-hard, thus complementing the suspension perfectly. At the back, a rigid axle, semi-elliptic springs, and piston shock absorbers, and at the front telescopic shock absorbers, coil springs, and sliding pillars, just about protect the occupants from the worst the roads can throw up.

This was also an opportunity for the company's dormant ties with Ford to be revived—not without digging up a small piece of lightly rusted-over tradition at the same time. The 100E engine below the narrow hood of the Series II 4/4 (whose top, for reasons of economy, no longer boasted parallel rows of air inlets) was derived from the four-cylinder motor that powered the later three-wheelers. It was cheap, reliable and easy to service, though its 1172cc and 36 bhp provided the 4/4 driver with no more than a contemplative, leisurely means of locomotion. This engine taps timidly on the 60 mph (100 kph) barrier—but only after taking a half-minute run-up. In this it was not helped by having just three gears at its disposal, the gearshift sticking out from the dashboard and operated by means of a handy push-pull system.

Subsequent Ford units that found shelter at various times under the hood of the 4/4 livened up this rather sluggish starter-level Morgan considerably. The first to be given this honor was the 105E, with its modest 997cc, which had great tuning potential and even saw active and energetic racing service in the 1-liter class. This 39 bhp engine, introduced in 1961 (Series III), brought with it four-speed transmission.

The introduction of the Series IV in 1962 saw the replacement of Girling front drum brakes with disc brakes from the same manufacturer. The 1340cc of its 109E engine increased bhp to 54. Series V followed a year later with full synchromesh transmission, a normal gearshift and the 116E Cortina engine (1498cc offering 60 bhp and 78 bhp in the competition model).

Engines come, engines go, but Morgans stay the same. While other car manufacturers trumpet the technical and even visual brilliance of their engines, the units used to power Morgans, as a result of constant change, remain invisible to the point of anonymity. The star is the car itself, an eternal evergreen. Here we see the classic front end of the Morgan in profile.

The inevitable consequence of the Plus 4's absence between 1970 and 1984 was to boost the appeal of the entry-level Morgan 4/4, all the more so as the latter was a nimble and by no means underpowered machine – the vehicle shown here is a 1983 model with 1600 Ford CVH engine. Small aeroscreens proclaiming the defiant message "just try stopping me!" constituted a useful weapon in the constant battle against airflow.

The next engine, the larger 1598cc unit offering initially 74 and later 88 bhp, came from the same stable and made its home under the Morgan 4/4 1600's hood between spring 1968 and 1982. This was the first 4/4, enthused John Bolster in the well-known British racing magazine *Autosport* in March 1974, to manage "more than a ton" (British slang for 100mph). He also went into raptures over the Morgan's throaty exhaust sound. 43 percent of the 3512 cars produced during this period were four-seaters—their purchasers evidently placed more of an emphasis on practicality than on aesthetics.

An Italian interlude between 1981 and 1983 (during which time the Ford engine was replaced by a 1.6-liter power unit borrowed from Fiat's Mirafiori sedan—the first twin overhead cam engine in Morgan's history) was cruelly punished by Morgan enthusiasts, who withheld their affection. Only 96 two-seater and four-seater examples with this configuration were sold. The interloper was still the subject of their dislike when another Ford engine, the 1597cc CVH (Compound Valve Hemispherical) was introduced. As well as offering the same capacity, at 96 bhp it was also nearly as powerful as the unpopular Italian unit. As a consequence, subsequent Ford developments were adopted by Morgan and in 1991 the 100 bhp 1600 EFI (Electronic Fuel Injection)

unit gave Malvern Link its initial entry into a lead-free, clean-emission world. In 1993 this engine was replaced by the 1800 Zetec, whose originally announced 128 bhp shrank to 114 bhp upon closer inspection. The chassis of all three Morgan models had to be modified the same year when Girling withdrew from the small manufacturer sector and Lockheed brakes were fitted instead.

During its long life, careful attention has always been given to the design of the 4/4, and it was soon equipped with some of the features that initially stood out on the Plus 8: new rear lights, a dual-circuit brake system, and crash padding on the dashboard. In the mid-1970s bucket seats were introduced as standard following the adoption of further safety measures, and in 1986 the car was endowed with improved rust and weather protection for the more sensitive of the traditionally rain- and cold-resistant Morganistas. In summer 1997, airbags, accompanied by the necessary modifications to the fabric of the vehicle, were introduced throughout the range, reducing the risk of injury.

None of these changes are ever very conspicuous, for progress in merely homoeopathic doses is to some extent included in the purchase price of the 8397 Morgan 4/4s sold up to and including the year 2000.

The term dashboard could not be more appropriate as it remains flat and simple below its protective padding, an aesthetic continued in the emphatically plain steering wheel chosen here. The glove compartment is just a gaping hole: Morgan owners are also characterized by their faith in human nature. The Rostyle wheels shown here were standard at the time, but the luggage rack was not.

The English are apparently incapable of carrying out a tumultuous revolution. Coups are expected to take place in as discreet and gentlemanly a manner as possible, ideally well documented and bearing an official seal (e.g. the Magna Carta of 1225) rather than conducted to the sound of noisy detonations (e.g. the failed Gunpowder Plot of 1605).

Another prime example is the genesis of the Morgan Plus 8. Anyone ambling past the small family firm's stand at the 1968 London Motor Show in Earl's Court would initially gain the reassuring impression that all was as serene as usual at the old-established company. The host of Morgan disciples, however, brothers in gentle fanaticism, had known for a long time that a change of shattering proportions had occurred at the company's Pickersleigh Road factory in Malvern Link. The Plus 4 had just been laid to rest—at least temporarily—as engine supplier Standard had stopped making its long-stroke TR4 Triumph engine. The six-cylinder TR5 was too heavy and unwieldy, the Ford Capri's V6 a great lump of iron, the Lotus Cortina twin-cam too

MORGAN PLUS 8

jittery and the latest Triumph V8 was still in the grip of childhood illnesses. But just at the right moment, along came Rover's compact aluminum V8 power unit. This expatriate American unit, from the arsenal of General Motors' subsidiary Buick, had been used to power the Rover P6 3500 since April of that year.

This large-bore engine altered the external appearance of the Morgan slightly and its character and image completely. The car's wheelbase was extended from 96 inches (2440 mm) to 98 inches (2490 mm), the front track widened by just over an inch to 48 inches (1220 mm) and the rear track by 2 inches to 50 inches (1280 mm), bringing about subtle changes to the vehicle's lines. The 15-inch (381-mm) alloy wheels replaced the previous wire wheels.

The Plus 8 is capable of casually throwing off a performance Morgan drivers could previously only dream of, especially when the optional aluminum body, which reduces its weight by a further 99 lb (45 kg), has been specified. All drivers need to do is open up the throttle valves of the giant

SU carburetors by easing down the delicate roller gas pedal. Whenever this happens the dull throb of the eight-cylinder is overlaid with the roar of the Moss gearbox, which punishes any gearshift not executed to its satisfaction with an indignant crunching noise. Later Rover gearboxes—four-speed from April 1972 and five-speed from October 1976—show greater tolerance in this respect.

Most Morgan enthusiasts are not particularly keen on testing out the Plus 8's top speed of 125 mph (201 kph). Even at 87 mph (140 kph), the noises of roar, flutter, and hiss permeate the cabin, reducing communication to visual signs and single, screamed syllables. The wind that whistles around the vehicle seeks continually to gain entrance to the interior and manages it too, through the side windows. The unattractive choice means, as Klaus Westrup notes in *auto motor und sport* in 1970, that one must content oneself with lower speeds or become deaf. But the Plus 8 maltreats its occupants from below too: as soon as the quality of the road deteriorates, its annoyance is transmitted to those seated above.

Resembling the lid of a concert grand, this Morgan's open hood gives us a glimpse of the business end of the car: the Rover V8 that gives the car its rumbling appeal—it may make music but there are no piano strings here. Purists like the owner of this 1978 example were saddened by the introduction of feedback catalytic converters, which take away some of its character. Nonetheless, it still deserves to be well ventilated by its four rows of louvers.

Things are not that different in the Sports Lightweight model introduced in the fall of 1975, whose wider fenders accommodate thicker tires. Two years later the chassis was widened giving a track width of 53 inches (1346 mm) at the front and 54 inches (1372 mm) at the rear, the engine moved slightly rearward in order to improve balance and the wheels reduced to a diameter of 14 inches (356 mm), a measure reversed in 1981. The usual steel bumpers protecting the bodywork from minor bumps and dents were later replaced by aluminum ones. In 1983 rack and pinion steering was introduced, initially as an optional extra and later as standard.

The performance of the carburetor versions of the engine used up to this point fluctuated from an original 168 bhp via 143 bhp in 1973 to 155 bhp in 1976. This was increased to 190 bhp by the 1984 Vitesse engine whose liquid nourishment was delivered by Lucas electronic fuel injection. While the 3.9-liter version that came on the scene in 1990 brought no further increase in power, it did improve torque, and was further optimized by the introduction of cleaner emissions in later examples.

This is also the area in which the 4.6-liter Range Rover engine excelled. This unit first found its way into a prototype in 1997, the year the Plus 8 and its siblings were given airbags along with the necessary modifications. It did not stay long: issue 4 of the Morgan company newsletter, *The Malvern Link*, announced that due to the Euro III emissions standards, from November 2000 the Plus 8 would only be available with the new 4-liter V8, the environmentally most friendly version of the well-known 3.9-liter unit. A never-ending story: the symbiotic relationship between the Worcestershire-based roadster and the Rover eight-cylinder has already endured for 22 years, with 5400 examples built.

Those who are trapped in the new motoring monoculture have the consolation of being able to choose from 34,000 colors, but a Morgan—so its advertising goes—allows you to escape the mediocre.

For eight years from 1977 the Plus 8 could be identified by its eight-hole Milrace 14-inch (356 mm) wheels, which made a small but significant contribution to the increasingly sturdy appearance of the top-of-the-range Morgan. The three small windshield wipers were standard features from the outset, while the luggage rack over the back wheel is an optional extra that can be ordered from Malvern Link.

The Morgan Motor Company unveiled its Aero 8, which is positioned somewhere between yesterday and tomorrow, classic and modern, tradition and innovation, at the 2000 Geneva Motor Show, coinciding perfectly with the start of the new millennium.

Its venerable name speaks of past glories and refers specifically to the nimblest of the three-wheelers produced between 1919 and 1936—streamlined and open to the elements like its (twice-as-fast) descendent. Despite the dramatic and slightly bizarre reinterpretation of the original idea, there is indeed something familiar about the overall look of the newcomer—the flowing lines of its fenders, the interminable, two-part hood, its waterfall radiator. Keen observers will not be caught completely unawares by the new Morgan's aesthetic innovations: the GT2 racing car built by the company for the 1997 FIA Championships looked very similar. A sense of *déjà vu* greets those lucky enough to open the door (which features a leather top strip), thread themselves through the wide aperture into the confined cockpit and ease themselves into the narrow leather seat.

A commitment to hand-craftsmanship is another aspect firmly rooted in the company philosophy. As before, there is no place here for heartless, soulless robots. The Aero 8 does not leave the Malvern Link works during the entire production process, from the initial stage of the mass of individual puzzle pieces to finished product. Company boss Charles Morgan adheres unbendingly to the structural use of wood in the car: "A Japanese manufacturer recently promised to plant a tree for each of their cars," he declares wrily, "while we, on the other hand, put a tree in every car. In future, our

MORGAN

Aero production will require between six and ten ash trees to be felled every week."

The wooden frame is no longer load-bearing, however. Outside suppliers now supply Malvern Link with perfect made-to-measure, thermoplastically shaped aluminum sections, such as fenders and trunk lids, cut to size using laser technology. The ultra-stiff chassis is bonded and riveted together from aluminum alloy parts made by German manufacturer Alcan. In contrast to the pliable classic cars from the same stable, nothing gives down below any more. And that's quite an achievement as the Aero's roadholding and lateral acceleration of up to one G are guaranteed by mighty 18-inch (457-mm) magnesium wheels with correspondingly large tires and a generous track width, all-round independent suspension based on long cantilever upper arms with Eibach springs and Koni shock absorbers, and intelligent underbody construction that exploits the venturi effect of passing airflow. Innocent passengers and drivers of any vehicles behind be warned: should Aero drivers care to make maximum use of their AP ventilated racing

brakes, their eyes will pop out of their sockets and the Morgan will be standing there motionless like a newly landed plane on an aircraft carrier. And don't bother looking for a fifth wheel. If you get a blowout, which is to be avoided at all costs, an attentive monitoring system on the middle console will immediately alert you to the decreasing tire pressure and an emergency safety system will be activated.

Talking of airplanes, in terms of speed the Aero leaves its predecessors standing. Weighing in at 2205 lb (1000 kg), it is brought into and sustained in motion by the phenomenal 286 bhp of a 4398cc BMW V8 motor, which draws attention to its presence beneath the curves of the car's front end with a sonorous rumble akin to that of a large propeller engine. Although it immediately begins to purr immaculately when the illuminated green starter button is pressed, the Bavarian power unit is no plaything. It responds to the gas pedal like a dachshund to the postman. At 2000 rpm in the first of its Getrag transmission's six gears, its thick rear Dunlop tires are already fighting for traction. The speed of 60 mph (100 kph) is reached within the space of a deep breath and top speed is 160 mph (258 kph)—this engine does not believe in self-imposed restrictions.

And airflow is no longer a problem. Thanks to sophisticated aerodynamics, the Morgan promises a drag co-efficient of 0.39 with its stiff fabric top either up or down. The fact that the Morgan's traditional cutaway doors have been dispensed with also plays a part here. An unaccustomed degree of humanity in the workplace, coupled with comfort—luxury even—is evident in other respects too: all-round heated windows, a stylish Connolly leather interior,

AERO 8

elegant solid ash trim, a Blaupunkt entertainment center, and air conditioning.

The trunk, which can be opened from the cockpit, offers enough space to accommodate a set of golf clubs (the welfare of golfers seems to be a priority for all supercar manufacturers), but businessmen are also catered for: instead of a glove compartment, there is a removable leather Mulberry case which can easily accommodate the ubiquitous laptop.

These items will need to belong to high earners, however, as the Morgan Aero 8 comes with a price tag approaching £60,000 (around $90,000).

The front of the Morgan Aero 8 (shown here parked in front of a rugby field not far from the Malvern Link works where it is made), sports a characteristic cross-eyed look and combines old and new elements. Its rear end, on the other hand—at least when seen from this angle—is characterized by a jumble of lights and dual exhaust pipes that project menacingly.

The solid and sturdy appearance of this Morgan for the new millennium gives more than a hint of the forces that lurk beneath its hood. The power, readiness for battle and mood of its BMW V8 engine are controlled by a wealth of sophisticated instruments. Parts of the aluminum monocoque, conveying a sense of stubborn rigidity, can be glimpsed here beneath the open hood.

CHARLES MORGAN
IN THE DRIVER'S SEAT

The small world of English sports car manufacturing can be seen as a microcosm of human existence in general: the constant battle for survival in a world characterized by a dog-eat-dog attitude; the familiar pattern of rise and fall; the difficulty of preserving one's individuality.

In the midst of this rampant biotope, the Morgan Motor Co, which has occupied the same premises on Pickersleigh Road in Malvern Link, Worcestershire, since time immemorial, seems to be the hereditary leaseholder of a comfortable niche, to have become an idyll of continuity and steadfastness. The company has been passed on like the family silver from grandpa Henry Frederick Stanley Morgan to son Peter and thence to grandson Charles. The freezing of progress into familiarity and the deceleration of a fast-moving world into slow-motion are curiously reflected in the company's products, which remain recognizably similar to the 1936 original. How reassuring—and how boring.

But appearances can be deceptive. Naturally, Charles Morgan's visits to his grandfather in Maidenhead (not far from London) as a boy made a deep impression on him. Charles was born in 1952 and HFS died when he was nine years old: "He came across to his customers and even employees as shy. But he was a loving family man and an inventor par excellence. There were always these splendid pedal cars there, full of ingenious gimmicks and even at that time sporting pneumatic tires, which I was allowed to whiz around the garden in."

And of course he was over the moon when his father took him along to motor racing events and even allowed him to enter—naturally in a Morgan ("for a long time the most economical way of getting from A to B quickly in a car"). But then he fled the safety of family tradition, taking to his heels in fright at the prospect of continuing this comfortable, mapped-out existence: "In order to find oneself, a man with this kind of background has to do something else, at least for a while."

This something else was 10 years in the television industry as a news cameraman and journalist with ITV and ITN. Charles Morgan became a member of the global village. He traveled Iran and the Far East, was in Rhodesia when it became Zimbabwe, and risked life and limb when the Russians marched into Afghanistan: "I wanted to stay for two weeks, but ended up spending three months there and lost 33 lb (15 kg)." His father never placed any obstacles in his way, was always interested in what he did and even encouraged him in his chosen career.

ABOVE: The Morgan Motor Company has long been one of Malvern Link's main attractions and a few years ago the local council drew attention to its existence by putting an imaginative sign up on the opposite side of the street.
LEFT: As Charles Morgan is involved in every aspect of his company he is seldom to be found in his office.

The entrance to the second oldest of the factory's buildings dates from 1919, the year of the Morgan dawn. It contrasts symbolically with the purposeful and unadorned building at the other end of the site where the Aero 8 is built.

In 1985 the prodigal son returned to Pickersleigh Road worldly and experienced: "It's not enough to simply take things over. Each generation has to invent them all over again." This is how passion develops. Not as a result of something being passed down to you, but because you have had a choice and have decided on a course of action for yourself. Oh yes, acknowledges Charles Morgan, the Morgan Motor Co is in his blood and every day his passion for it grows a little bit stronger. And this is how he escapes the commonly expressed prejudice that "he is a member of the clan and has no other alternatives."

Shortly after his arrival he sniffed the Morgan air, so to speak, and sensed a need for change: "In terms of performance there was a growing discrepancy between our cars and modern sports cars." Something new was needed, but it had to be in keeping with the spirit of the company—something that would build on the past rather than breaking radically with it, that would be both traditional and progressive like the 4/4 half a century before. And he began playing with ideas for the Aero. These were not developed seriously, however, until 1996.

When Charles Morgan talks about his car for the new millennium, he takes on a sense of urgency and mission. This is infectious and has been transmitted to his two small daughters, Harriet and Kate, who unveiled the prototype at the 2000 Geneva Motor Show to the excited murmur of the onlookers: "They're already completely car mad."

And the Aero 8 is the perfect embodiment of these aims—the creation as projection and symbol of its creator. Backward-looking are certain retro elements in the car's styling and an adherence to traditional craftsmanship. Ultimately, the company's ambition is not only to tap into new markets but also to retain the old stalwarts among its customer base. Forward-looking elements, on the other hand, include the car's performance, which is nothing short of breathtaking, the adoption of CAD methods, the latest aluminum bonding techniques and the high-tech BMW power unit.

In terms of "performance, size, weight, economy, and low emissions, this is the best V8 in the world," declares Charles Morgan in praise of his Bavarian partner. And to have the opportunity to lean on such a strong shoulder does no harm at all. What marks out true conservatism is that while firmly rooted in the safe ground of the present, it is also prepared to venture little by little into new territory.

Charles, the third boss in the Morgan dynasty, has already gone considerably further than this.

MORGAN MOTOR COMPANY LIMITED
TIME-HONORED METHODS

RIGHT: *Wooden door frames being fitted into the body of a Plus 8. Being individually crafted, doors are neither interchangeable nor easily replaced from stock in the event of damage.*

Planks of ash just as they are delivered to Pickersleigh Road. Morgan uses five tons/tonnes a year.

The same pieces, now roughly shaped, before entering the wood shop.

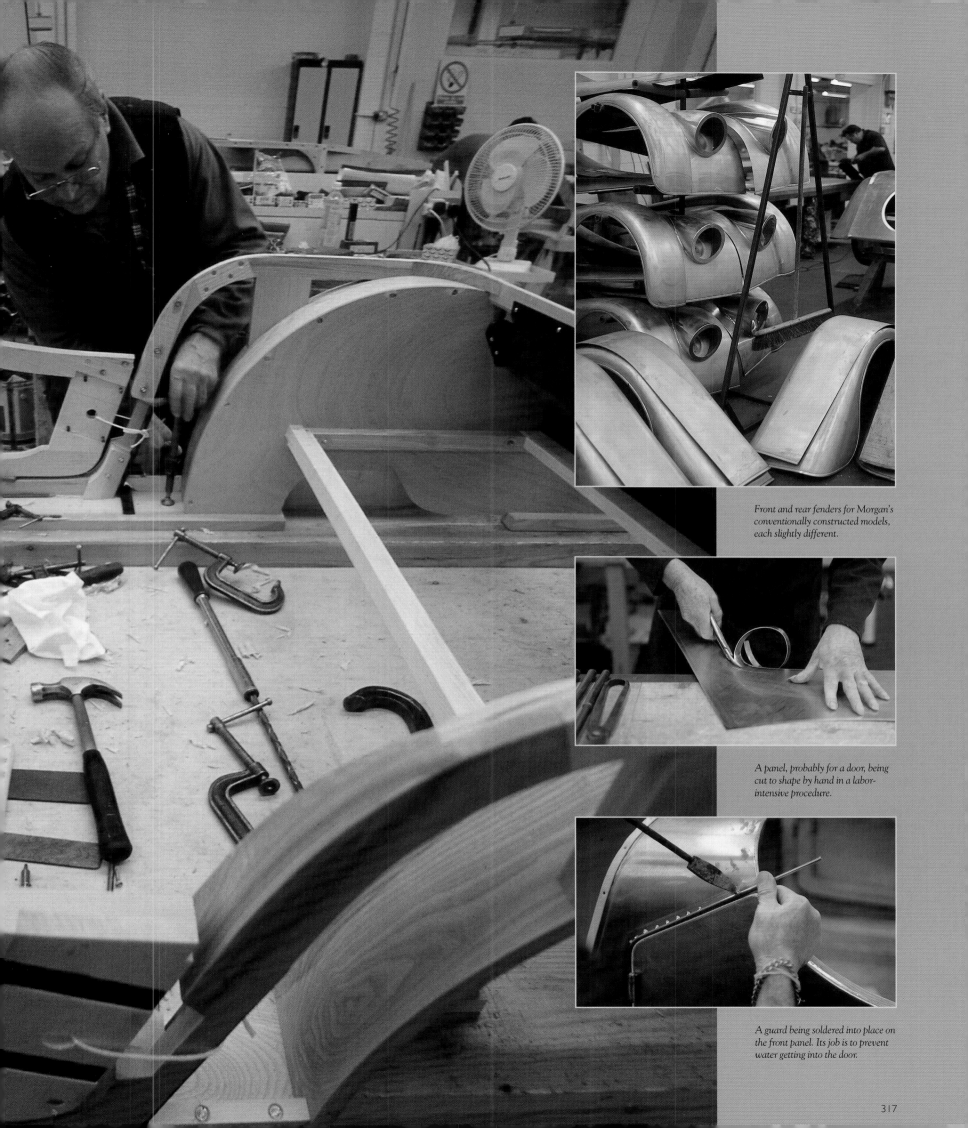

Front and rear fenders for Morgan's conventionally constructed models, each slightly different.

A panel, probably for a door, being cut to shape by hand in a labor-intensive procedure.

A guard being soldered into place on the front panel. Its job is to prevent water getting into the door.

RIGHT: *The fenders being fitted to a traditional car body, in this case a Morgan 4/4, recognizable from its four-cylinder engine.*

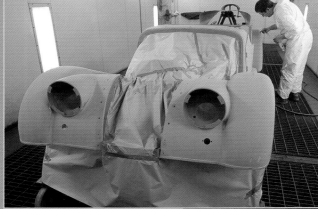

A vehicle during undercoating. Seven coats of paint are normally applied.

Mick Hand takes pains to remove every speck of dust prior to delivery. This car has already undergone a test drive.

The wooden framework and aluminum panels of an Aero 8 being fitted to the chassis.

An Aero 8 whose wings and front spoiler have just been fitted. The production process is a combination of the old and the new.

PANTHER KALLISTA

With the founding of Panther West Winds Ltd in 1971, engineer Bob Jankel filled a new market niche. What his firm (based at the picturesque address of Oatlands Chase, Weybridge, Surrey, England) essentially set out to do was to turn his boyhood (and possibly also adult) dreams into reality.

This was evident from his very first creation, which looked like a Rolls-Royce from times gone by. Following this, the 1972 Panther J72 V12 was inspired by the Jaguar SS100 and the 1974 FF appeared in 1974 in the attire of Ferrari's firstborn, the 125 S of 1947. The engineering under its retro-styled shell (supplied by Maranello) was that of the 330 GTC. The De

Ville, dating from the same year, was based on the Bugatti Royale, while the Panther Super Six of 1977 took its unusual inspiration from the Formula One car of the day: like Tyrrell's P34 monstrosity, it had six wheels and incorporated a host of superlative features such as a mid-positioned turbocharged 8.2-liter Cadillac V8 engine delivering 600 bhp, capable, according to the producer, of a top speed of 199 mph (320 kph). Fuel consumption was around 8 US gallons (30 liters) to the mile, and there was no fixed price. Not surprisingly, potential customers didn't exactly warm to this extreme car, and other than a pirated copy, only one example was ever built.

certain motifs from the Panther Lima (897 of which were built between 1976 and 1981), which exuded a certain slightly long-winded nostalgia of the 1930s. Whereas the Lima had a fiberglass shell and took its mechanical components from Vauxhall, the Kallista had an aluminum body and featured a jigsaw puzzle of Ford technology from different years: 1.6- and later 2.3-liter four-cylinder power units, 2.8- and subsequently 2.9-liter V6 units, four-speed transmission for the basic model and the option of automatic transmission for the six-cylinder.

Last but not least, the suspension, consisting of double wishbones and coil springs at the front and a rigid axle with two trailing arms, coil springs, and a Panhard rod at the rear, was also mostly picked up from Ford's shelves. The chassis and body were built in South Korea, shipped to England to be provided with the local ingredients and then transported to Weybridge—a stone's throw from the former British motor racing Mecca of Brooklands—where they were given the finishing touches. In 1986 the slim foreigner was relatively cheap by the company's former standards.

In February 1983 a well-disposed review of the variant shown here, which is actually a prototype with 6J × 14 inch alloy wheels and 205/60 Goodyear tires, appeared in a feature in *Classic and Sportscar* written by Mike McCarthy. In it he compares the newcomer with a Lima he had picked up from the factory a few years before. There had been no improvement to the lack of trunk space and elbow room—arms were still jammed between ribs and door—and also, as with the earlier car, there was wheelspin at full throttle even in second gear in spite of the fat Goodyear tires.

Just as before, however, the Panther excelled with fantastic handling and showed heaps of character. Apart from these aspects, noted the author, the Kallista was a completely new car. Whereas supple humility had previously been required in order to climb into the car when the top was up, the same operation was now perfectly simple, though Rolls-Royce drivers—partly, of course, because of old age—could hardly be expected to lower themselves (in both senses) to it.

The main beneficiary of a 3-inch (76-mm) increase in length was the cockpit, to such an extent in fact that drivers of small stature might even find themselves having difficulty reaching the pedals. The sitting position was now at last low, the previous high position having meant that a visible swelling in the canopy was a sure sign the driver was 6 ft 2 in (1m 90 cm) tall or more.

The article's author reserved special praise for the controlled suspension and precise steering, but observed that in contrast to the car's classic exterior styling, the dashboard had too little of the "Made in Britain" about it. This was easily remedied, however: the list of accessories contained 40 extortionately priced optional extras including (alongside the finest wood and leather fittings) a badly welded rear luggage rack, low-profile tires, and a stainless steel radiator grill.

By the end of 1991, when the Panther Kallista was consigned once and for all to the past, 1741 purchasers had succumbed to its charms.

By 1979, Jankel's bold retro look no longer suited the times and West Winds Ltd went into receivership. Salvation came from the other end of the global village when South Korean group Jindo Industries, under its dynamic boss Y.C. Kim, took pity on what was left of the company. His calculation was that there was potential to do well with West Wind's unusual sports cars given the low production costs at home—especially as two other manufacturers of airy two-seaters, MG and Triumph, had just quit the market.

In fall 1982 Panther roared back to life with a new model, the Kallista. Clear to all was the way this model took up

RELIANT SCIMITAR SS1

Talented engineer T.L. Williams was in no doubt at all about one thing: the future had three wheels. Inspired by his credo of the arch-rational and arch-modest, he founded the Reliant Motor Company Ltd, rolled up his shirt sleeves in a simple workshop located in the garden of his property in Tamworth, Staffordshire, and succeeded in licensing his first three-wheeler, a miniature truck, which went on sale on January 1, 1935.

Elementary transport for three or four persons was afforded by the Regal, which was to become a familiar sight on British streets soon after its launch in 1953, and while designing the body of the 1956 Regal Mk II, the company came upon the material out of which future Reliant dreams were made: fiberglass.

In 1961 the firm took its first hesitant steps on new territory, having made the decision to enliven the dry everyday prose of minimalist motoring with a smattering of poetry in the form of a fully-grown sports car or two. It made its debut in this field with the Sabre, commissioned originally by an Israeli company. This curiously designed creation with man-made body was none too successful, and the following Scimitar GT, produced between 1965 and 1970, was similarly meager. The long-lived Scimitar GTE (Grand Touring Estate), on the other hand, (which remained in production from August 1968 until fall 1986), eventually became a cult object. This pleasingly shaped notchback coupé looked as if made for the transportation of scepters, purple robes, and other regalia, or a generous assortment of golfing equipment at the very least. It immediately attracted favor from the highest quarters—serving as Prince Philip's private mode of transport (rather than his official car) for a year, and providing Princess Anne, who took out a kind of long-term subscription in the form of seven consecutive models during the 1980s, with subversive driving pleasure.

There were high expectations of the next offspring of the Scimitar family, the small open two-seater known as the Scimitar SS1 (standing simply for Small Sports Car Number 1). The conditions were also right: a massive decline in the number of roadsters being produced at the end of the 1970s had led to a thinning out of the world market. The unveiling of a pearly white prototype at the 1984 London Motor Show, however, met with general disappointment. "The missed opportunity of the year," moaned *Performance Car*, and another publication went even further, declaring ill-naturedly (and showing acute disdain for the principle that no ill should be spoken of the dead) that Michelotti would have done better to have broken his own arm. The universally respected designer (known affectionately in Tamworth as "Micho"), had been commissioned to design the SS1's bodywork, but died soon after delivering his initial designs to Reliant on December 11, 1978. His role was taken over by a team led by Richie Spencer, but they did not make a terribly good job of it. The decision to keep down the insurance costs through the use of easy-to-manufacture, easily exchangeable composite pressed parts did not do the car's overall appearance any favors.

On the insipid side and somewhat anachronistic, it was distorted by various grooves and bulges. On top of this came technical blunders such as badly fitting panels. Neither was the interior by Jevon Thorpe, a 25-year-old student at Lancaster Polytechnic, well received. Consisting of elements borrowed from Austin and the Mini Moke, it gave the impression of having been thrown together carelessly and discordantly.

The new model went into production in 1985 with 1.3- and 1.6-liter Ford power plants from the current Escort program. The name SS1 was dropped as inappropriate when in July 1986 the 1800ti model appeared, featuring the Nissan Silvia turbo engine. This model can be recognized from its alloy wheel rims and a black spoiler added to the trunk lid. Delivering 138 bhp without catalytic converter and capable of more than 125 mph (200 kph), it put an end to the prejudice that the Scimitar was something of a sluggard. As a consequence of cleaning up emissions, however, output was cut by 16 bhp, and in Germany in 1987 and 1988 there were only three takers for the environmentally friendly variant. The basic model was also modestly upgraded in 1987 when its innocuous 1.3-liter motor gave way to an only slightly less innocuous 1.4-liter unit.

Where the Scimitar did score extremely well was on roadholding, which it owed not least to its carefully co-ordinated independent suspension: double wishbones and coil springs in front, diagonal arms and coil springs at the rear, sway bars at either end.

But a good meal has to appeal to the eye too, and as the SS1 was not very satisfying in this respect, Reliant Cars Limited only sold 1507 units up to the end of production in 1990, having originally dreamed of 2000 per year.

RILEY BROOKLANDS NINE

Riley's earliest known racing victory occurred in 1899. The driver, noted a contemporary chronicler, was Robert Crossley, and the vehicle was a motorized three-wheeler built by the young company.

Motor racing was always part and parcel of the philosophy of Riley Ltd of Durbar Avenue, Foleshill, Coventry, and for very good reason: it boosted a company's image and therefore sales—especially in the case of Riley, whose racing cars were noted for their extraordinary reliability. A vehicle that had proven its worth under the sustained pressure of the racetrack had the ability to confer a valuable stamp of quality on its series production counterpart. The marque's first purebred sports model was the 10-horsepower Speed of 1909, which sat threateningly low on its detachable wire wheels and had a displacement of 1390cc from a "quadratic" bore and stroke of 3.78 inches (96 mm).

In 1922 and 1923 a new generation of Riley sports cars burst noisily onto the scene. These were the Eleven Two Seat and Four Seat Sports, for which the factory guaranteed respective top speeds of 70 mph (113 kph) and 60 mph (97 kph), as well as a Short Wheelbase Sports. With their 1498cc engines, they were admirably equipped for success in the international "F Class" of up to 1.5 liters.

Since 1926, the Riley Nine had been known as the Wonder Car, due to its very obvious qualities, and in 1928 the company embarked upon the most successful sporting decade in its history with the racing versions of it. Initially, they were built by Thomson and Taylor—in situ, so to speak, in the racing Mecca of Brooklands—and were initially called the Speed Model, then the Brooklands Speed Model and finally simply the Brooklands. The inspiration for building the fastest Nine to date (with a speed guarantee of 80 mph (129 kph)), was the success of J.G. Parry-Thomas and Reid Railton in the car's predecessor, and their experience contributed significantly to the newcomer's development.

Around 100 examples of this wind-dodger, the lowest-ever Riley, were built between 1926 and 1932 in a wide variety of two-seater bodies. Its backbone consisted of a framework of U-profile sections running underneath the rear axle and ending in goosenecks at the front. It had a wheelbase of 96 inches (2438 mm) with suspension consisting of rigid axles and semi-elliptic springs.

The long front fenders fell away diagonally from their highest point above the wheels to their lowest beneath the door hinges, while the sturdy and close-fitting rear wings formed a simple curve over the tops of the rear (driving) wheels. All four wheels could be changed very quickly by the racing team.

In the early models a wooden frame supported a steel body provided with standard weather gear that delivered rather less than it promised. The flat windshield could be folded down and two tiny doors provided access to the spartan cabin. The vehicles entered in the 1929 Tourist Trophy offered no such luxury, however, and the occupants had to sit over the flanks. The boat-like "stern" of these racing versions was shortened, the frames were made of metal and the bodies of aluminum. The doorless lightweight versions were also entered at Le Mans in 1933 and 1934.

The engine, with a displacement of 1087cc and Treasury-rated horsepower of 9.01 (in keeping with the Royal Automobile Club norm) deviated from that of the standard Nine in that it had a water pump driven by the same shaft as its magneto ignition. Oil could quickly be fed into the large oil pan through an inlet at the front, though its cap, equipped with a strong spring, had a tendency to snap shut on careless fingers, earning it the respectful nickname of the "rat trap."

Even the Brooklands's early progress was strewn with records. With H.W. Purdy at the wheel it set new speeds of between 85 and 87 mph (137 and 140 kph) in the 200-kilometer and 200-mile, 500-kilometer and 500-mile races, as well as in the three and six-hour races.

Three works cars were entered in the 1928 Tourist Trophy on the Ards circuit as well as two private Speeds driven by Edgar Maclure and K.S. Peacock. The latter won his class with an average speed of 59 mph (95 kph). A year later a fleet of seven Rileys entered the same event, taking first, second and third places. Winner Sammy Davis was to become a legend in his own lifetime.

In 1930 a private entrant stole the works drivers' show. C.R. Whitcroft, driving his own two-year-old Riley, registration PK 2721, won the 1100cc class in the Brooklands Double Twelve with ease, achieving an average speed of 70 mph (113 kph) over the 24 hours. In second place came Mrs Scott. As if to show that this was not all mere chance, Whitcroft again won his class in the 1932 Tourist Trophy and Joan Richmond and Elsie Wisdom secured first place in the Brooklands 1,000-Mile Race.

Riley's most successful year on the track, however, was yet to come. In the 24 Hours of Le Mans in 1934 it took overall second, third, fifth, sixth, twelfth, and thirteenth places, was class winner in the 1.1 and 1.5-liter categories and carried off the Team Prize and Rudge Whitworth Cup. And on top of this, Miss Dorothy Champney and Mrs Kay Petre achieved the distinction of being the fastest all-woman team in the history of the race. All the six Rileys and their teams then had to do was to make their way home—which they managed under their own steam.

The pointed "stern" of the Brooklands Nine was normal racing practice for the day and could also be seen on various Bugattis as well as the Aston Martin International. Like them, the Riley had only token fenders, which could be rapidly removed. The winged filler cap also reveals the model's racing aspirations. The middle section is deliberately wide in order to accommodate two people.

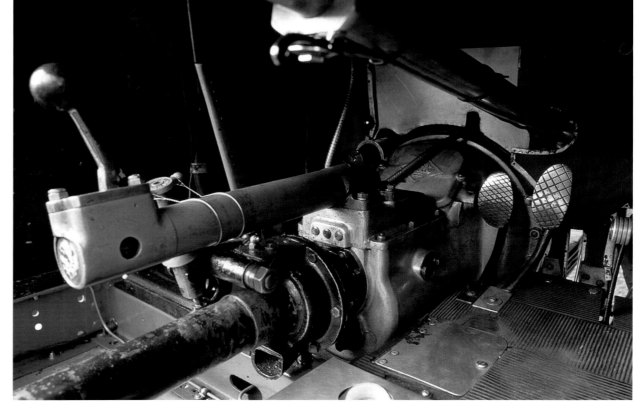

The idea for the Brooklands originated with J.G. Parry-Thomas, who began work developing a sports car out of the "civilian" Nine towards the end of 1926. Because of the way the frame was constructed, the resulting vehicle was so low that its occupants could touch the ground with the flat of their hands. They also had to suffer being cheek by jowl with the car's mechanicals.

The steering column extends into the cockpit almost horizontally. The most important of the instruments—the tachometer—stands out as by far the largest dial on the dashboard. The sprightly little engine could deliver around 50 bhp at 6000 rpm.

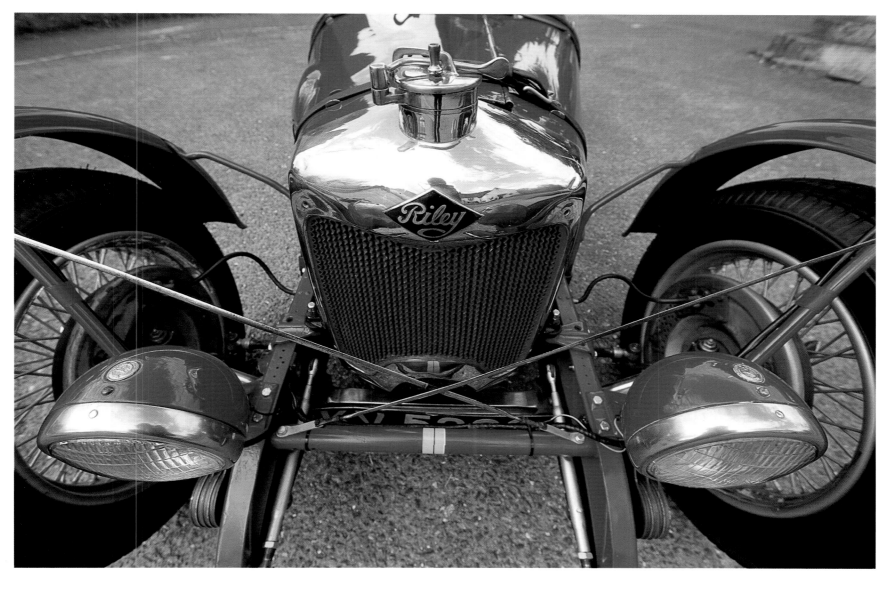

The overhead valves of this small four-cylinder unit are operated by two camshafts positioned high up on the sides of the engine block. The sports variant was given further attention with high-compression pistons, special camshafts, twin carburetors, a four-tube exhaust manifold, and an alternative oil pump.

RILEY SPRITE

In the beginning was the engine: since 1928 the tradition of the four-cylinder, 1.5-liter engine had gradually dried up at Riley (Coventry) Limited, meaning that an attractive market segment was lying fallow. The transmission specialist Hugh Rose was given the job of plugging the gap as quickly as possible. This decision seems to have been preceded by a dispute between the Riley brothers: Victor and Stanley were in favor of four cylinders; Percy would have preferred six.

The new engine was ready in September 1934: a modern design with two high cams, hemispherical combustion chambers with crossflow cooling, a crankshaft with three bearings, and a Zenith carburetor that was later replaced by two Zenith or SU carbs. In terms of performance this little marvel was no slouch: the standard version produced 45 and later 46 bhp, a Special-Series variant delivered 52 bhp and the Sprite version 59 and later 61 bhp. This power plant was Rose's parting gift to his employers: later that year he moved to a new job at Lea-Francis.

Not believing in doing things by halves, the Rileys wanted to make further changes. The new engine was soon joined by a newly designed box frame with solid crossmembers that rendered it extremely rigid and strong. Furthermore, within the context of an all-encompassing burst of innovation, the exteriors of the pre-existing Kestrel sedan and Lynx models were polished up and the Falcon sedan was proudly presented with fashionable "aero-line" styling—a kind of prehistoric fastback. This provided more space fore and aft as well as more headroom, and also fully synchronized four-speed transmission. Its tires and attractive wire wheels with central spinners were made by Dunlop (as were those of the other models in the 1.5-liter range) and its wedge brakes by Girling.

As usual, the reception from the motoring press was extremely favorable, but the company had no intention of resting on its laurels. On the contrary, this was the beginning of the most productive phase in the marque's history. Over the next year numerous improvements were introduced and new products, such as the aesthetically flawless Riley Six Light Kestrel, appeared as if by magic.

It slightly overshadowed Riley's Sprite sports, an elegant open-top two-seater with increased streamlining, whose chassis consisted of longitudinal members that bent up and around at the front and ran underneath the rear axle. An early brochure shows the Sprite with the traditional Riley radiator grill, but this was to make way on the first completed production model (registration BDU 727), and at the car's debut at the 1935 London Motor Show, to an agreeably shaped, more streamlined front.

On most of the Sprite production vehicles, as well as on the Riley 2-liter Racing Six, a sloping grill with widely spaced chrome bars afforded a good view inside.

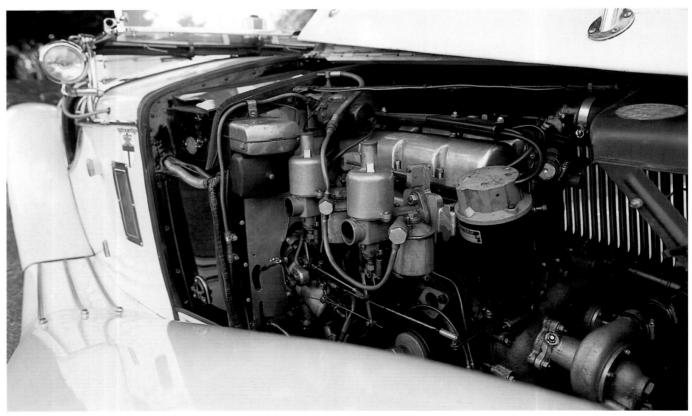

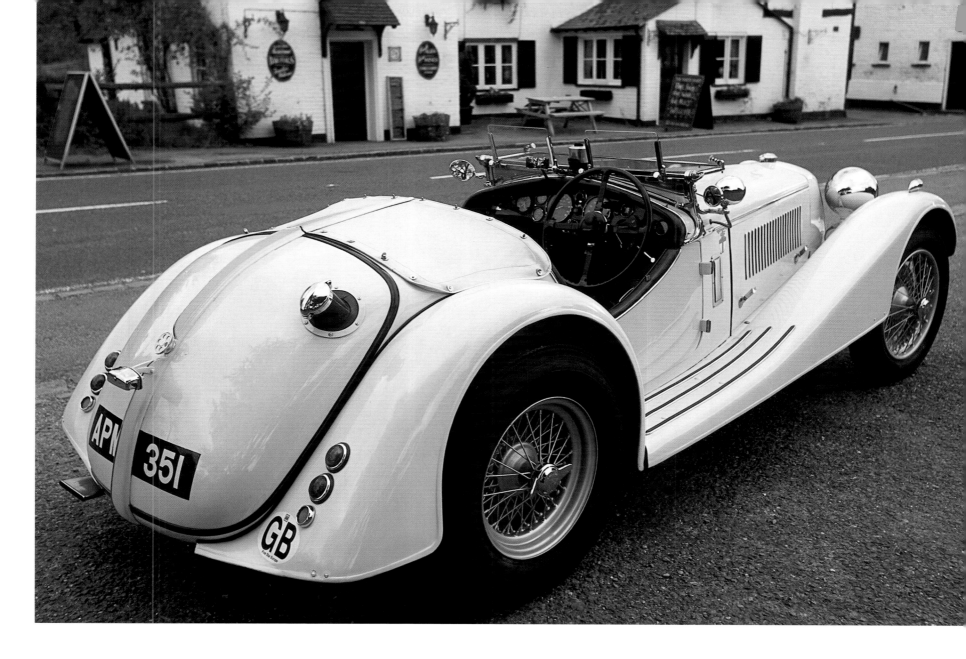

The Sprite was powered by a tuned-up version of Riley's 1496cc 12/4 engine. Later versions were equipped with crossflow cylinder head cooling, designed to allow higher compression using 80-octane gasoline. Razor-sharp tailfins, admittedly only hinted at here, could also be found on contemporaries such as the Lagonda M45 R Le Mans.

The TT competition variant, which was available in full battle readiness with either the same engine, a six-cylinder of almost identical displacement or rebored variants of the latter, offering 1808 and occasionally 1986cc, was never meant for general sale. While the 2-liter TT did appear in a 1936 company brochure with a price tag of £550, this must have been more for information than as a real invitation to buy. The small Riley six had a number of manifest qualities—silky running, plenty of power, and rugged reliability—which were put to good use in powering the supercharged racers built by ERA (English Racing Automobiles), for example, but it was allowed to lapse into rarity status, having never been given the opportunity to prove its worth in any of the major production series.

The Sprite's four-cylinder engine, on the other hand, was destined for greater things. It was made available initially to the Kestrel and Lynx models, and from 1937 to the entire 1.5-liter range, for an extra charge of £48. In the final year of its production the price of the Sprite was increased by £25 to £450, which had a big impact on sales: just 47 examples are known from registration details to survive today, around half the original production. A manual version was offered as an alternative to the pre-select transmission, but this was rejected by potential purchasers for being too crude, and hardly anyone bought it.

At around the same time, the ambitious family firm succumbed to a devastating financial crisis. Sir W.H. Peat was appointed official receiver and company manager, taking the helm of the damaged ship on February 24, 1938. In September the same year, Lord Nuffield acquired what was left of the company for £143,000, and Riley (Coventry) Ltd (whose slogan was: "As old as the industry, as modern as the hour") was reborn under the name Riley (Coventry) Successors Ltd. The company achieved a kind of protected species status based on a promise wrested from the new owner that he would not interfere with the very special character of the company.

Soon after, however, Nuffield sold his new acquisition to Morris Motors Ltd—for a pound, as was rumored at the time, giving rise to the unusual situation in which an entire car manufacturer could be bought for less than the price of one of its products.

RILEY RMC

Riley's Coventry production plant was reduced to rubble by World War II, a state of affairs viewed overwhelmingly by the firm as an opportunity. Under the leadership of appropriately named project manager Harry Rush, a fresh sheet of paper was produced and a team set to work without delay on writing a new chapter. This work was stoked by a new sense of cohesion and corporate mission like that of the early 1920s—evident in the company's use of resonant advertising slogans such as "Rileyability." The new products were helped on their way—quite justifiably as it turned out—by the tag-line, "Magnificent Motoring." Another spur may have been the blow to corporate pride inflicted by Lord Nuffield when he incorporated the traditional family firm into his combine in September 1938: the name of the new entity, RM (standing for Riley Motors), speaks of a defiant reassertion of the unit's own identity.

The first post-war Riley, a sedan offering tasteful, classic styling with generous sweeping fenders and running boards, a vertical grill and partially integrated headlamps, was announced in late summer 1945 and was ready by spring 1946. It was based on a box frame with front independent suspension consisting of twin wishbones and torsion bars, and a rigid axle resting on semi-elliptic springs at the back. Two different wheelbases were created, accompanied by corresponding differences in the dimensions of the hood and the front wings: 113 inches (2858 mm) for the smaller of the two engines (1496cc) in the RMA and 119 inches (3023 mm) for the larger, with displacement of 2443cc (the "world's largest four-cylinder") in the RMB, which was designed to appeal to a discriminating clientele.

Although the two engines had their roots in different epochs of Riley's history, they resembled each other in that they were both long-stroke units with camshafts set high into the sides of the engine block and both had hemispherical combustion chambers and crossflow units on top of their cylinder heads. Power was transmitted to the rear axle via a torque tube, and from 1952, when the hydro-mechanical brakes were replaced by fully hydraulic ones, by means of a cardan shaft.

The RMC Roadster, built on the same chassis as the 2.5-liter saloon, was aimed predominantly at the lucrative North American market, as indicated by its deep fenders (with emphatic overriders) that wrapped around the vulnerable sides. Its bench seat could accommodate two people comfortably and three with a bit of a squeeze. Room for the third had been created by moving the gearshift onto

First impressions did not deceive: the Riley RMC Roadster was as solid as it looked. Despite the lack of fixed roof the bodywork did not shake and sway thanks to an unusually strong chassis structure. Both front and rear of this

ROADSTER

the steering column. A button had to be pressed on the knob of the gearshift in order to engage reverse gear. Women in short frocks were doubly inconvenienced when sitting in the middle as they were required to straddle the wide propshaft tunnel and suffer the pronounced curve of the lower edge of the dashboard in their lap.

The purpose of the fishtail at the end of the exhaust pipe was to generate a refined and sporty designer sound. The enormously long rear of the Riley roadster combined three separate elements: a well into which the easy-to-operate fold-back top disappears completely from view, an unusually large luggage space, and a capacious fuel tank that was filled via two nozzles beneath the trunk lid. It could hold 24 US gallons (91 liters), giving a maximum traveling distance on English roads of 450 miles (725 km)—as *Autocar* was happy to record in its issue of September 24, 1948—even on the inferior gasoline available during those post-war years.

In fact, the magazine revealed itself to be very taken with the fast roadster. A speed of 98 mph (158 kph) had been electrically recorded (in two directions, with the windshield down) along a stretch of Belgian highway. Under normal conditions, and not motivated by any desire to break records—or so noted the article's author—a glance at the speedometer had shown that the car was traveling at 75 mph (120 kph). As an open-topped addition to the marque's fixed-roof products, the roadster was following in a tradition that dated from before the war, he observed. With the same transmission, the same power, and roughly the same weight, the performance was similar, and like its fixed-roof siblings, the open sports even displayed an agreeable rigidity—on poor surfaces too.

Steering was accurate and smooth, though the car had to be given extra gas at low speeds (when parking, for example). As one would expect with a Riley, the car conveyed an impression of extreme solidity and high quality. The author even commented approvingly on the semi-integrated head-lamps positioned between fenders and hood, seeing them as a nod to the spirit of the times but by no means out of keeping with the roadster's very British looks.

Around 507 RMCs were produced between September 1948 and January 1951, 121 of them at the old Coventry plant. In 1949, at the behest of combine head Lord Nuffield, who wanted to bring together all his firm's sports and exclusive marques under one roof, it was announced that Riley would be moving to the MG works in Abingdon.

The 2.5-liter roadster was therefore the last of its type.

three-seater were protected by substantial fenders – incorporating strong double overriders—that wrapped around the sides of the car. The lightly angled radiator grill takes up a feature introduced by Riley before the war.

When folded back, the canopy disappeared completely into a space behind the back of the seat. Beneath the rear hump was a luggage compartment of remarkable proportions, and behind this the fuel tank, whose twin filler caps were shielded from view by the trunk lid. Like Riley's sedans, the car had a two-part hood.

SINGER ROADSTER

In many respects, the history of Singer Motors Ltd of Coventry can be seen as a paradigm of the history of British car firms in general: modest beginnings as manufacturer of bicycles (1874) and then tricycles, entry into the motorcycle (1900) and then automobile (1905) markets, glory days, decline and collapse, hostile takeover (1955 by Rootes), and finally a phantom existence as a mere name on another company's products (Chrysler).

In 1933 the company turned its hand to sports models, but suffered a severe setback on September 7, 1935 when three works cars spun out of control on the same curve on the Ards circuit, all sustaining damage to their steering. Fortunately nobody was injured but a photographer was present and the resulting pictures were shown all over the world. This caused the Singer Smile, an optimistic product of the company's advertising, to fade from even the hardest-bitten Singer enthusiast.

The company was not remotely lost for words, however: publicity material for the launch of the Nine Roadster in Singer's London showroom on March 6, 1939, for example, featured the following breezy invitation: "Singer invite You to the Season's most important coming out." The accompanying picture showed two cheerful young women, one of them at the large triple-spoked wheel of the open four-seater, and a rather uncomfortable-looking man. The copy claimed that the vehicle was "The greatest little roadster of our Time."

The best thing about the big-acting car was its engine, though despite its overhead camshaft this was a modest 1074cc affair delivering a moderate 36 bhp, and Nine Roadster drivers had to make do with only three speeds. The chassis was thoroughly conventional: a box frame with rigid axles. The simple bodywork design, which featured an element of streamlining in the form of an upward-curving ducktail rear, was made of aluminum and, like the rest of the vehicle, was hand-crafted. As the back-seat passengers were positioned high above the rear axle, they were exposed to the full force of the wind. With the windshield folded down, this privilege could be democratically shared by all four occupants.

Production had hardly begun when it was brought to an abrupt end by World War II, but was rapidly resumed after the end of hostilities. Enhancements were initially unusually few and far between. The 4A variant of 1949 offered four speeds and its metamorphosed successor, the 4AB, which appeared in October 1950, took the bold step of introducing independent front (wishbones and coil springs) suspension.

The 4AB was well into its dotage and barely sellable any longer by the time Singer's attempt at combining classic and modern, the SM Roadster (also known as the 4AD), was unveiled at the 1951 Geneva Road Show. Continuity with its predecessor was afforded by its chassis and also bodywork, with a few retouches here and there including altered rear lighting. The new model was represented by an increase in engine size to 1497cc and in power to 48 bhp with a single carburetor.

September 1952 saw the appearance of a 1.5-liter twin-carb version producing 58 bhp. With the help of the second carb, the gritty little machine gained an extra six or so miles (around 10 km) per hour, but came up against its limits at around 80 mph (129 kph) due to wind resistance. Sightlines to the rear were improved at the same time, more legroom created for the back-seat passengers and the fenders were wrapped around the corners and equipped with robust overriders. This demonstrates where Singer continued to see its main market: among a core of steadfast Anglophiles in the United States, not dissimilar to the purchasers of MG's competing TC and TD models.

By the time the new model was launched on the domestic market in 1954, it was already being rumored that Singer's

days as an independent company were numbered. Nonetheless, a total of 3440 examples had sold by 1955, and the car received good reports in the British motoring press. *The Motor*, for example, opined that the new Singer was extremely well suited for carrying four people with a relatively small amount of luggage on short journeys or two people with plentiful luggage on long ones. *The Autocar* declared that there was no question the vehicle filled a market niche and its existence was therefore justified, going on to observe that while it may not belong to the noble supersports class, it nevertheless guaranteed four people a pleasant ride in the fresh air, giving them far more fun than the average family jalopy. Its closing remark was that the SM was a compact, willing little car of lively disposition.

The 4AB, declared a full-page advert in *The Autocar* of February 9, 1951, was the famous Nine Roadster with a new look, offering a new driving experience and licensed for the domestic market. Independent front suspension, it continued, was taking the car to new heights in terms of performance, comfort and ease of handling. The comment about a new look, if not the rest, is a charming exaggeration, as the changes consisted merely of relieving the front wings of some of their volume and lowering the hood slightly.

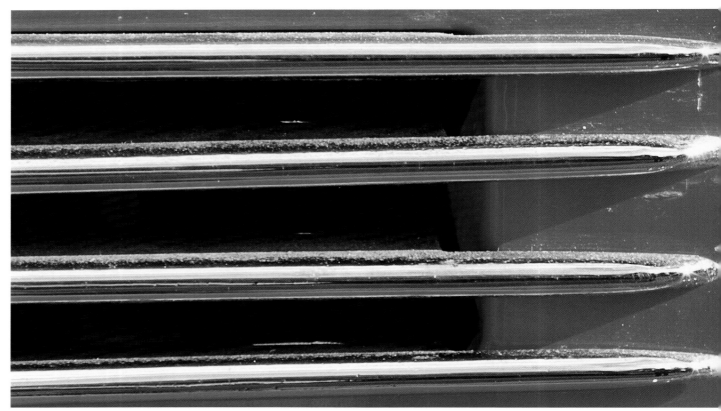

The small roadster exhibited refined craftsmanship and a devotion to detail, evident here in its uncluttered dashboard with attractive curving frame. Passenger and driver sat huddled together behind the tiny engine and were afforded protection from the wind by a windshield of Gothic proportions. The little car gleams with plentiful chrome decoration.

SUNBEAM ALPINE

For the generation born around the turn of the twentieth century, the name Sunbeam was, during the early 1950s, synonymous with motor racing. For certain periods between 1911 and 1925, the marque had been Great Britain's sole representative in the Grand Prix. One year that stands out in particular from the inter-war period is 1923, when Henry Segrave won the French Grand Prix in Tours for the company and Sunbeams also took second and fourth places.

Between 1937 and 1953, however, the car world at large had to make do without the distinguished products from the firm's Wolverhampton (and later Coventry) works. In 1935 that multi-headed corporate Hydra, the Rootes group, swallowed Sunbeam competitor Talbot and three years later Sunbeam itself.

For a while the illustrious Sunbeam-Talbot name was used as a badge to adorn the staid luxury machines of Hillman and Humber, but efforts were being made at the same time to revive the enfeebled sporting myth of the two

Rootes subsidiaries. A suitable forum for this was the Alpine Rally, and a range of trophies bear witness to successes in 1932, 1934, 1948, 1950, and 1951 in particular.

A stroke of luck led to Norman Garrad, the dynamic head of the Competition Department, enlisting the services of the young Stirling Moss. Moss, who was keen to enter the Monte Carlo Rally, made some casual enquiries while strolling through the 1951 London Motor Show and was enthusiastically taken on. He even waived the princely fees his manager Ken Gregory normally demanded in his name. In the Alpine Rally of 1952, the elite team of Moss/Cutts, Hawthorn/Chipperton, and Murray-Frame/Pearman won the manufacturers' team prize in Sunbeam-Talbot 90s and also the Challenge Cup of the Automobile Clubs of Marseille and Provence.

The same year, George Hartwell, a Rootes dealer in Bournemouth and a passionate rally driver known for his aggressive treatment of his vehicles, converted a Sunbeam-

In the early 1950s a car truly capable of 95 mph (153 kph) with adequate luggage space was a rarity, particularly when it happened to be an open two-seater. The Sunbeam Alpine was an exception and its elegant trunk contained a spacious, if somewhat flat storage space. The car's slightly cumbersome and stolid appearance was more than made up for by a carefully managed publicity offensive that focused on its rallying accomplishments. The person who was actually responsible for its appealing lines—a mixture of the conventional and the bang up to date—has been lost in the mists of time.

Talbot 90 Mk II A drophead coupé into an open two-seater for his own use. The exact genesis of the car's body shape has been lost in the mists of time, but it is likely that Hartwell himself produced an initial design that was refined (at the very least) by car stylist Raymond Loewy at his studios in South Bend, USA.

Striking features include the long, rounded trunk behind two bucket seats and the multiple louvers in the top of the hood. The box frame of the original four-seater was strengthened through the substitution of more robust longitudinal members and an additional crossmember beneath the engine. The suspension remained unchanged: wishbones and coil springs in front, a rigid axle and semi-elliptic springs to the rear. The output of the 2.3-liter engine was increased by four to 81 horsepower as a result of a small improvement in compression, a new valve mechanism and a new carburetor.

A slightly sleepy family car was thus transformed into a rather less stolid and indubitably attractive two-seater of harmonious proportions. It was also equipped with all the luxuries that vehicles of this marque normally offered. Despite its sporting origins, a sure sign that the car came in peace was its gearshift on the steering column.

When Hartwell drove to Coventry and showed his creation to Bernard Winter, the head of Sunbeam-Talbot's construction department, Winter immediately decided to adopt the foundling and include it in his production plans. The name that presented itself as the most suitable was the Alpine, because of the well-known achievements of the marque in the European rally of the same name. And since statistics counted for more in the sports than in the non-sports world, an early Alpine, registration plate MWK 969, was taken to Belgium for testing, where a stretch of highway in the vicinity of Jabbeke was ideal for high-speed excesses that were not possible in the British Isles. The driver in charge of the vehicle was Sheila van Damm, a sturdy racing Amazon who had acquired the reputation of being completely fearless. The story went that on one occasion she lifted and held up the corner of a car for as long as it took to change a wheel. With a few modifications such as a tarp over the passenger seat, an undertray and protective driver's overalls instead of a windshield, she achieved 120 mph (193 kph) over the flying kilometer. This figure flatters the car's fundamentally rather phlegmatic character, however: the overdrive introduced on the car as standard in fall 1954 brought the top speed down to barely 100 mph (160 kph). Stirling Moss, who along with team mates Murray-Frame, van Damm, and John Fitch won a Coupe des Alpes in 1953, confided 30 years later to motoring author Graham Robson that his car had been excruciatingly slow. Nevertheless he repeated his success in 1954, making it three in a row. During this time more and more rally victories were confronted by fewer and fewer sales, partly because the Triumph TR2 and the Austin-Healey 100 represented better-value, faster alternatives. And so, having sold around 3000 units, the first-generation Sunbeam Alpines failed to see out 1955.

SUNBEAM TIGER

The second-generation Sunbeam Alpine, furnished with clear lines by Rootes designers Kenneth Howes and Roy Axe, was without doubt an attractive car. One small problem was that the tail-fins, the product of a striving for overall horizontality, were a little too long and the body line was a little too low for contemporary taste. In 1964 the tail-fins were trimmed back to more traditional proportions. The scope for further changes was limited by the fact that the Alpine was built on the floorpan of the Hillman Husky.

As a result the car came to be dogged by a reputation for innocuousness, although the five series produced between July 1959 and January 1968 found 69,251 takers and the Mark V version of 1965 was capable of 100 mph.

The lack of machismo was a source of great irritation to Ian Garrad, manager of Rootes subsidiary Rootes Motors Inc on the American west coast. His latent displeasure turned to angry determination when his tweaked Alpine was left standing at traffic lights one day by a little old lady in a sedan. The worst thing about the incident was that the culprit did not even notice the humiliation she had caused the ambitious salesman.

This was the starting point for the Tiger. Formula One world champion Jack Brabham advised Garrad to replace the Alpine's sensible 1.6-liter four-cylinder motor with an American V8 unit. The engine he had in mind might not be the best from a technological point of view, but was powerful, effortless, and reliable. Garrad asked his service manager Walt McKenzie to carefully measure the engine bay of the Alpine and to his surprise found that the compact 4.2-liter, 164-bhp Ford Fairline small block unit, the lightest cast iron V8 in the world, fitted, even if it did take up every inch.

In the end the conversion was carried out by Carroll Shelby, who had made a name for himself in the world of macho motoring with his work on the AC Cobra and who had good connections with Ford. After a meeting with Shelby himself, his development engineer and test driver Ken Miles and Ford representative Ray Geddes at his American plant in Venice, California, Ian Garrad gave the project the green light. For a $10,000 fee and a royalty for every car sold, the Texan undertook to create a prototype in eight (actually it turned out to be 12) weeks.

The prototype was ready for inspection and initial test driving on April 29, 1963. The V8 was fitted as far back as possible, the bulkhead strengthened in order to stiffen the whole structure, the Alpine's steering replaced by that of the MGA, and the battery moved to the rear. The front suspension (wishbones and coil springs) remained basically unchanged while a Panhard rod was added at the back in order to keep the rear rigid axle and semi-elliptic leaf springs in check.

Teething problems were sorted out by Ken Miles and Garrad then put in 40,000 miles behind the wheel of the white test vehicle, making sure the necessary final adjustments were made. After briefly testing the vehicle out himself, Lord Rootes revealed himself to be utterly smitten, even though the handbrake had been left on, filling the car with a pungent smell. At a hastily arranged meeting in the Bahamas, Henry Ford III agreed to supply 3600 engines a year with the proviso that Lee Iacocca agreed. He did.

The first choice of sobriquet for the fleet-footed hybrid was Thunderbolt, but it turned out that Chrysler had already acquired the rights to this name. In the end the newcomer was christened Tiger in memory of Sunbeam's glory days—specifically Henry Segrave's 1926 world record-breaking machine. The Tiger debuted at the New York Auto Show in spring 1964.

Meanwhile it occurred to Lord Rootes that they had made a fatal mistake: the car lacked the necessary threatening appearance to go with its feral name. While competitors Cobra and Corvette Sting Ray wore their power on their sleeves, the muscle variant of the Alpine was the very model of English understatement, a Tiger in sheep's clothing, so to speak. The only indications of the beast lurking beneath the hood, that this was not just another much-maligned run-of-the-mill Alpine going peaceably about its business, were a narrow chrome strip along the sides, and the Tiger logo.

Due to a lack of capacity, production was farmed out to Jensen Motors of West Bromwich, Birmingham. Following an initial run of 6495 units, the model was made fiercer still through the substitution of a larger Ford unit in 1966. A 4.7-liter engine now pumped out 200 bhp, producing primordial torque. In addition, some careful retouching now made the Anglo-American wildcat look a shade more aggressive too. In the meantime, however, Chrysler had gained control of the Rootes Group. The consequences of this were the same as those of the Indian settlement of the Punjab: there was no longer any place for the tiger. The last of 571 examples of the second-series Tiger left the factory in West Bromwich on June 30, 1967.

A peculiarly English virtue—understatement—was the car's undoing. The Sunbeam Tiger was a wolf in sheep's clothing, but in a world in which appearances count for everything, nobody noticed because it came along in the completely unchanged guise of the Sunbeam Alpine. This look initially included rather over-long tail fins that were only trimmed in the Mark V version.

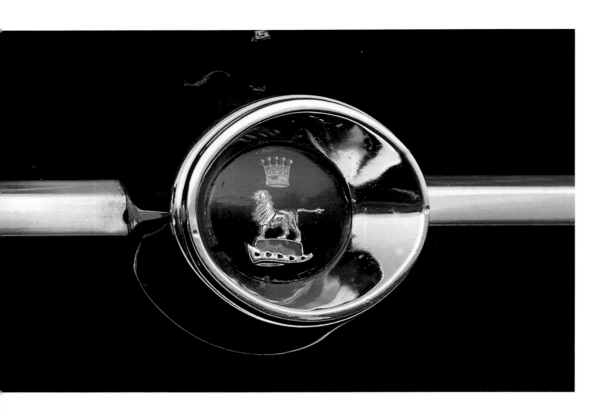

Even in the cockpit of the Tiger there is not the slightest indication that a Ford small block V8 had taken up residence beneath the car's forward-lifting hood. The only hints are the narrow chrome strip along the sides, the discreet Tiger logo and the low growl of the exhaust. Nevertheless, an aggressive advertising campaign in the USA was based on the idea that the car deserved to be shown respect: "Down cats—here comes the real Tiger."

SWALLOW DORETTI

If the name Swallow Coachbuilding provokes a sense of *déjà-vu*, this is because it is the company Sir William Lyons founded before moving away to pastures new in the 1930s, a departure which led to the creation of Standard Swallow and then Jaguar. The time-honored firm with which he first won his spurs subsequently changed owners more times than a worn cent before ending up under the umbrella of Tube Investments.

At around the same time it was decided that a fundamental change of direction was necessary. The company had made its name, and held its head above the water, with sidecars, but the market was in rapid decline. A public with greater purchasing power now preferred the bubble car, which offered elementary weather protection, if not something even more substantial.

It was decided that the company should build a sports car and so Swallow Coachbuilding Co (1935) Ltd entered into negotiations at its new site at Walsall Airport, Staffordshire, with Standard-Triumph boss Sir John Black to find out whether, in the light of earlier co-operation between the two companies, he would be prepared to support the project by supplying Triumph components such as the TR2 engine, transmission, suspension parts, and axles. To the astonishment of many observers, who suspected that he could be nurturing a viper in his bosom, Black gave his assent.

The task of developing the vehicle was handed to Frank Rainbow, an engineer with Tube Investments. A lattice framework was constructed using Reynolds 531 tubing and given an aluminum body over an inner skin of sheet steel.

The result, unveiled just 10 months later in 1954, was the Swallow Doretti, the latest star in the firmament of the British sports car. The rights to the name Doretti, with its melodious southern European ring, had been secured back in the 1930s, but it had been lying around gathering dust since then. The car's superior finish and excellent roadholding attracted high praise. Its pretty lines also went down well and resulted in an immediate influx of orders, above all from sunny California. The Triumph bosses and their dealers throughout the land were alarmed—the Doretti seemed to be developing into a real threat to their own products. Even

Tube Investments's customer Jaguar began to be affected by the competition, and they quickly suggested to Swallow's owners that, unless they took the rival off the market, the company ran the considerable risk of losing a lucrative parts-supply contract.

These broad hints, in the meanwhile, proved unnecessary. Another 10 months and 276 sales down the line it became clear that this was not to be the company's route to salvation. This swallow only made one summer and Triumph's triumph could not, in the end, be held back. The Doretti foundered as a result of inherent contradictions and factors that were entirely foreseeable.

The positioning of engine and transmission well back in the chassis benefited handling, but reduced the cabin to claustrophobic proportions, with small seats that offered inadequate support. And while the look of the robust two-seater was enhanced by the fact that the canopy, when opened, disappeared completely from view into a well behind the seats, this also meant there was very limited luggage space in the remaining part of the trunk, a defect that Swallow attempted to remedy by supplying a set of tailor-made leather cases with the vehicle as standard.

The main factor in the Doretti's undoing, however, was that it had to compete in the same league as the TR2, which had come on the market at the same time. While the Doretti may have been the Triumph's equal in terms of looks and maneuverability, in all other respects it lagged behind. Whereas the Triumph's top speed—a vital consideration for all potential sports cars buyers—was 103 mph (166 kph), the Doretti could only squeeze 97 mph (156 kph) from the same 1991cc, 90 bhp unit. Where the Triumph could reach 60 mph (100 kph) in 11.2 seconds, the Doretti took a second and a half longer, wounding statistical pride if nothing else. Where the Coventry roadster could be had for £844, its purchasers thus benefiting from TR's higher production volume and lower unit cost, customers for the Walsall roadster had to pay £1102—30 percent more—in return for a dubious abstract benefit: greater exclusivity. Where Standard-Triumph could offer a large, well-trained customer service network, Swallow owners had to be prepared to go out of their way to find service, care, and maintenance.

Ultimately, the car's downfall came through no fault of its own: in fall 1953 Sir John Black had had an accident in a Doretti, and Swallow's board used this as their official reason for axing it. Three examples of a more comfortable 2+2 successor, the Sabre, had already been built, but the new model was dropped. In the end, two superlatives could at least be applied to the Doretti: it was able to go down in history as both the first and last car to be built by Swallow Coachbuilding Co. Ltd.

The attractive lines of the Swallow Doretti intimate that its downfall would not result from any lack of appeal, but from its potential for success: manufacturer Tube Investments feared the wrath of Jaguar and one-time Swallow boss William Lyons and opted to take its own product quietly off the market rather than sacrificing a contract to supply its larger competitor with everyday automotive accessories such as door handles and fenders.

In designing the Doretti, Frank Rainbow borrowed certain ideas from the Austin-Healey 100, while the car's engine and suspension were taken wholesale from the Triumph TR2. In terms of market positioning, it also shared the same target customers as these, although it was very pricey, even taking into account comforts such as heating and tailor-made luggage sets.

TRIUMPH ROADSTER

In 1887, in the middle of the flourishing cycling boom at the end of the nineteenth century, two Germans named Siegfried Bettmann and Mauritz Johann Schulte founded the New Triumph Cycle Co Ltd in Coventry. The word Triumph—meaning the same in German as it does in English—is used in many European languages, and the new owners had no intention of hiding their light under a bushel.

The first Triumph car appeared in 1923, but Schulte's part had meanwhile been taken over by Lieutenant Colonel Claude Holbrook, and in 1913 the hard-working Bettmann had risen to be mayor of Coventry, as the only foreigner among 559 colleagues.

The new model was the 10/20, but it left no lasting impression on the motoring populace. It announced a racy and well equipped range of models for the 1930s, which belonged in the upper-middle class motoring sector and was a genuinely worthy alternative to the products of archrival SS Cars Ltd. Nevertheless, like so many others, the Triumph Motor Company got into deep water and in 1939 had to declare bankruptcy. On November 24, 1944 the boss of the Standard Motor Company, Sir John Black, took the sad remains of the moribund firm under his wing. A neo-aristocrat, he was an authoritarian who ran his company to the great satisfaction of his shareholders, and made both sober and sobering judgements. One such was that the Triumph collapse was not accidental but rather the final word on the wrong policy. Moreover, German air raids had already laid waste to a considerable part of the production plant in November 1940, so a comprehensive new beginning was needed, and as quickly as possible.

Rationalization was the order of the day: two different models would be created, but on the same technical base. Many parts were to be siphoned off the Standard production lines, but it was dictated that the established Triumph label would not be allowed to degenerate into a mere fig leaf for badge engineering. Steel, the blue gold of the late war and early post-war years, had to be used sparingly. But Black also had a personal account to settle: with his new models he wanted to make forays into the territory where SS Jaguar chief William Lyons felt so uniquely secure.

In early March 1946 the new models were taking shape, emerging as the Triumph 1800 Roadster and the 1800 Town and Country Saloon. For their chassis both used a tubular structure taken under the rear axle and designed by Ray Turner, enabling two different wheelbases to be used—108 inches (2740 mm) for the limousine and 100 inches (2540 mm) for the open tourer. The front wheels had

independent suspension using triangular track control arms above, with a transverse leaf spring beneath, set behind on a rigid axle that was supported by semi-elliptical springs and fitted with a stabilizer bar.

The engine, a four-cylinder unit of 1776cc and 63 bhp, taken from the Flying Standard model, was supplied exclusively to Jaguar until 1939 and was still being used in the rival factory's current touring models. Triumph used the same four-gear transmission as Jaguar, but preferred to keep its gearshift at the steering wheel.

For its silhouette, the saloon designer Walter Belgrove, who worked for Triumph from 1933 to 1955, revived the sharply accentuated knife edge of the 1930s—there were similarly shaped models by Rolls-Royce, Bentley, and Daimler. Frank Callaby was responsible for the swinging curves of the Roadster. He presented his first drafts to Black as early as October 1944 and finally got the go-ahead for a drawing at an eighth of the full size.

As so often was the case, Sir John happily assumed the sketch could have been his own, secretly envying William Lyons' creative trait. Before being hung over an ash frame, the aluminum panels of the Roadster were shaped with rubber presses, as used in aircraft manufacture during the war.

While the detailing of the section from the window B-pillar rearward was handled by Callaby's colleague and friend Arthur Ballard, Black only suggested one real anachronism: in addition to the three narrow seats on a single front bench, two dickey seats would be included behind, accessed by opening a dual cover over the trunk, the front half of which would be raised to form a second windshield like a pair of spectacles. Passengers clambered into the emergency accommodation up tiny steps set at the ends of the bumper.

But the result was controversial—particularly on the hoped-for market across the Atlantic, where response proved to be barely lukewarm. When the company tried again with a retouched version at the Earl's Court Motor Show in 1948 it included the 2088cc power plant from the Standard Vanguard fitted with two carburetors; simple, long-lived and easy to maintain, but with only 5 bhp more it was very little faster, particularly as the Vanguard, with its mere three-gear transmission, could accelerate up to 60 mph (100 kph) only a fraction faster—in just under half a minute.

In October 1949 the Triumph Roadster 2000 lapsed into obscurity as unnoticeably as it had survived, with a dismal tally of 2000 models sold. The fact that only 148 examples were exported tells us of the extent of this tale of woe.

Unlike the sharp contours of the 1800 saloon from which it was derived, the Triumph Roadster was gently rounded, but with its striking front fenders and corresponding historical references behind, it took up motifs distinctly belonging in the past. Both bodies were made by Mulliners in Birmingham.

The folding seats under the two rear covers were the latest thing in the 1920s, but they greatly restricted trunk space, and passengers in the back must have felt in some way underprivileged. It was fairly difficult to get into the dickey seats, access being up little steps to the left and right of the bumper. It was fairly certain that the Triumph Roadster would be the last model built in this way.

TRIUMPH TR2

Sir John Black, Standard-Triumph's chief, had three things to worry about in 1950. Jaguar, the rival he most loved to hate, was soaring into unassailable heights with its victorious XK120. The Roadster successor, known as the TRX, indifferently styled by in-house designer Walter Belgrove, was as round as a huge boiled sweet licked smooth. The three prototypes flopped, while the sharp-edged MG TC, with its suggestion of antiquity, was selling like hot cakes, particularly abroad. Meanwhile, the Morgan clan was manfully resisting the energetic magnate's check book and his efforts to persuade them to seek a new home for the motor company that had grown old with honour, and escape financial worries under the Standard roof.

No wonder Black was eager for satisfaction. The last two had to be beaten on their own ground, with a simple, light and fast two-seater roadster. As always, the designers were told to realise the project with the minimum of cost and labor, and to use as many components as possible from current production. Capacities were still tied up in a new small Standard model, the Eight, and the new sports model could only really come on line in July 1952. But time was already pressing on—the deadline was the opening of the London Motor Show in October.

John Turnbull was given the order for the chassis, and he remembered with pleasure that a few box frames from the pre-war Flying Nine model were still lying around in Standard's attic. He modified one of them for his new model, transforming it with the Triumph Mayflower suspension, radial control arms with coil springs at the front, and for the rear, the usual rigid axle attached to semi-elliptical leaf springs.

The engine was a revised version of the two-carburetor engine of the TRX with 1991cc and 75 bhp, and the transmission was from the Standard Vanguard model, although this version had four gears and the gearshift lever was in the centre. The shape—again from Walter Belgrove's drawing board and composed of cleanly shaped panels that were easy to cut—essentially anticipated the TR2 but ended in a short, clumsily rounded back. The spare wheel was enthroned above it piggy-back—another whim of Black's, who was not always distinguished by stylistic refinement. The model shown at Earl's Court under the name "The Triumph Sports Car" was in fact the TR1—it's just that nobody had at that stage thought of serial numbering.

Reception was cool, largely because of the car's uninspiring rear section. Ken Richardson, a former BRM engineer and racing driver, took the Triumph round the block a few times to gain a first impression and handed it back with the dismayed comment: "It's a bloody death trap!"

Black's response was wise; he involved Richardson in developing the model further, and Richardson responded by

pounding innumerable miles at full speed in all weathers on the MIRA test run, the straight roads of Warwickshire and the bumpy mountain roads of Wales. In co-operation with Triumph veterans John Turnbull and Harry Webster he worked a veritable miracle in the next three months—visually as well.

The ugly duckling TR1 was turning into the beautiful TR2 swan. On December 10 the men reported to their boss that they were ready to go. The chassis, at first greatly inclined to twist and turn, had become much firmer, and nothing remained of the Flying Nine frame. The engine was now a four-cylinder 90 bhp unit, its power increased in careful stages with no cost to life expectancy. Most importantly, the designers had changed the rear, placing the petrol tank above the axle instead of behind it, and packing

the spare wheel away flat under its own cover with the license plate on top, so freeing a large amount of welcome space in the trunk and blending the whole with the successful front section, into one single, swinging line.

So the Triumph TR2, first shown at the Geneva Motor Show in March 1953, had almost imperceptibly become an automotive personality. It was mature, it had a certain something, moreover it was economical and more nimble than had been hoped for. Richardson could easily cruise round the MIRA track above the magic 100 mph (160 kph) in stretches. In fact, in May he reached 115 mph (185 kph) over the standing-start kilometer on a stretch of the Belgian autobahn near Jabbeke.

Two months later, production started. The first 1400 chassis were made by Standard-Triumph themselves, then the specialist firm Sankey took over. The bold target of 100 units a week had already been reached by spring 1954 and from June that year the company ordered 600 bodies a month from the coachbuilders Mulliners in Birmingham. Business in accessories such as overdrives and wire spoke wheels was already booming, and a fibreglass hard top became available for the car that fall. Altogether, 8628 examples of the second version, cured of a few early hiccups and with its doors set higher and shortened, were sold by October 1955.

An ironic quirk of fate: in January that year the first enthusiastic test report appeared in an English auto magazine, yet in the very same week Sir John Black resigned as Chairman of Standard-Triumph.

When the top is not visible the pleasing, practical shape of the TR2 is very enticing. Compared with the model shown at Earls Court in October 1952 its rear end is aesthetically satisfying and has been revised to carry on the sweeping line of the body overall. Adequate space is now available in the trunk and the spare wheel has its own compartment. The front windshield could easily be removed for drivers wanting to feel the wind in their face.

Test reports at the time stressed the excellent vision through the big windshield held by filigree columns. Another happy idea was the unusually shaped tunnel that channels the ram-air of forward motion to the radiator, so keeping the engine at moderate temperature. Hot air is expelled via suitable outlets at the windshield end of the bonnet.

The dials, as *Light Car* reported in July 1953, are sensibly arranged, particularly the big round speedometer and the rev counter. The handbrake and gearshift are placed just where the driver most likes them. The big glove compartment can be locked, a great virtue at the time.

The handsome rear of the TR2 was a view that many motorists would get to see—to the great delight of ambitious customers. The Triumph TR2 was acknowledged to be a "real" sports car: the 124 mph (200 kph) that test driver Ken Richardson achieved near Jabbeke in Belgium in spring 1953 was a very motivating sales coup. The tank, with its opening in the center, is located between the seat backs and the trunk.

TRIUMPH TR3

Karl Ludvigsen put it in a nutshell in March 1958. Writing in *Sports Cars Illustrated* he commented that he had rarely, if ever, met a man who had bought a TR2 or TR3 and regretted it. He said he could still remember the first time, in 1954, that he climbed into a TR2. After a day with the car he could only marvel at how they had managed to put so much together for so little money. It was one of those rare vehicles that one really did not want to get out of.

The article was already referring to the TR3A, which was fed into the market from September 9, 1957. But all these models had that quality: they were made as if to illustrate the dictionary entry "Roadster," with their archetypal shape and a macho toughness bordering on stability in concept but mobility in detail. .

The TR3 appeared in October 1955, in good time to take up the cudgels with the MGA. With its basic price of £650 (without purchase tax) it was £55 more expensive than its rival, but much more lively and almost 6 mph (10 kph) faster. Where in the earlier model a grill at the end of the funnel-shaped shaft between the horns of the front bumper kept the worst impact from the radiator behind, a grill simply set into the surrounding metal blocked that view.

Emergency seating was installed behind the narrow backs of the front seats, should it be required for a third passenger, who would sit at right angles to the direction of travel. The extra 5 bhp above the earlier model's performance were countered by greater weight. An overdrive by Laycock de Normanville was available as an option, and gears two to four could be switched on electrically using a switch directly beside the steering wheel. A GT Kit, as it was called, comprised a steel hard top and the outside door handles.

From chassis number TS 13046 of October 1956 the TR3 could offer a spectacular innovation: disc brakes at the front, in the middle of the strange empty space behind the hollow disc wheels. These were the first British series-produced vehicles to have them, while the world pioneer was the Chrysler Crown in 1949. In 1955 three works cars were entered for the Le Mans 24 Hours: one had Dunlop disc brakes all round, while the other two had a mixed system using drums at the rear and Girling discs in front. All three finished the event with little between them, but the hybrid solution was preferred for series production. Racing improves the breed—as did the purgatory of the Sarthe Marathon, where a mildly tuned cylinder head was forged that quickened the metabolism of the engine and added five more bhp until midsummer 1956, when it was replaced by the High Port head.

After 13,377 models had left the production line the TR3 was replaced by the TR3A, secretly and literally with no shout of triumph. A new model was already under discussion, but the firm nonetheless decided to update the existing, very successful car. Ironically, what was meant as an interim model became a bestseller, with 58,326 produced by October 1961.

It can be recognized by its broadly grinning radiator grill, scarcely hooded headlights above the corners of its mouth, and series-produced external handles for the doors and trunk, with more space behind the seating. The four growling cylinders and 100 bhp were obviously in their element. Reinhard Seiffert surmised in *auto motor und sport* in 1958 that this was not just a car to write about, rather that its very sound was being converted—consciously and deliberately by the makers—into a powerful public acoustic image.

Triumph boss Alick Dick and the directors at his side had long been enjoying intoxicating success. The US seemed to be insatiable. In the boom year of 1959, Mulliners, supplying the bodies, had to make up to 2000 a month. The customer could now order a 2138cc engine with 34-inch (860-mm)

The formal evolution of the popular Triumph Roadster can literally be read off from the appearances of the TR2 through to the TR3B. The TR3A of 1957 differs from its predecessor, the TR3, with a broader grill with parking lights set in the corners, part of a new front with more robust bumpers and headlights set further back. At the rear braking lights and indicators, previously close together, now lived separate lives. The doors and the lid of the trunk were given handles for the first time.

bore, well proven in numerous sports events, and as sound and reliable as the Standard engine. In the winter the firm overhauled the braking system and made a few small improvements to the cockpit, the windshield and the roof fastenings.

In December 1960 the sales curve dropped dramatically. The TR3B brought a brief upswing, with 3331 made by the Forward Radiator Company between March and October 1962—all for export to the United States. The 2138cc engine and fully synchronized gears in the last 2801 units were a forecast of things to come in the TR4. And then … a legend died, if only physically.

As early as 1957 *Autosport* had summarized the virtues of the TR3: it was fast, economical and extremely good value by the standards of its day. Its performance was good enough

for its entry in rallies, but its true strength was fast travelling over long distances—grand touring, if you will. Above all it was a practical car well fitted for bad weather conditions, offering adequate comfort and considerable luggage space for a car of its ilk.

The surging outline with the deep hollow just behind the middle of the car is one of the great attractions of this model. It was retained, as was the design of the engine, which, according to *Sports Cars Illustrated* in March 1958, released 100 very active horsepower. The magazine was much impressed by the sensible mechanical arrangement under the bonnet and the easy accessibility of important items such as the carburetor, spark plugs, and oil dipstick.

TRIUMPH
TR4 & TR5

Whatever was to take over the difficult inheritance of the aging superstar TR3 would need to be better in every respect and offer considerably more—maybe Italian dress sense would be the answer. So in summer 1957 Giovanni Michelotti was engaged to clothe the new model. Triumph's list of requirements left room for visions, but also imposed limits: it had to be a dream sports car based on the much-loved predecessor.

All things need time. Diverse prototypes were produced, like the Zest and the Zoom, and the best was filtered out for the final version. Series production of the body was assigned to a subsidiary company in Liverpool, the former Hall Engineering (Holdings) Ltd. The mistrust of the rather conservative US dealers was countered with the promise that the TR3 would continue to be built in a "B" variant for some time. The first production TR4 model left the factory in August 1961 and was presented to the public a month later. "Alick Dick's last Triumph" headlined an English publication with ironic *double entendre*—Standard-Triumph was taken over by Leyland Motors at the start of the year and the Triumph boss had just been fired.

Michelotti certainly started a revolution. He dropped the diagonals, stylistic features that had survived from the 1930s, and installed horizontals. Altogether he jettisoned the concept of the classical English sports roadster. Gone was the era of oblique door sections from which one could so elegantly dangle one's lower arm. Gone, too, was the era of soft side windows blowing in the wind. The resultant lack of ideology was made good by simple practical advantages, windows to wind down, for instance, and a big trunk. But the product was simply beautiful. It swept up, low and wide, its track widened at the front from 45 inches (1140 mm) to 48 inches (1220 mm), and at the rear from 46 inches (1160 mm) to 49 inches (1245 mm). The engine cover was wide and low, with a decorative raised section on the right to provide the necessary "headroom" for the two SU carburetors that fed the 2138cc 100 bhp engine (the 2-liter version was available as an option). Another option was a chic hard top, originally designed by Michelotti for a Ferrari and consisting of an aluminum frame at the rear with a pressed steel plate on top. It provided "limousine comfort" and an excellent all-round

The Triumph TR5 was the first of a new TR generation with six cylinders, and it only sold for 15 months. Apart from the relevant markings, the lines of its forerunners, the TR4 and TR4A, remained unchanged. The designers even left the drop-shaped raised section on the right of the engine cover in place. It was originally created by Giovanni Michelotti to provide the four-cylinder version with the necessary space for the dashpots of the two SU carburetors.

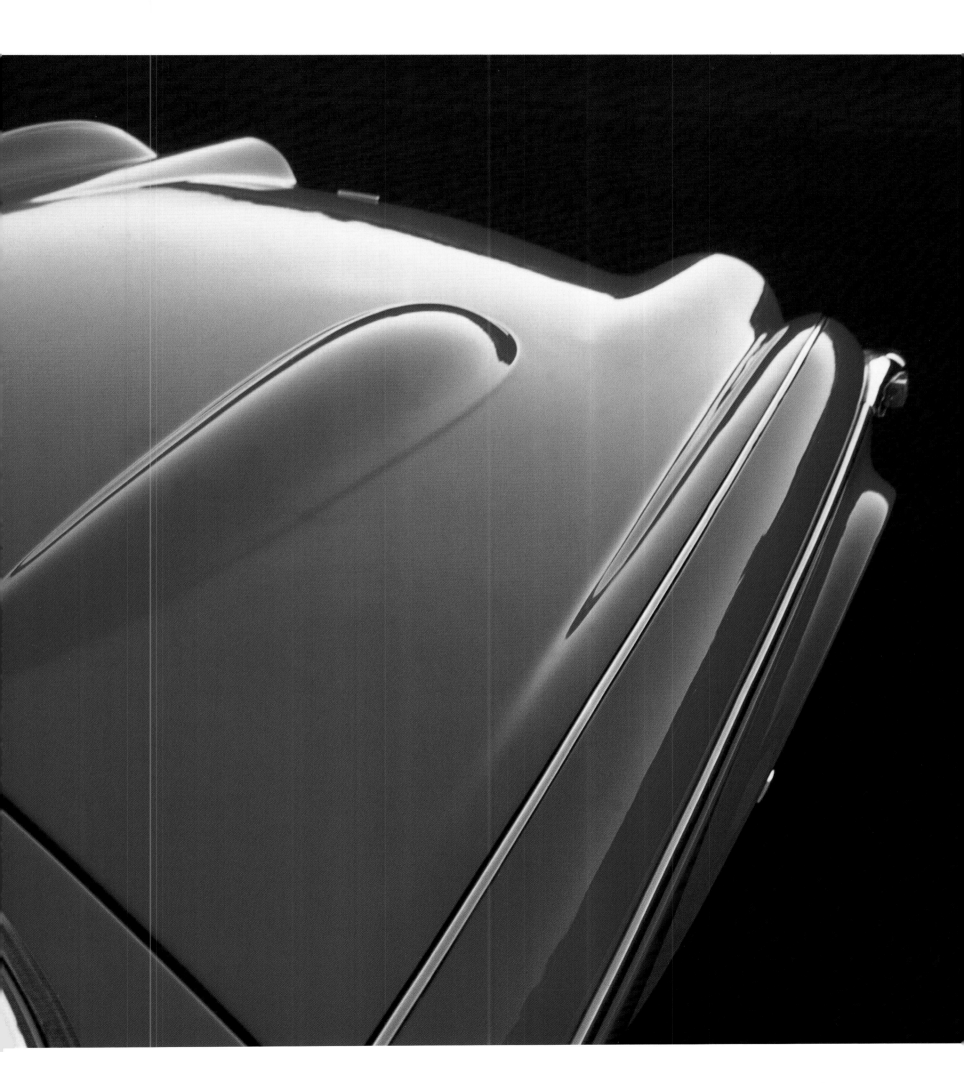

view. An option that proved less popular was the so-called Surrey Top, a light support with a vinyl cover. It was later developed into the Targa roof by Porsche.

At the end of 1962 the first 100 TR4s were fitted with Zenith-Stromberg Type 175CD carburetors, and after around 4000 had been made, the geometry of the front suspension was improved, smaller and lighter brake arms were installed and the seats were reworked. But regrettably, the Triumph still jolted its occupants unmercifully, not least thanks to its underslung layout that left little room for suspension springs.

In January 1965 the company acceded to the many requests and (after producing 40,253 TR4s) brought out the TR4A. Externally, it could be seen to have a new front grill, different indicators and be slightly more decorative. More importantly, it featured independent suspension. However, first the resistance of the dealers in the United States had to be overcome; they feared additional cost and the inevitable

extra weight, so they were promised a delivery of the conventional version, which duly arrived. For the new version, the strong, profiled frame was changed slightly. Analogous to the Triumph 2000 sedan, two arms to the right and left took widely-set aluminum radius rods. Coil springs performed the function performed previously by leaf springs. But a shortage of space meant that an undesirable historical feature would be retained in the form of lever-arm dampers. The last of 28,465 TR4As rolled off the line on August 2, 1967. At the end of the car's life, Triumph was claiming that the honorably graying four-cylinder engine was producing 104 bhp—for all the difference it made.

The announcement of a successor in October showed firstly that the top men at Triumph could brush aside the rule that A must necessarily be followed by B, for the TR4A remained like an English queue consisting of only one person. The new model was the TR5 (known as TR250 in the US), with an engine compartment containing a far-reaching

innovation. This was the six-cylinder version, of which a total of 11,431 examples would be made, although its roots went back to the Standard Eight of the late 1940s. With 2498cc the TR5 offered 150 bhp with Lucas mechanical injection, although in regard for the American emission laws 8484 models had carburetors instead, detuning the performance right down to 104 bhp. The model also continued an old British tradition with its low piston speeds. Even at high engine speeds the rpm dial showed figures worthy of a ship's diesel. At 100 mph (160 kph) in fourth gear with overdrive engaged the crankshaft registered a comfortable 3800 rpm. But in both variants the model rode so hard on the road that cynics urged drivers to fit a protective back support before tackling bad highway surfaces.

Disc wheels had long been the norm, spokes cost extra. The six-cylinder models, fed by Lucas fuel injection developed specifically for the TR5, fitted into the engine compartment as if made to measure—once the radiator was set a fraction further forward. Only the chassis beneath needed any worthwhile modification.

TRIUMPH SPITFIRE

Giovanni Michelotti, the tiny designer from Turin, was driven by a restless compulsion to create; he was obsessed with form and ideas simply bubbled out of him. If he was invited out for a meal he would scribble auto silhouettes and studies of details on any menu card he could get hold of, leaving them for his hosts and the waiters as souvenirs. As Alick Dick, then head of Triumph, recalled, the best thing about him was that he could adjust totally to his customers, and conjure something on paper that would appeal to them within five minutes.

That is how he created what the department headed by Triumph engineer Harry Webster—with their fondness for telling four-letter words—called the "bomb." In September 1960 it received Alick Dick's blessing. When Leyland Motors took control of Standard-Triumph in April 1961 they found a prototype standing in a corner covered in cobwebs. Michelotti's chic bodywork concealed the chassis from the Triumph Herald, albeit with an appropriately shortened wheelbase, and its 1147cc and 63 bhp four-cylinder engine. There it crouched, a little shyly, behind the mighty front cover, the whole of which could be lifted, allowing unhindered access to the entire front part of the vehicle.

The instruction for the project sounded militant, as was indeed the aim, namely to tackle competitors, such as the Austin-Healey Sprite and the MG Midget, on their own ground. The name eventually chosen for the little Roadster—Spitfire—was also aggressive. It came from the fearsome World War II RAF fighter plane, and it was agreed, despite doubts by some of the more educationally-minded management at Triumph, that it could induce a wild style of driving.

But the sabre-rattling was purely verbal. The floating axle at the rear on a transverse leaf spring led a choleric independent life in the border area, and induced drivers to keep calm when handling the fire-spitter, while the front wheels on their track control arms and coil springs kept the course mostly reliable. But the new model did burst onto the enemy's territory like a bomb. It was more attractive and faster than the Spridgets, and unlike them, fitted with disc brakes at the front. It shot above their sales figures in the twinkling of an eye. As a further attraction, delighted reviewers all over the world mentioned the small turning circle, the generous trunk and the separate frame on which the outside panels were attached, making them easy to change should they be damaged. Only late in 1963 did a hard top, spoke wheels and overdrive become available as welcome options. Then in March 1965 came a II version with 4 bhp more.

A true moneymaker was a bigger engine available from the spring of 1967. With 1296cc and 75 bhp it responded willingly, allowing the Spitfire to come boldly up to the 100 mph (160 kph) mark. At the same time the front bumper appeared to be guarding the radiator grill, so to speak, in reaction to bad parking habits and stricter laws in the United States. Journalists agreed that this was the generation with the bit between its teeth, but they found the wooden veneer on the dashboard and the smaller steering wheel something of an attraction. At the end of that year the company happily celebrated Spitfire Number 100,000—out of the total of 314,338 they would go on to make.

But the original design was already showing a few wrinkles and crows' feet, and in 1968 Maestro Michelotti was again consulted. The fruit of keeping him at the desk was embodied in the Mark IV, which appeared in 1970 shortly

after the Earl's Court Motor Show. Its appearance was touched up, the rear was more sharply contoured, and the hard top had sharper corners. The dashboard was given a new layout with the dials grouped in the center immediately in the driver's view. The first gear was now synchronized, the rear axle transmission longer, although this did not bring an increase in top speed. The best news came last: roadholding was much improved, as the rear transverse leaf spring was not supported on a pivot on the differential housing. Not that this prevented Harry Webster's successor, Spen King, from somersaulting during a trial drive.

But British Leyland's engine range was aging, and parts were clearly past their sell-by date. Owing to radical intervention to reduce pollution, the US variant was reduced

to a rickety 48 bhp in 1972, and a year later it was given a 1493cc engine together with ugly rubber bumpers. Admittedly, the new engine provided an additional 9 bhp. The fifth version of the model was fitted with this, and it was available on the European from 1974 with a powerful 71 bhp. It inspired its former rival, the MG Midget, to better its performance, as the new Spitfire was again around the 100 mph (160 kph) mark at top speed and could reach 60 mph (100 kph) in 13.2 seconds. The 1500 of 1980 was the apotheosis of the series, and also marked its end. By then the entire concept had grown old and was raising doubts, if only because the major components that had made the Triumph Spitfire such amazingly good value were no longer available.

Apart from the doors and covers, the body of the Triumph Spitfire was moulded from a single sheet, and was astonishingly resistant. The windscreen was bequeathed by its big brother, the TR4. For the Mark III of 1967 the company revamped the front section; most striking was the front bumper, raised to the height of the radiator. Like a soldier, the Spitfire carried its weapon at the ready.

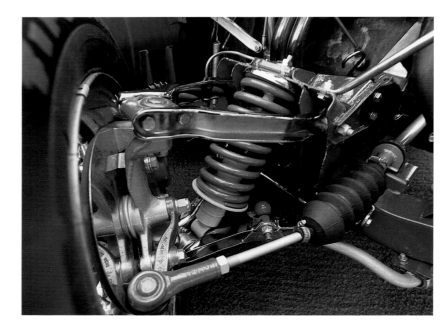

The luggage rack was an extra, like overdrive and the spoke wheels. The Spitfire's roomy engine compartment now had 1296cc, carefully maintained and lovingly prepared. It had found a home here and could take the car to 100 mph (160 kph) in 12.5 seconds; and it also took it into the important league of 100-mph (160-kph) cars. The driver could see how his engine was doing by glancing above the gear tunnel in the center, and if he lifted the big hood he could also see the front suspension.

TRIUMPH GT6

It was to be a noble Spitfire, with a steel hard top and lots of luxury, a Gran Turismo that would honor its name. People were to want to get in for a long journey, and not want to get out again. If it looked like an E-Type Jaguar that had shrunk in the wash, then never mind. That simply reflected the facts. Triumph had spent a lot less than Jaguar and anyway, a jockey's size and the suppleness of youth were what drivers and passengers wanted.

Co-operation between Giovanni Michelotti and Harry Webster produced a prototype at the end of 1963 based on the Roadster, but fully enclosed and with a big hatchback opening above a huge luggage space. The new model was to be introduced in 1964 as the Spitfire GT, with the same four-cylinder engine as the open model, and in the spring of that year it went on a short pilgrimage to Le Mans, the Lourdes among motor sports' holy places, its name alone bearing enough pulling power to bring the British freaks across the Channel.

But then events came thick and fast. Rumors started that MG was planning a fastback variant of the MGB for the fall

of 1965, and Standard-Triumph International Ltd would certainly not stand aside. They were determined to offer a match for the prestige project by their rival in Abingdon, and the GT6—as it was agreed the new model would be called—was given the green light in May. The number six in GT6 referred to the number of cylinders arranged in a row in the 2-liter engine that the GT6 shared with the Triumph Vitesse—introduced at the same time, in October 1966. An elongated swelling on the bonnet also announced the presence of those silkily purring six cylinders. They were wedded to a transmission with fully synchronized gears—one that had already been doing good service in the racing Spitfire for quite some time.

Once the passenger had humbly ducked his head and edged in through the narrow door he was welcomed into a rather close and intimate space, with luxuries such as walnut veneer encasing black instrument dials, sweetly clicking switches, and soft carpeting on the floor—an upgrade that the standard Spitfire did not possess. The building-block

In principle the Triumph GT6 was a Spitfire with six cylinders and a full fastback body. The rear window was also the door to the trunk. The GT6 appeared in 1968 as a Mark II, sporting the improvements that the third-generation Spitfire had been given, including a higher-set front bumper. The cylinder head came from the TR5 and the addition of another camshaft did much to bolster performance.

principle seemed to have flourished here, without unduly weighing down the Triumph budget.

But a few mistakes had been made in the hasty design of the coupé. The ventilation was wretched and the glass panes misted up at the slightest opportunity. Worst of all, the engine was placed so far forward that on fast corners the GT6 proved very nose-heavy and indulged in wicked understeer that was almost impossible to control. If the everyday Spitfire had roadholding problems owing to its floating axle, then this version was best described as diabolical, proving almost too much for even the most experienced drivers. Dramatic photos in trade journals were more likely to put potential customers off. In many photographs of the GT6 in motion, all four wheels seemed to be in what could be called "democratic dissent" over which direction should ultimately be taken. On bad roads the little Briton lost its cool altogether; it stamped and jerked, slipped and jumped, its all-too-weak shock absorbers simply unable to quell the suspension's constant quarreling.

Nevertheless, 15,818 untroubled fans had bought the first job lot by 1968. For the second, of which 12,066 were sold by 1970, the car's dangerous moodiness was cured with its revised rear suspension from the Vitesse Mark II—an elaborate and costly procedure involving the introduction of telescopic shock absorbers and proper control arms for the previously lively swing-axle arrangement. The transverse leaf spring remained in place. Like the third-generation Spitfire the GT6 now also had its front bumper set before the radiator. The cockpit fittings and ventilation were much better and played their part in an upgrade, which at only £79 over the earlier price of £800 represented a truly modest increase. The engine performance was upped by 10 bhp to 105 bhp with the use of the TR5 cylinder head and sharper camshafts, and the little racer could now hold its own—on German autobahns, for instance, against rapid German limousines traveling at 112 mph (180 kph).

The cleaner US version had to be content with only 95 bhp, and the annual painful sacrifices on the altar of the American emission regulations bled the virility of the actually very agile 2-liter model, bringing it down to a mere 79 bhp in the very sad year of 1972.

The third series, between 1970 and 1973 (13,042 sold) was given the same styling update as the Mark IV Spitfire—a revamped front and a square back end. And in the last year of its model life its optimized rear chassis design helped the GT6 behave better on the road. But by then the sales curve had already dropped sharply, and where demand ceases supply always eventually dries up. The Triumph GT6 had in any case always been overshadowed by its older brother.

TRIUMPH TR6

In June 1976 the last of a total of 94,619 TR6 bodies left Triumph's Number 1 factory, the former Hall Engineering works in Liverpool, to be united with their mechanical halves in Coventry and made ready for sale. The event gave chroniclers, statisticians, and analysts plenty of material on which to draw conclusions, trace developments, and produce penetrating comments of every kind. One conclusion, for instance, was that time had overtaken the series; the TR2 of 1953, where it all began, was a state-of-the-art machine, but with the TR6 they were bidding farewell to the last dinosaur. It was in truth the end of the mass-produced sports car "with hairs on its chest," as the English motor historian Graham Robson put it in a dark physical metaphor.

The two models now had nothing in common, but the two milestones of TR history are linked by a chain of ceaseless evolution with clearly recognizable joints. They include the change from the diagonal to the horizontal in the TR4 (ordered by Giovanni Michelotti), the transition from rigid axle to independent suspension in the TR4A, and the replacement of the four-cylinder engine with the six-cylinder in the TR5. In a certain manner, this process reflects the history of the firm after the war: building up, expanding, converting, then expanding again.

The TR5 was still alive and in the best of health when the firm was already thinking about its successor. Again they consulted the maestro in Turin, but this time he was not interested—too many commitments. In search of a substitute, the Triumph emissaries finally arrived at the German body manufacturer, Karmann, in Osnabrück, a firm well known for its Ghia versions for Volkswagen, and its work for Porsche. Agreement was reached. What Triumph wanted from their Westphalian partners was no mere trifle. The present line was to be cleaned up and brought up to date, as far as possible at "neutral" cost, and the machine tools needed for series production were to be provided and sent to Liverpool—all within 14 months. Only 15 months after the TR5 was introduced the TR6 followed hot on its heels, in January 1969.

Karmann solved the problem elegantly, and punctually. The pleasing right angle they incorporated in the car's styling became a keynote. Michelotti's silhouette was freed of all its opulent additions and simplified, reducing it to what the maestro had actually intended. The current, rather swollen

From January 1969 the TR5 and TR250 were replaced by the TR6. In principle the basic shape of the TR4, designed by Michelotti, was retained, but in response to requests from Triumph, the German partners at Karmann redesigned the front and rear to bring them up to date. This involved simplifying the radiator, changing the fenders, smoothing the hood by taking out the redundant swelling on the right and improving the abruptly concluded rear end.

TR face underwent plastic surgery, as the headlights were taken out of their half-exposed high setting and located on each side of a clearly divided matt-black grill. The asymmetrical raised section on the right of the hood had degenerated into a merely decorative relic of four-cylinder days long past, and so it was removed. Two decorative strips on the sides that had led into the indicator lights and parking lights also went the way of the wind, and the rear lighting ensembles, now set horizontally, were taken round at right angles to the sides.

The rear, jutting out considerably beyond the wheels, was made even more square, with the trunk inside it even larger. There was one small regression, though: where heavy cases had previously only had to be lifted to the upper edge of the bumper, now they had to be heaved over a rear wall. The hard top was also more sharply cornered; it was made from a single piece and supplied by Triumph itself as an extra, as were the overdrive and wire spoke wheels. The TR6 rolled on 5.5-inch (140-mm) wheels, and with a wider track of 1 inch (25 mm) at the front and 0.9 inches (24 mm) behind, plus a strong front sway bar, this ensured far more neutral roadholding.

The traditional hard ride was still present, and on bad roads the car jolted, while the body—from the original Roadster—shuddered and groaned uncontrollably. In themselves these signs of unease taught drivers to relax and drive defensively. The six-cylinder engine did the rest by

providing robust power, even at low revs, but could not come to terms with delivering much higher up the range. Altogether, fitted with a more robust transmission from 1970, it behaved like an unsophisticated country boy. In 1973 a milder camshaft improved its manners, but also cost it a few bhp. At the same time the unavoidable spoiler lip was projecting from beneath the front bumper, and to compound matters, a few years later black protuberances sprouted here too, in the versions destined for exportation to North America. These models were known in factory jargon as the TR6 Carb (carburetor) to distinguish them from the TR6 PI (petrol injection), and they had to be content with a mere 104 bhp, like their forerunners the TR4A and TR250. New

Stromberg carburetor jets provided an extra 2 bhp from 1972, and fortunately, a further reduction of the compression ratio from 8.5 to 7.5:1 had no effect on ultimate speed.

In many regards Americans are more inclined to keep to what is familiar and they've proved their loyalty better than have their cousins on the other side of the Atlantic. The TR6 Carb still had faithful customers two years after the TR7 came onto the market in the USA.

The cockpit of the TR6 was safer, as the Triumph advertisements proclaimed, because, for instance, the switches were set further back in the dashboard. As for the rest, the TR5 layout was retained here. The gearbox appeared outwardly unchanged, but as time went by the manners of the transmission improved noticeably after some careful internal surgery.

TRIUMPH STAG

As with the story of the Spitfire, the saga of the Stag begins with the discovery of a Michelotti creation hidden in a corner. On a routine visit to the Maestro's studio early in 1966 Harry Webster, technical manager at Triumph, spotted a sleek and lithe four-seater cabriolet, a sports version of the Triumph 2000, designed by Michelotti himself. The tireless genius from Turin had elevated a battered prototype that had done general service during the Spitfire debut in Le Mans in 1964. What was he planning to do with it, asked Webster. Well, he might send it to a few shows as a one-off eye-catcher, but no more than that, said Michelotti in his musical English.

But Webster spontaneously decided to adopt the attractive foundling, and, as was to be expected, his fellow managers back home fell in love with Michelotti's folly. Plans were drawn up, and the first parts made. An annual output of 12,000 should be possible—customers could surely be won from Alfa Romeo and Lancia, maybe even Mercedes. The world was to learn about the new Triumph in 1968. It was called the Stag during its development phase, and the name was kept for the final version, because they all liked it. Only—although nobody knew it at the time—that was the start of the Stag's path of sorrows, for while the Spitfire became a general favorite, the Stag enjoyed a less glorious progress.

First, it was caught up in the wheels of politics. The mammoth "marriage" of Leyland Motors and British Motor Holdings in January 1968, with the British government as best man, was in sight. With the difficulties of co-existence between such strong and well-developed corporate identities as Austin-Morris, Triumph-Standard, MG, and Jaguar-Daimler, much sensitivity and claim to prestige, as well as many established positions had to be taken into account, and the big new organization needed a structure.

Secondly, the project turned out to be much more expensive than planned, particularly as it moved further and further away from the mass-produced Triumph 2000. Originally the six-cylinder from the TR5 was to be the engine, but then, to the annoyance of the Triumph men, the Rover V8 came under discussion. It had the advantage of being ready for series production, but it did not quite fit into the Stag's engine compartment.

Finally, the choice fell on a company engine of the same configuration, with two of the Dolomite's four cylinders set

Again and again the designers of the Stag studied the North American safety regulations, and consequently a T-shaped rollover bar appeared. "Stag" was initially the company's codename for the developing car, but was retained for the final marketing—unique in Triumph history.

obliquely, each with a camshaft above. Its 3-liter version overstrained existing components, and so Webster's successor, Spen King, reluctantly gave the green light for a more powerful transmission in 1968, with a more robust rear axle, bigger brakes, and larger 14-inch (356-mm) wheels. In any case, although the original concept had not, by and large, been changed, thousands of details had. For example, a defiant T-shaped rollover bar disfigured the pure line of Michelotti's design, although mercifully it could be hidden by a massive, and fortunately beautiful hard top, which came at a higher price and changed the Stag into a roomy Grand Tourer. And the headlights, originally half-hidden behind an electrically retractable grid to left and right of the radiator grill, were now fully revealed. Not a single panel of the monocoque body now resembled the 2000. It was assembled in the first Liverpool factory, sprayed and given opulent trimmings in the brand new second works, and united with its mechanical other half at the Canley production plant.

Nevertheless, underneath the appearance everything was as planned, with power steering, front disc brakes and elaborate independently sprung wheels, attached to MacPherson struts located by track control arms at the front, and coil springs and semi-trailing arms behind.

In the climate of October 1968—a minefield of merger confusion where fatal mistakes were all too easy to make—the company just managed to complete a second prototype. Even in June 1970, when the Stag had officially already seen the light of day, potential customers had to contain themselves and be patient for a while. Then came the long faces: it seemed that reliability was not the Stag's greatest asset. The company's homegrown V8 had not really been fully thought through. Hastily cobbled together under great time constraint, it struggled with considerable thermal problems. Gaskets burned through, cylinder heads distorted, and premature bearing wear became apparent, as did endless warranty claims from a disgruntled clientele. The Stag's design—old hat even when first shown—aged rapidly into the 1970s. Above all, the North American market did not respond with the hoped-for enthusiasm: of the total 25,877 Triumph Stags that were made—5446 in the best year, 1973—only 6780 were exported.

And so in June 1977 the curtain came down on the Stag—to the secret relief of the accountants, who had been helping it to survive for far too long.

TRIUMPH TR7 & TR8

Much more delicate than its predecessors, the TR4 to TR6, the Triumph TR8 Convertible pushed forward like a simple wedge into the wind. This visual concept was highlighted when the electrically operated headlights receded back into the silhouette. The open version looked more lithe than the coupé and was certainly the more successful of the two. In the cockpit, however, the right-angle reigned supreme, as did all-too familiar cheap plastic.

After Leyland Motors and British Motor Holdings merged in 1968 to form British Leyland the symbiosis of the irreconcilable had become an everyday reality, and the policy makers in the new corporate federation were already racking their brains and knocking their heads over the future range.

It was soon the TR's turn. Of course, the TR6 had just been put on track for the 1970s, but a more up-to-date concept would soon be needed, following the Dolomite series. The body would be of monocoque design, the form fit for the future, with automatic transmission offered as an option. The traditional arrangement of front engine and rear drive would be retained, and rather ruefully, the company returned to a rigid rear axle. Spencer King, Triumph's head engineer, could only warm to independent suspension for the rear wheels in its more elaborate—that is, expensive—forms, and the engineers were also bound by the stringent North American regulations on emissions and safety, which dictated

a number of points. A hard top was compulsory in case the car overturned.

A body design put on paper by Harris Mann, stylist in the beauty studio of Leyland's subsidiary, Austin-Morris in Longbridge, was quickly made full-size in clay and approved in December 1971. Immediately, squabbling broke out over who was to do what and where. Even "badge engineering" was under discussion—possibly in tandem with former arch-rival MG.

The decision was taken in April 1972. The new model would be built entirely in Liverpool, the complex panels pressed in Works 1, all the rest in Works 2. At the time no-one knew that the model was facing a difficult time and that moving production from one plant to another would one day be the norm. From mid-1978 the body parts would be ordered from the Pressed Steel Co. in Cowley, near Oxford, and as before, assembly would be in Canley. In 1980 assembly was transferred to the modern Rover factory in Solihull.

No wonder stability and continuity were lost, as were the plans to establish a TR7 family against the threatening background of strikes, energy crises, and constant increases in the value of the pound.

When the hard top coupé, which marked the start of this series, was finally presented in January 1975, inevitably the question was asked whether anything had really improved. Mockingly, critics sneered that one clumsy lump had been followed by a clumsy wedge. The unusually high waist and low side windows did indeed hamper vision as much as they detracted from the visual appeal, as did the hood, which fell away steeply, impishly leaving the driver unsure where his vehicle actually ended. And one could argue forever over the aesthetic virtues of the sloping rear, while the cell-like lack of space for the passengers was a big demerit.

The same lack of space was evident under the hood, where a short-stroke four-cylinder overhead-cam engine of 1998cc and 105 bhp was installed canted by 45 degrees. It was a unit familiar to lovers of the the Saab 99 and Triumph Dolomite. The originally promised 16-valve Sprint variant was never built, although 25 pre-series models were in fact tested. In the US version 13 bhp was throttled out of the equation by two Stromberg 175CD SEV carburetors instead of the SU HS6 units, along with a compression ratio reduction to 8:1 from 9.25:1. But in no way did any of this affect the popularity of the TR7 in the United States. The front wheels were independently located on transverse arms, the rear wheels, as planned, on a rigid axle, although well located and well sprung, with trailing and diagonal control arms and coil springs.

After a break for the transfer of premises the TR7 was back on the market from the fall of 1978, now with five gears as standard. The introduction of the TR7 Drophead was delayed to the summer of 1979; it was shipped first only to the United States, and then to the rest of the world from March 1980. With its more tilted windshield and bolder A-pillars it didn't also need an ugly rollover bar, and presented an altogether more pleasing and generally balanced sight than its covered siblings. The TR8, also long awaited and introduced far too late, embarked on its journey—exclusively overseas—in January 1980. It was in fact a TR7 with the hugely popular 3.5-liter Rover V8 engine, which made it a really fast car. Even in the officially prescribed, more environmentally-friendly version with carburetors it managed 133 bhp and could reach more than 118 mph (190 kph), to the devilish delight of all who so wanted to show the state troopers a clean pair of heels. But by then Triumph was feeling a cold wind in its face. In mid-1980 the pound rose from $1.80 to $2.40; moreover the thirst of the mighty V8 was being called into question.

There never was any joy on the British market, for British Leyland was losing heavily on every TR sold. The requiem came in October 1981 after the last of a total of 112,368 TR7s left the factory. The TR8 achieved a sad total sales figure of of 2722.

TVR GRANTURA

Trevor Wilkinson from Blackpool was creative and highly individual even in the choice of name for the company he founded with his friend Jack Pickard in his native town in 1947. They were going to make sports cars that would be special in every way, and the name chosen was TVR Engineering. For the first part of the name, Wilkinson just left a few letters out of his first name, and the second part was a delightful exaggeration, for at first the men largely trusted to rather uncertain inspiration, and much was guesswork.

But while the technical standard and finish of their products steadily improved, financing the TVR venture proved a desperate enterprise for a long time. The sale of two early prototypes gave Wilkinson the funds to build a third model, which he kept for his own use for a long time, driving it mainly in local rallies. Other models followed, and some actually found their way into the United States under the Jomar badge. This name was a combination of the names John and Margaret, the children of Wilkinson's business associate and future TVR importer, Ray Saidel, in Manchester, New Hampshire. By 1958 the company on the Hoo Hill Industrial Estate in Blackpool was operating a well-practised scenario: a fiberglass body would just be dropped over a tubular frame made by the company itself, while the mechanical components came from a series-production manufacturer.

In the same year a Grantura forerunner was already displaying the TVR profile that would become typical for the marque over the next few years, with its gnome-like brevity. It had a gradually rising front, a tiny cockpit for just two occupants, and a rear that dropped abruptly over the driven wheels in a design that Trevor Wilkinson had crystalized from a mass of random drawings. The front steering elements were from a Volkswagen, and used multiple torsion rods as the springing medium to provide independent suspension for the wire spoke wheels at both front and back. To avoid purchase tax the sports dwarf was initially supplied solely in the United Kingdom as a kit for self-assembly. The home car builder could choose between a range of engines, from the elderly Ford 100E of 1172cc and 35 bhp, through the MGA of 1489cc and 72 bhp, to the Coventry Climax motor of 1216cc and 83 bhp.

In 1960 the black clouds of bankruptcy began to gather over the little firm. Nevertheless, after around 100 of the first-series Grantura had been produced, a Mark II version arrived, altogether better and 110 lb (50 kg) heavier, with rack and pinion steering and the MGA engine as standard. With front disc brakes and that 1622cc, 86 bhp MGA power

unit, it sold as the Grantura Mk IIA from 1961. The Mk II and the Mk IIA together achieved sales of about 400.

The Mk III, shown at the New York Motor Show in April 1962, brought changes for the better in many respects. A rigid chassis, divided into triangles and designed by TVR engineer John Thurner, replaced the former, rather clumsy tubular structure, and at the same time freed the fiberglass superstructure from its role of assisting chassis rigidity. All four wheels were now hung on track control arms and suspended by coil springs, and the wheelbase was extended by 1.5 inches (38 mm) to 85 inches (2170 mm). In September 1963 the Mk II 1800 appeared with the MGB 1798cc 95 bhp engine. The magazine *Motor*, in its issue of October that year, stressed the better traction of the new Grantura; the rear wheels held unswervingly to the asphalt on even the most hilly and winding moorland roads.

About 90 Mk IIIs were built for customers, some by selected dealers, and then in the middle of the year came the Grantura 1800S. It was recognizable by the Manx back, as it was called, with the striking rear lights of the Ford Cortina and the bigger rear screen that curved round into the sides. When TVR was taken over by the wealthy Lilley family in November 1965, 90 of the 1800S cars had been made— about on the same level as all the earlier production figures. Manager Martin Lilley, however, whose father became Chairman of the new TVR Engineering Ltd, wanted precise accounting. It showed that between February and September 1966 another 38 1800S models were made, but between July 1966 and October 1967 78 of the all-round optimized Mk IV 1800S cars were produced, all with the MGB 1800 engine.

Why, for Heaven's sake, *Cars & Car Conversions* asked itself and any interested reader in May 1967, should anyone buy a Grantura Mk IV 1800S if it owed so much to MGB? But then a whole list of good reasons was provided. It weighed 440 lb (200 kg) less than the MGB, had bigger wheels, a shorter wheelbase, and wider track and so was much easier to handle. It was a fully developed vehicle, well thought-out and well made, comfortable, fast, and very sporty. Moreover, it aroused considerable interest in every public parking lot, no doubt a plus-point if you like that kind of thing.

The reviewer had last driven a TVR eight years before, and he clearly concluded that the progress made in that period was enormous.

The most striking feature of the TVR "dwarf" was the steeply dropping hood and the big panoramic rear screen that curved into the sides. The bumpers were more gratuitous than protective.

The steering wheel was set straight onto a densely packed dashboard. Big spokes like those on the popular Nardi wheel would partly conceal the view of the speedometer and the rpm indicator.

This warning to passengers was no doubt a little joke on the part of the present or a former owner. But it was a serious failing for anyone who couldn't stand being enclosed in so small a space.

PASSENGERS RIDE AT THEIR OWN RISK

The rather clumsy, amateurish TVR logo with the winged V in the centre immortalized the founder Trevor Wilkinson but involved sacrificing three letters of his first name.

The company founded by Wilkinson operated as Layton Engineering from 1954 through 1957, and until 1962 as Layton Sports Cars Ltd. In the following year the name was changed to Grantura Engineering Ltd.

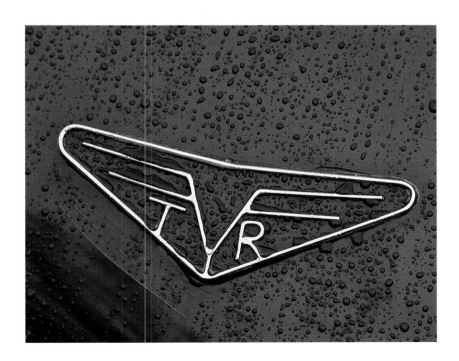

TVR VIXEN

The premiere came in 1967 when the Vixen was the first TVR to be presented at the prestigious Earl's Court Motor Show. Otherwise father and son Lilley, under whose direction the financial situation in the little factory on Hoo Hill in Blackpool had been calmed and steadied while the workforce was on a constant high, were feeding progress to their customers in homeopathic doses.

The new model was actually just a Grantura 1800S with an engine transplant to improve it. After the first 12 of the 117 Vixens of the first series—built between October 1967 and the same month a year later—it was no longer the familiar MGB engine that nestled in the compartment, but the crossflow 1599cc engine from the Ford Cortina GT, producing 88 bhp. Its presence was evident from a clearly different exhaust and a broader, flatter air vent in the middle of its fiberglass hood that supplied fresh air to the Weber double-downdraft carburetor.

Autocar welcomed this solution in its issue of June 26, 1969. The Ford four-cylinder was the ideal choice for a sports car, as it provided good punch. For the rest, the TVR was as striking in appearance as ever, arousing admiration wherever it went. And the driver found himself in familiar surroundings: the relatively long hood was fully in view, although it took up half the length of the vehicle, while a voluminous tunnel down the middle of the cabin ensured he maintained a decent distance from his passenger. At the back the TVR stopped very abruptly. Finally, the chassis was familiar too—a tubular construction which formed the support for racing car suspension using double wishbones and coil springs for all four wheels, and no less than four dampers behind.

The Vixen S2 proved even more popular, with 438 examples being built, and it sold for precisely two years from October 1968. It was improved in no fewer than 75 areas, as TVR Engineering assured its faithful and future customers. Most importantly, the wheelbase was extended by 2.8 inches (70 mm) to 90 inches (2290 mm), allowing wider doors to give better access to the driving seat—a long-overdue

improvement. The body was no longer glued to the chassis but screwed on, so that it could be lifted off in its entirety if need be. The rear lights, borrowed from the Cortina Mk II, now cut squarely into the sides, while a long, slim bulge rose over the engine. From spring 1969 it would be flanked in front by two air vents.

Between October 1970 and April 1972 168 Vixen S3s bore witness to the constant concern of their creators for detail. The first vehicles were delivered while the company was moving to Blackpool's Bristol Avenue. Cast aluminum wheel rims like those on the TVR Tuscan V6 became standard, while filigree chromium grills from the Ford Zephyr and Zodiac models covered the side vents to left and right under the bonnet. They fed air to the Ford Capri 1600GT engine; with 86 bhp it was slightly less powerful than its predecessor, but it had a more even temperament.

The backbone of the fourth and last Vixen generation of only 23 units—22 in 1972 and only one in 1973—was the M-frame, as it was called. It was a joint creation by company boss Martin (hence the M) Lilley and Mike Bigland, using tubes of different strength and square elements, more rigid than the earlier structure, but easier to manufacture.

The series was rounded off by the TVR 2500, with which the Lilleys caused much discussion in Earl's Court in 1970. Their latest creation could claim two superlatives: it was the shortest six-cylinder car in the world and also the most compact 2.5-liter vehicle of all time. At 146 inches

(3695 mm) it was hardly longer than a Renault 4. By 1973 385 non-conformists had seized the chance to stand out from the mass of normal motorists by buying the 2500, while secretly moving themselves up from other TVR enthusiasts. But they could not easily leave them behind on the road, for it was the declared aim of TVR to get at least a foothold on the American market with its little giant. To reduce its emissions the cast iron standard engine, which was also destined for export to the United States in the Triumph TR250 and TR6 models, had bled 46 bhp and could therefore only struggle along with 104 bhp. Nonetheless the TVR 2500 could still manage 120 mph (190 kph), enough to engage the ire of highway cops.

The owners of the 15 initial TVR 1300s built in 1971 and 1972 for only £50 less than a normal Vixen S3 could not enjoy such law-breaking peak performance, as they simply lacked the necessary power. Their Spitfire engines had only 63 bhp to spare.

In purely quantitative terms the customer bought a lot of engine with the TVR Vixen 2500, but not much car. He really needed to be small himself, for the distribution of space clearly favored the car and not its driver, with a long hood, little room inside and narrow seating. The back broke off abruptly after a short overhang, and a lot of space here was taken up by the spare wheel. There was no trunk as such and the rear window could not be opened.

Under the hood was the errant TR5 and TR6 six-cylinder engine, although it was greatly weakened by emission-stifling measures. Combined with a weight of only 2028 lb (920 kg) and the TVR's exemplary handling it nevertheless endowed the Vixen with a fiery enough character.

Once settled into his bucket seat the driver would always have to make compromises with the TVR, on account of the huge central tunnel and doorsteps that took up far too much room. The Triumph gearbox was intended for a bigger car, and in the TVR its ratios were too high. The dashboard of the Vixen 2500, illustrated here, was not standard, and nor were the spoked wheels.

TVR M-SERIES

The many curious onlookers who refused to budge from the TVR stand at the 1971 Earl's Court Motor Show were chiefly waiting for the return of two young topless models who had made a brief appearance there. The smart PR trick was aimed at rudimentary male urges and hardly served to increase anyone's knowledge of the new car. Nor did the ladies create a serious basis for a new family of cars, although that was precisely what the skilfully illuminated exhibit was intended to do.

In fact, the 2500M was excellently equipped for the job. It was the first really new TVR since father and son Lilley had taken over the wilting firm in 1965. The frame, consisting of lengths of tubing of varying wall-strength and both round and square profiles, was by Martin (hence the M) Lilley and Mike Bigland. To it was attached elaborate suspension using triangular control arms, coil springs, and telescopic dampers (two for each rear wheel). Anchored between the four main supports was the standard 2498cc six-cylinder engine (hence the 2500 in the designation) from the Triumph TR6; it was emission-reduced for the US market and so brought down to 106 bhp. In the fiberglass superstructure over this rigid frame the designers had released hidden possibilities from the Grantura shape, which in this model emerged as more elongated, more balanced, more roomy, and somehow more classical in the sense of ageless simplicity. Work on the first production 2500M started in March 1972.

In June that year came two additions. Firstly, as successor to the TVR 1300, the economy version 1600M with its cheerful 1599cc crossflow Ford Capri engine worth 86 bhp

was doing a satisfactory job. After the first lot up to April 1973 production faltered with the introduction of VAT in England, which pretty well put paid to the advantages of building kit cars. Until then many mechanically-minded customers had bought the 1600M as a kit and built it themselves, at considerably reduced cost. A second batch, all now fully assembled, followed between 1973 and 1975.

The next addition, preferably for the domestic market, was the 3000M. Under its hood another Ford engine was at work—the Essex V6 of 2994cc, which developed 136 bhp. With a top speed of 124 mph (201 kph) and the ability to sprint to 60 mph (100 kph) in just eight seconds, the TVR was much faster but nevertheless incomparably more economical with its fossil fuel than was the Capri, the other big series-production car in which this compact power unit performed. That helped the model to survive the artificially instigated energy crisis of 1974. Variations on the 3000M theme were the ML (L for luxury) of 1973, with expensive wood and carpets providing costly comfort, and the Martin, with which the successful decade under

the Lilley regime was celebrated in 1976, in a limited edition of 10 models.

However, more extensive interventions were needed before the TVR Taimar could make its entrance bow at the London Motor Show in the same year. The name recalled a river between Devon and Cornwall. The new model was the response to many requests for a hatchback without any changes to the silhouette of the 3000M. In earlier TVRs shopping bags, cases, and coats literally had to be pushed in over and behind the seats for storage.

In 1978 the series culminated in a convertible, identical to the coupé except for the different windshield—something of a jewel that rapidly became an eagerly sought-after rarity. The exclusivity of the very small number produced was guaranteed by acquisition of one of the 63 Turbo TVRs between 1975 and 1979, whose Essex engines had been tuned to produce a robust 230 bhp under the skilful hands of horsepower extortionist Ralph Broad (and aided by a turbocharger by Broadspeed, Holset, or AiResearch). This model behaved with discipline and also without the lag

usually attendant with turbocharging, and greatly benefited the image of TVR Engineering Ltd. But it also turned out to be an unholy drunkard, guzzling fuel at a rate of less than 22 miles per US gallon (15 liters per 100 kilometers). The main appeal of this TVR, said a test report in *Motor* of April 28, 1979, was its total lack of compromise. No other sports car of the time was more worthy to follow in the footsteps of the legendary AC Cobra. The owner of this car could show everything and everyone on the road an exceedingly clean pair of heels.

By the end of the M-Series production in 1979, 947 2500Ms, 148 1600Ms, 674 3000Ms (20 of these turbo), 425 Taimar (30 turbo), and 271 convertibles (13 turbo) had been made.

The last link in TVR's extensive M family was the convertible of 1978 and 1979. Occasionally it was also known as the 3000S. The rolling chassis was identical to that of its fully enclosed brother, as was the front section. The fenders, windshield, doors, and all the rear section were made to measure. The side windows could either be pushed up and down or taken out altogether.

TVR TASMIN & DERIVATIVES

Three men and a girl played a part in the design of the Tasmin, TVR's model for the 1980s. The young lady was an attractive friend of company boss Martin Lilley, and she contributed a touch of secret charm, as well as her name, which had the very desirable echo of Maserati's Khamsin.

The men's contribution was more visible. Lilley himself directed the ambitious project. Two former Lotus men assisted him: Oliver Winterbottom, who was entrusted with designing the shape in 1977, and Ian Jones, who was responsible for the mechanicals. The TVR faith in plastic bodies, tubular frames, and Ford engines was maintained, but it also left room for new ideas and contemporary innovations. In the end Winterbottom's severe interpretation of the current wedge shape enveloped a tubular frame permanently

revamped by Jones, with the independent suspension set into it using track control arms from the Ford Cortina at the front, and a home-made axle *à la* Lotus behind. The V6 engine from the German Ford Capri had now taken residence in the engine compartment, with its 2792cc, Bosch mechanical fuel injection, and 160 bhp output. It was altogether of quite different dimensions from its British Essex colleague; moreover, it was emission-reduced in accordance with the regulations, so there was no obstacle to exporting it to the United States.

In this configuration the Tasmin appeared at the Brussels Motor Show in January 1980, a two-seater fastback coupé for the individualist who wanted to go his own way off the beaten track. By the time of the Earl's Court Show in October Lilley was already following up, offering the option of a three-speed automatic transmission by Ford, a convertible and a +2 variant. To make room for two tight seats at the back behind the front chairs the last fraction of available space had been squeezed out—this was only possible by extending the wheelbase by 4 inches (100 mm) over the 3000M, to 94 inches (2385 mm). The front of the +2 was shorter, the back longer; and the line of the roof was different, as were the cut-outs for the wheels. The apron-shaped sections between them were new. These features were transferred to both closed versions in a second series available from April 1981. In October that year the range was rounded off at the lower end in the form of the Tasmin 200 with a Ford Pinto four-cylinder engine of 1993cc and 101 bhp.

The receding headlights of the TVR 350i, initially known as the Tasmin, had good and bad aspects. The good was that when not in use they fitted seamlessly into the smoothly rising front of the convertible and then became a positive element in its styling as it carved its way into the wind. The bad aspect was that when called into service, they were more obtrusive and also cost several mph. The lights between the bumper and the shovel-shaped front spoiler provided additional long-distance lighting.

The 350i marked the top end of the range, available from mid-1983—from 1984 the name Tasmin was only used internally. The simple abbreviated designation was a sign of revolutionary change, for the engine compartment now contained the omnipresent alloy V8 from the Rover Vitesse, that could generate 193 bhp from 3532cc, and do so in an incredibly gentle manner. It was a cultural event, said John Miles, a former Lotus driver and competent tester, in *Autocar* of August 27, 1983. It had been sparked off by reaction in an Arabian country, where there was great interest in the Tasmin. But the mere mention of the name Ford had had the same effect as would a Tournedos Rossini on a vegetarian owing to the mega-concern's connections with Israel. The decision in favor of the British V8 also turned into a game of chess, with which the TVR management got themselves out of a difficult situation in another respect.

The Turbo Tasmin, introduced at the Birmingham Motor Show in fall 1982, was a flop. It remained on the shelf and

was now altogether superfluous. Above all, the 350i proclaimed a new policy of strength. Peter Wheeler, who had been running TVR Engineering Ltd since 1982, had only contempt for certain rickety jalopies that had limped along in the past flattered by the description "sports car." The latest TVR truly did not need to face that accusation. It not only set about things quite differently from its sisters with the Ford V6, Miles went on, it also had a much better chassis, and its handling and comfort were certainly up to the standard one expected from a super sports car. It was in fact an entirely new car—the TVR Tasmin 350i.

And so it continued. The various expansion stages of the Rover V8 came just at the right time for Wheeler; in the year it was introduced, the new model was upgraded to the 390 SE, whose 275 bhp inspired the Blackpool lightweights to great dynamic performance.

In 1986 came the 300 bhp 420 E, with composite components made of Kevlar and carbon fiber, and the awkward

SEAC (Special Equipment Aramid Composite) addition. 1987 saw the demise of the TVR 280i with Ford engine, and in 1988 came the 400 SE with a revamped shape, new interior fittings, and a moderate 286 bhp, while the owners of the 450 SE of 1989 enjoyed 319 bhp. With this they could face any trial of strength with other, renowned sports cars. In 1990 the series began to dry up. The last 350i was made in August, the last 450 SE in December, the last 400 SE in October 1991. With sales totaling 2618, however, the model had certainly bolstered TVR.

Like the Formula One Lotus 72 or the Triumph TR7, the TVR took as its model the aerodynamic efficiency of the basic wedge shape. Under its long hood, however, were very much more robust forces, mobilized from the Rover V8, whose capacity provided the car's name; by 1988 its power had reached 200 bhp. The cockpit of the TVR 350i convertible also provided a far more attractive ambience to spoil the driver, with its use of expensive wood and high-quality instruments (from 1986 supplied by VDO).

TVR GRIFFITH

The TVR Griffith hit the Birmingham Motor Show in 1990 like a bomb. It was so close to true greatness that it hurt, enthused *Autocar & Motor*, and many who saw it asked themselves why certain competitors had to employ an exorbitantly expensive Italian couturier when something as fine as this could come from a home firm. At peak times during the Motor Show the TVR representatives were taking an order every eight minutes, and by the end of the Show they had 350 in their book. Some enthusiasts were actually ready to make a big down-payment to be among the first to get the beau from Blackpool.

What TVR boss Peter Wheeler had created with John Ravenscroft was indeed a sight for sore eyes—sensual, brutal, and beautiful. Straight lines, corners, and sharp edges had all been consistently avoided, a tendency that was underlined by the bold decision to drop the bumpers. An unmistakable feature of the styling on the GFK body was the way the doors had been brought forward below the level of the front fenders, their handles hidden behind the rear edge. The round swelling as leitmotif was continued inside, where the central shelf below the radio rose into a gentle "hill." The handbrake and the gear shifter emerged from this, half-hidden in two hollows. The roof could be removed and just fitted into the trunk, although many later owners ignored this, preferring to entrust themselves happily to the vagaries of the weather.

Some of these features already looked forward to the version produced from 1992, for the first Griffith owners had to exercise patience before they could present the rounded Roadster to the curious and eager eyes of their fellows. The idea behind the new model was to help Tasmin derivative S3 to new heights with as little expenditure as possible, using a V8. But the existing structure was not up to such a trial of strength, so the designers decided to adapt the chassis of the TVR Tuscan for the new job. The backbone of the standard Griffith was an extremely rigid tubular frame, galvanized, primed, and finally powder-coated. Strong, widely splayed trapezoidal control arms with telescopic dampers, coil springs, and sway bars were attached to the frame in front and behind, while the omnipresent Rover V8 was set far back to ensure good balance and create space for the exhaust catalyzers of future generations. Customers could choose between 3948cc and 240 bhp or 4280cc and 280 bhp—the latter for those who liked their driving really hot. Should there be a—no doubt rare—encounter of a hostile kind with

The TVR Griffith offered a large number of attractive details that culminated in its overall sensual appeal. There is no doubt that the whole constituted rather more than the sum of the parts.

a Porsche Turbo or a Ferrari Testarossa, the TVR driver could certainly hold his own, at any rate as far as acceleration was concerned. *Autocar & Motor* registered 11.1 seconds for the sprint to 100 mph (160 kph) in the more powerful version, with just under 160 mph (260 kph) as the top speed—a speed at which a cabriolet certainly becomes uncomfortable. The magazine was very impressed by the finish of the Griffith, and journalists Mark Hales and Andrew English expressed similar approval in *Performance Car*, saying: "This 'Blackpool Flyer' is the best TVR ever in terms of design and finish."

The same view was held by the many customers who were able to buy the Griffith in a wide range of colors that frankly extended into the exotic. In 1992 alone this model accounted for 73 percent of TVR's production, at 602 units. The rest of the range was pushed into the background in the tight space of the Blackpool Bristol Avenue factory, literally becoming niche models. Into the middle of this modern fairytale of one who came, saw, and conquered, burst the

announcement that from December that year the firm would withdraw for a time from the domestic market, where the model had mainly been sold. They wanted to give exports, particularly to the United States, a chance, settle the installation of the catalyzer with proper care, and prepare a less expensive version, to be called the Chimaera.

But demand continued unabated and in August 1993 the company responded with the Griffith 500. The number referred to the five liters (to be precise, 4988cc) of the latest evolutionary stage of the 325 bhp Rover motor. A long time spent in preparation invariably brings good results. The model was actually intended for that capacity when it was first conceived in the 1960s. The greater power was achieved by increasing the stroke from 2.8 to 3.5 inches (71.12 to 90 mm) while retaining the same cylinder bore. The improvement went hand in hand with a slight modification to the front of the car, where additional headlights found refuge in the corners of the radiator opening. In Japan and Portugal the

Griffith was also available with a 4-liter engine, and by special request, everywhere with 4.5 liters. The last 100 (by June 2001, 2253 had been produced altogether) were made as a special edition, with the front and back retouched again, new rear mirrors and their interior brought up to the standard of the more recent models of the series.

The obituaries that will be written one day for this model will have only good things to say, particularly that the Griffith made a huge contribution to the survival of TVR Engineering Ltd.

The cockpit was also a work of art in its forms, materials, visual impression, and ergonomic appeal. The great curving central tunnel hid parts of the tubular frame. Space under the smooth front was as cramped as a snack bar, for the robust 5-liter engine—a feast for the eyes—would suffer nothing beside it. But it did accommodate the big catalyzer.

TVR CERBERA

An excursion into Greek mythology only explains part of this. Cerberus was the hound of hell who watched at the entrance to Hades. He is generally shown with three heads and a snake tail, and unlike the nightclub bouncers of today the red-eyed beast could be relied upon 100 percent not to allow anyone to leave the inhospitable place. Instinctively one expects his female counterpart to be worse, particularly as the word in Italian means ill-tempered, domineering woman. The TVR Cerbera certainly shared the potential wildness of its legendary namesake, as it was bursting with strength. But once one was on good terms with it, as most of its 1350 owners to date became, it could certainly be tamed—carefully, and only with a firm and expert hand.

The 2+2 seater coupé, only 48 inches (1220 mm) high, started life as a styling study by TVR engineers. Their sketch appealed to the management, who rapidly gave the green light for a mock-up to be built in full size. This time they dropped the two-dimensional abstraction on paper and the cold creativity of the computer and modeled the final shape in foam blocks. A fully functioning prototype appeared at the London Motorfair in 1993, a maneuver often used by TVR to sound out public opinion and market prospects. The reception was extremely encouraging, as it had been for the Griffith three years earlier. A large number of orders were taken, a gratifying 276 at the Cerbera's official debut at the Birmingham Show in 1994 alone.

A rollover bar was integrated in the composite body, of the same strength as the structures that kept the worst away from the drivers in the hair-raising accidents suffered by the TVR Tuscan racing model. In other ways, too, the Cerbera tamer could feel safe. The backbone of this lightweight was a robust tubular frame, carefully galvanized and powder-coated to prevent corrosion. Racing technology fathered the suspension. The car had internally air-cooled dual-circuit disc brakes, double trapezoidal track control arms with coil springs and gas pressure dampers all round. There were sway bars in front and behind, although they were relatively soft to provide motoring in the Gran Turismo manner, further aided by higher-profile tires for greater comfort and reduced road noise. Nor did the traveller have to do without contemporary luxury of the superior kind. Expensive wood veneer and color glazing were part of the standard fittings, as were electrically operated windows, an anti-theft alarm system, and adjustable foot-pedals. The fact that this fast flat vehicle was primarily targeted at customers in the United Kingdom, was evident in that it was only made available with right-hand steering.

Originally the engine was to be the Rover V8, as modified by TVR for its range. It was indeed to be found under the hood in pre-series models, but then the company embarked on an unusual venture for a small manufacturer, and decided

to develop its own engine. In 1990 TVR boss Peter Wheeler met fellow Lancastrian, Al Melling, then an engine designer in Rochdale. It was said that Melling had been the real brains behind leading racing projects in the 1980s but modestly kept his light under a bushel. The two men bonded immediately, and decided to make an eight-cylinder aluminum engine under the works code AJP8. After an incubation period of only eight months an early version was unveiled at the Earl's Court Motor Show in 1992. In principle this light and compact V8 was similar to Formula One units like the Cosworth HB, with its cylinder banks set at 75 degrees to each other. However, its architecture only partly followed familiar patterns, as Melling was content with two valves per cylinder and one camshaft above each row of cylinders. The engine had not yet emitted its first cry on a test bed and there was still a lot of work to be done. Consequently the AJP8 could not be considered for the Griffith, for which it was originally intended.

With its 4185cc the original version could happily pump out 360 bhp. Before the 420 bhp of a 4475cc variant in 1998 could be achieved a number of changes had to be made to the vehicle and its transmission, such as bigger tires and brakes and the "thinking" Hydratrac differential. A short time later the Cerbera Speed Six range was added. With a six-cylinder 24-valve engine under its hood, 3966cc and 350 bhp it could set to work almost as energetically as its V8 colleagues, and sounded beautiful. Press and television journos alike were delighted. This was progress in strength, sound, and tempo, they enthused. The brakes were extremely efficient, too. It was the most user-friendly TVR ever, as Angus Frazer said in 1998 in the BBC's *Top Gear Magazine*. Not that the work of taming the hound of hell was complete. For the 2000 model the lines of the roof, the seats, and the headlights were all changed, and with doors and hood made of aluminum, the 4.5-liter version lost a bit more weight.

The sprint to 60 mph (100 kph) that could be achieved in 4.1 seconds had been leaving occupants breathless even in the earlier version.

The small and punchy two-spoke steering wheel of the TVR Cerbera performed a number of functions but still allowed a full view through its upper and lower halves of the crucial dashboard behind. Leather fittings were standard, as was the expensive wood veneer on the dashboard.

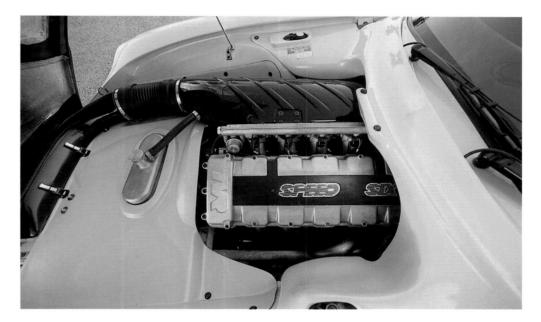

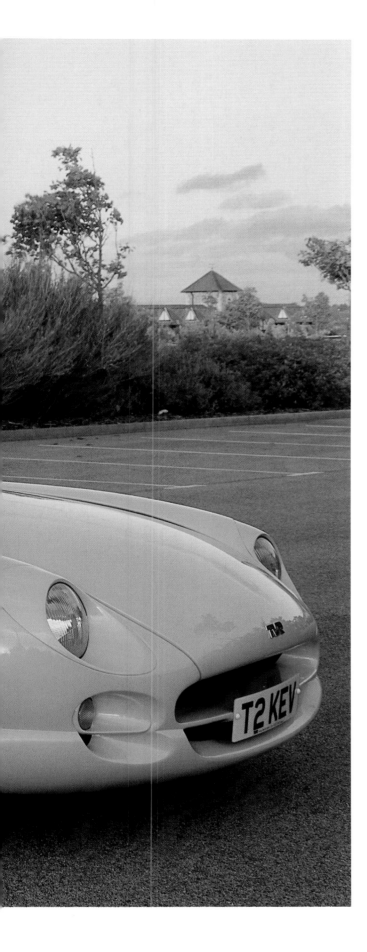

Slightly over-angled and rather rugged, the composite coupé lacked the consistent flowing lines of the Griffith, although it shared with it, among other things, its sporty wheels. The Speed Six was the first TVR with the company's own six-cylinder engine, and it sang in a sonorous *bel canto*. Beside sportiness the car offered luxurious comfort, with its softer suspension and higher-profile tires.

TVR TUSCAN

The official announcement of the TVR Tuscan in August 1988 made the model sound like Jekyll and Hyde. Firstly, it was firmly rooted in the history and philosophy of the firm. It was a name from the past and a challenge for the future. The new model was named after one of the fastest TVRs ever, a version from the 1960s. At the same time as the Tuscan, a specially prepared racing version, the Tuscan Challenge, would be introduced from 1989.

But it all turned out differently. The road variant, which was also dashingly publicized at the races, was dropped. Fragmentation loomed. The S and 350i to 450 SE models,

and particularly the Griffith, were tying up the funds and the workforce at TVR Engineering Ltd in Blackpool. But from 1989 the Tuscan Challenge became a fixture in the British racing scene. Again company chief Peter Wheeler provided key ideas for the styling of the nimble roadster, which was much more rounded than earlier TVRs. The headlights had withdrawn behind covers and the blunt back proclaimed the aerodynamic efficiency of even the tiniest cut-off cross-section.

The long-stroke 4.4-liter version of the Rover V8 provided 400 bhp, so the frame and transmission had to be

modified to suit this bursting extra power. More defiant than ever, the typical TVR lattice tubular frame resisted the forces that pulled at it, lifted it, and twisted it. The control arms were broadly splayed all round, the rear lower ones robustly equipped with torque control arms attached at four points. The Rover five-speed transmission was not up to the primeval force of the growling eight cylinders and it was consequently replaced by a Borg Warner unit similar to those used in the Ford Sierra Cosworth and RS 500.

At £16,000 plus VAT the Tuscan was extraordinarily good value. However, a condition was attached. The buyer

had to enter for at least six of the twelve Challenge races, otherwise the same amount was payable again. At the first start in Donington in 1989 there were already 21 entrants. The sport turned out to be spectacular and hugely entertained the crowd. For the Tuscan was, so to speak, faster than its tires on their 9-inch (229-mm) rims, and too fast for its brakes. Peter Dron, writing in *Fast Lane* magazine, admitted: "We are as crazy as the TVR people and should really be put in padded cells. Just think about it—400 bhp for a mere 1764 lb (800 kg)!" *Autosport*, on the other hand, warned that this car was only for the extremely skilful, or for

The extravagant exterior of the TVR Tuscan Speed Six revealed its dual nature as coupé and roadster in one. With a top it was a roomy traveling car for all weathers, when open a spectacular sight for onlookers. When the roof and rear window were stored in the 73-gallon (275-liter) trunk the traveler had to practice severe self-restraint in regard to how much luggage he could bring with him.

In its interior the Tuscan also offered some bizarre detailing, as the small manufacturer had allowed itself great freedom of creativity without losing sight of function. The aluminum arch above the dashboard was also part of the frame. And as in a racing car, little lights above the steering wheel indicated when it was advisable to change gear, in the interest of the health of that very audible six-cylinder engine. Green at 6000 rpm, yellow at 6500 rpm, and red at 7000 rpm.

the fearless. And as late as 2001 TVR racer Steve Guglielmi was advising Tuscan novices and bemused colleagues to get into the beast's mind, get it on their side, and make friends with it.

Hardly less inconsiderate but somehow more friendly in its method was the Tuscan Speed Six, a convertible fit for two people and their luggage for a month's holiday. At least so its parents said when a prototype was shown in Birmingham in 1996 as bait. But it was not on sale until the year 2000. "We went on developing it all that time," said TVR public relations man Ben Samuelson.

Evidently the detailed work paid off. A British car to be proud of, said *Autocar* in reverent praise on May 10, 2000. The magazine could report that 1600 customers had already made a down-payment. The Six in the name stood for the 4-liter, six-cylinder engine of the test model, produced by TVR themselves with 24 valves and dry-sump lubrication. With a weight of only 2425 lb (1100 kg) its 360 bhp did indeed produce speed in spades. Like its racing counterpart the Tuscan reached 60 mph (100 kph) in four seconds. The works literature put its top speed at above 180 mph (290 kph). It was also an aural delight—*Autocar* mentioned its *bel canto* in direct company with the pleasing sounds of the Ferrari 360 Modena and the Lamborghini Diablo.

A team under Peter Wheeler and Damien McTaggart were responsible for the highly individual shape of the Speed Six. Worms seemed to have burrowed through the low, snuffling nose, and the decorative hole motif continued around the front lights, where gas-discharge lamps gave out piercing light. In keeping with the trend of the time, the composite convertible looked like a hard-top coupé, but by renouncing all things material the upper panel and the rear window could be stowed away in the trunk. Wheeler and company had obeyed the timeless maxim that form follows function, and the curving aluminum element above the dashboard also served as a cross-strut for the frame.

The determination to seek new paths off the beaten track was also manifest inside the Tuscan Speed Six, even to the point of incredibility and bizarre aestheticism. Wherever one looked, said *Autocar* in amazement, one could find a candidate for the list of sexiest car components of all time. *Evo* magazine put it in a nutshell in June 2000: only very few cars looked as spectacular as this, sounded so sensational, and offered comparable value for money. One year later 800 customers were already enjoying all of that.

TVR ENGINEERING LIMITED

IN TREVOR'S FOOTSTEPS

1. *The parts of the lattice tubular frame as supplied. They are already arranged in accordance with the cross-section and their future position in the chassis.*

2. *The rough cut of the tubes for the chassis, which is largely identical in the Chimaera and the Griffith. Subsequently the tubes are cut to exact length using templates.*

3. *Parts of the under-flooring for a Cerbera Speed Six. TVR claims that more workmen are employed on this model per car than is the case for any other marque.*

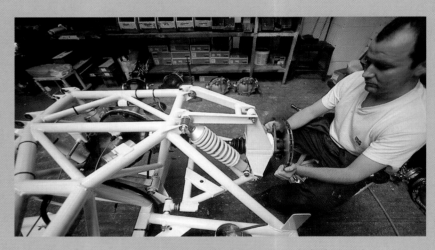

4. *Installing a disc brake. The chassis is first welded and then powder-coated. The many frame triangulations give the structure great strength and rigidity.*

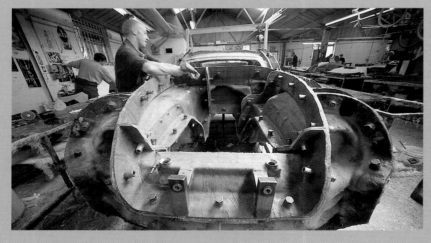

5. *A forming tool for a pressed Cerbera body panel.*

6. *The chassis and superstructure are already screwed together here, a process that takes 18 hours.*

RIGHT: *The assembly of the tubular frame is nearly complete. Altogether it takes 16 hours of six-man shifts. Each chassis is numbered for the future owner.*

RIGHT: *The body is given four coats of primer, each of which is baked at 143.6 degrees F (62 degrees C) for 30 minutes. Then the coating is smoothed down before the customer's choice of color (out of a range of 12,000) is sprayed on. A fan of brown paper protects the suspension parts behind.*

The hood of a Chimaera is strengthened with metal strips around the hinges.

Shaping the airconditioning outlets. Even a Cerbera does not have to be spartan.

Parts of the space for the occupant's feet in a Griffith or a Chimaera are being cut out here. Handling plastic has become a science at TVR.

Painting starting on a Chimaera.
Previously it has been hardened in
a heat chamber for eight hours.

To smooth out small irregularities
filler is applied with a trowel.

The team smooth and polish
reverently until the superstructure
is ready for its first coat of paint.

A six-cylinder engine is united with its frame and body in the final stage.

The Rover V8 has moved into the engine compartment of a Chimaera and is being given its ancillary components.

The central tunnel of the Chimaera being covered in leather. Twenty-four different colors are available for such coverings.

The final coat of paint for the Chimaera. In only a few hours it will be on its way to its new owner.

These Cerberas—each one is unique—have already rolled off the seven production lines.

After a short road test of about 30 miles (50 km) and a final inspection, the open road and adventure beckon.

WESTFIELD SEVEN

In the variety of species that flourishes in the garden of the automobile world, Colin Chapman's Lotus Seven marks an extreme development, very close to the spartan purity of the racing car and well remote from the commodious sterility of today's rolling high-tech boudoirs. Some call it a racing car thinly disguised with a few alibi measures to enable it to be driven on normal roads. Others put it more bluntly, suggesting things such as: "Chapman has built a bridge between two pairs of wheels, squeezed out just enough space for two people and an engine, and with ill grace thrown a body and four mudguards over it. Like a bikini they just cover the minimum, and the most decisive parts." The Seven, in other words, is no more than a tool to create speed.

Of course this minimalism *à la* Chapman has its attractions. Basically, said Peter Egan in *Road & Track* in March 1996, this is not design, it is a state of mind, a mood that keeps recurring. And as always in such cases it has followers and freaks right through to impassioned fundamentalists—and epigones, although Chapman installed Caterham chief Graham Nearn as guardian of the pure Seven doctrine in 1973. Imitation, as we all know, is the sincerest form of flattery.

Westfield Sports Cars Ltd. in Kingswinford in the English West Midlands also dipped into the bubbling fountain of ideas left by the inventive Lotus driver and pioneer. It was done no doubt partly from a sense of elective affinity. The founder of the firm, Chris Smith, was warmly attached to Lotus and still enters for historical races with Formula One cars of the early 1960s. His Westfield Eleven of 1983 with its fiberglass robe was based on the Lotus of the same name. A year later, when he followed it up with an open plagiarism of the Seven, there was trouble. There were court proceedings and in 1987 Smith was ordered to modify the design and give it an individual profile. So the men of Gibbons Industrial Park, Kingswinford set about surgical operations—some also beneath the tiny car's skimpy vest. The rear wheels of the Westfield Seven were attached to double track arms while the Caterham version used De Dion tube suspension. As time went on a large number of muscular lodgers progressively found refuge in the narrow engine compartment of the Westfield Seven. They ranged from the barely calmed Ford Formula motor through the 16-valve Ford Zetec, with 2700 units available as a kit from 1992 through July 2001, and 630 units fully assembled, to the tuned turbo-diesel

version from the same donor manufacturer. The Mega Bird and Mega Busa versions with motorcycle engines by Honda and Suzuki currently account for two thirds of production. These distortions are—according to Smith—to keep step with his changing clientele. A growing number of bikers want to change to a vehicle that is essentially the same as a bike, except that it has four wheels.

An impudent venture on sale since 1991 is the Westfield Seight, a contamination formed rather clumsily out of the letters SE and the number eight. In fact, a lot has been combined here. The availability of the Rover V8, in its various versions and states of tune up to 300 bhp (and more) had as big an impact on the British sports car world as the Cosworth DFV did in Formula One from 1967. The Seight shares this engine with such similar and dissimilar bedfellows as the Morgan Plus 8 and the Land Rover Discovery. Coupled with a car weight of only 1587 lb (720 kg), driving the Seight really should require a weapons license, even in its current 3950cc, 200 bhp version. The 0–60 mph (up to 100 kph) figure of 4.3 seconds is held in huge esteem by the Westfield cognoscenti, and is certainly brisk enough to prevent a passenger from lighting his cigarette. Purists regret the lack of roar that delighted Seight drivers up until 1996 and gave passers-by big frights. As the Westfield, nimble as a weasel, has gradually been incorporated into peaceful co-existence with "normal" cars on British roads, for the last few years two three-way exhaust catalyzers have prevented the infernal noise the engine used to unleash. The speed, as the honorable trade journal *Autocar* complained on October 30 that year, is no longer felt quite so intensely now. The magazine commented on the car's affordability: only £25,950 for the fully assembled Seight, a fraction of what supercars of comparable performance cost, £6000 less for the kit version and only £4000 more for the Morgan Plus 8. But it was absurd to offer a car of this speed without a cover on the glove compartment, for when the driver accelerated smartly its contents spilled out into the passenger's lap. Nevertheless, the Seight was a Seven that had reached graduation.

In June 2001, after 653 of these cars were sold, these virtues were evidently no longer desired. The Seight, Chris Smith admitted, had become an end-of-sale model, just like its Zetec-motorized counterpart.

The evolution of the Seven was slow. The ZEi differed from its predecessor, the Westfield SEi, with small cosmetic changes to its fiberglass body, and a different grill. The letter "i" stood for independent rear suspension. The ZEi could be ordered with motorcycle mudguards or long extending fenders.

Initially one could recognize the model by the power bulge on the right of the hood, providing room for the respiratory tracts of the Ford Zetec engine. Its intake manifold was first made of aluminum, later plastic, enabling the panels above to be flattened again. Nevertheless, the owner of this Seven ZEi prefers the so-called V8 hood, which usually covers the much bigger Rover V8.

SPECIFICATIONS

AC Ace 1953–1963
1954 model

Engine	Configuration	in-line six-cylinder, overhead camshafts
	Displacement	1991cc
	Bore and stroke	65 × 100 mm
	Carburetion	three horizontal SU H2 carburetors
	Power	86 bhp at 4500 rpm
	Transmission	four-speed manual
Chassis	Frame	tubular frame with crossmembers
	Front suspension	lower wishbones, upper transverse leaf springs
	Rear suspension	lower wishbones, upper transverse leaf springs
Dimensions	Wheelbase	90 in (2286 mm)
	Length × width × height	149 × 59.5 × 49 in (3780 × 1510 × 1240 mm)
	Weight	1667 lb (765 kg) (curb)
Maximum speed		104 mph (167 kph)

Allard J2X 1952–1954
Allard J2X Le Mans 1952

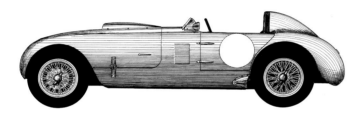

Engine	Configuration	V8
	Displacement	5420cc
	Bore and stroke	96.8 × 92 mm
	Carburetion	single Rochester four-barrel downdraft carburetor
	Power	162 bhp at 4800 rpm
	Transmission	four-speed Cadillac Seville
Chassis	Frame	box frame with tubular crossmembers
	Front suspension	swinging half-axles, coil springs
	Rear suspension	De Dion axle, coil springs, triangulated anti-roll mechanism, sway bar
Dimensions	Wheelbase	100 in (2540 mm)
	Length × width × height	154 × 63 × 46 in (3910 × 1600 × 1170 mm)
	Weight	2015 lb (914 kg) (curb)
Maximum speed		125 mph (201 kph)

Alvis TB 21 1950–1953
1951 model

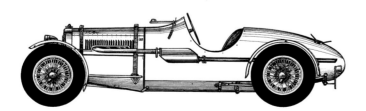

Engine	Configuration	in-line six-cylinder
	Displacement	2993cc
	Bore and stroke	84 × 90 mm
	Carburetion	twin SU H4 carburetors
	Power	93 bhp at 4000 rpm
	Transmission	four-speed manual
Chassis	Frame	U-profile longitudinal members with crossbraces
	Front suspension	double wishbones, coil springs
	Rear suspension	rigid axle, semi-elliptic leaf springs
Dimensions	Wheelbase	111.6 in (2832 mm)
	Length × width × height	177.3 × 70 × 54.8 in (4500 × 1780 × 1390 mm)
	Weight	3020 lb (1370 kg)
Maximum speed		97 mph (156 kph)

Aston Martin International 1929–1932
1930 model

Engine	Configuration	in-line four-cylinder, overhead camshafts
	Displacement	1494cc
	Bore and stroke	69 × 99 mm
	Carburetion	twin horizontal SU carburetors
	Power	56 bhp at 4250 rpm
	Transmission	four-speed manual
Chassis	Frame	steel U-profile sections
	Front suspension	rigid axle, leaf springs
	Rear suspension	rigid axle, leaf springs
Dimensions	Wheelbase	102 in (2590 mm)
	Length × width × height	153.7 × 64.6 × 51.2 in (3900 × 1640 × 1300 mm) (windshield up)
	Weight	1896 lb (860 kg)
Maximum speed		78 mph (125 kph)

Aston Martin 2-Liter Sports (DB1) 1948–1950
1950 model

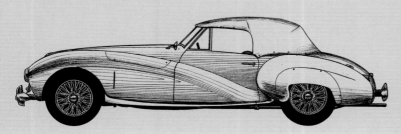

Engine	Configuration	in-line four-cylinder
	Displacement	1970cc
	Bore and stroke	82.55 × 92 mm
	Carburetion	twin SU TH4 485 carburetors
	Power	90 bhp at 4750 rpm
	Transmission	four-speed manual
Chassis	Frame	lattice frame construction
	Front suspension	trailing arms, coil springs
	Rear suspension	rigid axle, trailing arms, coil springs, Panhard rod
Dimensions	Wheelbase	108 in (2740 mm)
	Length × width × height	176 × 67.4 × 55.6 in (4470 × 1710 × 1410 mm)
	Weight	2525 lb (1145 kg) (curb)
Maximum speed		79 mph (127 kph)

Engine	Configuration	in-line six-cylinder, twin overhead camshafts	**Aston Martin DB2** 1950–1953
	Displacement	2580cc	*1953 model*
	Bore and stroke	78 × 90 mm	
	Carburetion	twin horizontal SU H4 carburetors	
	Power	108 bhp at 5000 rpm	
	Transmission	four-speed manual	
Chassis	Frame	lattice frame construction	
	Front suspension	coil springs, lateral arms	
	Rear suspension	coil springs, rigid axle, trailing arms, Panhard rod	
Dimensions	Wheelbase	99 in (2511 mm)	
	Length × width × height	162.7 × 65 × 53.6 in (4130 × 1650 × 1360 mm)	
	Weight	2601 lb (1180 kg) (curb)	
Maximum speed		110 mph (177 kph)	

Engine	Configuration	in-line six-cylinder, twin overhead camshafts	**Aston Martin DB4** 1958–1963
	Displacement	3670cc	*1961 model*
	Bore and stroke	92 × 92 mm	
	Carburetion	twin horizontal SU HD8 carburetors	
	Power	243 bhp at 5500 rpm	
	Transmission	four-speed manual	
Chassis	Frame	platform frame with interlaced ribs	
	Front suspension	wishbones, coil springs	
	Rear suspension	rigid axle, trailing arms, coil springs, Watts linkage	
Dimensions	Wheelbase	98 in (2489 mm)	
	Length × width × height	176 × 66 × 51.6 in (4480 × 1680 × 1310 mm)	
	Weight	2857 lb (1296 kg) (curb)	
Maximum speed		140 mph (225 kph)	

Engine	Configuration	in-line six-cylinder, twin overhead camshafts	**Aston Martin DB6** 1965–1970
	Displacement	3995cc	*1967 model*
	Bore and stroke	96 × 92 mm	
	Carburetion	three horizontal SU HD8 carburetors	
	Power	286 bhp at 5500 rpm	
	Transmission	five-speed manual	
Chassis	Frame	tubular platform frame	
	Front suspension	wishbones, coil springs	
	Rear suspension	rigid axle, trailing arms, coil springs, Watts linkage	
Dimensions	Wheelbase	101.7 in (2580 mm)	
	Length × width × height	182 × 66.2 × 53.6 in (4620 × 1680 × 1360 mm)	
	Weight	3252 lb (1475 kg) (empty)	
Maximum speed		148 mph (238 kph)	

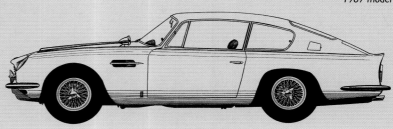

Engine	Configuration	V8, four overhead camshafts	**Aston Martin DBS V8/V8** 1969–1989
	Displacement	5340cc	*1972 model*
	Bore and stroke	100 × 85 mm	
	Carburetion	Fuel injection	
	Power	315 bhp at 5000 rpm	
	Transmission	three-speed Borg-Warner automatic	
Chassis	Frame	platform chassis	
	Front suspension	wishbones, coil springs	
	Rear suspension	De Dion axle, coil springs, Watts linkage	
Dimensions	Wheelbase	102.8 in (2610 mm)	
	Length × width × height	180.6 × 72 × 52.2 in (4585 × 1830 × 1325 mm)	
	Weight	3807 lb (1727 kg) (empty)	
Maximum speed		150 mph (242 kph)	

Engine	Configuration	V8, four overhead camshafts, four valves per cylinder	**Aston Martin Virage/V8** 1989–2000
	Displacement	5340cc	*Aston Martin Virage Volante 1993*
	Bore and stroke	100 × 85 mm	
	Carburetion	Weber-Marelli electronic fuel injection	
	Power	330 bhp at 5300 rpm	
	Transmission	five-speed manual	
Chassis	Frame	platform chassis	
	Front suspension	wishbones, coil springs	
	Rear suspension	De Dion axle, Watts linkage, diagonal trailing arms, coil springs	
Dimensions	Wheelbase	102.8 in (2610 mm)	
	Length × width × height	187 × 73 × 55 in (4745 × 1855 × 1400 mm)	
	Weight	4409 lb (2000 kg) (empty)	
Maximum speed		157 mph (253 kph)	

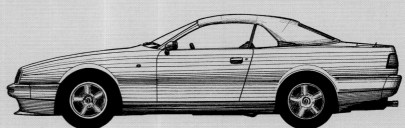

Aston Martin DB7 1994 to present
1995 model

Engine	Configuration	in-line six-cylinder, two overhead camshafts, four valves per cylinder
	Displacement	3239cc
	Bore and stroke	91 × 83 mm
	Carburetion	electronic injection, single Roots (Eaton) compressor
	Power	317 bhp at 5500 rpm
	Transmission	four-speed automatic GM Hydramatic
Chassis	Frame	monocoque
	Front suspension	double wishbones, coil springs
	Rear suspension	trailing arms and wishbones, links, coil springs
Dimensions	Wheelbase	102 in (2591 mm)
	Length × width × height	183 × 72 × 48.8 in (4645 × 1830 × 1238 mm)
	Weight	3748 lb (1700 kg)
Maximum speed		160 mph (258 kph)

Aston Martin Vanquish from 2001
2001 model

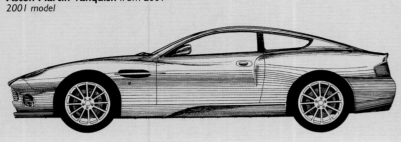

Engine	Configuration	V12, four overhead camshafts, four valves per cylinder
	Displacement	5935cc
	Bore and stroke	89 × 79.5 mm
	Carburetion	electronic engine management
	Power	457 bhp at 6500 rpm
	Transmission	six-speed manual with Auto Shift or Select Shift
Chassis	Frame	aluminum and carbon fiber monocoque
	Front suspension	double wishbones, coil spring and damper combination
	Rear suspension	double wishbones, coil spring and damper combination
Dimensions	Wheelbase	106 in (2690 mm)
	Length × width × height	183.8 × 75.8 × 52 in (4665 × 1923 × 1318 mm)
	Weight	4045 lb (1835 kg) (empty)
Maximum speed		190 mph (306 kph)

Austin-Healey 100 1953–1959
Austin-Healey 100S 1955

Engine	Configuration	in-line four-cylinder
	Displacement	2660cc
	Bore and stroke	87.3 × 111.1 mm
	Carburetion	twin horizontal SU H6 carburetors
	Power	132 bhp at 4700 rpm
	Transmission	four-speed manual
Chassis	Frame	underslung box frame with crossbraces
	Front suspension	wishbones, coil springs
	Rear suspension	rigid axle, semi-elliptic leaf springs
Dimensions	Wheelbase	90.2 in (2290 mm)
	Length × width × height	148 × 60 × 41.8 in (3760 × 1525 × 1060 mm)
	Weight	1873 lb (850 kg) (curb)
Maximum speed		119 mph (191 kph)

Austin-Healey Sprite Mk I 1958–1961
1958 model

Engine	Configuration	in-line four-cylinder
	Displacement	948cc
	Bore and stroke	62.9 × 76.2 mm
	Carburetion	two S4 HI semi-downdraft carburetors
	Power	42.5 bhp at 3300 rpm
	Transmission	four-speed manual
Chassis	Frame	box frame welded to body
	Front suspension	wishbones, coil springs
	Rear suspension	rigid axle, quarter-elliptic leaf springs, double trailing arms
Dimensions	Wheelbase	80 in (2030 mm)
	Length × width × height	137.5 × 53 × 47.7 in (3490 × 1350 × 1210 mm)
	Weight	1411 lb (640 kg) (curb)
Maximum speed		78 mph (126 kph)

Austin-Healey 3000 1959–1968
Austin-Healey 3000 Mk I BN7 1960

Engine	Configuration	in-line six-cylinder
	Displacement	2912cc
	Bore and stroke	83.34 × 88.9 mm
	Carburetion	two SU HD 6 semi-downdraft carburetors
	Power	124 bhp at 4600 rpm
	Transmission	four-speed manual
Chassis	Frame	tubular frame with diagonal crossbracing
	Front suspension	wishbones, coil springs
	Rear suspension	rigid axle, semi-elliptic leaf springs
Dimensions	Wheelbase	91.8 in (2329 mm)
	Length × width × height	157.6 × 60 × 49.2 in (4000 × 1524 × 1250 mm)
	Weight	2381 lb (1080 kg) (curb)
Maximum speed		114 mph (183.5 kph)

Bentley 4½-Liter Supercharged 1929–1931
1930 model

Engine	Configuration	in-line four-cylinder, overhead camshafts, four valves and two spark plugs per cylinder, Amherst Villiers supercharger
	Displacement	4298cc
	Bore and stroke	100 × 140 mm
	Carburetion	twin horizontal SU HVG 5 carburetors
	Power	182 bhp at 3900 rpm
	Transmission	four-speed manual
Chassis	Frame	tubular, with longitudinal runners and crossmembers,
	Front suspension	rigid axle, semi-elliptic leaf springs
	Rear suspension	rigid axle, semi-elliptic leaf springs
Dimensions	Wheelbase	117.6 in (2984 mm)
	Length × width × height	176 × 70 × 60 in (4470 × 1778 × 1524 mm)
	Weight	3814 lb (1730 kg) (curb)
Maximum speed		105 mph (169 kph)

Engine	Configuration	in-line six-cylinder
	Displacement	1971cc
	Bore and stroke	66 × 96 mm
	Carburetion	three Solex 32 BI downdraft carburetors
	Power	107 bhp at 5000 rpm
	Transmission	four-speed manual
Chassis	Frame	platform frame with box girders
	Front suspension	upper wishbones, lower transverse leaf springs
	Rear suspension	rigid axle, longitudinal torsion bars
Dimensions	Wheelbase	96 in (2445 mm)
	Length × width × height	173.3 × 68 × 54.8 in (4400 × 1727 × 1390 mm)
	Weight	2293 lb (1040 kg) (curb)
Maximum speed		105 mph (169 kph)

Bristol 404 1953–1955
1954 model

Engine	Configuration	in-line four-cylinder, two overhead camshafts, four valves per cylinder
	Displacement	1998cc
	Bore and stroke	86 × 86 mm
	Carburetion	twin horizontal Weber 45 DCOE carburetors
	Power	175 bhp at 6000 rpm
	Transmission	five-speed manual
Chassis	Frame	tubular frame
	Front suspension	wishbones, coil springs
	Rear suspension	De Dion axle, coil springs
Dimensions	Wheelbase	88.7 in (2250 mm)
	Length × width × height	133 × 61.9 × 42.9 in (3380 × 1570 × 1090 mm)
	Weight	1301 lb (590 kg) (empty)
Maximum speed		126 mph (202.7 kph)

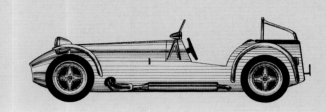

Caterham Seven from 1973
Caterham Seven HPC 1992

Engine	Configuration	in-line four-cylinder, two overhead camshafts, four valves per cylinder
	Displacement	1795cc
	Bore and stroke	80 × 89.3 mm
	Carburetion	electronic fuel injection
	Power	190 bhp at 7500 rpm
	Transmission	six-speed manual
Chassis	Frame	tubular frame
	Front suspension	wishbones, coil springs
	Rear suspension	De Dion axle, Watts linkage, trailing arms, coil springs
Dimensions	Wheelbase	87.7 in (2225 mm)
	Length × width × height	152.9 × 62.3 × 41 in (3880 × 1580 × 1045 mm)
	Weight	1433 lb (650 kg) (curb)
Maximum speed		137 mph (220 kph)

Caterham 21 1994–2000
2000 model

Engine	Configuration	V8
	Displacement	2548cc
	Bore and stroke	76.2 × 69.85 mm
	Carburetion	twin SU HD 6 semi-downdraft carburetors
	Power	140 bhp at 5800 rpm
	Transmission	four-speed manual
Chassis	Frame	box frame with diagonal crossbracing
	Front suspension	wishbones, coil springs
	Rear suspension	rigid axle, semi-elliptic leaf springs
Dimensions	Wheelbase	92 in (2337 mm)
	Length × width × height	160.8 × 60.7 × 50.9 in (4080 × 1540 × 1292 mm)
	Weight	2090 lb (948 kg) (curb)
Maximum speed		120 mph (193.6 kph)

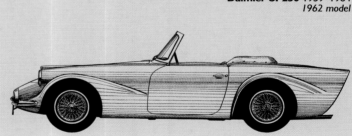

Daimler SP250 1959–1964
1962 model

Engine	Configuration	in-line four-cylinder
	Displacement	1588cc
	Bore and stroke	75.6 × 88.9 mm
	Carburetion	twin horizontal SU H4 carburetors
	Power	78 bhp at 5500 rpm
	Transmission	four-speed manual
Chassis	Frame	tubular frame with crossbraces
	Front suspension	wishbones, coil springs
	Rear suspension	rigid axle, coil springs, trailing arms, Panhard rod
Dimensions	Wheelbase	90 in (2286 mm)
	Length × width × height	154 × 59.5 × 46.5 in (3912 × 1511 × 1180 mm)
	Weight	1429 lb (648 kg) (curb)
Maximum speed		103 mph (165 kph)

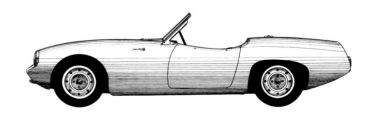

Elva Courier 1958–1968
Elva Courier Mk II 1960

Engine	Configuration	in-line six-cylinder
	Displacement	1971cc
	Bore and stroke	66 × 96 mm
	Carburetion	three Solex downdraft carburetors
	Power	101 bhp at 5000 rpm
	Transmission	four-speed manual
Chassis	Frame	tubular frame
	Front suspension	upper wishbones, lower transverse leaf springs
	Rear suspension	rigid axle, longitudinal torsion bars, triangulated anti-roll mechanism
Dimensions	Wheelbase	88.3 in (2240 mm)
	Length × width × height	150 × 57.9 × 50.8 in (3810 × 1470 × 1290 mm)
	Weight	1808 lb (820 kg) (curb)
Maximum speed		124 mph (200 kph)

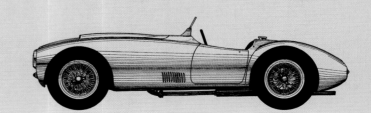

Frazer Nash Mille Miglia 1950–1952
1952 Model

Ginetta G4 1961–1968
Ginetta G4 Series II 1964

Engine	Configuration	in-line four-cylinder
	Displacement	1498cc
	Bore and stroke	80.96 × 72.65 mm
	Carburetion	single Weber 38 double-downdraft carburetor
	Power	78 bhp at 6000 rpm
	Transmission	four-speed manual
Chassis	Frame	spaceframe
	Front suspension	wishbones, coil springs
	Rear suspension	rigid axle with coil springs
Dimensions	Wheelbase	80 in (2030 mm)
	Length × width × height	132 × 56 × 37 in (3353 × 1422 × 940 mm)
	Weight	1124 lb (510 kg) (empty)
Maximum speed		115 mph (185 kph)

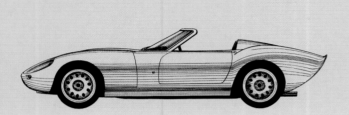

Ginetta G27 from 1985
1999 model

Engine	Configuration	in-line four-cylinder, overhead camshafts
	Displacement	2093cc
	Bore and stroke	93 × 76.93 mm
	Carburetion	single horizontal Dell'Orto 45 twin carburetor
	Power	145 bhp at 5800 rpm
	Transmission	five-speed manual
Chassis	Frame	spaceframe with central support
	Front suspension	double wishbones, coil springs
	Rear suspension	rigid axle, trailing arms, Panhard rod
Dimensions	Wheelbase	84.6 in (2148 mm)
	Length × width × height	145.3 × 62.4 × 41 in (3690 × 1583 × 1040 mm)
	Weight	1609 lb (730 kg) (empty)
Maximum speed		128 mph (206 kph)

Healey Silverstone 1949–1951
1949 model

Engine	Configuration	in-line four-cylinder
	Displacement	2443cc
	Bore and stroke	80.5 × 120 mm
	Carburetion	twin horizontal SU H4 carburetors
	Power	100 bhp at 5300 rpm
	Transmission	four-speed manual
Chassis	Frame	box frame with diagonal crossbracing
	Front suspension	trailing arms, coil springs
	Rear suspension	rigid axle, coil springs
Dimensions	Wheelbase	102 in (2591 mm)
	Length × width × height	157.6 × 58.3 × 40.2 in (4000 × 1480 × 1020 mm)
	Weight	2072 lb (940 kg) (curb)
Maximum speed		100 mph (160 kph)

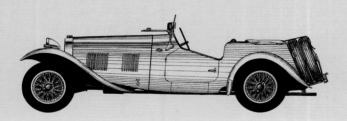

H.R.G. 1500 1939–1956
1948 model

Engine	Configuration	in-line four-cylinder, overhead camshafts
	Displacement	1496cc
	Bore and stroke	68 × 103 mm
	Carburetion	twin horizontal SU carburetors
	Power	61 bhp at 4800 rpm
	Transmission	four-speed manual
Chassis	Frame	underslung frame with longitudinal supports and crossbraces
	Front suspension	rigid axle, quarter-elliptic leaf springs
	Rear suspension	rigid axle, semi-elliptic leaf springs
Dimensions	Wheelbase	102.8 in (2610 mm)
	Length × width × height	146.2 × 56.5 × 52 in (3710 × 1435 × 1320 mm) (windshield down: 42.4 in/1075 mm)
	Weight	1623 lb (736 kg)
Maximum speed		87 mph (140 kph)

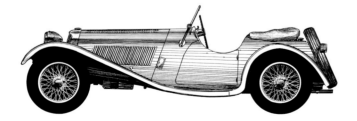

Jaguar SS100 1936–1940
1936 model

Engine	Configuration	in-line six-cylinder
	Displacement	3485cc (originally 2.5 liter)
	Bore and stroke	82 × 110 mm
	Carburetion	twin horizontal SU carburetors
	Power	125 bhp at 4250 rpm
	Transmission	four-speed manual
Chassis	Frame	box frame with diagonal crossbracing
	Front suspension	rigid axle, semi-elliptic springs, friction dampers
	Rear suspension	rigid axle, semi-elliptic leaf springs, hydraulic dampers
Dimensions	Wheelbase	104 in (2642 mm)
	Length × width × height	150 × 62 × 55 in (3810 × 1575 × 1397 mm)
	Weight	2601 lb (1180 kg) (curb)
Maximum speed		101 mph (163 kph)

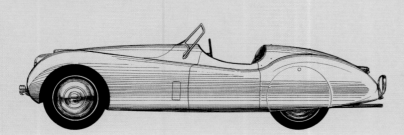

Jaguar XK120 1948–1954
Jaguar XK120 Roadster 1951

Engine	Configuration	in-line six-cylinder, two overhead camshafts
	Displacement	3442cc
	Bore and stroke	83 × 106 mm
	Carburetion	twin horizontal SU H6 carburetors
	Power	162 bhp at 5200 rpm
	Transmission	four-speed manual
Chassis	Frame	box frame, longitudinal members with crossbracing
	Front suspension	wishbones, longitudinal torsion bars
	Rear suspension	rigid axle, semi-elliptic leaf springs
Dimensions	Wheelbase	102 in (2590 mm)
	Length × width × height	173.6 × 62 × 52.5 in (4406 × 1574 × 1332 mm)
	Weight	2469 lb (1120 kg) (curb)
Maximum speed		121 mph (194 kph)

Engine	Configuration	in-line six-cylinder, two overhead camshafts
	Displacement	3781cc
	Bore and stroke	87 × 106 mm
	Carburetion	twin horizontal SU HD6 carburetors
	Power	220 bhp at 5500 rpm
	Transmission	four-speed manual
Chassis	Frame	X-frame with box girders
	Front suspension	wishbones, longitudinal torsion bars
	Rear suspension	rigid axle, semi-elliptic leaf springs
Dimensions	Wheelbase	102 in (2590 mm)
	Length × width × height	176 × 64.6 × 55 in (4470 × 1640 × 1395 mm)
	Weight	3131 lb (1420 kg) (curb)
Maximum speed		136 mph (219 kph)

Jaguar XK150 1957–1960
Jaguar XK150 coupé 2+2
3.8 Litre 1960

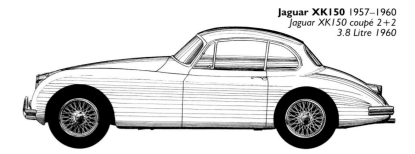

Engine	Configuration	in-line six-cylinder, two overhead camshafts
	Displacement	3781cc
	Bore and stroke	83 × 106 mm
	Carburetion	three horizontal Weber 45 DCO3 carburetors
	Power	265 bhp at 5500 rpm
	Transmission	four-speed manual
Chassis	Frame	lattice frame with self-supporting exterior skin
	Front suspension	wishbones, longitudinal torsion bars
	Rear suspension	rigid axle, trailing arms, longitudinal torsion bars, triangular anti-roll mechanism
Dimensions	Wheelbase	89.4 in (2270 mm)
	Length × width × height	156 × 65.4 × 40 in (3960 × 1660 × 1015 mm)
	Weight	2019 lb (916 kg) (curb)
Maximum speed		125 mph (200 kph)

Jaguar XKSS 1957
Jaguar D-Type 1955, brought up to road-going specifications

Engine	Configuration	in-line six-cylinder, two overhead camshafts
	Displacement	4235cc
	Bore and stroke	92.07 × 106 mm
	Carburetion	three horizontal SU HD8 carburetors
	Power	265 bhp at 5400 rpm
	Transmission	four-speed manual
Chassis	Frame	monocoque construction
	Front suspension	wishbones, longitudinal torsion bars
	Rear suspension	lower wishbones, upper double driveshaft links, trailing arms, double coil springs
Dimensions	Wheelbase	96 in (2438 mm)
	Length × width × height	175.3 × 65.4 × 48 in (4450 × 1660 × 1220 mm)
	Weight	2601 lb (1180 kg) (empty)
Maximum speed		149 mph (240 kph)

Jaguar E-Type 1961–1971
Jaguar E-Type 4.2 Liter cabriolet 1967

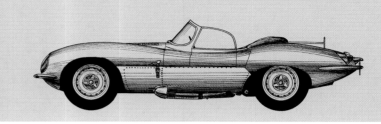

Engine	Configuration	V12, two overhead camshafts
	Displacement	5343cc
	Bore and stroke	90 × 70 mm
	Carburetion	four horizontal Zenith 175 CD SE carburetors
	Power	276 bhp at 5850 rpm
	Transmission	four-speed manual
Chassis	Frame	monocoque construction
	Front suspension	wishbones, longitudinal torsion bars
	Rear suspension	upper wishbones, lower double driveshaft links, trailing arms, double coil springs
Dimensions	Wheelbase	105 in (2667 mm)
	Length × width × height	184.6 × 66.2 × 51.4 in (4685 × 1680 × 1305 mm)
	Weight	3331 lb (1511 kg) (empty)
Maximum speed		121 mph (228 kph)

Jaguar V12 1971–1975
Jaguar 5.3 E-Type coupé 2+2 1972

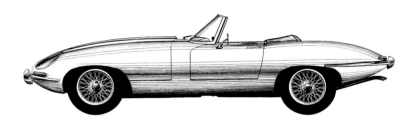

Engine	Configuration	V12, two overhead camshafts
	Displacement	5343cc
	Bore and stroke	90 × 70 mm
	Carburetion	indirect electronic fuel injection
	Power	289 bhp at 5570 rpm
	Transmission	three-speed automatic
Chassis	Frame	monocoque construction
	Front suspension	wishbones, coil springs
	Rear suspension	lower forked guide arms, upper drive links and trailing arms
Dimensions	Wheelbase	102 in (2591 mm)
	Length × width × height	187.7 × 70.7 × 49.3 in (4765 × 1795 × 1250 mm)
	Weight	4233 lb (1920 kg) (empty)
Maximum speed		150 mph (241 kph)

Jaguar XJ-S 1975–1995
Jaguar XJ-S V12 cabriolet 1991

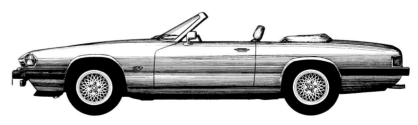

Engine	Configuration	mid-mounted V6 engine, four overhead camshafts, four valves per cylinder, twin Garrett turbochargers, two intercoolers
	Displacement	3498cc
	Bore and stroke	94 × 84 mm
	Carburetion	electronic engine management
	Power	549 bhp at 7200 rpm
	Transmission	five-speed manual
Chassis	Frame	alloy monocoque
	Front suspension	double wishbones, coil spring and damper units
	Rear suspension	multiple wishbones, coil spring and damper units
Dimensions	Wheelbase	104 in (2640 mm)
	Length × width × height	194.2 × 79.2 × 45.3 in (4930 × 2010 × 1150 mm)
	Weight	3031 lb (1375 kg) (empty)
Maximum speed		217 mph (349 kph)

Jaguar XJ220 1992–1994
Pre-production chassis 1992

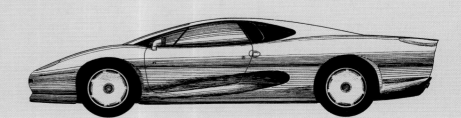

Jaguar XK8 from 1996
1996 model

Engine	Configuration	V8, four overhead camshafts, four valves per cylinder
	Displacement	3996cc
	Bore and stroke	86 × 86 mm
	Carburetion	electronic fuel injection
	Power	284 bhp at 6100 rpm
	Transmission	five-speed automatic
Chassis	Frame	monocoque construction with auxiliary front and rear frame
	Front suspension	double wishbones, coil springs
	Rear suspension	lower wishbones, drive links, coil springs
Dimensions	Wheelbase	102 in (2590 mm)
	Length × width × height	187.5 × 72 × 50.8 in (4760 × 1830 × 1290 mm)
	Weight	3560 lb (1615 kg) (empty)
Maximum speed		156 mph (251 kph)

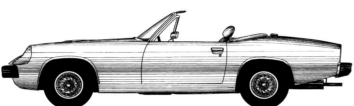

Jensen 541 1954–1961
1954 model

Engine	Configuration	in-line six-cylinder
	Displacement	3993cc
	Bore and stroke	87 × 111 mm
	Carburetion	three horizontal SU HD6 carburetors
	Power	131 bhp at 3700 rpm
	Transmission	four-speed manual
Chassis	Frame	box frame with tubular longitudinal and crossmembers
	Front suspension	wishbones, coil springs
	Rear suspension	rigid axle, trailing arms, coil springs
Dimensions	Wheelbase	105.2 in (2670 mm)
	Length × width × height	174 × 63 × 53.2 in (4420 × 1600 × 1350 mm)
	Weight	2690 lb (1220 kg) (curb)
Maximum speed		104 mph (168 kph)

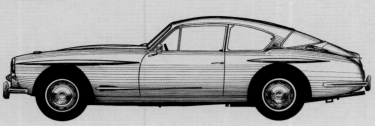

Jensen-Healey 1972–1976
Jensen-Healey Mk II 1975

Engine	Configuration	in-line four-cylinder, two overhead camshafts, four valves per cylinder
	Displacement	1973cc
	Bore and stroke	95.2 × 69.3 mm
	Carburetion	twin horizontal Stromberg 175 CD 2SE carburetors
	Power	140 bhp at 6500 rpm
	Transmission	five-speed manual
Chassis	Frame	monocoque construction
	Front suspension	wishbones, coil springs
	Rear suspension	rigid axle, lower trailing arms, upper diagonal arms
Dimensions	Wheelbase	92.2 in (2340 mm)
	Length × width × height	165.7 × 63.4 × 47.7 (4205 × 1610 × 1210 mm)
	Weight	2161 lb (980 kg) (with full 13.2–US-gal/50-liter tank)
Maximum speed		119 mph (191.5 kph)

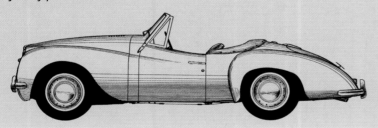

Jowett Jupiter 1950–1954
Jowett Jupiter Mk IA 1954

Engine	Configuration	four-cylinder boxer
	Displacement	1486cc
	Bore and stroke	72.5 × 90 mm
	Carburetion	twin Zenith 30 VM downdraft carburetors
	Power	63 bhp at 4500 rpm
	Transmission	four-speed manual
Chassis	Frame	tubular frame with longitudinal supports and diagonal crossbracing
	Front suspension	wishbones, longitudinal torsion bars
	Rear suspension	rigid axle, double trailing arms, longitudinal torsion bars
Dimensions	Wheelbase	93 in (2360 mm)
	Length × width × height	168.2 × 61.9 × 55.9 (4270 × 1570 × 1420 mm)
	Weight	2083 lb (945 kg) (curb)
Maximum speed		90 mph (145 kph)

Lea Francis 2½-Liter Sports 1950–1953
1950 model

Engine	Configuration	in-line four-cylinder, two side camshafts
	Displacement	2496cc
	Bore and stroke	85 × 110 mm
	Carburetion	twin horizontal SU H3 carburetors
	Power	106 bhp at 4000 rpm
	Transmission	four-speed manual
Chassis	Frame	box frame
	Front suspension	wishbones, torsion bars
	Rear suspension	rigid axle, semi-elliptic leaf springs
Dimensions	Wheelbase	99 in (2514 mm)
	Length × width × height	165 × 63 × 54 in (4190 × 1600 × 1370 mm)
	Weight	2575 lb (1168 kg) (curb)
Maximum speed		98 mph (158 kph)

Lotus Elite 1957–1963
1960 model

Engine	Configuration	in-line four-cylinder, overhead camshafts
	Displacement	1216cc
	Bore and stroke	76.2 × 66.6 mm
	Carburetion	single horizontal SU H4 carburetor
	Power	76 bhp at 6100 rpm
	Transmission	four-speed
Chassis	Frame	monocoque construction
	Front suspension	wishbones, strut units
	Rear suspension	thrust rods, strut units, driveshaft links
Dimensions	Wheelbase	88 in (2235 mm)
	Length × width × height	144.2 × 57.9 × 46 in (3660 × 1470 × 1170 mm)
	Weight	1290 lb (585 kg) (curb)
Maximum speed		112 mph (181 kph)

Engine	Configuration	in-line four-cylinder, two overhead camshafts
	Displacement	1558cc
	Bore and stroke	82.6 × 72.8 mm
	Carburetion	two horizontal Weber 40 DCOE carburetors
	Power	125 bhp at 6200 rpm
	Transmission	four-speed
Chassis	Frame	spaceframe with supporting outer skin
	Front suspension	wishbones, strut units
	Rear suspension	rigid axle, trailing arms, strut units
Dimensions	Wheelbase	89 in (2260 mm)
	Length × width × height	133 × 61 × 37 in (3378 × 1550 × 940 mm)
	Weight	1257 lb (570 kg) (empty)
Maximum speed		112 mph (181 kph)

Lotus Seven 1957–1973
Lotus Seven S3 Twin Cam SS 1969

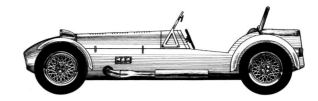

Engine	Configuration	in-line four-cylinder, two overhead camshafts
	Displacement	1558cc
	Bore and stroke	82.55 × 2.75 mm
	Carburetion	twin Weber 40 DCOE carburetors
	Power	105 bhp at 5500 rpm
	Transmission	four-speed manual
Chassis	Frame	backbone chassis
	Front suspension	wishbones, coil springs
	Rear suspension	lower wishbones, diagonal strut units
Dimensions	Wheelbase	83.9 in (2130 mm)
	Length × width × height	146 × 56 × 44 in (3670 × 1420 × 1120 mm)
	Weight	1367 lb (620 kg) (empty)
Maximum speed		108 mph (174 kph)

Lotus Elan 1962–1973
1963 model

Engine	Configuration	in-line four-cylinder mid-mounted engine
	Displacement	1470cc
	Bore and stroke	76 × 81 mm
	Carburetion	single horizontal Solex 35 DIDS A2 carburetor
	Power	82 bhp at 6000 rpm
	Transmission	four-speed manual
Chassis	Frame	backbone chassis
	Front suspension	wishbones, coil springs
	Rear suspension	trailing arms, wishbones, strut units
Dimensions	Wheelbase	83.9 in (2310 mm)
	Length × width × height	157.2 × 64.6 × 42.9 in (3990 × 1640 × 1090 mm)
	Weight	1345 lb (610 kg) (empty)
Maximum speed		115 mph (185 kph)

Lotus Europa 1966–1975
Lotus Europa S2 1969

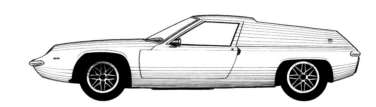

Engine	Configuration	in-line four-cylinder, two overhead camshafts
	Displacement	1558cc
	Bore and stroke	82.55 × 72.75 mm
	Carburetion	two twin-choke Weber 40 DCOE carburetors
	Power	118 bhp at 6250 rpm
	Transmission	four-speed manual
Chassis	Frame	backbone chassis with front and rear forks
	Front suspension	wishbones, coil springs
	Rear suspension	lower wishbones, diagonal strut units
Dimensions	Wheelbase	96.5 in (2450 mm)
	Length × width × height	169 × 66.2 × 46.9 in (4290 × 1680 × 1190 mm)
	Weight	2083 lb (945 kg) (empty)
Maximum speed		120 mph (193 kph)

Lotus Elan +2 1969–1974
Lotus Elan +2S 1970 model

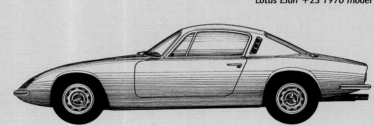

Engine	Configuration	in-line four-cylinder, two overhead camshafts, four valves per cylinder
	Displacement	1973cc
	Bore and stroke	95.3 × 69.3 mm
	Carburetion	two twin-choke horizontal Dell'Orto DHLA 45E carburetors
	Power	155 bhp at 6500 rpm
	Transmission	five-speed manual
Chassis	Frame	backbone chassis with front and rear forks
	Front suspension	upper and lower wishbones, coil springs
	Rear suspension	diagonal arms, diagonal struts, coil springs
Dimensions	Wheelbase	97.7 in (2480 mm)
	Length × width × height	175.6 × 71.6 × 47.6 in (4457 × 1816 × 1207 mm)
	Weight	2579 lb (1170 kg) (empty)
Maximum speed		124 mph (199.5 kph)

Lotus Elite 1974–1983
Lotus Elite S1 1975

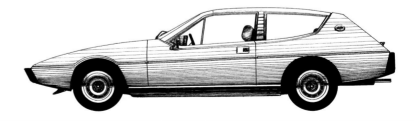

Engine	Configuration	in-line four-cylinder, two overhead camshafts, four valves per cylinder
	Displacement	2174cc
	Bore and stroke	95.25 × 6.2 mm
	Carburetion	two twin-choke horizontal Dell'Orto DHLA 45 carburetors
	Power	162 bhp at 6500 rpm
	Transmission	five-speed manual
Chassis	Frame	backbone chassis with auxiliary spaceframe
	Front suspension	upper and lower wishbones, strut units
	Rear suspension	wishbones, longitudinal struts, strut units
Dimensions	Wheelbase	96 in (2440 mm)
	Length × width × height	165 × 73.3 × 43.7 in (4190 × 1860 × 1110 mm)
	Weight	2249 lb (1020 kg) (empty)
Maximum speed		134 mph (215 kph)

Lotus Esprit 1975–1990
Lotus Esprit S3 1982

Lotus Esprit Turbo from 1980
Lotus Esprit Turbo SE 1989

Engine	Configuration	in-line four-cylinder mid-mounted engine, two overhead camshafts, four valves per cylinder, turbocharger, intercooler
	Displacement	2174cc
	Bore and stroke	95.29 × 76.2 mm
	Carburetion	electronic fuel injection (Venturi)
	Power	264 bhp at 6500 rpm
	Transmission	five-speed manual
Chassis	Frame	backbone chassis with auxiliary spaceframe
	Front suspension	upper and lower wishbones, strut units
	Rear suspension	wishbones, longitudinal struts and strut units
Dimensions	Wheelbase	96 in (2440 mm)
	Length × width × height	16.9 × 73.3 × 45.3 in (4330 × 1860 × 1150 mm)
	Weight	2952 lb (1339 kg) (empty)
Maximum speed		155 mph (249 kph)

Lotus Elan 1989–1995
Lotus Elan S2 Turbo 1995

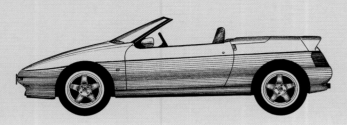

Engine	Configuration	transverse in-line four-cylinder, two overhead camshafts, four valves per cylinder, turbocharger, intercooler
	Displacement	1588cc
	Bore and stroke	80 × 79 mm
	Carburetion	electronic fuel injection
	Power	158 bhp at 6600 rpm
	Transmission	five-speed manual
Chassis	Frame	backbone chassis with auxiliary front structure
	Front suspension	double wishbones, coil springs
	Rear suspension	double wishbones, coil springs
Dimensions	Wheelbase	88.7 in (2250 mm)
	Length × width × height	149.8 × 68.3 × 48.5 in (3803 × 1734 × 1230 mm)
	Weight	2370 lb (1075 kg) (empty)
Maximum speed		137 mph (221 kph)

Lotus Elise from 1995
2000 model

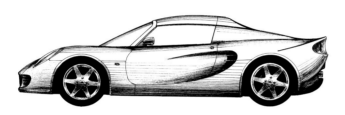

Engine	Configuration	in-line four-cylinder, two overhead camshafts, four valves per cylinder
	Displacement	1795cc
	Bore and stroke	80 × 89.3 mm
	Carburetion	electronic fuel injection
	Power	120 bhp at 5500 rpm
	Transmission	five-speed manual
Chassis	Frame	epoxy-bonded extruded aluminum chassis
	Front suspension	double wishbones, spring and damper units
	Rear suspension	wishbones and diagonal arms, spring and damper units
Dimensions	Wheelbase	90.6 in (2300 mm)
	Length × width × height	146.8 × 67 × 47.3 in (3726 × 1700 × 1200 mm)
	Weight	1616 lb (733 kg) (full 10.57–US-gal/40-liter tank)
Maximum speed		125 mph (202 kph)

Lotus Exige from 2000
2000 model

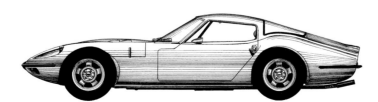

Engine	Configuration	in-line four-cylinder, two overhead camshafts, four valves per cylinder
	Displacement	1795cc
	Bore and stroke	80 × 89.3 mm
	Carburetion	electronic fuel injection
	Power	179 bhp at 7800 rpm
	Transmission	five-speed manual
Chassis	Frame	epoxy-bonded extruded aluminum chassis with integral steel roll-over structure
	Front suspension	double wishbones, strut units
	Rear suspension	double wishbones, strut units
Dimensions	Wheelbase	90.6 in (2300 mm)
	Length × width × height	148.9 × 67.8 × 6.9 in (3780 × 1720 × 1175 mm)
	Weight	1735 lb (787 kg) (empty)
Maximum speed		135 mph (218 kph)

Marcos GT 1800 to 3-Liter 1964–1971
Marcos GT 1800 1964

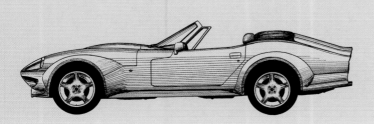

Engine	Configuration	in-line four-cylinder
	Displacement	1780cc
	Bore and stroke	84.14 × 80mm
	Carburetion	twin horizontal Stromberg 17S carburetors
	Power	114 bhp at 5800 rpm
	Transmission	four-speed manual
Chassis	Frame	self-supporting wooden semi-monocoque
	Front suspension	wishbones, coil springs
	Rear suspension	rigid axle, diagonal guide arms, coil springs
Dimensions	Wheelbase	88.7 in (2250 mm)
	Length × width × height	161 × 62.3 × 41.4 in (4090 × 1580 × 1050 mm)
	Weight	1455 lb (660 kg) (empty)
Maximum speed		124 mph (199 kph)

Marcos Mantara 1993–1998
1997 model

Engine	Configuration	V8
	Displacement	3946cc
	Bore and stroke	94 × 80 mm
	Carburetion	electronic fuel injection
	Power	190 bhp at 4750 rpm
	Transmission	five-speed manual
Chassis	Frame	tubular steel frame
	Front suspension	wishbones, strut units
	Rear suspension	wishbones, coil springs
Dimensions	Wheelbase	89.6 in (2273 mm)
	Length × width × height	157.8 × 66.2 × 45.3 in (4005 × 1680 × 1150 mm)
	Weight	2249 lb (1020 kg) (half-filled 12–US-gal/47-liter tank)
Maximum speed		131 mph (211 kph)

Engine	Configuration	mid-mounted V12 engine, four overhead camshafts, four valves per cylinder
	Displacement	6064cc
	Bore and stroke	86 × 87 mm
	Carburetion	electronic fuel injection
	Power	627 bhp at 7400 rpm
	Transmission	six-speed transverse transmission
Chassis	Frame	carbon-fiber monocoque
	Front suspension	double wishbones, inner spring and damper units
	Rear suspension	double wishbones, inner spring and damper units
Dimensions	Wheelbase	107 in (2718 mm)
	Length × width × height	168.9 × 71.7 × 44.9 in (4288 × 1820 × 1140 mm)
	Weight	2500 lb (1134 kg) (empty)
Maximum speed		230 mph (371 kph)

McLaren F1 1992–1998
1994 model

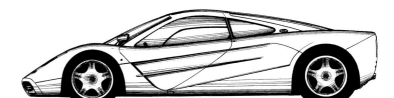

Engine	Configuration	in-line four-cylinder
	Displacement	847cc
	Bore and stroke	57 × 83 mm
	Carburetion	two SU semi-downdraft carburetors
	Power	36 bhp at 5500 rpm
	Transmission	four-speed manual
Chassis	Frame	box frame
	Front suspension	rigid axle, semi-elliptic leaf springs
	Rear suspension	rigid axle, semi-elliptic leaf springs
Dimensions	Wheelbase	86 in (2184 mm)
	Length × width × height	126 × 50.8 × 48.9 in (3200 × 1290 × 1240 mm)
	Weight	1565 lb (710 kg) (empty)
Maximum speed		70 mph (112 kph)

MG J2 1932–1934
1934 model

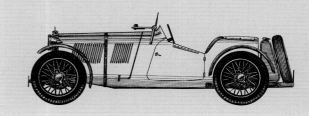

Engine	Configuration	in-line four-cylinder
	Displacement	1292cc
	Bore and stroke	63.5 × 102 mm
	Carburetion	two SU semi-downdraft carburetors
	Power	52.4 bhp at 5000 rpm
	Transmission	four-speed manual
Chassis	Frame	box frame with U-profile sections
	Front suspension	rigid axle, semi-elliptic leaf springs
	Rear suspension	rigid axle, semi-elliptic leaf springs
Dimensions	Wheelbase	94 in (2388 mm)
	Length × width × height	138 × 57.5 × 49.3 in (3350 × 1460 × 1250 mm)
	Weight	1940 lb (880 kg) (empty)
Maximum speed		78 mph (125 kph)

MG TA 1936–1939
1936 model

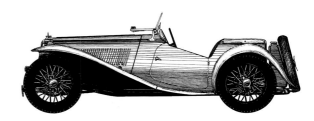

Engine	Configuration	in-line four-cylinder
	Displacement	1250cc
	Bore and stroke	66.5 × 90 mm
	Carburetion	two SU H2 semi-downdraft carburetors
	Power	54.4 bhp at 5200 rpm
	Transmission	four-speed remote control
Chassis	Frame	underslung box frame
	Front suspension	rigid axle, semi-elliptic leaf springs
	Rear suspension	rigid axle, semi-elliptic leaf springs
Dimensions	Wheelbase	94 in (2388 mm)
	Length × width × height	139.6 × 56 × 53 in (3543 × 1422 × 1346 mm)
	Weight	1737 lb (788 kg) (empty)
Maximum speed		78 mph (124.9 kph)

MG TC 1945–1949
1947 model

Engine	Configuration	in-line four-cylinder
	Displacement	1250cc
	Bore and stroke	66.5 × 90 mm
	Carburetion	two SU H2 semi-downdraft carburetors
	Power	54.4 bhp at 5200 rpm
	Transmission	four-speed manual
Chassis	Frame	box frame with tubular crossbraces
	Front suspension	wishbones, coil springs
	Rear suspension	rigid axle, semi-elliptic leaf springs
Dimensions	Wheelbase	94 in (2388 mm)
	Length × width × height	143 × 58.7 × 53 in (3630 × 1489 × 1346 mm)
	Weight	1951 lb (885 kg) (curb)
Maximum speed		83 mph (132.9 kph)

MG TD 1949–1953
1950 model

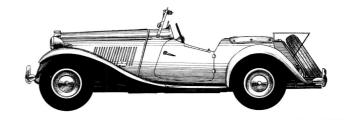

Engine	Configuration	in-line four-cylinder
	Displacement	1466cc
	Bore and stroke	72 × 90 mm
	Carburetion	two SU H4 semi-downdraft carburetors
	Power	63 bhp at 5000 rpm
	Transmission	four-speed manual
Chassis	Frame	box frame with tubular crossbraces
	Front suspension	wishbones, coil springs
	Rear suspension	rigid axle, semi-elliptic leaf springs
Dimensions	Wheelbase	94 in (2388 mm)
	Length × width × height	147 × 59.8 × 52.4 in (3730 × 1517 × 1330 mm)
	Weight	1929 lb (875 kg) (curb)
Maximum speed		88 mph (141.9 kph)

MG TF 1953–1955
1954 model

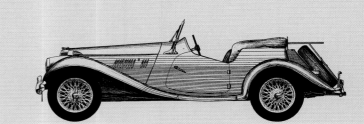

MGA 1955–1962
MGA coupé 1957 model

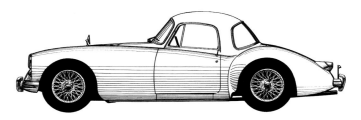

Engine		
	Configuration	in-line four-cylinder
	Displacement	1489cc
	Bore and stroke	73 × 88.9 mm
	Carburetion	two SU semi-downdraft carburetors
	Power	72 bhp at 5500 rpm
	Transmission	four-speed manual
Chassis	Frame	box frame with tubular crossbraces
	Front suspension	wishbones, coil springs
	Rear suspension	rigid axle, semi-elliptic leaf springs
Dimensions	Wheelbase	94 in (2388 mm)
	Length × width × height	156 × 58 × 50 in (3960 × 1473 × 1270 mm)
	Weight	2105 lb (955 kg) (curb)
Maximum speed		100 mph (160 kph)

MG Midget 1961–1979
MG Midget Mk II 1966

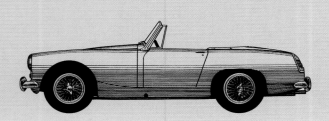

Engine		
	Configuration	in-line four-cylinder
	Displacement	1098cc
	Bore and stroke	64.58 × 83.72 mm
	Carburetion	two SU HS2 semi-downdraft carburetors
	Power	56 bhp at 5750 rpm
	Transmission	four-speed manual
Chassis	Frame	box frame welded to body
	Front suspension	wishbones, coil springs
	Rear suspension	rigid axle, semi-elliptic leaf springs
Dimensions	Wheelbase	80 in (2030 mm)
	Length × width × height	137.5 × 53.2 × 49.6 in (3500 × 1350 × 1260 mm)
	Weight	1530 lb (694 kg) (empty)
Maximum speed		85 mph (137 kph)

MGB 1962–1980
MGB Roadster 1967

Engine		
	Configuration	in-line four-cylinder
	Displacement	1798cc
	Bore and stroke	80.26 × 89 mm
	Carburetion	two SU HS4 semi-downdraft carburetors
	Power	95 bhp at 5400 rpm
	Transmission	four-speed manual
Chassis	Frame	monocoque construction
	Front suspension	wishbones, coil springs
	Rear suspension	rigid axle, semi-elliptic leaf springs
Dimensions	Wheelbase	91 in (2311 mm)
	Length × width × height	153.3 × 59.9 × 49.3 in (3890 × 1520 × 1250 mm)
	Weight	2028 lb (920 kg) (empty)
Maximum speed		104 mph (167.3 kph)

MGF from 1995
2001 model

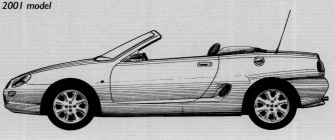

Engine		
	Configuration	in-line four-cylinder, two overhead camshafts, four valves per cylinder
	Displacement	1795cc
	Bore and stroke	80 × 89.3 mm
	Carburetion	electronic fuel injection
	Power	120 bhp at 5500 rpm
	Transmission	Steptronic
Chassis	Frame	monocoque construction with front and rear auxiliary frame
	Front suspension	double wishbones
	Rear suspension	double wishbones, Hydragas springing
Dimensions	Wheelbase	94 in (2380 mm)
	Length × width × height	154 × 64.2 × 50 in (3910 × 1630 × 1270 mm)
	Weight	2337 lb (1060 kg) (empty)
Maximum speed		120 mph (193 kph)

Morgan Threewheeler 1909–1951
Super Sports Aero 1932

Engine		
	Configuration	V2
	Displacement	1096cc
	Bore and stroke	85.7 × 95 mm
	Carburetion	single Amal carburetor with twin float
	Power	25 bhp at 2400 rpm
	Transmission	three-speed manual
Chassis	Frame	tubular backbone
	Front suspension	vertical sliding pillars, coil springs
	Rear suspension	double links, leaf springs
Dimensions	Wheelbase	87 in (2209 mm)
	Length × width × height	115 × 56.8 × 32.7 in (2921 × 1442 × 831 mm)
	Weight	994 lb (451 kg) (curb)
Maximum speed		81 mph (130 kph)

Morgan 4/4 Series I 1936–1950
Morgan 4–4 1936

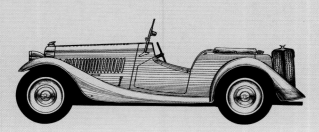

Engine		
	Configuration	in-line four-cylinder
	Displacement	1122cc
	Bore and stroke	63 × 90 mm
	Carburetion	single Solex 30 HBFG downdraft carburetor
	Power	39 bhp at 4500 rpm
	Transmission	four-speed manual
Chassis	Frame	box frame with crossmembers
	Front suspension	vertical sliding pillars, coil springs
	Rear suspension	rigid axle, semi-elliptic leaf springs
Dimensions	Wheelbase	98 in (2489 mm)
	Length × width × height	137 × 52.4 × 43.4 in (3480 × 1330 × 1100 mm)
	Weight	1583 lb (718 kg) (curb)
Maximum speed		74 mph (120 kph)

Engine	Configuration	in-line four-cylinder, two overhead camshafts, four valves per cylinder
	Displacement	1994cc
	Bore and stroke	84.5 × 89 mm
	Carburetion	electronic fuel injection
	Power	138 bhp at 6000 rpm
	Transmission	five-speed manual
Chassis	Frame	box frame with diagonal crossbracing
	Front suspension	vertical sliding pillars, coil springs
	Rear suspension	rigid axle, semi-elliptic leaf springs
Dimensions	Wheelbase	96 in (2440 mm)
	Length × width × height	153.3 × 59 × 53.2 in (3890 × 1500 × 1350 mm)
	Weight	2161 lb (980 kg) (empty)
Maximum speed		121 mph (195 kph)

Morgan Plus 4 1950–2000
Morgan Plus 4 Tourer 1990

Engine	Configuration	in-line four-cylinder, overhead camshaft
	Displacement	1597cc
	Bore and stroke	80 × 79.5 mm
	Carburetion	single Weber 32/34 DFT twin-choke downdraft carburetor
	Power	96 bhp at 6000 rpm
	Transmission	five-speed manual
Chassis	Frame	box frame with diagonal crossbracing
	Front suspension	vertical sliding pillars, coil springs
	Rear suspension	rigid axle, semi-elliptic leaf springs
Dimensions	Wheelbase	96 in (2440 mm)
	Length × width × height	144.2 × 55.9 × 51 in (3660 × 1420 × 1295 mm)
	Weight	1620 lb (735 kg) (empty)
Maximum speed		104 mph (167 kph)

Morgan 4/4 from 1955
Morgan 4/4 1600 1983

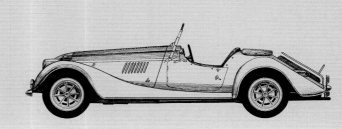

Engine	Configuration	V8
	Displacement	3532cc
	Bore and stroke	88.9 × 71.12 mm
	Carburetion	two SU HIF6 semi-downdraft carburetors
	Power	155 bhp at 5250 rpm
	Transmission	five-speed manual
Chassis	Frame	box frame with diagonal crossbracing
	Front suspension	vertical sliding pillars, coil springs
	Rear suspension	rigid axle, semi-elliptic leaf springs
Dimensions	Wheelbase	98 in (2490 mm)
	Length × width × height	147.4 × 62 × 52 in (3740 × 1575 × 1320 mm)
	Weight	1830 lb (830 kg) (empty)
Maximum speed		125 mph (201 kph)

Morgan Plus 8 from 1968
1978 model

Engine	Configuration	V8, four overhead camshafts, four valves per cylinder
	Displacement	4398cc
	Bore and stroke	82.7 × 92 mm
	Carburetion	electronic engine management
	Power	286 bhp at 5500 rpm
	Transmission	six-speed manual
Chassis	Frame	chassis of bonded and riveted aluminum sections, ash frame
	Front suspension	wishbones, trailing link arms, spring and damper units
	Rear suspension	double wishbones, lower tie rods, spring and damper units
Dimensions	Wheelbase	99.7 in (2530 mm)
	Length × width × height	161 × 69 × 43 in (4089 × 1753 × 1092 mm)
	Weight	2205 lb (1000 kg) (empty)
Maximum speed		160 mph (258 kph)

Morgan Aero 8 from 2001
2001 model

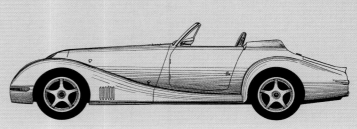

Engine	Configuration	V6
	Displacement	2792cc
	Bore and stroke	93 × 68.5 mm
	Carburetion	mechanical fuel injection
	Power	150 bhp at 5700 rpm
	Transmission	five-speed manual
Chassis	Frame	box frame
	Front suspension	wishbones, coil springs
	Rear suspension	rigid axle, coil springs, upper and lower trailing arms, Panhard rod
Dimensions	Wheelbase	100.5 in (2550 mm)
	Length × width × height	153.9 × 67.4 × 49 in (3905 × 1710 × 1245 mm)
	Weight	1918 lb (870 kg) (empty)
Maximum speed		123 mph (198 kph)

Panther Kallista 1982–1991
1984 model

Engine	Configuration	in-line four-cylinder, overhead camshaft, turbocharger
	Displacement	1809cc
	Bore and stroke	83 × 83.6 mm
	Carburetion	electronic fuel injection
	Power	135 bhp at 6000 rpm
	Transmission	five-speed manual
Chassis	Frame	box frame with auxiliary frame
	Front suspension	double wishbones, coil springs
	Rear suspension	diagonal arms, coil springs
Dimensions	Wheelbase	84 in (2135 mm)
	Length × width × height	153 × 62.3 × 48.9 in (3885 × 1580 × 1240 mm)
	Weight	1852 lb (840 kg) (empty)
Maximum speed		129 mph (208 kph)

Reliant Scimitar 1984–1989
Reliant Scimitar 1800Ti 1986

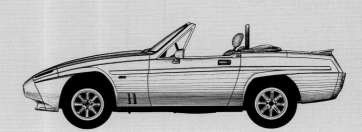

Riley 9 h.p. Brooklands Speed 1928–1932
Riley Brooklands Speed 1930

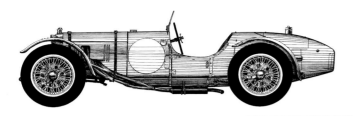

Engine	Configuration	in-line four-cylinder, two camshafts
	Displacement	1087cc
	Bore and stroke	60.3 × 95.2 mm
	Carburetion	two horizontal SU OM carburetors
	Power	never published
	Transmission	four-speed manual
Chassis	Frame	U-profile sections with goosenecks in front, underslung at rear
	Front suspension	rigid axle, leaf springs
	Rear suspension	torque tube axle, leaf springs
Dimensions	Wheelbase	96 in (2438 mm)
	Length × width × height	150 × 57 × 41 in (3810 × 1450 × 1040 mm)
	Weight	1543 lb (700 kg) (curb)
Maximum speed		109 mph (175 kph)

Riley 12 h.p. Sprite 1936–1938
Riley Sprite 1937

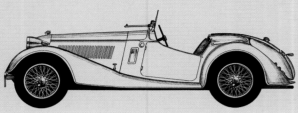

Engine	Configuration	in-line four-cylinder, two camshafts
	Displacement	1496cc
	Bore and stroke	69 × 100 mm
	Carburetion	two horizontal SU HV2 carburetors
	Power	45 bhp at 4650 rpm
	Transmission	four-speed manual
Chassis	Frame	box frame with diagonal crossbracing
	Front suspension	rigid axle, leaf springs
	Rear suspension	rigid axle, leaf springs
Dimensions	Wheelbase	97.6 in (2476 mm)
	Length × width × height	137.5 × 56.5 × 48 in (3500 × 1435 × 1220 mm)
	Weight	2017 lb (915 kg) (empty)
Maximum speed		85 mph (137 kph)

Riley RMC Roadster 1948–1951
1949 model

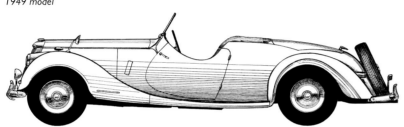

Engine	Configuration	in-line four-cylinder, two camshafts
	Displacement	2443cc
	Bore and stroke	80.5 × 120 mm
	Carburetion	two horizontal SU H4 carburetors
	Power	100 bhp at 4400 rpm
	Transmission	four-speed manual
Chassis	Frame	box frame with diagonal crossmembers
	Front suspension	wishbones, torsion bars
	Rear suspension	rigid axle, semi-elliptic leaf springs
Dimensions	Wheelbase	119 in (3023 mm)
	Length × width × height	186 × 66.2 × 54.8 in (4720 × 1680 × 1390 mm)
	Weight	3056 lb (1386 kg) (empty)
Maximum speed		98 mph (158 kph)

Singer Roadster 1939–1955
Singer Roadster 4AB 1952

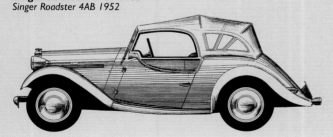

Engine	Configuration	in-line four-cylinder, overhead camshafts
	Displacement	1074cc
	Bore and stroke	60 × 95 mm
	Carburetion	single horizontal Solex carburetor
	Power	36 bhp at 5000 rpm
	Transmission	four-speed manual
Chassis	Frame	box frame with diagonal crossmembers
	Front suspension	wishbones, coil springs
	Rear suspension	rigid axle, semi-elliptic leaf springs
Dimensions	Wheelbase	92 in (2337 mm)
	Length × width × height	145.6 × 58 × 58.5 in (3696 × 1473 × 1486 mm)
	Weight	1735 lb (787 kg) (empty)
Maximum speed		69 mph (112 kph)

Sunbeam Alpine 1953–1955
1953 model

Engine	Configuration	in-line four-cylinder
	Displacement	2267cc
	Bore and stroke	81 × 110 mm
	Carburetion	single Stromberg DAA 36 downdraft carburetor
	Power	81 bhp at 4200 rpm
	Transmission	four-speed manual
Chassis	Frame	underslung box frame with diagonal crossmembers
	Front suspension	wishbones, coil springs
	Rear suspension	rigid axle, semi-elliptic leaf springs
Dimensions	Wheelbase	97.6 in (2476 mm)
	Length × width × height	167.8 × 62.3 × 60.7 in (4260 × 1580 × 1540 mm)
	Weight	2857 (1296 kg) (curb)
Maximum speed		95 mph (153 kph)

Sunbeam Tiger 1964–1967
1965 model

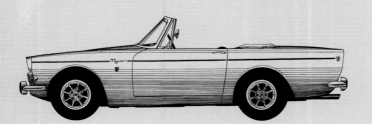

Engine	Configuration	V8
	Displacement	4261cc
	Bore and stroke	96.5 × 73 mm
	Carburetion	single Ford C4DF 9510 downdraft carburetor
	Power	164 bhp at 4400 rpm
	Transmission	four-speed manual
Chassis	Frame	monocoque construction
	Front suspension	wishbones, coil springs
	Rear suspension	rigid axle, semi-elliptic leaf springs
Dimensions	Wheelbase	85.9 in (2180 mm)
	Length × width × height	155.2 × 60.8 × 51.6 in (3940 × 1540 × 1310 mm)
	Weight	2524 lb (1145 kg) (empty)
Maximum speed		117 mph (188 kph)

Engine	Configuration	in-line four-cylinder
	Displacement	1991cc
	Bore and stroke	83 × 92 mm
	Carburetion	twin horizontal SU H4 carburetors
	Power	90 bhp at 4800 rpm
	Transmission	four-speed manual
Chassis	Frame	tubular frame
	Front suspension	wishbones, coil springs
	Rear suspension	rigid axle, trailing arms, semi-elliptic leaf springs
Dimensions	Wheelbase	95 in (2410 mm)
	Length × width × height	152 × 61 × 51.2 in (3860 × 1550 × 1300 mm)
	Weight	2028 (920 kg) (curb)
Maximum speed		97 mph (156 kph)

Swallow Doretti 1954–1955
1954 model

Engine	Configuration	in-line four-cylinder
	Displacement	2088cc
	Bore and stroke	85 × 92 mm
	Carburetion	single Solex 32 BIPC downdraft carburetor
	Power	68 bhp at 4200 rpm
	Transmission	three-speed manual
Chassis	Frame	underslung box frame with tubular struts
	Front suspension	upper wishbones, lower transverse leaf springs
	Rear suspension	rigid axle, semi-elliptic leaf springs
Dimensions	Wheelbase	100 in (2540 mm)
	Length × width × height	168.6 × 64 × 56 in (4280 × 1626 × 1422 mm)
	Weight	2544 lb (1154 kg) (empty)
Maximum speed		77 mph (124 kph)

Triumph Roadster 1946–1949
Triumph Roadster 2000 1949

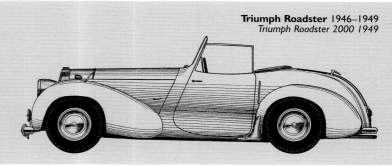

Engine	Configuration	in-line four-cylinder
	Displacement	1991cc
	Bore and stroke	83 × 92 mm
	Carburetion	twin horizontal SU H4 carburetors
	Power	90 bhp at 4800 rpm
	Transmission	four-speed manual
Chassis	Frame	box frame with diagonal crossbracing
	Front suspension	wishbones, coil springs
	Rear suspension	rigid axle, semi-elliptic leaf springs
Dimensions	Wheelbase	88 in (2235 mm)
	Length × width × height	78.2 × 55.6 × 50 in (3480 × 1410 × 1270 mm)
	Weight	1984 lb (900 kg) (curb)
Maximum speed		104 mph (167.3 kph)

Triumph TR2 1953–1955
1954 model

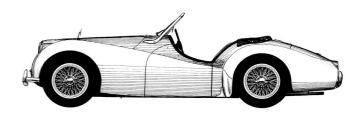

Engine	Configuration	in-line four-cylinder
	Displacement	1991cc
	Bore and stroke	83 × 92 mm
	Carburetion	two SU H6 semi-downdraft carburetors
	Power	101 bhp at 5000 rpm
	Transmission	four-speed manual
Chassis	Frame	box frame with diagonal crossbracing
	Front suspension	wishbones, coil springs
	Rear suspension	rigid axle, semi-elliptic leaf springs
Dimensions	Wheelbase	88 in (2235 mm)
	Length × width × height	137 × 55.6 × 50 in (3480 × 1410 × 1270 mm)
	Weight	2072 lb (940 kg) (curb)
Maximum speed		103 mph (166 kph)

Triumph TR3 1955–1962
Triumph TR3A 1958

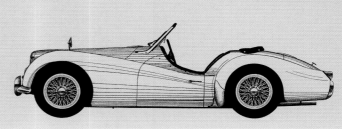

Engine	Configuration	in-line six-cylinder
	Displacement	2498cc
	Bore and stroke	74.7 × 95mm
	Carburetion	fuel injection
	Power	150 bhp at 4800 rpm
	Transmission	four-speed manual
Chassis	Frame	box frame with diagonal crossbracing
	Front suspension	wishbones, coil springs
	Rear suspension	diagonal arms, coil springs
Dimensions	Wheelbase	88.3 in (2240 mm)
	Length × width × height	89.8 × 57.9 × 50 in (3900 × 1470 × 1270 mm)
	Weight	2280 (1034 kg) (empty)
Maximum speed		118 mph (189.5 kph)

Triumph TR5 1967–1968
Triumph TR5 PI 1968

Engine	Configuration	in-line 4-cylinder
	Displacement	1296cc
	Bore and stroke	73.7 × 76 mm
	Carburetion	two horizontal Weber 40 DCOE carburetors
	Power	80 bhp at 6000 rpm
	Transmission	four-speed manual and overdrive
Chassis	Frame	box frame with crossmembers
	Front suspension	wishbones, coil springs
	Rear suspension	jointed cross-shaft axle, transverse leaf springs, longitudinal thrust rod
Dimensions	Wheelbase	83 in (2110 mm)
	Length × width × height	146.6 × 57 × 47.5 in (3721 × 1448 × 1205 mm) (with top up)
	Weight	1649 lb (748 kg) (empty)
Maximum speed		100 mph (160 kph)

Triumph Spitfire 1962–1980
Triumph Spitfire Mark 3 1969

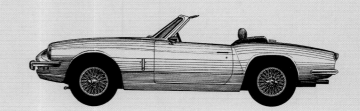

Triumph GT6 1966–1973
Triumph GT6 Mark 2 1969

Engine	Configuration	in-line six-cylinder
	Displacement	1998cc
	Bore and stroke	74.7 × 76 mm
	Carburetion	twin Stromberg 1.50 CD horizontal carburetors
	Power	105 bhp at 5300 rpm
	Transmission	four-speed manual
Chassis	Frame	box frame with crossmembers
	Front suspension	wishbones, coil springs
	Rear suspension	reverse wishbones and thrust rods, upper transverse leaf springs
Dimensions	Wheelbase	83 in (2110 mm)
	Length × width × height	147 × 57 × 47 in (3735 × 1450 × 1195 mm)
	Weight	2017 lb (915 kg) (empty)
Maximum speed		115 mph (180 kph)

Triumph TR6 1968–1976
1974 model

Engine	Configuration	in-line six-cylinder
	Displacement	2498cc
	Bore and stroke	74.7 × 95 mm
	Carburetion	fuel injection
	Power	127 bhp at 5000 rpm
	Transmission	four-speed manual
Chassis	Frame	box frame with diagonal crossbracing
	Front suspension	wishbones, coil springs
	Rear suspension	diagonal arms, coil springs
Dimensions	Wheelbase	88.3 in (2240 mm)
	Length × width × height	155.2 × 57.9 × 50 in (3940 × 1470 × 1270 mm)
	Weight	2370 lb (1075 kg) (with full 13.47–US-gal/51-liter tank)
Maximum speed		120 mph (193.5 kph)

Triumph Stag 1970–1977
1970 model

Engine	Configuration	V8, two overhead camshafts
	Displacement	2997cc
	Bore and stroke	86 × 64.5 mm
	Carburetion	twin Stromberg 175 CDS horizontal carburetors
	Power	145 bhp at 5500 rpm
	Transmission	four-speed manual
Chassis	Frame	monocoque construction
	Front suspension	vertical sliding pillars, lower wishbones with diagonal struts, coil springs
	Rear suspension	wishbones, coil springs
Dimensions	Wheelbase	100 in (2540 mm)
	Length × width × height	174 × 63.4 × 49.6 in (4420 × 1610 × 1260 mm)
	Weight	2810 lb (1275 kg) (empty)
Maximum speed		120 mph (193 kph)

Triumph TR8 1980–1981
1981 model

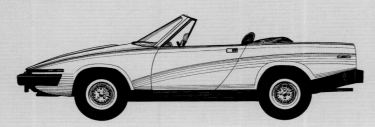

Engine	Configuration	V8
	Displacement	3528cc
	Bore and stroke	88.9 × 71.1 mm
	Carburetion	fuel injection
	Power	137 bhp at 5000 rpm
	Transmission	five-speed manual
Chassis	Frame	monocoque construction
	Front suspension	MacPherson struts, lower wishbones
	Rear suspension	rigid axle, coil springs, two trailing arms, two diagonal arms
Dimensions	Wheelbase	85 in (2160 mm)
	Length × width × height	164.5 × 66.2 × 50 in (4175 × 1680 × 1270 mm)
	Weight	2568 lb (1165 kg) (empty)
Maximum speed		121 mph (194 kph)

TVR Grantura 1958–1967
TVR Grantura MK IIA 1962

Engine	Configuration	in-line four-cylinder
	Displacement	1340cc
	Bore and stroke	80.96 × 65.07 mm
	Carburetion	twin SU H4 horizontal carburetors
	Power	69 bhp at 4900 rpm
	Transmission	four-speed manual
Chassis	Frame	spaceframe
	Front suspension	longitudinal torsion bars, lateral arms
	Rear suspension	longitudinal torsion bars, lateral arms
Dimensions	Wheelbase	84 in (2132 mm)
	Length × width × height	138 × 64 × 48 in (3505 × 1626 × 1219 mm)
	Weight	1543 lb (700 kg) (empty)
Maximum speed		98 mph (158 kph)

TVR Vixen 1967–1973
TVR Vixen 2500 1972

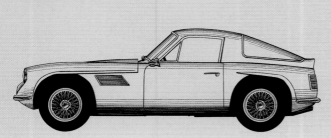

Engine	Configuration	in-line six-cylinder
	Displacement	2498cc
	Bore and stroke	74.7 × 95 mm
	Carburetion	twin Stromberg 175 CD 2SE horizontal carburetors
	Power	104 bhp at 4950 rpm
	Transmission	four-speed manual
Chassis	Frame	lattice frame
	Front suspension	wishbones, coil springs
	Rear suspension	wishbones, coil springs
Dimensions	Wheelbase	90.2 in (2290 mm)
	Length × width × height	145.6 × 64 × 48 in (3695 × 1625 × 1220 mm)
	Weight	2028 lb (920 kg)
Maximum speed		118 mph (190 kph)

Engine	Configuration	V6
	Displacement	2994cc
	Bore and stroke	90.67 × 72.42 mm
	Carburetion	single Weber 38 DGAS twin downdraft carburetor
	Power	136 bhp at 5300 rpm
	Transmission	four-speed manual
Chassis	Frame	lattice frame
	Front suspension	wishbones, coil springs
	Rear suspension	wishbones, double coil springs
Dimensions	Wheelbase	90 in (2286 mm)
	Length × width × height	155 × 64 × 46.9 in (3930 × 1625 × 1190 mm)
	Weight	2161 lb (980 kg) (with full 14.5—US-gal/55-liter tank)
Maximum speed		125 mph (201 kph)

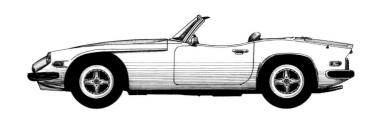

TVR M-Series 1972–1979
TVR 3000S convertible 1979

Engine	Configuration	V8
	Displacement	3532cc
	Bore and stroke	88.9 × 71.12 mm
	Carburetion	electronic fuel injection
	Power	193 bhp at 5280 rpm
	Transmission	five-speed manual
Chassis	Frame	tubular steel frame
	Front suspension	wishbones, coil springs
	Rear suspension	wishbones and trailing arms, supporting half axles, coil springs
Dimensions	Wheelbase	94 in (2385 mm)
	Length × width × height	158.2 × 68.2 × 47.5 in (4015 × 1730 × 1205 mm)
	Weight	2469 lb (1120 kg) (empty)
Maximum speed		136 mph (219 kph)

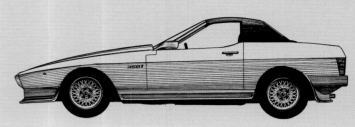

TVR 350i 1983–1990
TVR 350i convertible 1988

Engine	Configuration	V8
	Displacement	4988cc
	Bore and stroke	94 × 90 mm
	Carburetion	electronic fuel injection
	Power	325 bhp at 5500 rpm
	Transmission	five-speed manual
Chassis	Frame	tubular steel frame
	Front suspension	double wishbones, coil springs
	Rear suspension	double wishbones, coil springs
Dimensions	Wheelbase	90 in (2286 mm)
	Length × width × height	153.3 × 76.6 × 47.5 in (3892 × 1943 × 1205 mm)
	Weight	2337 lb (1060 kg) (empty)
Maximum speed		167 mph (269 kph)

TVR Griffith 1992–2001
TVR Griffith 500 1998

Engine	Configuration	in-line six-cylinder, two overhead camshafts, four valves per cylinder
	Displacement	3966cc
	Bore and stroke	96 × 92 mm
	Carburetion	electronic fuel injection
	Power	350 bhp at 6800 rpm
	Transmission	five-speed manual
Chassis	Frame	tubular steel frame
	Front suspension	double wishbones, coil springs
	Rear suspension	double wishbones, coil springs
Dimensions	Wheelbase	101 in (2565 mm)
	Length × width × height	168.6 × 73.5 × 48 in (4280 × 1865 × 1220 mm)
	Weight	2271 lb (1030 kg) (empty)
Maximum speed		170 mph (273 kph)

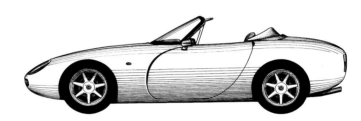

TVR Cerbera from 1994
TVR Cerbera Speed Six 1999

Engine	Configuration	in-line six-cylinder, two overhead camshafts, four valves per cylinder
	Displacement	3996cc
	Bore and stroke	96 × 92mm
	Carburetion	electronic fuel injection
	Power	360 bhp at 7000 rpm
	Transmission	five-speed manual
Chassis	Frame	tubular steel frame
	Front suspension	double wishbones, coil springs
	Rear suspension	double wishbones, coil springs
Dimensions	Wheelbase	93 in (2360 mm)
	Length × width × height	166.9 × 71.3 × 47.3 in (4235 × 1810 × 1200 mm)
	Weight	2425 lb (1100 kg) (empty)
Maximum speed		over 180 mph (290 kph)

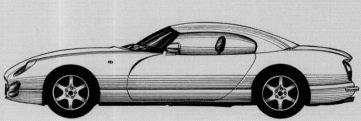

TVR Tuscan Tuscan from 1989, Speed Six from 2000
TVR Tuscan Speed Six 2000

Engine	Configuration	in-line four-cylinder, two overhead camshafts, four valves per cylinder
	Displacement	1796cc
	Bore and stroke	80.6 × 88 mm
	Carburetion	electronic fuel injection
	Power	170 bhp at 4800 rpm
	Transmission	five-speed manual
Chassis	Frame	synthetic-coated spaceframe
	Front suspension	double wishbones, spring and damper units
	Rear suspension	double wishbones, spring and damper units
Dimensions	Wheelbase	93 in (2360 mm)
	Length × width × height	132.4 × 65 × 46.9 in (3360 × 1650 × 1190 mm)
	Weight	1521 lb (690 kg)
Maximum speed		134 mph (215 kph)

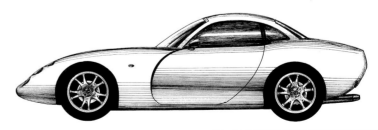

Westfield Seven from 1983
Westfield Seven ZEi 2000

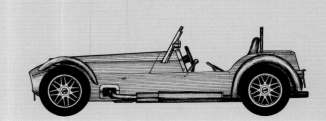

INDEX

ACKNOWLEDGEMENTS

I would like to thank the following for giving us access to their vehicles:

Joachim Adloff, Axel Anders, Horst Auer, Martin Baas, Werner Bald, Horst Ballé, Thomas Berther, Rocky Boecher, Peter Brodt, Wolfgang Buchholz, Hans-Hermann Christensen, Muhammed Darr, Markus Deppert, Johannes Ditz, Simon Draper, Hans Dreger, Erik Ehing, Walter Einhäuser, Herbert Engel, Jorge Ferreira-Basso, Thomas Fischer, Christof Flugel, Jean-Pierre Frottier, Miriam Geisler, Richard Gerstner, Eberhard Göcke, Karl-Heinz Gombert, Hermann Graf Hatzfeldt, Werner Groh, Dieter Haack, Peter Hart, Hans Hausmann, Heribert Herold, Michael Höfer, Kai-Uwe Hohn-Simons, Dr Hans Jantsch, Wolf-Dieter Juchem, Klaus Keck, Peter Klee, Matthias Klemp, Alexander C. Knapp-Voith, Lorenz Koch, Rainer Köllmann, Helmut Kopp, Fredy Kumschick, Robert Leyba, Hans Lienhard, Martin Lorscheider, Werner Lübke, Martin Lützeler, Werner Maurer, Günter Memminger, Kevin Moore, Tony O'Keeffe, Arved Otto, Lucas Patras, Daniel Paulus, Barbara Prince, Dr Wolf Pröpsting, Dr Georg Prugger, Reinhard Rebel, Klaus Rehm, Matthias Reuter, Joachim Rimpl, Karlheinz Rüdebusch, Klaus Salomon, Joachim C. Schairer, Dr. Ralf Scheffler, Paul Schinhofen, Hugo Schneider, Ulrich Schödel, Norbert Schumann, Thorsten Seegräber, Frank Seitz, Wolfgang Seitz, Marcel Spiess, Klaus Steinmetz, Dirk Strassl, David & Lucas Tasa, Peter Taylor, Frank Teschner, Richard Thomson, Joos Tollenaar, Chris Tubbs, Klaus Tweddell, Wolfgang Vogt, Barbara Volkenandt, Dr Manfred Westphal, Graham White, Kurt Wilms, Guido Wittig, Johannes Woskowski, Ernst Zahnweh, Peter Zimmermann, Peter Zizka, Erich Zöller.

Special thanks to:

Mark Aston, John Atkins, John Blunsden, Clive Chapman, Adriano Cimarosti, Howard R. Davies, Debby Feeley, Hans Griebling, Sandra Hayashi, Anthony L. Hussey, Beate Jung, Ian Law, Hartmut Lehbrink, Heinz-Josef Meeßen, Lord Montagu, Charles Morgan, Jochen von Osterroth, Barbara Prince, Dr Manfred Schlick, Christopher K. Smith, Tim Ward, Ralf Weber.

I would also like to thank the management of Egelsbach, Michelstadt, Karlsruhe-Forchheim, Oberschleißheim airfields, Siegerland Airport, and the Mainz-Finthen Flying Club for their valuable co-operation.

And I would like to thank the Könemann team for their commitment to this project: Sally Bald, Peter Feierabend, and Sabine Gerber, as well as Roman Bold & Black: Malgorzata Calusinka and Thomas Lindner.

Rainer W. Schlegelmilch

© 2005 KÖNEMANN*, an imprint of Tandem Verlag GmbH, Königswinter

Original title: *Englische Sportwagen*
ISBN 3-8331-1046-5

Art director and design: Peter Feierabend
Project manager: Sally Bald
Editor: Sabine Gerber
Design: Roman Bold & Black, Cologne

English edition:
© 2005* KÖNEMANN*, an imprint of Tandem Verlag GmbH, Königswinter
Translation: Richard Elliott, Malcolm Green, Eileen Martin, Philip Radcliffe, Les Telford in association with Cambridge Publishing Management Ltd, Cambridge UK.
Editor: Ivor Carroll in association with Cambridge Publishing Management Ltd.
Typesetting: Cambridge Publishing Management Ltd.
Project Management: Mine Ali for Cambridge Publishing Management Ltd.

*KÖNEMANN is a registered trademark of Tandem Verlag GmbH

Printed in Germany

ISBN 3-8331-1154-2

10 9 8 7 6 5 4 3 2 1
X IX VIII VII VI V IV III II I

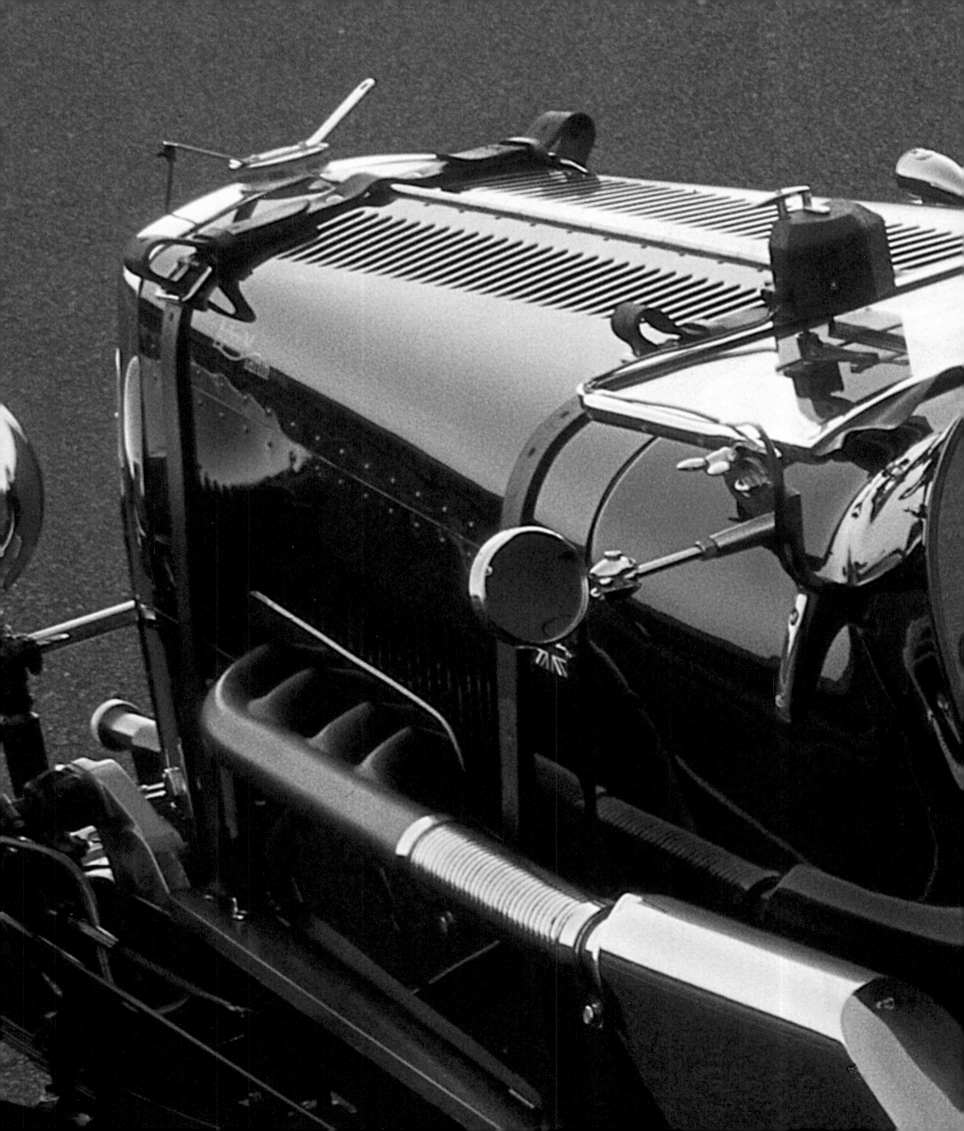